Cardigan

Robert W. Chambers

Alpha Editions

This edition published in 2024

ISBN : 9789364737296

Design and Setting By
Alpha Editions
www.alphaedis.com
Email - info@alphaedis.com

As per information held with us this book is in Public Domain.
This book is a reproduction of an important historical work. Alpha Editions uses the best technology to reproduce historical work in the same manner it was first published to preserve its original nature. Any marks or number seen are left intentionally to preserve its true form.

Contents

INTRODUCTION .... - 1 -
PREFACE .... - 3 -
CHAPTER I .... - 4 -
CHAPTER II .... - 18 -
CHAPTER III .... - 34 -
CHAPTER IV .... - 47 -
CHAPTER V .... - 54 -
CHAPTER VI .... - 71 -
CHAPTER VII .... - 82 -
CHAPTER VIII .... - 100 -
CHAPTER IX .... - 116 -
CHAPTER X .... - 134 -
CHAPTER XI .... - 160 -
CHAPTER XII .... - 176 -
CHAPTER XIII .... - 188 -
CHAPTER XIV .... - 208 -
CHAPTER XV .... - 225 -
CHAPTER XVI .... - 239 -
CHAPTER XVII .... - 258 -
CHAPTER XVIII .... - 279 -
CHAPTER XIX .... - 285 -
CHAPTER XX .... - 295 -
CHAPTER XXI .... - 308 -
CHAPTER XXII .... - 324 -
CHAPTER XXIII .... - 343 -
CHAPTER XXIV .... - 355 -

CHAPTER XXV .... - 363 -
CHAPTER XXVI .... - 384 -
CHAPTER XXVII .... - 408 -
CHAPTER XXVIII .... - 430 -
CHAPTER XXIX .... - 440 -
THE END .... - 453 -

INTRODUCTION

This is the Land of the Pioneer,

Where a life-long feud was healed;

Where the League of the Men whose Coats were Red

With the Men of the Woods whose Skins were Red

Was riveted, forged, and sealed.

Now, by the souls of our Silent Dead,

God save our sons from the League of Red!

Plough up the Land of Battle

Here in our hazy hills;

Plough! to the lowing of cattle;

Plough! to the clatter of mills;

Follow the turning furrows'

Gold, where the deep loam breaks,

While the hand of the harrow burrows,

Clutching the clod that cakes;

North and south on the harrow's line,

Under the bronzed pines' boughs,

The silvery flint-tipped arrows shine

In the wake of a thousand ploughs!

Plough us the Land of the Pioneer,

Where the buckskinned rangers bled;

Where the Redcoats reeled from a reeking field,

And a thousand Red Men fled;

Plough us the land of the wolf and deer,

The land of the men who laughed at fear,

The land of our Martyred Dead!

Here where the ghost-flower, blowing,
Grows from the bones below,
Patters the hare, unknowing,
Passes the cawing crow:
Shadows of hawk and swallow,
Shadows of wind-stirred wood,
Dapple each hill and hollow,
Here where our dead men stood:
Wild bees hum through the forest vines
Where the bullets of England hummed,
And the partridge drums in the ringing pines
Where the drummers of England drummed.
This is the Land of the Pioneer,
Where a life-long feud was healed;
Where the League of the Men whose Coats were Red
With the Men of the Woods whose Skins were Red
Was riveted, forged, and sealed.
Now, by the blood of our Splendid Dead,
God save our sons from the League of Red!

R. W. C.

BROADALBIN.

PREFACE

Those who read this romance for the sake of what history it may contain will find the histories from which I have helped myself more profitable.

Those antiquarians who hunt their hobbies through books had best drop the trail of this book at the preface, for they will draw but a blank covert in these pages. Better for the antiquarian that he seek the mansion of Sir William Johnson, which is still standing in Johnstown, New York, and see with his own eyes the hatchet-scars in the solid mahogany banisters where Thayendanegea hacked out polished chips. It would doubtless prove more profitable for the antiquarian to thumb those hatchet-marks than these pages.

But there be some simple folk who read romance for its own useless sake.

To such quiet minds, innocent and disinterested, I have some little confidences to impart: There are still trout in the Kennyetto; the wild ducks still splash on the Vlaie, where Sir William awoke the echoes with his flintlock; the spot where his hunting-box stood is still called Summer-House Point; and huge pike in golden-green chain-mail still haunt the dark depths of the Vlaie water, even on this fair April day in the year of our Lord 1900.

THE AUTHOR.

CHAPTER I

On the 1st of May, 1774, the anchor-ice, which for so many months had silver-plated the river's bed with frosted crusts, was ripped off and dashed into a million gushing flakes by the amber outrush of the springtide flood.

On that day I had laid my plans for fishing the warm shallows where the small fry, swarming in early spring, attract the great lean fish which have lain benumbed all winter under their crystal roof of ice.

So certain was I of a holiday undisturbed by school-room tasks that I whistled up boldly as I sat on my cot bed, sorting hooks according to their sizes, and smoothing out my feather-flies to make sure the moths had not loosened wing or body. It was, therefore, with misgiving that I heard Peter and Esk go into the school-room, stamping their feet to make what noise they were able, and dragging their horn-books along the balustrade.

Now we had no tasks set us for three weeks, for our schoolmaster, Mr. Yost, journeying with the post to visit his mother in Pennsylvania, had been shot and scalped at Eastertide near Fort Pitt—probably by some drunken Delaware.

My guardian, Sir William Johnson, who, as all know, was Commissioner of Indian Affairs for the Crown, had but recently returned from the upper castle with his secretary, Captain Walter Butler; and, preoccupied with the lamentable murder of Mr. Yost, had found no time to concern himself with us or our affairs.

However, having despatched a messenger with strings and belts to remonstrate with the sachems of the Lenni-Lenape—they being, as I have said, suspected of the murder—we discovered that Sir William had also written to Albany for another schoolmaster to replace Mr. Yost; and it gave me, for one, no pleasure to learn it, though it did please Silver Heels, who wearied me with her devotion to her books.

So, hearing Esk and fat Peter on their way to the school-room, I took alarm, believing that our new schoolmaster had arrived; so seized my fish-rod and started to slip out of the house before any one might summon me. However, I was seen in the hallway by Captain Butler, Sir William's secretary, and ordered to find my books and report to him at the school-room.

I, of course, paid no heed to Mr. Butler, but walked defiantly down-stairs, although he called me twice in his cold, menacing voice. And I should have continued triumphantly out of the door and across the fields to the river had not I met Silver Heels dancing through the lower hallway, her slate and pencil under her arm, and loudly sucking a cone of maple sugar.

"Oh, Michael," she cried, "you don't know! Captain Butler has consented to instruct us until the new schoolmaster comes from Albany."

"Oh, has he?" I sneered. "What do I care for Mr. Butler? I'm going out! Let go my coat!"

"No, you're not! No, you're not!" retorted Silver Heels, in that teasing sing-song which she loved to make me mad withal. "Sir William says you are to take your ragged old book of gods and nymphs and be diligent lest he catch you tripping! So there, clumsy foot!"—for I had tried to trip her.

"Who told you that?" I answered, sulkily, snatching at her sugar.

"Aunt Molly; she set me to seek you. So now who's going fishing, my lord?"

The indescribable malice of her smile, her sing-song mockery as she stood there swaying from her hips and licking her sugar-cone, roused all the sullen obstinacy in me.

"If I go," said I, "I won't study my books anyway. I'm too old to study with you and Peter, and I won't! You will see!"

Sir William's favourite ferret, Vix, with muzzle on, came sneaking along the wall, and I grasped the lithe animal and thrust it at Silver Heels, whereupon she kicked my legs with her moccasins, which did not hurt, and ran up-stairs like a wild-cat.

There was nothing for me but to go to the school-room. I laid my rod in the corner, pocketed the ferret, dragged my books from under the library table, and went slowly up the stairs.

At sixteen I was as wilful a dunce as ever dangled feet in a school-room, knowing barely sufficient Latin to follow Cæsar through Gaul, loathing mathematics, scorning the poets, and even obstinately marring my pen-writing with a heavy backward stroke in defiance of Sir William and poor Mr. Yost.

As for mythology, my tow-head was over-crammed with kennel-lore and the multitude of small details bearing upon fishing and the chase, to accommodate the classics.

Destined, against my will, for Dartmouth College by my guardian, who very well understood that I desired to be a soldier, I had resolutely set myself against every school-room accomplishment, with the result that, at sixteen, I presented an ignorance which should have shamed a lad of ten, but did not mortify me in the least.

And now, to my dismay and rage, Sir William had set me once more in the school-room—and under Mr. Butler, too!

"Master Cardigan," said Mr. Butler when I entered the room, "Sir William desires you to prepare a recitation upon the story of Proserpine."

I muttered rebelliously, but jerked my mythology from the pile of books and began to thumb the leaves noisily. Presently tiring of dingy print, I moved up to the bench where sat the children, Peter and Esk, a-conning their horn-books.

Silver Heels pulled a face at me behind her French grammar book, and I pinched her arm smartly for her impudence. Then, casting about for something to do, I remembered the ferret in my pocket, and dragged it out. Removing the silver bit I permitted the ferret to bite Peter's tight breeches, not meaning to hurt him; but Peter screeched and Mr. Butler birched him well, knowing all the while it was no fault of Peter's; yet such was the nature of the man that, when angry, the innocent must suffer when the guilty were beyond his wrath.

I had remuzzled the ferret, and Peter was smearing the tears from his cheeks, when Sir William came in, very angry, saying that Mistress Molly could hear us in the nursery, and that the infant had fallen a-roaring with his new teeth.

"I did it, sir," said I, "and Mr. Butler punished Peter—"

"Silence!" said Sir William, sharply. "Put that ferret out the window!"

"The ferret is your best one—Vix," I answered. "She will run to the warren and we shall have to dig her out—"

"Pocket her, then," said Sir William, hastily. "Who gave you leave to pouch my ferrets? Eh? What has a ferret to do in school? Eh? Idle again? Captain Butler, is he idle?"

"He is a dunce," said Mr. Butler, with a shrug.

"Dunce!" echoed Sir William, quickly. "Why should he be a dunce when I have taught him? Granted his Latin would shame a French priest, and his mathematics sicken a Mohawk, have I not read the poets with him?"

Mr. Butler, a gentleman and an officer of rank and fortune, whose degraded whims led him now to instruct youth as a pastime, sharpened a quill in silence.

"Gad," muttered Sir William, "have I not read mythology with him till I dreamed of nymphs and satyrs and capered in my dreams till Mistress Molly—but that's neither here nor there. Micky!"

"Sir," I replied, sulkily.

Then he began to question me concerning certain gods and demi-gods, and I gaped and floundered as though I were no better than the inky rabble ruled over by Mr. Butler.

Sir William lounged by the window in his spurred boots and scarlet hunting-coat, and smelling foul of the kennels, which, God knows, I do not find unpleasant; and at every slap of the whip over his boots, he shot me through and through with a question which I had neither information nor inclination to answer before the grinning small fry.

Now to be hectored and questioned by Sir William like a sniffling lad with one eye on the birch and the other on Mr. Butler, did not please me. Moreover, the others were looking on—Esk with ink on his nose, Peter in tears, a-licking his lump of spruce, and that wild-cat thing, Silver Heels—

With every question of Sir William I felt I was losing caste among them. Besides, there was Mr. Butler with his silent, deathly laugh—a laugh that never reached his eyes—yellow, changeless eyes, round as a bird's.

Slap came the whip on the polished boot-tops, and Sir William was at it again with his gods and goddesses:

"Who carried off Proserpine? Eh?"

I looked sullenly at Esk, then at Peter, who put out his tongue at me. I had little knowledge of mythology beyond what concerned that long-legged goddess who loved hunting—as I did.

"Who carried off Proserpine?" repeated Sir William. "Come now, you should know that; come now—a likely lass, Proserpine, out in the bush pulling cowslips, bless her little fingers—when—ho!—up pops—eh?—who, lad, who in Heaven's name?"

"Plato!" I muttered at hazard.

"What!" bawled Sir William.

I felt for my underlip and got it between my teeth, and for a space not another word would I speak, although that hollow roar began to sound in Sir William's voice which always meant a scene. His whip, too, went slap-slap! on his boots, like the tail of a big dog rapping its ribs.

He was perhaps a violent man, Sir William, yet none outside of his own family ever suspected it or do now believe it, he having so perfect a control over himself when he chose. And I often think that his outbursts towards us were all pretence, and to test his own capacity for temper lest he had lost it in a long lifetime of self-control. At all events, none of us ever were the worse for his roaring, although it frightened us when very young; but we soon came to understand that it was as harmless as summer thunder.

"Come, sir! Come, Mr. Cardigan!" said Sir William, grimly. "Out with the gentleman's name—d'ye hear?"

It was the first time in my life that Sir William had spoken to me as Mr. Cardigan. It might have pleased me had I not seen Mr. Butler sneer.

I glared at Mr. Butler, whose face became shadowy and loose, without expression, without life, save for the fixed stare of those round eyes.

Slap! went Sir William's whip on his boots.

"Damme!" he shouted, in a passion, "who carried off that slut Proserpine?"

"The Six Nations, for aught I know!" I muttered, disrespectfully.

Sir William's face went redder than his coat; but, as it was ever his habit when affronted, he stood up very straight and still; and that tribute of involuntary silence which was always paid to him at such moments, we paid, sitting awed and quiet as mice.

"Turn the children free, Captain Butler," said Sir William, in a low voice.

Mr. Butler flung back the door. The children followed him, Esk bestowing a wink upon me, Peter grinning and toeing in like a Devon duck, and that wild-cat thing, Silver Heels—

"You need not wait, Captain Butler," said Sir William, politely.

Mr. Butler retired, leaving the door swinging. Out in the dark hallway I fancied I could still see his shallow eyes shining. I may have been mistaken. But all men know now that Walter Butler hath eyes that see as well by dark as by the light of the sun; and none know it so well as the people of New York Province and of Tryon County.

"Michael," said Sir William, "go to the slate."

I walked across the dusty school-room.

"Chalk!" shouted Sir William, irritated by my lagging steps.

I picked up a lump of chalk, balancing it in my palm as boys do a pebble in a sling.

Something in my eyes may have infuriated Sir William.

The next moment he had me by the arm, then by the collar, whip whistling like the chimney wind—and whistling quite as idly, for the blow never fell.

I freed myself; he made no effort to hold me.

"Keep your lash for your hounds!" I stammered.

He did not seem to hear me, but I planted myself in a corner and cried out that he dare not lay his whip on me, which was a shameful thing to taunt him with, for he had promised me never to lay rod to me; and I knew, as all the world knows, that Sir William Johnson had never broken his word to man or savage.

But still I faced him, now hurling safe defiance, now muttering revenge, until the scornful rebuke in his eyes began to shame me into silence. Tingling already with self-contempt, I dropped my head a little, not so low but what I could see Sir William's bulk motionless before me.

Presently he said, as though to himself: "If the boy's a coward, no man can lay the sin to me."

"I am not a coward!" I burst out, all a-quiver again, "and I ask your pardon, sir, for daring you to lay whip on me,—knowing your promise!"

Sir William scowled at me.

"To prove it," I went on, desperately, still trembling at the word "coward," "I will give you leave to drive a fish-hook through my hand and cut it out with your knife; and I'll laugh at the pain—as did that Mohawk lad when you cut the pike-hook out of his hand!"

"What the devil have I to do with your fish-hook and your Mohawks!" shouted Sir William, with a hearty oath.

Mortified, I shrank back while he fumed and cracked his whip and swore I was doomed to folly and a most vicious future.

"You assume the airs of a man," he roared—"you with your sixteen unbirched years—you with your gross ignorance and grosser impudence! A vicious lad, a bad, undutiful, sullen lad, ever at odds with the others, never diligent save with the fishing-rod—a lazy, quarrelsome rustic, a swaggering, forest-running fellow, without the polish or the presence of a gentleman's son! Shame on you!"

I set my teeth and shut both eyes, opening one, however, when I heard him move.

"I'll polish you yet!" he said, with an oath; "I'll polish you, and I'll temper you like the edge on a Mohawk hatchet."

"One red belt," I added, impudently, meaning that I defied him.

"Which you will cover with a white belt before the fires in this hearth are dead," he answered, gulping down the disrespect.

He laid his heavy hand on the door, then, turning, he bade me write with the chalk on the slate the history of Proserpine in verse, and await his further pleasure.

Sir William had shut the school-room door upon me. I listened. Had he locked it I should have kicked the panelling out into the hallway.

Standing there alone in the school-room beside the great slate, I read in dull anger the names of those who, tasks ended, were now free of the hateful place; here Esk had left his name above his sum, all smears; here fat Peter had written seven times, "David did die and so must I."

With a bit of buckskin I dusted these scrawls from the slate, slowly, for I was not yet of a mind to begin my task.

I opened the window behind me. A sweet spring wind was blowing. Putting up my nose to scent it, I saw the sky bluer than a heron's egg, and a little white cloud a-sailing up there all alone.

That year the snow had gone out in April, and the same day the blue-birds flew into the sheep-fold. Now, on this second day of May, robins were already running over the ground below the school-room window, a-tilting for worms like jack-snipes along the creek.

Folding my arms to lean on the sill, I could see a corner of the northern block-house, with a soldier standing guard below in the sunshine, and I peppered him well with spit-balls, he being a friend of mine.

His mystified anger brought but temporary pleasure to me. Behind me lay that villanous slate, and my task to deal with the ravishment of that silly creature, Proserpine—and that, too, in verse! Had it been my long-legged Diana with her view-halloo and her hounds and shooting her arrows like a Huron squaw from the lakes! But no!—my business lay with a puny, cowslip-pulling maid who had strayed from the stockade and got her deserts, too, for aught I know.

Leaning there in the breezy casement I tried to forget the jade, attentively observing the birds and the young fruit-trees, Sir William's pride. Now that the snow had melted I could see where mice, working under the crust in midwinter, had fatally girdled two young apple-trees; and I was sorry, loving apples as I do.

For a while my mind was occupied in devising a remedy against girdling; then the distant sparkle of the river caught my eye, and straightway my thoughts slipped into their natural channel, smoothly as the river flowed there in the sunshine; and I laid my plans for the taking of that bull-trout who had so grossly deceived and flouted me the past year—ay, not only me, but also that master of the craft, Sir William himself.

Thinking of Sir William, my lagging thoughts drifted back again to my desk. It madded me to pine here, making rhymes, while outside the sweet wind whispered: "Come out, Michael—come out into the green delight!"

Now Sir William had bidden me, not only to write my verses, but also to bide here awaiting his good pleasure. That meant he would return by-and-by. I had no stomach for further quarrels. Besides, I was ashamed of my disrespect and temper, and indeed, selfish, idle beast that I was, I did truly love Sir William because I knew he was the greatest man of our times—and because he loved me.

Resolved at last to accomplish some verses as proof of a contrite and diligent spirit, I set to work; and this is what I made:

"Proserpine did roam the hills,

Intent on culling daffydills;

Alas, in gleeful girlish sport,

She wandered too far from the fort,

Forgetting that no belt of peace,

Bound the people of Pluto from war to cease;

Alas, old Pluto lay in wait,

To ambush all who stayed out late;

And with a dreadful war-whoop he

Ran after the doomed Proserpine—"

Absorbed in my task, and, moreover, considerably affected by the piteous plight of the maid, I stepped back from the slate and for a moment conceived a generous idea of introducing somebody to rescue Proserpine and leave Pluto damaged—perhaps scalped. Reflection, however, dissuaded me from such a liberty, not that I found the anachronism at all discordant, for, living all my life in a family where Indians were oftener seen than white men, my hazy notions concerning classic myths were inextricably mixed with the reality of my own life, and were also gayly coloured by the legends I learned from my red neighbours. So, lazy dunce that I was, with but a fraction of my attention fixed on my tasks, mythology to me was but a Græco-Mohawk medley of jumbled fables, interesting only when they concerned war or the chase.

Still I did not feel at liberty to rescue Proserpine in my verses or plump a war-arrow into Pluto. Besides I knew it would enrage Sir William.

As I stood there, breathing hard, resolved to finish the wretched maiden quickly and let the metre go a-limping, behind me I heard the door stealthily open, and I knew that long-legged wild-cat thing, Silver Heels, had crept in, her moccasins making no noise.

I pretended not to notice her, knowing she had come to taunt me; and, for a space, she stood behind me, very still. Clearly, she was reading my verses, and I became angry. Not to show it, I made out to whistle and to draw a picture of a fish on the slate. Then she knew I had seen her and laughed hatefully.

"Oh," said I, "if there is somebody come a-prying, it must be Silver Heels!" And I turned around, pretending amazement at the justness of my hazard.

"You saw me," she answered, disdainfully.

"It is your hour for the stocks," I hinted.

"I won't go," she retorted.

To secure that grace of carriage and elegance of presence necessary for a young lady of quality, and to straighten her back, which truly was as straight as a pine, Sir William and Mistress Molly were accustomed to strap her to a pine plank and lock her in the stocks for an hour at noon, forbidding Peter, Esk, and me to tickle the soles of her feet.

It was noon now; I could hear the guard changing at the north block-house, tramp! tramp! tramp! across the stony way.

"If you don't go to the stocks now," I said, "you'll be sorry when you do go."

"If you tickle my feet, you great booby, I'll tell Sir William," she retorted, balancing defiantly from one heel to the other.

"Will you go, Silver Heels?" I insisted.

"My name isn't Silver Heels," she observed, still coolly tilting back and forth on heels and toes. "Call me by my right name and perhaps I'll go—and perhaps I won't. So there, Mr. Micky Dunce!"

"If I call you Felicity Warren, will you go?" I inquired cautiously.

"There! you have called me Felicity Warren!" she cried in triumph.

"I didn't," said I, in a temper; "I only said that there was such a person. But you are not that person! Anyway, you toe in like a Mohawk. Anyway, you're half wild-cat, half Mohawk."

"It's a lie!" she flashed; "I'm all white to the bones of my body!"

It was true. Indeed, she was kin to Sir William and niece to Sir Peter Warren, but, to torment her, we feigned to believe her one of Mistress Molly's brood, half Mohawk; and it madded her. Besides, had not the Mohawks dubbed her Silver Heels, a year ago, when, with naked flying feet, she had beaten us all in the foot-race before Sir William and half the people of the Six Nations?

The prize had been a Barlow jack-knife, which, before the race, I had looked upon as mine. Besides, I had rashly given my old knife to Esk, and that left me without a blade to notch whistles.

"You are a Mohawk," I said, resentfully; "also you are a cat-child beneath notice. When you are hungry you cry, 'Miau! *Eso cautfore!*—like Peter."

"I don't!" she said, stamping her moccasin.

"Anyway," said I, disdaining to torment her further, "the guard is changed these ten minutes, and Sir William will come to find you here a-prying. *Esogee cadagcariax*," I added, incautiously.

"Who is Mohawk, now!" she cried, clapping her hands. "Bah, Mister Micky, it is spoon-meat *you* require to make you run the faster after jack-knives!"

This outrageous taunt ruffled me, the more for her laughter. I attempted to hold my head in the air and look down at the presumptuous child, but it appeared she had grown very fast in the past months since the race, and I was disturbed to find her eyes already on a straight line with mine, though she was but fifteen and I sixteen.

"I'm as high as you," she said.

"I can jump and touch the ceiling," said I; and did so.

She strove in vain, then called me dunce, and vowed what brains I had were in my feet. For that, and because she pushed me, I seized the chalk and wrote high on the slate:

"Silver Heels is Mohock she toes in like ducks."

She caught up the buckskin to wipe out the taunt, jostling me till the ferret in my pocket jumped out and ran round and round the room.

I jostled her; then she gave me a blow and a quick shove, whereupon I stumbled, pulling her to the floor to rub her face with chalk. She twisted and turned, kicking and striking while I rubbed chalk into her skin, till of a sudden she coiled up and bit me clean through the hand.

I was on my feet with a bound; she also, all white in the face and her eyes aflame.

The blood began welling up, running into my palm and along the fingers to the floor. At that same instant I heard the door of the nursery open, and I knew that Sir William was coming through the hall to the school-room.

From instinct I thrust my wounded hand into my breeches-pocket.

"Don't tell!" whispered Silver Heels, in a fright; "don't tell—and here is the jack-knife."

She thrust it into my right hand, then sped across the floor to the open window, and over the sill, dropping light as a cat on the grass below.

My first impulse was to follow her and give her such a spank as Mistress Molly administered the day she trounced her for pushing Peter into the creek. However, it was already too late; Sir William came quickly along the hall, and I had scarce time to step to the slate when he marched in.

Sir William had changed his clothing for the buckskin hunting-shirt and breeches which he was accustomed to wear when angling. He carried, too, that light, seasoned rod, fashioned for him by Thayendanegea, and on his bosom he wore a bouquet of gayly coloured feather-flies, made by Mistress Molly during the winter.

He approached the slate whereon my verses stared white and unfinished; and at first his brows knitted and he said, "Fudge, fudge, fudge!" Then of a sudden he sat down on the bench, clapping his hand to his brow.

"Oh Lord!" said he, and fell a-laughing, while I, hot, ashamed, and a little dizzy, my breeches-pocket being full of blood, gnawed my lips and glowered askance.

"The Lord's will be done," said he, taking breath. "Who am I to ordain, when He who fashioned yon tow-head designed it to hold neither Latin nor the classics?"

"It pleases you to laugh, sir," I muttered.

"Pleases me! Pleases me, quotha! Lad, it stabs me like a French dirk, nor can I guard the thrust in tierce! I have been wrong. A friar is not made with a twisted rope nor a man hanged with words. If you are not born a scholar, 'twas the mint-mark I could not read aright; and no blame to you, lad, no blame to you. Micky boy! Shall we leave Cæsar to go marching with his impedimenta and his Tenth Legion? Shall we consign the hypothenuse of all triangles to those who mend pens from the quills of wild-geese which better men have brought down with a single ball?"

I was regarding him wildly, uncertain of his meaning.

"Shall we," cried Sir William, heartily, "bid the nymphs and dryads farewell forever, lad, and save our learning for Roderick Random and a bowl of cider and the bitter nights of December?"

His meaning was dawning upon me slowly, for what with the pain of my hand and the dizziness, I was perhaps more stupid than usual.

"No," said Sir William, with a thump of his fist on his knee, "the college which my Lord Dartmouth has endowed is a haven for those who seek it, not a prison for men to be driven to."

He paused.

"I should have sought it," he said, dropping his head. "No wilderness, no wintry terrors, neither French scalping parties nor the savages of all the Canadas could have kept me from instruction had I, in my youth, been favoured by the opportunity I offer you."

I gazed at him in silence while the blood, overrunning my leather pocket, ran down to my knee-buckles.

"I was poor, without means, without counsel, save for the letters Sir Peter Warren wrote me. I traded for my daily bread; I read Ovid by lighted pine splinters; I worked—God knows I worked my flesh to the bone."

He sat, fingering the bunch of scarlet feather-flies in his breast.

"Our Lord gives us according to our needs—*when we take it*," he said, without irreverence. "I could have gone to England, to Oxford; I had saved enough. I did neither; I did not take the instruction I wished for, and God did not teach me Greek in my dreams," he added, bitterly.

The blood was now stealing down my stocking towards my shoe. I turned the leg so he could not observe it.

"Come, lad," he said, brightening up; "learning lies not always between thumbed leaves. I only wish that you bear yourself modestly and nobly through the world; that you keep faith with men, that your word once given shall never be withdrawn.

"This is the foundation. It includes courage. Further than that, I desire you, once a purpose formed and a course set, to steer fearlessly to the goal.

"I know you to be brave and honest; I know you to be a very Mohawk in the forest; I believe you to be merciful and tender underneath that boy's thoughtless and cruel hide.

"As for learning, I can do no more for you than I have done and have offered to do. If it pleases you, you may go to England, and learn the arts, bearing, and deportment you can never acquire here with us. No? Well, then, stay with us. I want you, Micky. We Irish are fond of each other—and I am an old man now—I am nigh sixty years, Michael—sixty years of battle. I would be glad of rest—with those I love."

My heart was very soft now. I looked at Sir William with an affection I had never before understood.

"There is one last thing I wish to add," he said, gravely, almost sadly. "Perhaps I may again refer to it—but I pray that it may not be necessary."

I sat up and rubbed my eyes to clear them from the sickly faintness which stole upward from my throbbing hand.

"It is this," he continued, in a low voice. "If it ever comes to you to choose between his Majesty our King and—and your native land—which God forbid!—go to your closet and kneel down, and stay there on your knees, hours, days!—until you have learned your own heart. Then—then—God go with you, Michael Cardigan."

He rose, and his face was years older. Slowly the colour came back into his cheeks; he fumbled with the brass-work on his fish-rod, then smiled.

"That is all," he said; "let Pluto chase Proserpine to hell, lad; and a devilish good place they say it is for those who like it! Where is that ferret? What! Running about unmuzzled! Hey! Vix! Vix! Come here, little reptile!"

"I'll catch her, sir," said I, stumbling forward.

But as I laid my hand on Vix the floor rose and struck me, and there I lay sprawling and senseless, with the blood running over the floor; and Sir William, believing me bitten by the ferret, pouched the poor beast and lifted me to a bench.

He must have seen my hand, however, for, when a cup of cold water set me spluttering and blinking, I found my hand tied up in Sir William's handkerchief and Sir William himself eying me strangely.

"How came that wound?" he said, bluntly.

I could not reply—or would not.

He asked me again whether the ferret bit me, and I was tempted to say yes. Treachery was abhorrent to me; I hated Silver Heels, but could not betray her, and it was easy to clap the blame on Vix.

"Sir?" I stammered.

"I asked what bit you," he said, icily.

I tried to say Vix, but the lie, too, stuck in my throat.

"I cannot tell you," I muttered.

"Then," said Sir William, with a strange smile of relief, "I shall not force you, Michael. May I honourably ask you how you come by this jack-knife?"

I shook my head. My face was on fire.

"Very well," he said. "Only remember that you are a man, now—a man of sixteen, and that I have to-day treated you as a man, and shall continue. And remember that a man's first duty is to protect the weaker sex, and his second duty is to endure from them all taunts, caprice, and torments without revenge. It is a hard lesson to learn, Micky, and only the true and gallant gentleman can ever learn it."

He smiled, then said:

"Pray find our little Silver Heels and return to her the jack-knife, which was her wampum-belt of faith in the honour of a gentleman."

And so he walked away, smoothing the fur of the red-eyed ferret against his breast.

CHAPTER II

When Sir William left me in the school-room, he left a lad of sixteen puffed up in a glow of pride. To be treated no longer as a fractious child—to be received at last as a man among men!

And what would Esk say? And Silver Heels, poor little mouse harnessed in the stocks below?

I had entered the school-room that morning a lazy, sullen, defiant lad, heavy-hearted, with chronic resentment against the discipline of those who had sent me into a hateful trap from the windows of which I could see the young, thirsty year quaffing spring sunshine. Now I was free to leave the accursed trap forever, a man of discretion, responsible before men, exacting from other men the same courtesies, attentions, and considerations which I might render them.

What a change had come to me, all in one brief May morning! As I stood there, resting my bandaged hand in the palm of the other, looking about me to realize the fortune which set my veins tingling, a great tide of benevolent condescension for the others swept over me, a ripple of pity and good-will for the hapless children whose benches lay in a row before me.

I no longer detested Silver Heels. I walked on tiptoe to her bench. There lay her slate and slate-pen; upon it I read a portion of the longer catechism. There, too, lay her quill and inky horn and a foolscap book sewed neatly and marked:

FELICITY WARREN
1774
HER BOOKE.

Poor child, doomed for years still to steep her little fingers in ink-powder while, with the powder I should require hereafter, I expected to write fiercer tales on living hides with plummets cast in bullet-moulds!

Cramped with importance, I cast a contemptuous eye upon my poem which embellished the great slate, and scoured it partly out with the buckskin.

"My books," said I, to myself, "I will bestow upon Silver Heels and Esk;" and I carried out my philanthropic impulse, piling speller, reader, and arithmetic on Esk's bench; my Cæsar, my pair of globes, my compass, and my algebra I laid with Silver Heels's copy-book, first writing in the books, with some malice:

```
SILVER HEELS HER GIFT BOOKE FROM
MICHAEL CARDIGAN
BE DILIGENT AND OF GOOD THRIFT
KNOWLEDGE IS POWER.
```

For fat Peter, because I allowed Vix to bite his tight breeches, I left a pile of jacks beside his horn-book, namely, a slate-pen, three mended quills, a birchen box of ink-powder, a screw to trade with, two tops and an alley, pumice, a rule, and some wax.

Peter, though duck-limbed and half Mohawk, wrote very well in the Boston style, and could even copy in the Lettre Frisée—a poor art in some repute, but smelling to my nose of French flummery and deceit.

Having bestowed these gifts with a light heart, I walked slowly around the room, and I fear my walk was somewhat a strut.

I knew my small head was all swelled with vain imaginings; I saw myself in a flapped coat and lace, fingering the hilt of a sword at my hip, saluted by the sentries and the militia; I saw myself riding with Sir William as his deputy; I heard him say, "Mr. Cardigan, the enemy are upon us! We must fly!"—and I: "Sir William, fear nothing. The day is our own!" And I saw a lad of sixteen, with sword pointing upward and one hand twisted into Pontiac's scalp-lock, smile benignly upon Sir William, who had cast himself upon my breast, protesting that I had saved the army, and that the King should hear of it.

Then, unbidden, the apparition of Mr. Butler rose into my vain dreaming, and, though I am no prophet, nor can I claim the gift of seeing behind the veil, yet I swear that Walter Butler appeared to me all aflame and bloody with scalps bunched at his girdle—*and the scalps were not of the red men!*

Now my imagination smoking into fire, I saw myself dogging Mr. Butler with firelock a-trail and knife loosened, on! on! through fathomless depths of forest and by the still deeps of shadowy lakes, fording the roaring tumble of rivers, swimming silent pools as otters swim, but tracking him, ever tracking Captain Butler by the scent of his reeking scalps.

There was a dew on my eyebrows as I waked into sense. Yet again I fell straightway to imagining the glories of my young future. Truly I painted life in cloying colours; and always, when I accomplished gallant deeds, there stood Silver Heels to observe me, and to marvel, and to stamp her little moccasins in vexation that I, the pride and envy of all men, applauded, courted, nay, worshipped—I, the playmate she had in her silly ignorance flouted, now stood so far beyond her that she dared not twitch the skirt of my coat nor whisper, "Sir Michael, pray condescend to notice one who passes her entire life in admiring your careless exploits."

Perhaps I would smile at her—yes, I certainly should speak to her—not with familiarity. But I would be magnanimous; she should receive gifts, spoils from wars, and I would select a suitable husband for her from the officers of my household who adored me! No, I would not be hasty concerning a husband. That would be foolish, for Silver Heels must remain heart-whole and fancy-free to concentrate her envious admiration upon me.

In a sort of ecstasy I paraded the school-room, the splendour of my visions dulling eyes and ears, and it was not until he had called me thrice that I observed Mr. Butler standing within the doorway.

The unwelcome sight cleared my brains like a dash of spring-water in the face.

"It is one o'clock," said Mr. Butler, "and time for your carving lesson. Did you not hear the bugles from the forts?"

"I heard nothing, sir," said I, giving him a surly look, which he returned with that blank stare of the eyes, noticeable in hawks and kites and foul night birds surprised by light.

"Sir William dines early," he said, as I followed him through the dim hallway, past the nursery, and down stairs. "If he has to wait your pleasure for his slice of roast, you will await his pleasure for the remainder of the day in the school-room."

"It is not true!" I said, stopping short in the lower hallway. "I am free of that ratty pit forever! And of the old ferret, too," I added, insolently.

"By your favour," said Mr. Butler, "may I ask whether your erudition is impairing your bodily health, that you leave school so early in life, Master Cardigan?"

"If you were a real schoolmaster," said I, hotly, "I would answer you with a kennel lash, but you are an officer and a gentleman." And in a low voice I bade him go to the devil at his convenience.

"One year more and I could call you out for this," he said, staring at me.

"You can do it now!" I retorted, angrily, raising myself a little on my toes.

Suddenly all the hatred and contempt I had so long choked back burst out in language I now blush for. I called him a coward, a Huron, a gentleman with the instincts of a pedagogue. I heaped abuse upon him; I dared him to meet me; nay, I challenged him to face me with rifle or sword, when and where he chose. And all the time he stood staring at me with that deathly laugh which never reached his eyes.

"Measure me!" I said, venomously; "I am as tall as you, lacking an inch. I am a man! This day Sir William freed me from that spider-web you tenant, and now in Heaven's name let us settle that score which every hour has added to since I first beheld you!"

"And my honour?" he asked, coldly.

"What?" I stammered. "I ask you to maintain it with rifle or rapier! Blood scours tarnished names!"

"Not your blood," he said, with a stealthy glance at the dining-room door; "not the blood of a boy. That would rust my honour. Wait, Master Cardigan, wait a bit. A year runs like a spotted fawn in cherry-time!"

"You will not meet me?" I blurted out, mortified.

"In a year, perhaps," he said, absently, scarcely looking at me as he spoke.

Then from within the dining-hall came Sir William's roar: "Body o' me! Am I to be kept here at twiddle-thumbs for lack of a carver!"

I stepped back in an instant, bowing to Mr. Butler.

"I will be patient for a year, sir," I said. And so opened the door while he passed me, and into the dining-hall.

"I am sorry, sir," said I, but Sir William cut me short with:

"Damnation, sir! I am asking a blessing!"

So I buried my nose in my hollowed hand and stood up, very still.

Having given thanks in a temper, Sir William's frown relaxed and he sat down and tucked his finger-cloth under his neck with an injured glance at me.

"Zounds!" he said, mildly; "hell hath no fury like a fisherman kept waiting. Captain Butler, bear me out."

"I am no angler," said Mr. Butler, in his deadened voice.

"That is true," observed Sir William, as though condoling with Mr. Butler for a misfortune not his fault. "Perhaps some day the fever may scorch you—like our young kinsman Micky—eh, lad?"

I said, "Perhaps, sir," with eyes on the smoking joint before me. It was Sir William's pleasure that I learn to carve; and, in truth, I found it easy, save for the carving of a goose or of those wild-ducks we shot on the great Vlaie.

We were but four to dine that day: Sir William, Mr. Butler, Silver Heels, and myself. Mistress Molly remained in the nursery, where were also Peter and Esk, inasmuch as they slobbered and fouled the cloth, and so fed in the play-room.

Colonel Guy Johnson remained at Detroit, Captain John Johnson was on a mission to Albany, Thayendanegea in Quebec, and Colonel Claus, with his lady, had gone to Castle Cumberland. There were no visiting officers or Indians at Johnson Hall that week, and our small company seemed lost in the great dining-hall.

Having carved the juicy joint, the gilly served Sir William, then Mr. Butler, then Silver Heels, whom I had scarcely noticed, so full was I of my quarrel with Mr. Butler. Now, as Saunders laid her plate, I gave her a look which meant, "I did not tell Sir William," whereupon she smiled at her plate and clipped a spoonful from a dish of potatoes.

"Good appetite and good health, sir," said I, raising my wine-glass to Sir William.

"Good health, my lad!" said Sir William, heartily.

Glasses were raised again and compliments said, though my face was sufficient to sour the Madeira in Mr. Butler's glass.

"Your good health, Michael," said Silver Heels, sweetly.

I pledged her with a patronizing amiability which made her hazel-gray eyes open wide.

Now, coxcomb that I was, I sat there, dizzied by my new dignity, yet carefully watching Sir William to imitate him, thinking that, as I was now a man, I must observe the carriage, deportment, and tastes of men.

When Sir William declined a dish of jelly, I also waved it away, though God knew I loved jellies.

When Sir William drank the last of the winter's ale, I shoved aside my small-beer and sent for a mug.

"It will make a humming-top of your head," said Sir William. "Stick to small-beer, Micky."

Mortified, I tossed off my portion, and was very careful not to look at Silver Heels, being hot in the face.

Mr. Butler and Sir William spoke gravely of the discontent now rampant in the town of Boston, and of Captain John Johnson's mission to Albany. I listened greedily, sniffing for news of war, but understood little of their discourse save what pertained to the Indians.

Some mention, indeed, was made of rangers, but, having always associated militia and rangers with war on the Indians, I thought little of what they discussed. I even forgot my new dignity, and secretly pinched a bread crumb into the shape of a little pig which I showed to Silver Heels. She thereupon pinched out a dog with hound's ears for me to admire.

I was roused by Sir William's voice in solemn tones to Mr. Butler: "Now, God forbid I should live to see that, Captain Butler!" and I pricked up my ears once more, but made nothing of what followed, save that there were certain disloyal men in Massachusetts and New York who might rise against our King and that our Governor Tryon meant to take some measures concerning tea.

"Well, well," burst out Sir William at length; "in evil days let us thank God that the fish still swim! Eh, Micky? I wish the ice were out."

"The anchor-ice is afloat, and the Kennyetto is free, sir," I said, quickly.

"How do you know?" asked Sir William, laughing.

I had, the day previous, run across to the Kennyetto to see, and I told him so.

He was pleased to praise my zeal and to say I ran like a Mohawk, which praise sounded sweet until I saw Silver Heels's sly smile, and I remembered the foot-race and the jack-knife.

But I was above foot-races now. Others might run to amuse me; I would look on—perhaps distribute prizes.

"Some day, Sir William, will you not make me one of your deputies?" I asked, eagerly.

"Hear the lad!" cried Sir William, pushing back his chair. "On my soul, Captain Butler, it is time for old weather-worn Indian commissioners like me to resign and make way for younger blood! And his Majesty might be worse served than by Micky here; eh, Captain Butler?"

"Perhaps," said Mr. Butler, in his dead voice.

Sir William rose and we all stood up. The Baronet, brushing Silver Heels on his way to the door, passed his arm around her and tilted her chin up.

"Now do you go to Mistress Mary and beg her to place you in the stocks for an hour; and stay there in patience for your body's grace. Will you promise me, Felicity?"

Silver Heels began to pout and tease, hooking her fingers in Sir William's belt, but the Baronet packed her off with his message to Mistress Molly, and went out to the portico where one of his damned Scotch gillies attended with gaff, spear, and net-sack.

"Oho," thought I, "so it's salmon in the Sacondaga!" And I fell to teasing that he might take me, too.

"No, Micky," he said, soberly; "it's less for sport than for quiet reflection that I go. Don't sulk, lad. To-morrow, perhaps."

"Is it a promise, sir?" I cried.

"Perhaps," he laughed, "if the cards turn up right."

That meant he had some Indian affair on hand, and I fell back, satisfied that his rod was a ruse, and that he was really bound for one of the council fires at the upper castle.

So he went away, the sentry at the south block-house presenting his firelock, and I back into the hall, whistling, enchanted with my new liberty, yet somewhat concerned as to the disposal of so vast an amount of time, now all my own.

I had now been enfranchised nearly three hours, and had already used these first moments of liberty in picking a mortal quarrel with Mr. Butler. I had begun rashly; I admitted that; yet I could not regret the defiance. Soon or late I felt that Mr. Butler and I would meet; I had believed it for years. Now that at last our tryst was in sight, it neither surprised nor disturbed me, nor, now that he was out of my sight, did I feel impatient to settle it, so accustomed had I become to waiting for the inevitable hour.

I strolled through the hallway, hands in pockets, whistling "Amaryllis," a tune that smacked on my lips; and so came to the south casement. Pressing my nose to the pane, I looked into the young orchard where the robins ran in the new grass; and I found it delicious to linger in-doors, knowing I was free to go out when I chose, and none to cry, "Come back!"

In the first flush of surprise and pleasure, I have noticed that the liberated seldom venture instantly into that freedom so dearly desired. Open the cage of a thrush that has sung all winter of freedom, and lo! the little thing, creeping out under the sky, runs back to the cage, fearing the sweet freedom of its heart's desire.

So I; and mounted the stairway, seeking my own little chamber. Here I found Esk and Peter at play, letting down a string from the open window, baited with corn, and the pullets jumping for it with great outcry and flapping of wings.

So I played with them for a while, then put them out, and bolted the door despite their cries and kicks.

Sitting there on my cot I surveyed my domain serenely, proud as though it had been a mansion and all mine.

There were my books, not much thumbed save *Roderick Random* and the prints of Le Brun's *Battles of Alexander*. Still I cherished the others because gifts of Sir William or relics of my honoured father—the two volumes called *An Introduction to Sir Isaac Newton's Philosophy*; two volumes of *Chambers's Dictionary*; all the volumes of *The Gentleman's Magazine* from 1748; Titan's *Loves of the Gods*—an immodest print which I hated; my beloved "Amaryllis," called *A New Musical Design*, and well bound; and last a manuscript much faded and eaten by mice, yet readable, and it was a most lovely song composed long since by a Mr. Pepys, the name of which was "Gaze not on Swans!"

My chamber was small, yet pleasing. Upon the walls I had placed, by favour of Sir William, pictures of the best running-horses at Newmarket, also four prints of a camp by Watteau, well executed, though French. Also, there hung above the door a fox's mask, my whip, my hunting-horn, my spurs, and two fish-rods made for me by Joseph Brant, who is called Thayendanegea, chief of the Mohawk and of the Six Nations, and brother to Aunt Molly, who is no kin of mine, though her children are Sir William's, and he is my kinsman.

In this room also I kept my black lead-pencil made by Faber, a ream of paper from England, and a lump of red sealing-wax.

I had written, in my life, but two letters: one three years since I wrote to Sir Peter Warren to thank him for a sum of money sent for my use; the other to a little girl named Marie Livingston, whom I knew in Albany when Sir William took me for the probating of papers which I do not yet understand.

She wrote me a letter, which was delivered by chance, the express having been scalped below Fonda's Bush, and signed "your cozzen Marie," Mr. Livingston being kin to Sir William. I had not yet written again to her, though I had meant to do so these twelve months past. She had yellow hair which was pleasing, and she did not resemble Silver Heels in complexion or manner, having never flouted me. Her father gave me two peaches, some Salem sweets called Black Jacks, and a Delaware basket to take home with me, heaped with macaroons, crisp almonds, rock-candy, caraways, and suckets. These I prudently finished before coming again to Johnson Hall, and I remember I forgot to save a sucket for Silver Heels; and her anger when I gave her the Delaware basket all sticky inside; and how Peter licked it and blubbered while still a-licking.

Thus, as I sat there on my cot, scenes of my life came jostling me like long-absent comrades, softening my mood until I fell to thinking of those honoured parents I had never seen save in the gray dreams which mazed my sleep. For the day that brought life to me had robbed my honoured mother of her life; and my father, Captain Cardigan, lying with Wolfe before Quebec, sent a runner to Sir William enjoining him to care for me should the chance of battle leave me orphaned.

So my father, with Wolfe's own song on his lips:

"Why, soldiers, why

Should we be melancholy boys?

Why, soldiers, why?

Whose business 'tis to die—"

fell into Colonel Burton's arms at the head of Webb's regiment, and his dying eyes saw the grenadiers wipe out the disgrace of Montmorency with dripping bayonets. So he died, with a smile, bidding Webb's regiment God-speed, and sending word to the dying Wolfe that he would meet him a minute hence at Peter's gate in heaven.

Thus came I naturally by my hatred for the French, nor was there in all France sufficient wampum to wipe away the feud or cover the dear phantom that stood in my path as I passed through life my way.

Now, as I sat a-thinking by the window, below me the robins in all the trees had begun their wild-wood vespers—hymns of the true thrush, though not rounded with a thrush's elegance.

The tree-shadows, too, had grown in length, and the afternoon sun wore a deeper blazonry through the hill haze in the west.

Fain to taste of the freedom which was now mine, I went out and down the stairs, passing my lady Silver Heels strapped to a back-board and in a temper with her sampler.

"Oh, Micky," she said, "my bones ache, and Mistress Molly is with the baby, and the key is there on that brass nail."

"It would be wrong if I released you," said I, piously, meaning to do it, nevertheless.

"Oh, Micky," she said, with a kind of pitiful sweetness which at times she used to obtain advantages from me.

So I took the key and unlocked the stocks, giving her feet a pinch to let her know I was not truly as soft-hearted as she might deem me, nor too easily won by woman's beseeching.

And now, mark! No sooner was she free than she gave me a slap for the pinch and away she flew like a tree-lynx with the pack in cry.

"This," thought I, "is a woman's gratitude," and I locked the stocks again, wishing Silver Heels's feet were in them.

"Best have it out at once with Mistress Molly," thought I, and went to the nursery. But before I could knock on the door, Mistress Molly heard me with her ears of a Mohawk, and came to the door with one finger on her lips.

Truly the sister of Thayendanegea was a stately and comely lady, and a beauty, too, being little darker than some French ladies I have seen, and of gracious and noble presence.

Bearing and mien were proud, yet winning; and, clothed always as befitted the lady of Sir William Johnson, none who came into her presence could think less of her because of her Mohawk blood or the relation she bore to Sir William—an honest one as she understood it.

She ruled the Hall with dignity and with an authority that none dreamed of opposing. At table she was silent, yet gracious; in the nursery she reigned a beloved and devoted mother; and if ever a man's wife remained his sweetheart to the end, Molly Brant was Sir William's true-love while his life endured.

"Why did you release Felicity from the stocks, Michael?" said she, in a whisper.

So her quick Indian ear had heard the click of that lock!

"I had come to tell you of it, Aunt Mary," said I.

She looked at me keenly, then smiled.

"A sin confessed is half redressed. I had meant to release Felicity some time since, but the baby had fretted herself to sleep in my arms and I feared to put her down. But, Michael, remember in future to ask permission when you desire to play with Felicity."

"Play with Felicity!" I said, scornfully. "I am past the playing age, Aunt Molly, and I only released her because I thought her back ached."

Mistress Molly looked at me again, long and keenly.

"Little savage," she said, gently, "mock at my people no more. I should chide you for misusing Peter, but—I will say nothing. You make my heart heavy sometimes."

"I do honour and love you, Aunt Molly!" I said; "it was not that I mocked at Peter, but his breeches were so tight that I wondered if Vix could bite him. I shall now go to the garden and allow Peter to kick my shins. Anyway, I gave him all my quills and a plummet and a screw."

She laughed silently, bidding me renounce my intention regarding Peter, and so dismissed me, with her finger on her lips conjuring silence.

So I pursued my interrupted way to the garden where the robins carolled in every young fruit-tree, and the blue shadows wove patterns on the grass.

Peter and Esk were on the ground playing at marbles, with Silver Heels to judge between them.

Esk, perceiving me, cried out: "Knuckle down at taws, Micky! Come on! Alleys up and fen dubs!"

"Fen dubs your granny!" I replied, scornfully, clean forgetting my new dignity. "Dubs all, and bull's-eyes up is what I play, unless you want to put in agates?" I added, covetously.

Esk shook his head in alarm, muttering that his agates were for shooters; but fat Peter, sprawling belly down at the ring, offered to put up an agate against four bull's-eyes, two agates, and twelve miggs, and play dubs and span in a round fat.

The proposition was impudent, unfair, and thoroughly Indian. I was about to spurn it when Silver Heels chirped up, "Micky doesn't dare."

"Put up your agate, Peter," said I, coolly, ignoring Silver Heels; and I fished the required marbles from my pocket and placed them in the ring.

"My shot," announced Peter, hurriedly, crowding down on the line, another outrage which, considering the presence of Silver Heels, I passed unnoticed.

Peter shot and clipped a migg out of the ring. He shot again and grazed an agate, shouting "Dubs!" to the derision of us all.

Then I squatted down and sent two bull's-eyes flying, but, forestalled by Peter's hysterical "Fen dubs!" was obliged to replace one. However, I shot again and it was dubs all, and I pocketed both of my agates and Peter's also.

This brought on a wrangle, which Silver Heels settled in my favour. Then I sat down and, with deadly accuracy, "spun," from which comfortable position, and without spanning, I skinned the ring, leaving Peter grief-stricken, with one migg in his grimy fist.

"You may have them," said I, condescendingly, dropping my spoils into Silver Heels's lap.

She coloured with surprise and pleasure, scarcely finding tongue to say, "Thank you, Micky."

Peter, being half Indian, demanded more play. But I was satiated and, already remembering my dignity, regretted the lapse into children's pastimes. I quieted Peter by giving him the remainder of my marbles, explaining that I had renounced such games for manlier sport, which statement, coupled with my lavish generosity, impressed Peter and Esk, if it had not effect upon Silver Heels.

I sat down on the stone bench near the bee-hives and drew from my pocket the jack-knife given me by Silver Heels as a bribe to silence.

"Come over here, Silver Heels," I said, with patronizing kindness.

"What for?" she demanded.

"Oh, don't come then," I retorted, whereat she rose from the grass with her skirt full of marbles and came over to the stone bench.

After a moment she seated herself, eying the knife askance. I had opened the blade. Lord, how I hated to give it back!

"Take it," said I, closing the blade, but not offering it to her.

"Truly?" she stammered, not reaching out her hand, for fear I should draw it away again to plague her.

I dropped the knife into her lap among the marbles, thrilling at the spectacle of my own generosity.

She seized it, repeating:

"King, King, double King!

Can't take back a given thing!"

"You needn't say 'King, King, double King,'" said I, offended; "for I was not going to take it back, silly!"

"Truly, Michael?" she asked, looking up at me. Then she added, sweetly, "I am sorry I bit you."

"Ho!" said I, "do you think you hurt me?"

She said nothing, playing with the marbles in her lap.

I sat and watched the bees fly to and fro like bullets; in the quiet even the hills, cloaked in purple mantles, smoked with the steam of hidden snow-drifts still lingering in ravines where arbutus scents the forest twilight.

The robins had already begun their rippling curfew call; crickets creaked from the planked walk. Behind me the voices of Peter and Esk rose in childish dispute or excited warning to "Knuckle down hard!" Already the delicate spring twilight stained the east with primrose and tints of green. A calm star rose in the south.

Presently Silver Heels pinched me, and I felt around to pinch back.

"Hush," she whispered, jogging my elbow a little, "there is a strange Indian between us and the block-house. He has a gun, but no blanket!"

For a moment a cold, tight feeling stopped my breath, not because a strange Indian stood between me and the block-house, but because of that instinct which stirs the fur on wild things when taken unawares, even by friends.

My roughened skin had not smoothed again before I was on my feet and advancing.

Instantly, too, I perceived that the Indian was a stranger to our country. Although an Iroquois, and possibly of the Cayuga tribe, yet he differed from our own Cayugas. He was stark naked save for the breech-clout. But his moccasins were foreign, so also was the pouch which swung like a Highlander's sporran from his braided clout-string, for it was made of the scarlet feathers of a bird which never flew in our country, and no osprey ever furnished the fine snow-white fringe which hung from it, falling half-way between knee and ankle.

Observing him at closer range, I saw he was in a plight: his flesh dusty and striped with dry blood where thorns had brushed him; his eyes burning with privation, and sunk deep behind the cheek-bones.

As I halted, he dropped the rifle into the hollow of his left arm and raised his right hand, palm towards me.

I raised my right hand, but remained motionless, bidding him lay his rifle at his feet.

He replied in the Cayuga language, yet with a foreign intonation, that the dew was heavy and would dampen the priming of his rifle; that he had no blanket on which to lay his arms, and further, that the sentinels at the block-houses were watching him with loaded muskets.

This was true. However, I permitted him to advance no closer until I hailed a soldier, who came clumping out of the stables, and who instantly cocked and primed his musket.

Then I asked the strange Cayuga what he wanted.

"Peace," he said, again raising his hand, palm out; and again I raised my hand, saying, "Peace!"

From the scarlet pouch he drew a little stick, six inches long, and painted red.

"Look out," said I to the soldier, "that is a war-stick! If he shifts his rifle, aim at his heart."

But the runner had now brought to light from his pouch other sticks, some blood-red, some black ringed with white. These he gravely sorted, dropping the red ones back into his pouch, and naïvely displaying the black and white rods in a bunch.

"War-ragh-i-ya-gey!" he said, gently, adding, "I bear belts!"

It was the title given by our Mohawks to Sir William, and signified, "One who unites two peoples together."

"You wish to see Chief Warragh," I repeated, "and you come with your pouch full of little red sticks?"

He darted a keen glance at me, then, with a dignified gesture, laid his rifle down in the dew.

A little ashamed, I turned and dismissed the soldier, then advanced and gave the silent runner my hand, telling him that although his moccasins and pouch were strange, nevertheless the kin of the Cayugas were welcome to Johnson Hall. I pointed at his rifle, bidding him resume it. He raised it in silence.

"He is a belt-bearer," I thought to myself; "but his message is not of peace."

I said, pleasantly:

"By the belts you bear, follow me!"

The dull fire that fever kindles flickered behind his shadowy eyes. I spoke to him kindly and conducted him to the north block-house.

"Bearer of belts," said I, passing the sentry, and so through the guard-room, with the soldiers all rising at attention, and into Sir William's Indian guest-room.

My Cayuga must have seen that he was fast in a trap, yet neither by word nor glance did he appear to observe it.

The sun had set. A chill from the west sent the shivers creeping up my legs as I called a soldier and bade him kindle a fire for us. Then on my own responsibility I went into the store-room and rummaged about until I discovered a thick red blanket. I knew I was taking what was not mine; I knew also I was transgressing Sir William's orders. Yet some instinct told me to act on my own discretion, and that Sir William would have done the same had he been here.

A noise at the guard door brought me running out of the store-room to find my Cayuga making to force his way out, and the soldiers shoving him into the guest-room again.

"Fall back!" I cried, my wits working like shuttles; and quickly added in the Cayuga tongue: "Cayugas are free people; free to stay, free to go. Open the door for my brother who fears his brother's fireside!"

There was a silence; the soldiers stood back respectfully; a sergeant opened the outer door. But the Indian, turning his hot eyes on me, swung on his heel and re-entered the guest-room, drawing the flint from his rifle as he walked.

I followed and laid the thick red blanket on his dusty shoulders.

"Sergeant," I called, "send McCloud for meat and drink, and notify Sir William as soon as he arrives that his brothers of the Cayuga would speak to him with belts!"

I was not sure of the etiquette required of me after this, not knowing whether to leave the Cayuga alone or bear him company. Tribes differ, so do nations in their observance of these forms. One thing more puzzled me: here was a belt-bearer with messages from some distant and strange branch of the Cayuga tribe, yet the etiquette of their allies, our Mohawks, decreed that belts should be delivered by sachems or chiefs, well escorted, and through the smoke of council fires never theoretically extinguished between allies and kindred people.

One thing I of course knew: that a guest, once admitted, should never be questioned until he had eaten and slept.

But whether or not I was committing a breach of etiquette by squatting there by the fire with my Cayuga, I did not know.

However, considering the circumstances, I called out for a soldier to bring two pipes and tobacco; and when they were fetched to me, I filled one and passed it to the Cayuga, then filled the other, picked a splinter from the fire, lighted mine, and passed the blazing splinter to my guest.

If his ideas on etiquette were disturbed, he did not show it. He puffed at his pipe and drew his blanket close about his naked body, staring into the fire with the grave, absent air of a cat on a wintry night.

Now, stealing a glance at his scalp-lock, I saw by the fire-light the stumps of two quills, with a few feather-fronds still clinging to them, fastened in the knot on his crown. The next covert glance told me that they were the ragged stubs of the white-headed eagle's feathers, and that my guest was a chief. This set me in a quandary. What was a strange Cayuga chief doing here without escort, without blanket, yet bearing belts? Etiquette absolutely forbade a single question. Was I, in my inexperience, treating him properly? Would my ignorance of what was due him bring trouble and difficulty to Sir William when he returned?

Suddenly resolved to clear Sir William of any suspicion of awkwardness, and at the risk of my being considered garrulous, I rose and said:

"My brother is a man and a chief; he will understand that in the absence of my honoured kinsman, Sir William Johnson, and in the absence of officers in authority, the hospitality of Johnson Hall falls upon me.

"Ignorant of my brother's customs, I bid him welcome, because he is naked, tired, and hungry. I kindle his fire; I bring him pipe and food; and now I bid him sleep in peace behind doors that open at his will."

Then the Cayuga rose to his full noble height, bending his burning eyes on mine. There was a silence; and so, angry or grateful, I knew not which, he resumed his seat by the fire, and I went out through the guard-room into the still, starry night.

But I did not tarry to sniff at the stars nor search the dewy herbage for those pale blossoms which open only on such a night, hiding elf-pearls in their fairy petals. Straightway I sought Mistress Molly in the nursery, and told her what I had done. She listened gravely and without comment or word of blame or praise, which was like all Indians. But she questioned me, and I described the strange belt-bearer from his scalp-lock to the sole of his moccasin.

"Cayuga," she said, softly; "what make was his rifle?"

"Not English, not French," I said. "The barrel near the breech bore figures like those on Sir William's duelling pistols."

"Spanish," she said, dreamily. "In his language did he pronounce *agh* like *ahh*?"

"Yes, Aunt Molly."

She remained silent a moment, thoughtful eyes on mine. Then she smiled and dismissed me, but I begged her to tell me from whence my Cayuga came.

"I will tell you this," she said. "He comes from very, very far away, and he follows some customs of the Tuscaroras, which they in turn borrow from a tribe which lives so far away that I should go to sleep in counting the miles for you."

With that she shut the nursery door, and I, no wiser than before, and understanding that Mistress Molly did not mean I should be wiser, sat down on the stairs to think and to wait for Sir William.

A moment later a man on horseback rode out of our stables at a gallop and clattered away down the hill. I listened for a moment, then thought of other things.

CHAPTER III

At late candle-light, Sir William still tarrying, I went to the north block-house, where Mr. Duncan, the lieutenant commanding the guard, received me with unusual courtesy, the reason of which I did not at the time suspect.

"An express from Sir William has at this moment come in," said he. "Sir William is aware that a belt-bearer from Virginia awaits him."

"How could Sir William, who is at Castle Cumberland, know that?" I began, then was silent, as it flashed into my mind that Mistress Molly had sent an express to Sir William as soon as I had told her about the strange Cayuga. That was the galloping horseman I had heard.

Pondering and perplexed, I looked up to find Mr. Duncan smiling at me.

"I understand," said he, "that Sir William is pleased to approve your conduct touching the strange Cayuga."

"How do you know?" I asked, quickly, my heart warming with pleasure.

"I know this," said Mr. Duncan, laughing, "that Sir William has left something for you with me, a present, in fact, which I am to deliver to you on the morrow."

"What is it, Mr. Duncan?" I teased; but the laughing officer shook his head, retiring into the guard-room and pretending to be afraid of me.

The soldiers, lounging around the settles, pipes between their teeth, looked on with respectful grins. Clearly, even they appeared to know what Sir William had sent to me from Castle Cumberland.

As I stood in the guard-room, eager, yet partly vexed, away below in the village the bell in the new stone church began to ring.

"What is that?" I asked, in surprise.

The soldiers had all risen, taking their muskets from the racks, straightening belts and bandoleers. In the stir and banging of gun-stocks on the stone floor, my question perhaps was not heard by Mr. Duncan, for he stood silent, untwisting his sword knots and eying the line which the sergeant, who carried the halberd, was forming in the room.

A drummer and a trumpeter took station, six paces to the right and front; the sergeant, at a carry, advanced and saluted with, "Parade is formed, sir."

"'Tention!" sang out Mr. Duncan. "Support arms! Carry arms! Trail arms! File by the left flank! March!" And with drawn claymore on his shoulder he passed out into the starlight.

I followed; and now, standing by the block-house gate, far away in the village I heard the rub-a-dub of a drum and a loud trumpet blowing.

Nearer and nearer came the drum; the trumpet ceased. And now I could hear the tramp, tramp, tramp of infantry on the hill's black crest.

"Present arms!" cried Mr. Duncan, sharply.

A dark mass which I had not supposed to be moving, suddenly loomed up close in front of us, taking the shape of a long column, which passed with the flicker of starlight on musket and belt, tramp, tramp, tramp to the ringing drum-beats.

Then our drum rattled and trumpet sang prettily, while Mr. Duncan rendered the officer's salute as a dark stand of colours passed, borne furled and high above the slanting muskets.

Baggage wains began to creak by, great shapeless hulks rolling in on the black ocean of the night, with soldiers half asleep on top, and teamsters afoot, heads hanging drowsily and looped raw-hides trailing.

The last yoke of oxen passed, dragging a brass cannon.

"'Tention!" said Mr. Duncan. "Support arms! Trail arms! 'Bout face! By the right flank, wheel! March!"

Back into the block-house filed the guard, the drummer bearing his drum flat on his hip, the trumpeter swinging his instrument to his shoulder-knots.

Mr. Duncan sent his claymore ringing into the scabbard, wrapped his plaid around his throat, and strolled off towards the new barracks, east of the Hall.

"What troops were those, sir?" I asked, respectfully.

"Three companies of Royal Americans from Albany," said he. Then, noticing my puzzled face, he added, "There is to be a big council fire held here, Master Cardigan. Did you not know it?"

"No," said I, slowly, reluctant to admit that I had not shared Sir William's confidence.

"Look yonder," said Mr. Duncan.

Far out in the pale starlight, south and west of the Hall, I saw fires kindled, one by one, until the twinkle of their lights ran for a mile across the uplands. On a hill in the north a signal fire sent long streamers of flame straight up into the sky; other beacons flashed out in the darkness, some so distant that I could not be certain they were more than sparks of my imagination.

"It is the Six Nations gathering," said Mr. Duncan. "We expect important guests."

"What for?" I asked.

"I don't know," said Mr. Duncan, gravely. "Good-night, Mr. Cardigan."

"Good-night, sir," I said, thoughtfully; then cried after him, "and my present, Mr. Duncan?"

"To-morrow," he answered, and passed on his way a-laughing.

I walked quickly back to the Hall, where I encountered Esk and Peter, well bibbed, cleaning the last crumb from their bowls of porridge.

"Did you see the soldiers?" cried Esk, tapping upon his bowl and marching up and down the hallway.

"Look out of the back windows," added Peter. "The Onondaga fires are burning on the hills."

"Oneidas," corrected Esk.

"Onondagas," persisted Peter, smearing his face with his spoon to lick it.

"Where is Silver Heels?" I asked.

Mistress Molly came into the hall from the pantry, keys jingling at her girdle, and took Peter by his sticky fingers, bidding Esk follow.

"Bed-time," she said, with her pretty smile. "Michael, Felicity is being dressed by Betty. If Sir William does not return, you will dine with Felicity alone; and I expect you to conduct exactly like Sir William, and refrain from kicking under the table."

"Yes, Aunt Molly," said I, delighted.

Esk and Peter, being instantly hustled bedward, left lamenting and asserting that they too were old enough to imitate Sir William.

Silver Heels, with her hair done by Betty, and a blue sash over her fresh-flowered cambric, passed them on the stairs coming down, pausing to wish Mistress Molly good-night, and to slyly pinch fat Peter.

"Felicity," said Mistress Molly, "will you conduct as befits your station?"

"Oh la, Aunt Molly!" she answered, with that innocent, affected lisp which I knew was ever the forerunner of mischief.

She made her reverence, waiting on the landing until she heard the nursery door close, then flung both legs astride the balustrade and slid down like a flash.

"Have you seen the soldiers, Micky?—and the fires on the hills?" she cried. "To-morrow all the officers will be here, and I am to wear my hair curled, and my pink dress and tucker, with separate sleeves of silver gauze!"

We sat down on the stairs together as friendly and polite as though we never quarrelled; and she chattered on, smoothing her bib-apron with those silky hands of hers: "Betty rolled up my hair till I feared she meant to scalp me, and so told her.

"She coaxed me to endure, and called me her little Miss Honey-bee, but would not promise me a comfit; so I ran away before my cap was tied on. Micky, go and put on your silk breeches and lace cuffs and we will be gay and grand to dine!"

I ran to my chamber, bathed and dressed in all my finery, meaning to lord it in the dining-hall should Sir William not return.

And thus it fell out; for, when I descended the stairs, there was my lady Silver Heels parading before the pier-glass, and a gillie throwing open the doors of the dining-hall.

So that night Silver Heels and I supped alone together in the great hall, Mr. Butler having hurriedly ridden to his home, and Sir William not yet returned, though two hours past candle-light.

The hall was quiet and vast, and Silver Heels seemed exceedingly small, sitting in the big chair at the other end of the table. So I had the gillie lay her plate beside mine.

A single pair of candles lighted our supper, and those not of the best, for they smoked as the wind stirred the curtains.

"Do you not know what is due to quality?" said I, sternly, to the gillie—a raw yokel scented with whiffs of the stables.

The kilted oaf gaped at me.

"Do you not see it is dark here?" I said.

"'Tis far lichter than ye wud expeck for sae big a room, sir," said the gillie, with a foolish grin.

"Young Bareshanks," I retorted; "do you bring instantly a dozen wax candles and light them, idiot, in a seemly row! Also fetch Sir William's sherry and Madeira, and take away those pot-house pewters!"

The gillie made out to do as he was bidden, and I should have felt very grand and contented at being obeyed without questions had I not perceived him, through the buttery window, wink at the pantry-lad and put his mottled Scotch muzzle into my small-beer.

When the dozen waxen candles stood in a ring, all twinkling, and the decanters flanked me right and left, I bade the gillie leave us, mistrusting he might bear tales to Sir William touching our behaviour at table. But the dunce loitered, trimming wicks, and casting sidewise looks at me.

"Will you be gone?" said I, in a passion.

"Maister Michael," he whined; "ye'll no be soopin' till the blessing's said? Sir William gave us a grand discoorse this noon dinner, sir, verra suitable words, sir."

Mortified at my forgetfulness, I rose; so did Silver Heels, the candle-light sparkling under her half-closed lashes, for she ever kept one eye on duty.

In a rage I said grace before meat, then glared at the gillie.

"Aave heerd waur, sir," quoth he; "but aa never sleep the nicht without ma blessing, and aa'l no begin noo!"

"Get out, you Scotch loon," said I, "or I'll let this bottle fly with my blessing!"

He ran for it, at which Silver Heels and I laughed heartily until she spilled her wine on her knees, which spoiled her temper.

When the echoing of our laughter had died away in the dark corners of the room, an unaccustomed depression fell upon me. I peered up at the stags' shaggy heads, set around the wall; their dark glazed eyes reflected the little candle flames like fiery eyeballs of living bucks. The stillness in the familiar room troubled me.

Something of this Silver Heels also experienced, but the novelty of playing the grand lady with her sherry and her tea set her tongue a-swinging, clip-clap! She shrugged her shoulders and tossed her chin, pretending to trifle with a dish of cakes, vowing she had no appetite; but her hunger could not long withstand the pastry, and she ate all the suckets and cakes before I either perceived or prevented it.

Distressed at her greediness, I removed the caraways from the plate and pouched them to eat at my pleasure, whereupon she kicked my shins under the table.

But she would still play my Lady Languish, sighing and protesting she could not touch another morsel, and her cheeks full the while. Too, she drank of both sherry and Madeira, which was forbidden by Sir William, and became over-loud in speech until her humour changed to a fit of upbraiding me, and ended in the sulks.

I remember we had a brandied syrup, of which she also took too much, it making her pettish and sleepy; and after supper, when we sat together on the stairs, she harped ever on the same string, reproaching me for playing the high and mighty, whereas all could plainly see I was nothing but a boy like Esk and Peter and need give myself no plumes.

"My legs," she said, drowsily, "can touch the floor from the third stair as well as yours;" and she stretched them down to prove it, falling short an inch.

"If you are no longer a child," said I, "why do they harness you to the back-board and make you wear pack-thread stays?"

This madded her.

"You shall see," she said, in a temper, "you shall see me in flowered caushets, silk stockings, and shoes of Paddington's make, which befit my station and rank! You shall see me in padusoy and ribbons and a hat of gauze! I shall wear pompadour gloves and shall take no notice of you, with your big hands and feet, pardieu!"

"Nor I of you," said I, "tricked out in your silly flummery." And I drew a caraway from my pocket and bit deep.

"Yes, you will," said Silver Heels; "give me a caraway, piggy."

Sitting there in the dark, nibbling in silence, I could hear the distant stir of the convoy at the barracks, and wondered why the soldiers had come. Surely not because of danger to us at the Hall, for we had our Mohawks, our militia, and yeoman tenantry at beck and call. Besides, who would dare threaten Sir William Johnson, the greatest man in the colonies, and very dearly esteemed by our King?

"They say," said Silver Heels, "that there are men in Boston who have even defied the King himself."

"Never fear," said I, "they'll all hang for it."

"Would you like to fight for the King?" she asked, civilly, and without a trace of that mockery which left a sting, much as I pretended to despise it.

I said I should like to very much; that my father had died for his King, and that I should one day avenge him.

I would have said more, perhaps boasted, for Silver Heels was inclined to listen; but black Betty came down-stairs, her double ear-rings a-jingle, calling her "li'l Miss Honey-bee" to come to bed.

Silver Heels stood up, rubbing her eyes and stretching. I could not help noticing that she seemed to be growing very tall.

"Good-night, Micky," she said, with her mechanical curtsey, and took Betty's black hand.

Although there was now nobody to bid me retire, I went to my chamber gladly, for, what with the excitement of the morning, the arrival of the Cayuga, and, later, the soldiers—and also, I think, Sir William's sherry—my head was tired and confused.

I slept none too soundly. Dreams came crowding around my pillow; visions of Mr. Butler chasing Silver Heels awoke me.

I sat up in my bed and parted the curtains. Through the window I could see the watchful eyes of Indian fires glimmering from hill and hollow, and over all the little stars, all awake, watching the sleeping world.

A cock began crowing somewhere down in the village, although no tint of dawn appeared. But the crickets had ceased, and the stars grew paler, and that silence which is the dawn's true herald warned me to sleep again ere the red sun should steal over the edge of the world and catch me waking.

Then I slept soundly, and the sly sun had painted many a figure on my walls ere I waked to hear the bugle playing at the barracks, and Sir William's hounds baying in their kennels.

Dub! dub! rub-a-dub-dub! Dub! dub! rub-a-dub-dub!

The guard was changing at the block-house, while I, all shivers, dashed cold water over me from head to foot and rubbed my limbs into a tingle.

How sweetly came the matins of the robins! A kennel-lad, standing in the sunshine by the stables, wound his hunting-horn till the deep-jowled hounds drowned all with their baying.

In breeches and shirt I leaned from the open window to smell the young year, and saw Silver Heels's head at the next window, her hair in her eyes, and bare arms propping her chin.

She put out her tongue at me, but I bade her good-morning so civilly that she smiled and asked me if I had slept well.

"No," said I; "dreams disturbed me."

"It was the cakes and sherry," she observed, with a grimace.

"I also dreamed, and screamed until Betty came and rocked me in her arms. Which proves," she added, "that we are both too young to dine and wine imprudently. I am coming in to tell you what I dreamed. Open the door."

She entered, bundled in a wool blanket, and sat cross-legged on the bed, chattering of her dreams, how, in her sleep, she saw me mammocked by savages, among them Peter, who had grown big and sly and fierce like a fat bear cub in December.

Meanwhile I made of my hair a neat queue and tied it; then put on my buckskin vest with flaps, and my short hunting-shirt over it.

"Are you going to fish?" asked Silver Heels, enviously.

"If Sir William does," said I. "He sent me a present from Castle Cumberland last night. I doubt not that it may be a new fish-rod for salmon."

Presently she went away to be dressed by Betty, and I hastened down the stairs, impatient to find Mr. Duncan and have my present; nay, so fast and blindly did I speed that, swinging around the balustrade, I plumped clean into Sir William, coming up.

"What's to do! What's to do!" he exclaimed, testily. "Is there no gout in the world, then, wooden feet!"

"Oh, Sir William! My present from Castle Cumberland!" I stammered. "Is it a salmon-rod?"

"Now the wraith of old Isaac pinch ye!" said Sir William, half laughing, half angry. "What the devil have I to do with your presents and your fish-rods? Presents! Gad! It's a new algebra you need!"

"You promised not to," said I, stoutly.

"Did I?" said Sir William, with a twinkle in his eyes. "So I did, lad; so I did! Well, perhaps it is not an algebra book after all."

"Then let us go to Mr. Duncan and get it now," I replied, promptly.

"You may not want my present when you see it," argued Sir William, who did ever enjoy to plague those whom he loved best.

But I pulled him by the hand, and he pretended to go with reluctance and many misgivings.

At the door of the north block-house, Mr. Duncan rendered Sir William the officer's salute, which Sir William returned.

"Mr. Duncan," said he, "have you knowledge hereabouts of a certain present sent in your care for Mr. Cardigan here?"

"Now that you mention it, sir," replied Mr. Duncan, gravely, "I do dimly recall something of the sort."

"Was it not a school-book?" inquired Sir William.

"It was a parcel," replied Mr. Duncan, dubiously; "belike it hid a dozen good stout Latin books, sir."

I endured their plaguing with rising excitement. What could my present be?

"Take him in, Mr. Duncan," said Sir William at last. "And," to me, "remember, sir, that you forget not your manners when you return to me, for I shall await you here at the door."

Cramping with curiosity, I followed Mr. Duncan into his own private chamber, which connected with the guard-room. But I saw no parcels anywhere; in fact, there was nothing to be noticed save an officer's valise at the foot of Mr. Duncan's bed.

"It is for you," he said; "open it."

At the same moment I perceived my own name painted on the leather side, and the next instant I had stripped the lid back. Buff and gold and scarlet swam the colours of the clothing before my amazed eyes; I put out a trembling hand and drew an officer's vest from the valise.

"Here are the boots, Mr. Cardigan," said the lieutenant, lifting a pair of dress boots from behind a curtain. "Here is the hat and sword, too, and a holster with pistols."

"Mine!" I gasped.

"By this commission of our Governor," said Mr. Duncan, solemnly, drawing from his breast a parchment with seal and tape. "Mr. Cardigan, let me be the first to welcome you as a brother officer."

I had gone so blind with happy tears that I scarce could find his kind, warm hand outstretched, nor could I decipher the commission as cornet of horse in the Royal Border Regiment of irregulars.

He mercifully left me then, and I stood with head pinched in my fingers, striving to realize what had arrived to me.

But I did not tarry long to gape and devour my uniform with my eyes. One after another my hunting-shirt, vest, leggings, shoon, flew from me. I pulled on the buff breeches, and laced them tight, drew on the boots, set the vest close and buttoned it, then put on coat and hat, and lastly tied my silver gorget.

What I could see of myself in Mr. Duncan's glass left me dazed with admiration. I set my sword belt, hung the sword with one glove in the hilt, and so, walking on air, I passed the guard-room with all the soldiers at stiff attention, and came to Sir William.

He looked up sharply, without the familiar smile. But my wits were at work and I stopped short at three paces, heels together, and gave the officer's salute.

Sir William's lips twitched as he rendered the salute, then, casting his ivory cane on the grass, he stepped forward with arms outstretched, and I fell into them like a blubbering schoolboy.

To those contented and peaceful people who have never known that gnawing desire for the noblest of all professions, the soldier's, I can only say that I was contented. To those who themselves have known the longing it is needless to describe my happiness and pride, my gratitude to those who had honoured me, my impetuous thirst for service, my resolve to set heart and soul towards high ideals and thoughts, my solemn boyish prayers that I might conduct nobly in the eyes of all men, for God and King and country.

Something of my thoughts may have disclosed themselves in my face as Sir William laid both hands on my shoulders, for he looked at me a long while with kindly, steady eyes. His countenance was serene and benign when he spoke in that clear voice whose harmony and perfect cadence has charmed a thousand council fires, and turned feverish spleen and hatred into forbearance and reconciliation.

"My boy," he said, "the key to it all is faith. Keep faith with all men; keep faith with thyself. This wins all battles, even the greatest and last!"

Very soberly we returned to the Hall, where a small company were assembled for breakfast—Mistress Molly, Major Wilkes of the battalion which arrived the night before, Captains Priestly, Borrow, and McNeil, of the same regiment, my friend Lieutenant Duncan of the militia, and Silver Heels.

When Sir William and I entered the Hall the officers came to pay their respects to the Baronet, and I, red as a Dutch pippin, crossed the room to where Mistress Molly stood with Silver Heels.

Bending to salute her hand, cocked hat crushed under one arm, I discharged my duties with what composure I could command; but Mistress Molly put both arms around me and kissed me on both cheeks.

"I knew all about it," she whispered. "We are very proud, Sir William and I. Be tender and faithful. It is all we ask."

Dear, dear Aunt Molly! While life lasts can I ever forget those sweet, grave words of love, spoken to a boy who stood alone on the threshold of life?

Slowly I turned to look at Silver Heels, all my vanity, conceit, and condescension vanished.

She had turned quite pale; her eyes seemed set and fascinated, and she wished me happiness in a low voice, as though uncertain of her own words.

Chilled by her lifeless greeting, I returned to Sir William, who presented me to the guests with unconcealed pride:

"My kinsman, Mr. Cardigan, gentlemen; Captain Cardigan's only son!"

The officers, all in full dress, brilliant with the red, green, and gold of the Royal Americans, greeted me most kindly, some claiming acquaintance with my honoured father, and all speaking of his noble death before Quebec.

Before we sat at table, they gave me a standing toast, all touching glasses with me, and Sir William, smiling, with one arm around my shoulder.

So we sat down to breakfast, a breakfast I, being excited, scarcely tasted; but I listened with all my ears to the discourse touching the late troubles in New York and Massachusetts, concerning the importation of tea by the East India Company. The discussion soon became a monologue, for the subject was one which Sir William understood from A to Zed, and his eloquence upon it had amazed and irritated people of more importance than our Governor Tryon himself.

"Look you," said Sir William, in his clear voice like a bell; "look you, gentlemen; I yield to no man in loyalty and love to my King; but this I know and dare maintain here or at St. James: that his Majesty whom I serve and honour is misled by his ministers, and neither he nor they suspect the truth concerning these colonies!"

The officers were all attention, some leaning forward to lose no word or inflection; Mistress Molly poured the roundly abused tea, and her gentle dark eyes ever stole proudly towards Sir William.

"Gentlemen," said Sir William, blandly, "you all are aware that since last December the Atlantic Ocean is become but a vast pot of cold tea."

The laughter which followed sounded to me a trifle strained, as well it might be, considering the insolence of the people who had flung this defiance into the King's ocean.

"Very well," said Sir William, with that tight crease running around his jaw which meant his mind was made up. "This is the true history of that trouble, gentlemen. Judge for yourselves where lies the blame." And, leaning back in his chair, one hand lifted, he began:

"That damned East India Company, floundering about with the non-importation pill in its gullet, found itself owing the government fourteen hundred thousand pounds, with seventeen million pounds of unsold tea on its hands.

"Nobody likes bankruptcy, so off go the East India gentlemen with their petition to Parliament for permission to export their tea to America, free of duty, and so put it in the power of the company to sell tea here cheaper than in England. And now I ask you, gentlemen, whether in all these broad colonies there are not some few men whose motives are other than sordid?

"Your answers must be 'yes!'—because the colonists themselves so answered when they burned the *Gaspee*!—when they gathered at Griffin's wharf and made tea enough for the world to drink!—when John Lamb set his back to the portcullis of the fort and the tea commissioners ran like rabbits!

"God forbid that I, a humble loyal subject of my King, should ever bear out the work of rebels or traitors. But I solemnly say to you that the rebels and traitors are not the counterfeit Indians of Griffin's wharf, not the men who fired the *Gaspee* aflame from sprit to topmast, not that man who set his back to the fort in New York! But they are those who whisper evil to my King at St. James—and may God have mercy on their souls!"

In the silence which followed, Sir William leaned forward, his heavy chin set on his fists, his eyes looking into the future which he alone saw so clearly.

None durst interrupt him. The officers watched him silently—this great man—this great Irishman who had been the sole architect of his own greatness; this great American who saw what we, even now, cannot see as clearly as did he.

There he sat, dumb, eyes on vacancy; a plain man, a Baronet of the British realm, a member of the King's Council, a major-general of militia, and the superintendent of the Indian Department in North America.

A plain man; but a vast land-holder, the one man in America trusted blindly by the Indians, a man whose influence was enormous; a man who was as simple as a maid, as truthful as a child, as kind as the Samaritan who passed not on the other side.

A plain man, but a prophet.

There was a step at the door; Mr. Duncan spoke in a low tone with the orderly, then returned to Sir William.

"The Indian belt-bearer is at the block-house, sir," he said.

Sir William rose. The officers made their adieus and left. Only Sir William, Mistress Molly, Silver Heels, and I remained in the dining-hall.

The Baronet looked across at Mistress Molly, and a sad smile touched his eyes.

She took Silver Heels by the hand and quietly left the room.

"Michael," said Sir William; "listen closely, but remain silent concerning what this belt-bearer has to say. My honour is at stake, my son. Promise!"

"I promise, sir," said I, under my breath.

The next moment the door behind me opened and the Indian stole into the room.

CHAPTER IV

I now for the first time obtained a distinct view of the stranger as he stepped forward, throwing the blanket from him, and stood revealed, stark naked save for clout and pouch, truly a superb figure, and perfect, in the Greek sense, barring that racial leanness below knee and calf, and the sinewy feet planted parallel instead of diverging, as in our race.

But so splendid was his presence that Sir William, standing to receive him, unconsciously raised his chin and squared his shoulders as though bracing for a trial of strength with this tall red forester from the West.

For a space they stood face to face in silence; then the belt-bearer, looking warily around at the empty room, asked why Chief Warragh received his brother alone.

"My brother comes alone," replied Sir William, with emphasis. "It is the custom of the Cayuga to send three with each belt. Does my brother bear but a fragment of one belt? Or does he think us of little consequence that he comes without attestants?"

"I bear three belts," said the Indian, haughtily. "Nine of my people started from the Ohio; I alone live."

Sir William bowed gravely; and, motioning me to be seated, drew up an armchair of velvet and sat down, folding his arms in silence.

Then, for the first time in my life, I sat at a figurative council fire and listened to an orator of those masters of oratory, the peoples of the Six Nations.

Dignified, chary of gesture, clean, yet somewhat sad and over-grave of speech, the Cayuga, facing the Baronet, related briefly his name, Quider, which in Iroquois means Peter; his tribe, which was the tribe of the Wolf, the totem being plain on his breast. He spoke of his journey from the Ohio, the loss of the eight who had started with him; all dying from the small-pox within a week. He spoke respectfully of Sir William as the one man who had protected the Six Nations from unjust laws, from incursions, from white men's violence and deception. He admitted that Sir William was the only man in America who to-day retained the absolute trust and confidence of the Indians, adding that it was for this reason that he had come.

And then he began his brief speech, drawing from his pouch a black belt of wampum:

"*Brother*. With this belt we breathe upon the embers which are asleep, and we cause the council fire to burn in this place and on the Ohio, which are our proper fireplaces. With this belt we sweep this fireplace clean, removing from it all that is impure, that we may sit around it as brothers."

(*A belt of seven rows.*)

"*Brother.* The unhappy oppression of our brethren by Colonel Cresap's men, near the Ohio carrying-place, is the occasion for our coming here. Our nation would not be at rest, nor easy, until they had spoken to you about it. They have now spoken—with this belt!"

(*A black and white belt.*)

"*Brother.* What are we to do? Lord Dunmore will not hear us. Colonel Cresap and his men, to whom we have done no harm, are coming to clear the forest and cross our free path which lies from Saint Sacrement to the Ohio, and which path our brother's belts, which we still possess, have long since swept clear. What shall we do? Instead of polishing our knives we have come to our brother Warragh. Instead of seeking our kin the Mohawk and the Oneida with painted war belts to throw between us and them, we come to our brother and ask him, by this belt, what is left for us to do? Our brothers have taught us there is a God. Teach us He is a just God—by this belt!"

(*A black belt of five rows.*)

During this speech Sir William sat as still as death, neither by glance nor gesture nor change of colour betraying the surprise, indignation, and alarm which this exposure of Colonel Cresap's doings caused him.

As for me, I, of course, vaguely understood the breach of faith committed by Colonel Cresap in invading the land of our allies, and the danger we might run should this Cayuga chief go to our Mohawks and Oneidas with war-belts and inflammatory appeals for vengeance on Cresap and his men.

That he had instead come to us, braving all dangers, losing indeed all his comrades, on this mission of peace, most splendidly attested to the power and influence of Sir William among these savages whose first instinct is to draw the hatchet and begin the horrid vengeance which they consider their right when unjustly molested.

It is seldom the custom to reply to a speech before the following day. Custom and tradition rule among the Six Nations. Deliberation and profound reflection they give to all spokesmen who petition them, and they require it in turn, regarding with suspicion and contempt a hasty reply, which, they consider, indicates either premeditated treachery, or a shallow mind incapable of weighty and mature reflection.

I was prepared, therefore, when Sir William, holding in his right hand the three belts of wampum, rose and thanked the Cayuga for his talk, praising him and his tribe for resorting to arbitration instead of the hatchet, and promising an answer on the morrow.

The Cayuga listened in silence, then resuming his blanket turned on his heel and passed slowly and noiselessly from the room, leaving Sir William standing beside the arm-chair, and me erect in the embrasure of the casement.

Now, for the first time in my life, I saw a trace of physical decline in my guardian. His hand, holding the belts, had fallen a-trembling; he made a feeble gesture for me to be seated, and sank back into his arm-chair, listless eyes on the floor, absently running his fingers over the polished belts.

"At sixty," he said, as though to himself, "strong men should be in that mellow prime to which a sober life conducts."

After a moment he went on: "My life has been sober and without excess—but hard! very hard! I am an old man; a tired old man."

Looking up to meet my eyes, he smiled, watching the sympathy which twitched my face.

"All these wars! All these wars! Thirty years of war!" he murmured, caressing the belts and letting them slip through his fingers like smooth shining serpents. "War with the French, war with the Maquas, the Hurons, the Shawanese, the Ojibways! War in the Canadas, war in the Carolinas, war east and west and north and south! And—I am tired."

He flung the slippery belts to the floor, where they twisted and coiled up in a heap.

"I have worked with my hands," he said. "This land has drunk the sweat of my body. I have not spared myself in sickness or in health. My eyes are dim; I have used them by day, by starlight, by the glimmer of moons long dead, by candle-wood, by torch, by the flicker of smoke from green fires.

"My arms are tired; I have hewn forests away; my limbs ache; I have journeyed far through snow, through heat, from the Canadas to the Gulf—all my life I have journeyed on business for other men—for men I have never seen, and shall never see—men yet to be born!"

There came a flush of earnest colour into his face. He leaned forward towards me, elbow resting on the table, hand outstretched.

"Why, look you, Michael," he said, with childlike eagerness; "I found a wilderness and I leave a garden! Look at the valley! Can England grow such grain? Look at Tryon County! Look at this Province of New York? Ay—look farther—wherever my Indians have set their boundaries! There are roads, lad, roads where I found runways; turnpikes where I followed

Mohawk trails; mills turning where the wild-cat squatted, fishing with big flat paws! Lad, you cannot recall it, yet this village was but a carrying-place when I came. Look at it; look from the window, lad! Is it not fair and pretty to the eye? One hundred and eighty families! Three churches, counting my new stone church; a free school, a court-house, a jail, barracks—all built by me; stores with red and blue swinging signs, bravely painted, inns with the good green bush a-swing! Listen to the cock-crows; listen to the barking! Might it not be a Devonshire town? Ah—I forgot; you have never seen old England."

Smiling still, kind eyes dreaming, his head sank a little, and he clasped his hands in his lap.

"Lad," he said, softly, "the English hay smells sweet, but not so sweet as the Mohawk Valley hay to me. This is my country—my country first, last, and all the time. I am too old to change where in my youth I took root among these hills. To transplant me means my end."

The sunlight stole into the room through leaded diamond-panes and fell across his knees like a golden robe. The music from the robins in the orchard filled my ears; soft winds stirred the lace on Sir William's cuffs and collarette.

Presently he roused, shaking the dream from his eyes; and, watching him, it seemed to me I could see the very tide of life swelling flesh and muscle into new vigour. The colour came back into his face and hands; the light grew in his eyes.

"Come!" he said, in a voice that had lost its tremour. "Life has but one meaning—to go on, ever on, lad! 'Tis a long doze awaits us at the journey's end." And he fumbled for his snuff-box and lace hanker, blowing a vigorous blast and exclaiming, "Aha! Ho!" in deep tones which, when very young, awed me.

I bent and picked up the three belts, placing them on the table near him.

"Thank you, Michael," he said, heartily; "and I must say that in this matter of the Cayuga, you have conducted admirably. Mr. Duncan has told me all; it was wisely done. Had you received the Cayuga with less welcome or more suspicion, or had you met him haughtily, I do not doubt that he would have made mischief for me among my Mohawks."

"He had war-sticks painted red, in his pouch, sir," I replied.

"No doubt! No doubt! And a red war-belt, too, belike! They were meant for my Mohawks had he met with a rebuff here. Oh, I know them, Michael, I know them. A painted war-belt flung between that Cayuga and the sachems of my Mohawks would have set the whole Six Nations—save, perhaps, the Oneidas—a-shining up rifle and hatchet for Cresap and his men!"

Sir William struck the mahogany table with clinched fist.

"Damn Cresap!" he bawled, in one of his familiar fits of fury—fits which were never witnessed outside his family circle. "Damn the fatuous fool to go a-meddling with the Cayugas in their own lands, held by them in solemn covenant forever inviolate! What does the sorry ass want? A border war, with all this trouble betwixt King and colonies hatching? Does Colonel Cresap not know that a single scalp taken from the Cayugas will set the Six Nations on fire—ay, the Lenape, too?"

Sir William slapped the table again with the flat of his hand.

"Look, Michael; should war come betwixt King and colonies, neither King nor colonies should forget that our frontiers are crowded with thousands of savages who, if adroitly treated, will remain neutral and inoffensive. Yet here is this madman Cresap, on the very eve of a struggle with the greatest power in the world, turning the savages against the colonies by his crazy pranks on the Ohio!"

"But," said I, "in his blindness and folly, Colonel Cresap is throwing into our arms these very savages as allies!"

Sir William stopped short and stared at me with cold, steady eyes.

"Michael," said he, presently, "when this war comes—as surely it will come—choose which cause you will embrace, and then stand by it to the end. As for me, I cannot believe that God would let me live to see such a war; that He would leave me to choose between the King who has honoured me and mine own people in this dear land of mine!"

He raised his head and passed one hand over his eyes.

"But should He in His wisdom demand that I choose—and if the sorrow kills me not—then, when the time comes, I shall choose."

"Which way, sir?" I said, in a sort of gasp.

But he only answered, "Wait!"

Stupefied, I watched him. It had never entered my head that there could be any course save unquestioned loyalty to the King in all things; that there could be any doubt or hesitation or pondering or praying for light when it came time to choose between King and rebel.

I now recalled what Sir William had said to me in the school-room. Putting this with what he now said, or left unsaid, together with his anger at Colonel Cresap for endangering the peace betwixt the Indians and the colonies, I came to the frightened conclusion that Sir William's loyalty might be questioned. But by whom? Who in America was great enough to call Sir

William to account? Not Governor Tryon; not Lord Dunmore; not General Gage.

Feeling as though the bottom had fallen out of something, I sat there, my fascinated eyes never leaving Sir William's sombre face.

What then were these tea-hating rebels that Sir William should defend them at breakfast and in the faces of half a dozen of his Majesty's officers? I knew nothing of the troubles in Massachusetts save from soldiers' talk or the gossip of the townsmen, most of them being tenants of Sir William. I had heard vaguely about one turbulent fellow named Hancock, and a mischief-making jack-at-all-trades called Franklin. I knew that the trouble concerned taxes, but as all this bother appeared to be about a few pennies, and as I myself never wanted for money, I had little sympathy for people who made such an ado about a shilling or two. Moreover, if the King needed money, the idea of not placing one's all at his Majesty's disposal seemed contemptible to me. It is true that I had never earned a farthing in all my life, and so had nothing to offer my sovereign, save what fortune my father had left in trust for me. It is also true that I knew nothing of the value of money, having neither earned it nor wanted for it.

Something of these thoughts may have been easily read in my face, for Sir William said, with some abruptness:

"It is not money; it is principle that men fight for."

I was startled, although Sir William sometimes had a way of rounding out my groping thoughts with sudden spoken words which made me fear him.

"Well, well," he said, laughing and rising to stretch his cramped limbs; "this is enough for one day, Michael. Let the morrow fret for itself, lad. Come, smile a bit! Shall we have a holiday, perhaps the last for many a month? Nay, do not look so sober, Micky. Who knows what will come? Who knows; who knows?"

"I shall stand by you, sir, whatever comes," said I.

But Sir William only smiled, drawing me to him, one arm about me.

"Suppose," said he, "that you and I and Mr. Duncan and Felicity and Peter and Esk take rods and bait and go a-fishing in the Kennyetto by Fonda's Bush!"

"A peg-down fishing match!" cried I, enchanted.

"Ay, a peg-down match, and the prize whatever the victor wills—in reason. What say you, Michael?"

I was about to assent with enthusiasm when something occurred to me and I stopped.

"May I wear my uniform, sir?" I asked.

"Gad!" cried Sir William, in a fit of laughter. "'Tis a bolder man than I who dare separate you from your uniform!"

"Then I'll carry my pistols and go a-horse!" said I, delighted.

The Baronet, hands clasped behind him, nodded absently. That old gray colour came into his face again, and he lifted a belt from the table and studied it dreamily, picking at the wampum which glowed like a snake's skin in the sunshine.

CHAPTER V

To Fonda's Bush it is a good ten miles. I rode Sir William's great horse, Warlock, who plunged and danced at the slap of my sword-scabbard on his flanks, and wellnigh shook me from my boots.

"Spare spur, lad! Let him sniff the pistols!" called Sir William, standing up in the broad hay-wagon to observe me. "He will quiet when he smells the priming, Michael."

I drew one of my pistols from the holster and allowed Warlock to sniff it, which he did, arching his neck and pricking forward two wise ears. After this the horse and I understood each other, he being satisfied that it was a real officer he bore and no lout pranked out to shame him before other horses.

The broad flat hay-wagon, well bedded and deep in rye-straw, was filled with the company on fishing bent; Peter and Esk already disputing over their lines, red quills, and bob-floats; Silver Heels, in flowered cotton damask and hair rolled up under a small hat of straw, always observing me with lowered, uncertain eyes; Mr. Duncan, in fustian coat and leggings, counting out fish-hooks; Sir William, in yellow-and-brown buckskin and scarlet-flowered waistcoat, singing lustily:

"A-Maying!

A-Maying!

Oh, the blackthorn and the broom

And the primrose are in bloom!"

Behind the wagon, with punch-jugs swinging on his saddle-bags, like John Gilpin rode young Bareshanks the Scot, all a-grin; while upon either side of the wagon two mounted soldiers trotted, rifles slung and hangers sheathed.

Thus we set out for Fonda's Bush, which is a vast woods, cut into a hundred arabesques by the Kennyetto, a stream well named, for in the Indian language it means "Snake-with-its-tail-in-its-mouth," and, although it flows for forty miles, the source of it is scarce half a mile from the mouth, where it empties into the great Vlaie near to Sir William's hunting-lodge.

In the wagon Sir William turned to the windows and waved his hat at Mistress Molly, who stood behind the nursery curtains and kissed her fingers to him. And, as the wagon with its escort rolled off with slow wheels creaking, Mr. Duncan struck up:

"Who hunts, doth oft in danger ride;

Who hawks, lures oft both far and wide;

Who uses games, may often prove

A loser; but who falls in love,

Is fettered in fond Cupid's snare;

My angle breeds me no such care."

And Sir William and Mr. Duncan ended the song:

"The first men that our Saviour dear

Did choose to wait upon him here,

Blest Fishers were,—"

The shrill voices of Esk and Peter joined in, then were hushed as Silver Heels's dainty song grew from the silence like a fresh breeze:

"For Courts are full of flattery

As hath too oft been tried;

The City full of wantonness,

And both be full of Pride:

Then care away,

And wend along with me!"

So singing on their rye-straw couches, the swaying wagon bore them over the hilly road, now up, now rattling down-hill among the stones to ford some ice-clear brook, and away again across the rolling country, followed by Gillie Bareshanks, stone bottles flopping, and the trotting soldiers holding their three-cornered hats on with one hand, bridle-rein in t'other.

I galloped ahead, pistol poised, frowning at woodlands where I pretended to myself danger might hide, examining all wayfarers with impartial severity; and I doubt not that, seeing me in full uniform and armed, my countenance filled them with misgivings; indeed, some called out to know if the news from Boston was bad, if the Indians meant mischief hereabouts, or if the highwayman, Jack Mount, was abroad.

"Plague on your pistols!" shouted Sir William, as I waited at a ford for the wagon. "Gad! Michael, your desperate deportment is scaring my tenants along the way! Smile as you gallop, in Heaven's name! else they'll take you for Jack Mount himself!"

Somewhat mortified by Sir William's roar of laughter, I trotted on in silence, returning my pistol to its holster, and buckling the flap.

We now entered the slashings of the forest which is called Fonda's Bush, "bush" meaning land not yet cleared of woods. The sweet, moist shadow of the forest cooled me; I made Warlock stop, for I love to listen and linger in a woodland's quiet.

Here the field-birds which had sung everywhere by the roadside were silent, as they always are on the borders of deep forests. Slow hawks sailed along the edge of the woods; out in the clearing a few finches twittered timidly in the sunshine, but here among the hushed ranks of giant trees nothing stirred save green leaves.

But the solitude of forest depths is no solitude to those who know when and where to watch and listen. Faint sounds came to savant ears: the velvet rustle of a snake brushing its belly over soft mosses; the padded patter of the fox-hare; the husky quhit! quhit! of that ashy partridge whose eye is surmounted by a scarlet patch, and whose flesh is bitter as hemlock. Solitude! Nay, for the quick furry creatures that haunt water-ways live here, slipping among bowlders, creeping through crevices; here a mink with eyes like jet beads; here a whiskered otter peering from a cleft; now a musk-rat squatting to wash his face; now a red martin thrashing about in the thick tree-top like a mammoth squirrel at frolic.

If this be solitude, with the stream softly talking in that silly babble which is a language, too; if this be solitude, with the shy deer staring and the tiny wood-mouse in the windfall scraping busily; if this be solitude, then imprison me here, and not in the cities, where solitude is in men's hearts!

Five miles still lay before us over the moist, springy forest road, an excellent and carefully constructed thoroughfare which had been begun by Sir William and designed for a short and direct route to those healing springs of Saratoga which he loved, twenty-eight miles northeast of us. But this route had never been continued east of Fonda's Bush, partly because the winding Kennyetto interfered too often, demanding to be bridged a dozen times in a mile, partly because an easier though longer route had been surveyed by the engineer officers from Albany, and was already roughly marked as far as the Diamond Hill, from which, in clear weather, the Saratoga lake may be seen.

The road we travelled, therefore, came to an abrupt end on the banks of the Kennyetto; and here, in a sunny clearing which was a sugar-bush lately in use, the wagon and its passengers halted, and I dismounted, flinging my bridle to one of the soldiers.

"Souse the stone jugs in the stream!" called out Sir William to young Bareshanks, who came bumping up with his bottles a-knocking and his hat crammed on his ears.

Peter and Esk wriggled out of the straw, fighting over a red and blue bob-float, and fell with a thump upon the moss, locked in conflict. Whereupon Sir William fetched them a clip with his ivory cane across their buttocks, which brought them up snivelling, but reconciled.

Meanwhile Mr. Duncan had gone to the bank of the stream with six sharp pegs, all numbered; and presently Sir William joined him, where they consulted seriously concerning the proper ground, and took snuff and hummed and hawed with much wagging of heads and many eye-squints at the sky and water.

At last, the question being settled, Mr. Duncan set the six pegs ten yards apart and pushed them noiselessly down into the bank, while Sir William removed his hat and placed in the crown six bits of birch-bark with numbers written on each.

"Now, then, young wild-cats," he said, frowning at Esk and Peter, "and you, Felicity, you, too, Mr. Duncan, and Michael, also, come and draw lots for pegs. Zounds! Peter! Ladies first, sir! Now, Felicity!"

Silver Heels placed one hand over her eyes and groped in the hat until her fingers clutched a square of bark. Then she drew it out.

"Number six!" she said, shyly.

"Last peg to the left," announced Sir William. "Who next? Draw, Mr. Duncan!"

"Me! Me!" shouted Peter and Esk, charging at the hat and tearing their numbers from it.

Then Mr. Duncan drew, and then I drew number five.

"Get ready!" commanded Sir William, fumbling with his fish-rod. "Michael, take care of Felicity!"

Now the rules for a peg-down fishing match are few and simple. Each contestant must fish from the position which his peg indicates, and he must not leave his peg to fish elsewhere until the match is ended. Furthermore, he must fish courteously and with due regard for his neighbour's rights, employing no unfair means to attract fish to his own bait or to drive them from his neighbour's. The contestant securing the largest number of fish is the winner; he who bags the largest single fish is adjudged worthy of a second prize; he who secures the choicest individual fish receives a crown of young oak leaves.

At the words, "Take your stations!" we trooped to our pegs. Silver Heels was on the extreme left, I next, then Sir William, then Mr. Duncan, then Peter, and, last of all, Esk.

"Fish!" cried Sir William, and swung his rod from the wrist, sending a green and gray and scarlet feather-fly out into the water.

Silver Heels held her hook out to me and I garnished it with a bit of eel's skin and red flannel. My own line I baited with angle-worm, and together we cast out into the slow, deep current.

Farther along I heard Esk and Peter cast out with some heedless splashing, which was the occasion of mutual recrimination until Sir William silenced them.

Yet almost immediately fat Peter caught a fish, which is like all Indians. However, it was but a spiny sun-fish with blue and scarlet and yellow gills. Still it made Peter's score one.

"Does that count?" asked Silver Heels, turning up her nose. "See! Peter hath another one—a sun-fish, too! Pooh! Anybody can catch sun-fish."

"Better catch 'em then," said Sir William, laughing, and drawing his fly over the water to recover it for another cast.

Splash!—and Peter had a third sun-fish; and in another moment Esk jerked a fourth from the water, secured his prize with a scowl at Peter, and hurriedly rebaited, muttering and breathing thickly.

Then Mr. Duncan's yellow float bobbed under, once, twice, then bobbed so fast that the water dimpled all around and the little rings, spreading, succeeded each other so quickly that the wavelets covered the yellow float.

"A barbel-pout," quoth Mr. Duncan, coolly, and sure enough up came the bluish-black fish and flapped and squeaked, now on its white belly, now on its back, grinning with its gummy, whiskered maw agape and its three dagger fins ready to stab and poison him who rashly grasped it.

"Silver Heels," said I, politely; "you are having a nibble."

"Oh, so I am!" she cried, and drew a lovely blue and silver frost-fish to the surface, only to lose it by over-haste, and cry out in her vexation.

I explained to her how to strike the hook before pulling in, and she thanked me very modestly. There was a new and humble tone in her voice, delicate and grateful flattery to me, due, as I knew perfectly well, to my uniform. Nor did the tribute savour of any after-sting of jealousy or resentment for my new honours.

She recognized that I had climbed high in a single day, leaving the rounds of childhood behind forever; and she knew, too, which I did not, that she also was climbing the ladder very swiftly, a little behind me now, yet confident, and meaning to rejoin and pass me ere I dreamed of such a thing.

About this time Sir William hooked and landed a great pink and white Mohawk chub, which had risen silently from a black pool and had sucked in his feather-fly.

"Tush!" said Sir William. "I'll not count that!" And with a slack and a snip! he unhooked the fish, which at once slowly sank back into the black channel. Whereupon Sir William smoothed out his fly, and took snuff, singing merrily:

"A-Maying!

A-Maying!"

"You bade *us* make no noise, sir," spoke up Esk, reproachfully.

"So I did, lad! So I did! But not with thy mouth. Shout all day, and never a trout budges. Stamp thy feet—ay, brush but a stone in passing, and it's farewell, master troutling! Ho! What was that?"

A spattering and splashing arose from Peter's peg, and all turned to see the fat little Mohawk dragging a trout from the water and up the bank, where he fell upon the bouncing fish, whooping like the savage he was.

"Clearly," mused Sir William, "my eye has lost its cunning, and my arm its strength. So passes the generation that was born with me! Heigh-ho! Well done, Peter boy!"

Silver Heels was doomed to ill-fortune. She lost a second frost-fish, and was ready to weep. So I laid my rod on the bank, leaving the baited hook in the water, and went over to her, for she seemed discouraged, having broken her hook and quill.

"Fen dubs!" shouted Peter, from the other end of the line. "You can't do that, Michael! I'm ahead of you all, and it is not fair!"

"Mind your business," said I, sitting down beside Silver Heels; and truly enough he did, for, before I was seated, Peter jumped up, struggling with a fat white perch, which he landed, yelling and dancing in his vanity.

"Never you mind, Silver Heels," said I, tying a plated hook on her line, and covering it with a long silvery strip of skin and pin-feathers from a pullet's neck. "Now do as I say; toss the bait down stream, so! Now draw it slowly till it spins like a top."

Ere I could end my instructions I saw the nose of a great gold-green pike close after her bait.

"Slack!" I whispered. "He has it!"

She held the rod still. There came a twitch, more twitches, but so gentle you would have vowed 'twas a tender-mouthed minnow lipping the line.

"He gorged it," I muttered; "strike hard!"

"A log!" wailed Silver Heels, as she felt the rod stagger when the hook, deeply struck, embedded barb and shank.

But it was no log, for instantly the great fish shot into the air, and lay a-wallowing and thrashing in mid-stream.

"A chain-pike!" cried Sir William, briskly. "Do you net him, Michael, else Felicity will take a swim she has not bargained for!"

I ran to Sir William, who thrust the net at me, and back again as fast as my legs could move to Silver Heels, who had dropped the rod and now, sprawling on the moss, lay a-pulling at the line which was cutting her tender fingers.

"No fair!" bellowed fat Peter, jealously. "Let her bag her own game as I do! Hi-yi! Another trout!"

But spite of Peter's clamour and Esk's injured howls, I netted the floundering pike and flung it among the bushes, where young Bareshanks gaffed it and held it aloft.

There it hung, all spray and green and gold, marked with the devil's chain pattern; and its wolf-jaws gaping, lined with teeth.

"Oh, Michael," quavered Silver Heels, staring at her captive. She moved a little nearer to the fish, plucking up her skirts with her fingers, and bending forward, alarmed, amazed at the fierce, dripping creature.

"Ugh! There's blood on it!" she whispered, taking fast hold of my arm.

"Is it not a noble prize!" I urged, eagerly. But she shook her head and turned away, holding me tightly by the sleeve.

"Are you not proud?" I persisted, irritably. "It is the biggest fish any have yet caught. You will gain second prize, silly! What's the matter with you, anyhow!" I added, in a temper.

"I can't help it," she said, tremulously; "I'm not a man, and it frightens me to kill. I shall fish no more. Ugh—the blood!—and how it quivered when the gillie gaffed it! I could cry my eyes out for the life I took so lightly!"

I was disgusted and hurt, too, for I had thought to please her. I drew my sleeve from her fingers, but she only stood there like a simpleton harping on one string:

"Oh, the brave fish! Oh, the poor brave fish! I hurt it!—I saw blood on it, Michael."

"Ninny," said I; "there is blood on your fingers, too, where the line cut, and you've wiped it on my sleeve!"

She looked at her bleeding fingers in a silly, startled fashion, then held them out to me so pitifully that I could do no less than wipe them clean and bind them in my handkerchief, though it was my best, and flowered and laced at that.

"I don't care," she said, a-pouting at the water; "you told me that when you shot wild things it saddened you, too."

I pretended not to hear, yet it was true. And in sooth, to this day I never draw trigger on beast or bird that I do not thrill with pity.

I know not what fierce, resistless passion it may be that sets my nostrils quivering like a pointer's when I chase wild things—what savage craving drives me on, on, on! till the flash of the gun and the innocent death leave me standing sad and staring.

Could I but keep from the woods—but I cannot. And it were vainer to argue with a hound on a runway, or with the west wind in October, than with me.

I went to my rod, which I saw nodding its tip in the water, and found an eel fast to the bait, yet not hooked, so summoned Bareshanks to rid me of the snaky thing and strolled sulkily over to Sir William.

The Baronet had enticed and prettily netted a plump lake salmon, by far the choicest fish taken; so, the match being ended, and luncheon served under the pines, Silver Heels plaited a wreath of red-oak, and crowned Sir William for his third prize.

Peter with his motley string of fish, some two dozen brace in all, and mostly trout at that, clamoured for the first prize, which was a Barlow-knife like the one Silver Heels had gained in the foot-race a year ago; and he clutched his prize and straightway fell a-hacking the wagon till Sir William collared him.

Silver Heels received the other reward, a gold guinea; and she placed it in her bosom, and kissed Sir William heartily.

"Faith," said the Baronet, "you had best kiss your cousin yonder, who saved you from a bath in the brook with your pike!"

Silver Heels came up to me, laying both hands on my shoulders, and held up her lips. I kissed her maliciously and praised her skill, vowing that she was a very Huron for slaughter, which boorish jest set her face a sorrowful red.

Meanwhile young Bareshanks had laid a clean cloth upon the moss, and there was pot-pie and roast capon, and a dish of apples and gingerbread. Ale, too, and punch chilled in the brook, and small-beer for the children, with a few drops of wine to drink Sir William's health.

With a cup of ale in one hand and a slice of cold capon on a trencher of bread, I munched and drank and rallied Silver Heels because of her pity for the pike; but she did not like it, yet ventured no retort, such as was formerly her custom.

Presently, Sir William having done scant justice to pot-pie and ale, called for his rod and flies, and he and Mr. Duncan lighted their pipes and strolled off along the stream to lure those small plump salmon which abound in the Kennyetto's swiftest reaches.

Peter lay on the moss, a-stuffing himself Indian fashion until it hurt him to eat more, and he howled and licked his gingercake, lamenting because he could not contain it. So I grasped his heels and dragged him to the wagon, tossing him up in the straw to lie like a sucking pig and squeal his fill.

Bareshanks and the soldiers now fell upon the feast, and Silver Heels and I withdrew to play at stick-knife and watch Esk that he tumbled not into the water while turning flat rocks for cray-fish.

Seated there on the deep moss at stick-knife with the cold song of the stream in our ears, we conducted politely as became our quality, I asking pardon for plaguing her concerning the pike, she granting pardon and praising my skill in taking such a monster fish. That glow of amiability which suffuses man when he has fed, warmed me into a most friendly state of mind, and I permitted Silver Heels to win at stick-knife, and I drew the peg without protest.

Fat Peter had fallen asleep; Esk, nipped by a cray-fish, waddled to the wagon, and rolling himself into a ball like a raccoon, joined Peter in dreams of surfeit.

In a distant glade the soldiers and young Bareshanks played at cards; the horses, tethered near, snorted in their feed-bags, and whisked their tails at the gnats and forest flies.

A hush fell upon the woods, stiller for the gossip of the stream. Ringed pigeons in the trees overhead made low, melodious love; far in the forest dusk the hermit-bird sang, but so faint, so distant, that the whisper of leaves stirring effaced the hymn of the gray recluse.

"I had not thought that you were so nearly a man to be appointed cornet of horse," said Silver Heels, digging into the moss with her knife.

"And you," said I, magnanimously, "are almost a woman." But I said it from courtesy, not because I believed it.

"Yes," she replied, indifferently, "maids may wed at sixteen years."

"Wed!" I repeated, laughing outright.

"Ay. Mother was a bride at sixteen."

I was silent in my effort to digest such an absurd idea. Silver Heels marry in another year! I looked at the frail yet full arm, half bared, the slender neck, the round, clear hazel eyes, the faintly smiling mouth, which was the mouth of a child. Silver Heels wed? The idea was grotesque. It was also displeasing.

Not to rebuff her with scorn, I said: "Indeed, you are quite a woman. Perhaps in a year you will be one! Who knows?—for a year is such a long, long time, Silver Heels."

"It is a very long time," she admitted.

"And to love, one must be quite old," said I.

"Yes, that is true," she conceded, reluctantly; "but not always."

After a silence she said, "Michael, I have a secret."

The mere idea that Silver Heels possessed a secret which she had not at once revealed to me produced a complicated sensation in my breast. I was conscious of a sudden and wholly involuntary respect for Silver Heels, a hearty resentment, and a gnawing curiosity to learn the secret.

"Will you promise never, never to tell?" she asked, raising her eager eyes to me.

Again resentment and hurt pride stung me, but curiosity prevailed, and I promised, with pretended indifference, to soothe my weak loss of self-respect.

"Well, then," she said, lowering her voice, "I am sure that Mr. Butler is in love with me."

"Mr. Butler!" I cried out, in angry derision. "Why, he's an old man! Why, he's nearly thirty!"

Angry incredulity choked me, and I sat scowling at Silver Heels and striving to reconcile her serious mien with such a tomfool speech.

"If you shout my secret aloud," she said, "I shall tell you no more, Micky."

Again, troubled and astonished at her sincerity, I expressed my disbelief in a growl.

"He keeps me after school hours," she said; "once he would caress my hand, but I will have none of it. He sometimes speaks of the future, and certainly does conduct in most romantic manners, vowing he will wait for me, declaring that I must love him one day, that I am no longer a child, that he has adored me since I was but twelve."

"How long has this gone on?" I said, my face cold and twitching with rage.

"These three months," said Silver Heels, without embarrassment.

"And—and you never told me!"

She shook her head frankly.

"No, you were but a lad, and you could not understand such things."

For a moment I felt so small that I could have yelled aloud my vexation. What! I too young to be told the secrets of this chit of a child with her ridiculous airs and pretensions!

"But now that you are become a man," she continued, serenely, "I thought to tell you of this, because it tries my patience, yet pleases me, too, sometimes."

Boiling with fury and humiliation, I gave her a piece of my mind. I said that Mr. Butler was a sneak, a bully, and an old fool in his dotage to make love to a baby. I told her it did sicken me to hear of it; that there was no truth in it but vain imaginings, and that she had best confess to Sir William how this gentleman school-teacher did teach her his knowledge withal!

She listened, frowning and digging up moss with her knife.

"He is not old," she said, firmly; "thirty years is but a youth's prime, which you will one day comprehend."

Such condescension wellnigh finished me. I could find neither tongue nor words to speak my passion.

"He is a gentleman of rank and station," she said, primly. "If he chooses to protest his solicitous regard for me, I can but courteously discourage him."

"You little prig!" I exclaimed, grinding my teeth. "I will teach this fellow Butler to abuse Sir William's confidence!"

"I have your promise not to reveal this," said Silver Heels, coolly.

I groaned, then remembering that Mr. Butler had partly promised me a meeting, I caught Silver Heels by both hands and looked at her earnestly.

"I also have a secret," said I. "Promise me silence, and you shall share it."

"Truly?" she asked, a little pale.

"Truly, a secret. Promise. Silver Heels."

"I promise," she whispered.

Then I told her of my defiance, of the meeting which Mr. Butler had half pledged me, and I swore to her that I would kill him, eye to eye and hilt to hilt; not alone for his contempt and insults to me, but for Sir William's honour and for the honour of my kinswoman, Felicity Warren.

"The beast!" I snarled. "That he should come a-suing you without a word to Sir William! Do gentlemen conduct in such a manner towards gentlewomen? Now hear me! Do you swear to me upon your oath and honour never to stay again after school, never to listen to another word from this sneaking fellow until you are sixteen, never to receive his addresses until Sir William speaks to you of him? Swear it! Or I will go straight to Mr. Butler and strike him in the face!"

"Micky, what are you saying? Sir William knows all this."

Taken aback, I dropped her hands, but in a moment seized them again.

"Swear!" I repeated, crushing her hands. "I don't care what Sir William says! Swear it!"

"I swear," she said, faintly. "You are hurting my fingers!"

She drew her hands from mine. Where the fishing-line had cut a single drop of blood had been squeezed out again.

"First you bind my hand, then you tear it," she said, without resentment. "It is like all men—to hurt, to heal, then wound again."

I scarcely heard her, being occupied with my anger and my designs against Mr. Butler. Such hatred as I now felt for him I never had conceived could be cherished towards any living thing. My right hand itched for a sword-hilt; I longed to see him facing me as I never had craved for anything in this world or the next. And to think that Sir William approved it!

Unconsciously we had both risen, and now, side by side, we were moving slowly along the stream, saying nothing, yet in closer communion than we had ever been.

Little by little the hot anger cooled in my veins, leaving a refreshing confidence that all would come right. Such passions are too powerful for young hearts. Anger and grief heal their own wounds quickly when life is yet new.

With my sudden, astonished respect for Silver Heels came another sentiment, a recognition of her rights as an equal, and a strangely solicitous desire to control and direct her enjoyment of these rights. It is the instinct of chivalry, latent in the roughest of us, and which, in extreme youth, first manifests as patronage. Thus, walking with Silver Heels I unburdened my heart, telling her that I too had been in love, that the object of my respectful passion was one Marie Livingston, who would undoubtedly be mine at some distant date. I revealed my desire to see Silver Heels suitably plighted, drawing a pleasing portrait of an imaginary suitor who should fill all requirements.

To this she replied that she, too, had desired a suitor resembling the highly attractive portrait I had painted for her; that she found a likeness between that portrait and her secret ideal, and that she should be very glad to encounter the portrait in the flesh.

It hurt me a little that she had not recognized in me many of the traits I had painted for her so carefully, and presently I disclosed myself as the mysterious original of the portrait.

"You!" she exclaimed, in amazement. Then, not to hurt me, she said it was quite true that I did resemble her ideal, and only lacked years and titles and wealth and reputation to make me desirable for her.

"I believe, also," she said, "that Aunt Molly means that we marry. Betty says so, and she is wiser than a black cat."

"Well," said I, "we can't marry, can we, Silver Heels?"

"Why, no," she said, simply; "there's all those things you lack."

"And all those things which you lack," said I, sharply. "Now, Marie Livingston—"

"She is older than I!" cried Silver Heels.

"And those things I lack come with years!" I retorted.

"That is true," she answered; "you are suitable for me excepting your years, which includes all you ought to be."

"Suppose you wait for me?" I proposed. "If I wed not Marie Livingston, I will wed you, Silver Heels."

I meant to be generous, but she grew very angry and vowed she would rather wed young Bareshanks than me.

"I don't care a fig," said I; "I only meant you to be suitably wed one day, and was even willing to do so myself to save you from Captain Butler. Anyway I'll kill him next year, so I don't care whether you marry me or not."

"A sorry match, pardieu!" she snapped, and fell a-laughing. "Michael, I will warn you now that I mean to wed a gentleman of rank and wealth, and wear jewels which will blind you! And I shall wed a gallant gentleman of years, Michael, and scarred with battles—not so to disfigure a pleasing countenance, but under his clothes where none can see—and I shall be 'my lady!'—mark me! Michael, and shall be well patched and powdered as befits my rank! I shall strive to be very kind to you, Michael."

Her cheeks were aflame, her eyes daring and bright. She picked up her skirt and mocked me in a curtsey, then marched off, nose in the wind, to join Sir William and Mr. Duncan, who were returning along the bank with a few brace of fish.

The sun had dropped low behind the trees ere we were prepared to depart. Bareshanks brought around my horse, and I mounted without difficulty this time.

As the wagon moved off Mr. Duncan started a hymn of Watts, which all joined, the soldiers and young Bareshanks also singing lustily, it being permitted for servants to aid in holy song.

So among the woods and out into the still country, with the sun a red ball sinking through saffron mist and the new moon aslant and dim overhead.

As I rode, the whippoorwill called after me from the darkening woods; the crickets began from every tuft, and far away I heard the solitary hermit at vespers in the still pines.

It was night ere the lights of Johnstown glimmered out against the hill-side where, on the hillock called Mount Johnson, the candles in our windows spun little rings of fire in the evening haze.

As we passed through the village, the good people turned to smile and to doff their hats to Sir William, thinking not less of him for riding with his flock in the straw-lined wagon, and on they went; I pulling rein at the blacksmith's, as Warlock had cast a shoe on the stony way below.

While the smith was at his forge I dismounted and stood in the fire-glow, stroking Warlock's velvet nose, and watching the fiery flakes falling from the beaten metal.

And as I stood, musing now on Silver Heels, now on Mr. Butler, came one a-swaggering by the shop, and bawling loudly a most foolish lilt:

"Diddle diddle dumpling,

My son John

Went to bed with one shoe on;

One shoe off and one shoe on;

Diddle diddle dumpling,

My son John!"

Perceiving me in full uniform the songster halted and saluted so cheerfully that I rendered his salute with a smile. He was drunk but polite; a great fellow, six feet two at least, all buckskin and swagger and raccoon cap, with tail bobbing to his neck, a true coureur-de-bois, which is the term for those roaming free-rifles whose business and conduct will not always bear investigation, and who live by their wits as well as by their rifles.

"A fine horse, captain," quoth he, with good-natured, drunken freedom, which is not possible for gentlemen to either ignore or resent. "A fine horse, sir, and, by your leave, worthy of his master!" And he stood swaying there heel and toe, with such a jolly laugh that I laughed too, and asked the news from Canada.

"Canada!" he roared, in his voice of a giant. "I've not sniffed priest or Jesuit these six months! Do you take me for a Frenchy, captain?"

At that moment another man who had been pushing his nose against the window of a bake-shop crossed the street and joined the giant in buckskin, saluting me carelessly as he came up.

He was short and meagre and weasel-eyed, sharp-muzzled, and dingy as a summer fox. He was also drunk, yet his mouth was honest, and I judge not from such things, nor yet by the eye, but by men's lips and how they rest one upon the other, and how they laugh.

Waiting there for my horse, I paced up and down the doorway, sometimes glancing at the motley pair in their fringed buckskins, who were fondly embracing one another, sometimes watching the towns-people, passing before the lighted windows. There were soldiers strolling, two by two, lingering at bake-shops to sniff the ovens; there were traders, come to town to solicit permits from Sir William for the Canadas. At times the tall, blanketed form of a Mohawk passed like a spectre with the red forge light running along his rifle barrel, followed by his squaw, loaded with bags of flour, or a haunch of salted beef, or a bale of pelts crackling on her back.

My pair of buckskin birds, loitering before the tavern, had been observed and mistaken for French trappers by half a dozen soldiers of the Royal Americans, who were squatting in a row on the tavern porch, and a volley of chaff was fired at short range.

"Mossoo! Oh, Mossoo! I say, Mossoo! How's Mrs. Parleyvoo and the little Parleyvoos? What's the price of cat-stew in Canada? Take that cat-tail off your cap, Mossoo!"

The big ranger gave them a drunken stare, then burst into a laugh.

"Why, it's some of those lobster-backs. Hello! Old red-bellies! They're going to give another tea-party in Boston, I hear. Didn't they invite you?"

"Come across the street and we'll give you a tea-party, you damned Yankee!" cried the soldiers, unbuckling their leather belts and swinging them.

"Come over here and we'll drum the rogue's march on you!" shouted the little ranger, planting his legs wide apart and drawing the ramrod from his long rifle.

A watchman with rattle, pike, and lanthorn came hobbling up, threatening to sound his call. A group of towns-people gathered behind him, protesting against the disturbance.

But the two rangers flourished their ramrods and taunted the soldiers with inquiries which I did not understand at the time, such as: "How's Bully Tryon and his blood-pudding?" "I learn that Tommy Gage has the gout; too much Port-Bill; he needs bleeding, does Tommy Gage!"

Then the big ranger, addressing soldiers, watchman, and towns-people as "bloody-backs," "cow-rumps," and "scratch-wigs," advised them all to pickle their heads and sell them in Albany, where cabbage was much esteemed among the Dutchmen.

"Come up to the barracks and we'll show you what pickling is," shouted the soldiers, wrathfully.

"Come out in the woods and I'll show you something to beat pickled pig!" replied the little ranger, cheerfully.

Behind me I heard the trample of hoofs; the smith was backing Warlock out into the street. I paid him; he held my stirrup, and I mounted, walking my horse out between the soldiers, the people, and the two rangers.

"Come, boys," said I, pleasantly, "this town is no place for brawls. Let it end here—do you understand?—or Sir William shall learn of it!"

The soldiers had stepped forward to salute, the two rangers laughed scornfully, flung their rifles over their shoulders, and passed on into the darkness with noiseless, moccasined stride.

Waiting to see that the crowd dispersed without disorder, far down the dim street I heard the two rangers break out into a foolish catch:

"Who comes here?

A grenadier!

What d'ye lack?

A pot o' beer!

Where's your penny?

I forgot—

Get you gone, you red-coat sot!"

A most uncomfortable sensation came over me, although I did not fully understand that "red-coat" was a reproach. But the loose laughter, the disrespectful tone, the devil-may-care swagger of these fellows disturbed me. What had they meant by "lobster-back" and "Tommy Gage" and "Bully Tryon?" Surely they could not have referred to General Gage of Boston or to our Governor! Did they mean Sir William's son, John, by their "diddle dumpling?" What quarrel had they with the King's soldiers? They had been courteous enough to me, unless they intended their song as an insult.

The blood stung my face; I put Warlock to a gallop and overtook the pair. They were arm in arm, swaggering along, ogling the towns-people, jostling the crowd, sometimes mocking the bare shanks of a Highlander, sometimes hustling an Indian, or tweaking the beard of a Jew peddler, now doffing their caps to some pretty maid, now digging the ribs of a sober Quaker, and ever singing of "diddle diddle dumpling" or of the grenadier and his pot of beer.

Such license and freedom displeased me. I had never before observed it in our town or among those who came to the Hall. However, I now saw that I could not with dignity notice either their boorish gallantry, their mischief, or the songs they were pleased to bawl out in the street.

I therefore passed them in silence, and, loosening bridle, set Warlock at a gallop for home.

I did not comprehend it at the time; indeed, the whole matter passed from my mind ere the lights of the Hall broke out in the blue night. Yet the scene I had witnessed was my first view of the unrest which tormented the whole land, the first symptom of that new fever for which no remedy had yet been found.

CHAPTER VI

It was not yet dawn, though a few birds sang in the darkness around us, as Sir William and I set off for the Cayuga's lodge, which stood beyond the town on a rocky knoll, partly cleared of trees.

The air was cold and without fragrance, for in our country it is the sun that draws the earth's sweetness in early spring.

The stars lighted us through the streets of Johnstown, empty of life save for the muffled watchman dozing in his own lanthorn glow, who roused as he heard us, and shook his damp cloak. And far behind us we heard his sing-song:

"Four o'clock! A cold, fair morn, and all well!"

One inn there was, where the dim bush swung wet and sleek as a clinging bat, and where stale embers of the night's revelry still flickered; for, behind the lighted windows, men were singing, and we heard them as we passed:

"Oh, we're all dry

Wi' drinking on't—

We're all dry

Wi' drinking on't.

The piper kissed

The fiddler's wife;

And I can't sleep

For thinking on't!"

"Starbuck's Inn," muttered Sir William, grimly. "He's a Boston man; they drink no tea there."

And, as we strode on in the darkness, behind us, from the lighted hostelry, came a husky echo of that foolish catch:

"Diddle diddle dumpling,

My son John—"

So I knew that my buckskin birds were still chirping among us.

But now we were on the stony way and the town sank below us as we climbed towards Quider's lodge, knee-deep in dewy thistles.

The spark of a tiny council fire guided us. Coming nearer we smelled black birch burning, and we saw the long thread of aromatic smoke mounting steadily to the paling stars.

We passed a young basswood-tree from which hung a flint, symbol of the Mohawks. From another chestnut-sapling dangled the symbol of the Cayugas, a pipe. All at once we saw Quider, standing motionless before his lodge.

Sir William drew flint and tinder from his pouch, and sent a spark flying into the dry tobacco of his pipe. He drew it to a long glow, twice, and passed it, through the smoke of the fire, to Quider.

I saw the Cayuga's face then. It was a strange red, yet it was not painted. He seemed ill; his eyes glittered like the eyes of a lynx.

And now, as the Indian sank down into his blanket before the fire, Sir William produced a belt from the folds of his cloak and held it out. The belt was black with two figures woven in white on it. The hands of the figures were clasped together. It was a chain-belt.

"*Brother*," he said, slowly: "The clouds which hang over us prevent us from seeing the sun. It is, therefore, our business, with this belt, to clear the sky. And we also, with this belt, set the sun in its proper course, so that we may be enabled to see the narrow path of peace."

(*Gives the belt.*)

"*Brother.* We have heard what you have said about Colonel Cresap; we believe he has been misled, and we have rekindled the council fire at Johnstown with embers from Onondaga, with embers from the Ohio, with coals from our proper fireplace at Mount Johnson.

"We uncover these fires to summon our wisest men so that they shall judge what word shall be sent to Colonel Cresap, to secure you in your treaty rights which I have sworn to protect by these strings!"

(*A bunch of strings.*)

"*Brother.* By this third and last belt I send peace and love to my brethren of the Cayuga; and by this belt I bid them be patient, and remember that I have never broken my word to those within the Long House, nor yet to those who dwell without the doors."

(*A large black belt of seven rows.*)

Then Sir William drew from his girdle a belt of wampum, so white that, in the starlight, it shimmered like virgin silver.

"Who mourns?" asked Sir William, gently, and the Indian rose and answered: "We mourn—we of the Cayuga—we of three clans."

"What clans shall be raised up?" asked Sir William.

"Three clans lie stricken: the Wolf, the Plover, the Eel. Who shall raise them?"

"*Brother*," said Sir William, gravely. "With this belt I raise three clans; I cleanse their eyes, their ears, their mouths, their bodies with clean water. With this belt I clear their path so that no longer shall the dead stand in your way or in ours."

(*The belt.*)

"*Brother*. With these strings I raise up your head and beg you will no longer sorrow."

(*Three strings.*)

"*Brother*. With this belt I cover the graves."

(*A great white belt.*)

In the dead stillness that followed the northern hill-tops slowly turned to pink and ashes. The day had dawned.

When again we reached the village cocks were crowing in every yard; the painted weather-vanes glowed in the sun; legions of birds sang.

From Starbuck's Inn stumbled forth a blinking, soiled, and tipsy company, linking arms, sidling, shoving, lurching, and bawling:

"Oh, we're all dry

Wi' drinkin' on't!"

And I plainly saw my two coureurs-de-bois, boozy as owls, a-bussing the landlord's greasy wench while mine host pummelled them lustily, foot and fist.

So on through the cold shadowy street and out into the sun-warmed road again, and at last to the Hall where, on the sunny porch, stood Silver Heels, hair in her eyes, her naked white feet in moccasins, washing her cheeks in the dew.

"Tut! tut!" cried Sir William, sharply. "What foolishness is this, Felicity? Off to bed! with your bare legs!"

"Betty said that beauty grew with dew-baths at dawn," said Silver Heels, coolly. "I have bathed my limbs and my body in the grass and I'm all over leaves."

"Betty's a fool! Be off to bed!—you little baggage!" cried Sir William. And away up-stairs scampered Silver Heels, dropping both moccasins in her flight.

"Betty! Betty!" fumed Sir William. "I'll Betty her, the black witch!" And he stamped off to the nursery, muttering threats which I knew would never be fulfilled.

That day Sir William sat in his library writing with Mr. Butler, so there was no school, and Peter, Esk, Silver Heels, and I went a-fishing in the river. And I did not wear my uniform, for fear of soiling.

All day long, as we sat in the grass to watch our poles a-quiver, horsemen from our stables passed us, galloping east and south, doubtless bearing letters from Sir William to Albany and New York—and farther south, perchance—for there came one rider with six soldiers in escort, and two led horses well packed, all trotting and clattering away towards the Fort Pitt trail.

That day was the last of the old days for us; but how could we suspect that, as we waded in the shallows there, laughing, chattering, splashing each other, and quarrelling to our hearts' content. The familiar river, which every freshet changed just enough to sharpen our eyes for new pools, slipped over its smooth golden stones, inviting our dusty feet. Up to our knees we moved in the ice-cold stream, climbing out on the banks at times to warm our legs in the sun, and lie deep in the daisies, winking at the swallows in the sky.

We played all our old games again—but that we played them for the last time, none of us suspected. I held a buttercup under Silver Heels's snowy chin to prove her love for cheese; I played buzzing bee-songs on grass-blades; I whittled whistles for Peter and Esk; I skipped flat stones; I coloured Silver Heels's toes yellow with dandelion juice so she should ever afterwards wade in gold—this at her own desire.

Twice those tiny spotted lady-beetles perched on my hand, and Silver Heels, to ward off threatening evil, took them on the pink tip of her little finger, repeating:

"Lady-bird, Lady-bird, fly away home!

Thy lodge is afire! thy babies will burn!"

Which she said would save me from torture at the stake some day.

The late sun settled in the blue ashes of the western forests as we pulled on our stockings and moccasins and gathered up our strings of silvery fish.

For a whole day I had carefully forgotten that I was anything but a comrade to these children; but I did not know how wise I had been to lay by, in my memory, one more perfect day ere the evil days came and the years drew nigh wherein, God wot! I found no pleasure.

Silver Heels and I walked back together through the evening glow, and I remember that the windows of our house were all on fire from the sun as we climbed the hill under the splendour of the western sky.

As we came through the orchard I saw Sir William sitting on the stone seat near the bee-hives. His chin had fallen on his chest, both hands rested on his cane, and over his body fell the glory of the red sky.

He heard us as we came through the orchard, and he raised his head to smile a welcome. But there was that in his eyes which told me to stay there with him after the others had trooped in to be fed, and I waited.

Presently he said: "Quider is sick. Did you discover anything in his face that might betoken—a—a fever?"

"His eyes," I said.

"Was he blotched? My sight is dim these years."

"His face was over-red," I answered, wondering.

Sir William said nothing more. After a little while he rose, leaning on his cane, and passed heavily under the fruit-trees towards the house.

That night came our doctor, Pierson, galloping from the village with an urgent message for Sir William. Later I saw soldiers set out with bayonets on their muskets, and, with them, the doctor, leading his horse.

In the morning we knew that the small-pox had seized the Cayuga, and that our soldiers patrolled Quider's lodge to warn all men of the black pest.

The days which followed were busy days for us all—days fraught with bustle and perplexity—hours which hurried on, crowding one on another like pages turning in a book—turning too swiftly for me to cipher the ominous text.

All Sir William's hopes of averting war were now centred in the stricken Cayuga. He and I haunted the neighbourhood of Quider's lodge, staring for hours at the silent hut in the clearing, or, rambling by starlight, we watched the candle burning in the lodge door as though it were the flame of life, now flaring, now sinking in its socket.

On such rambles he seldom spoke, but sometimes he leaned on my shoulder as we walked, and his very hand seemed burdened with the weight of his cares.

Once, however, when from the sentinels we learned that Quider might live, Sir William appeared almost gay, and we walked to a little hill, all silvery in the light of the young moon, and rested on a rock.

"Black Care rides behind the horseman, but—I have dismounted," he said, lightly. "Quider will live, I warrant you, barring those arrows of outrageous fortune of which you have doubtless heard, Michael."

"What may those same arrows be marked with?" I asked, innocently.

"With the totem of Kismet, my boy."

I did not know that totem, and said so, whereupon he fell a-laughing and pinched my cheek, saying, "Are there no people in the world but the Six Nations of the Long House?"

I answered cautiously: "Oe-yen-de-hit Sar-a-ta-ke," meaning, "there are favourable signs (of people) where the tracks of (their) heels may be seen. I have not travelled; there may be other tracks in the world."

"Ten-ca-re Ne-go-ni," replied Sir William, gravely. "He scatters His people everywhere, Michael. The world lies outside of the Long House!"

"I shall say to the world I come from Ko-lan-e-ka, and that I am kin to you, sir," said I, dropping easily into that intimate dialect we children often used together, or in the family circle.

"The world will say: 'He comes from Da-o-sa-no-geh, the place without a name; let him return to The-ya-o-guin, the Gray-Haired, who sent him out so ignorant.'"

"Do you say that, sir, because I am ignorant of the poets?" I asked.

"Even women know the poets in these days," he said, smiling. "You would not wish to know less than your own wife, would you?"

"My wife!" I exclaimed, scornfully.

"Why, yes," said Sir William, much amused; "you will marry one day, I suppose."

After a moment I said:

"Is Silver Heels going to marry Mr. Butler?"

"I hope so," replied Sir William, a little surprised. "Mr. Butler is a gentleman of culture and wealth. Felicity has no large dower, and I can leave but little if

I provide for all my children. I deem it most fortunate that Captain Butler has spoken to me."

"If," said I, slowly, "Silver Heels and I are obliged to marry somebody, why can we not marry each other?"

Sir William stared at me.

"Are you in love with Felicity?" he asked.

"Oh no, sir!" I cried, resentfully.

"Is she—does she fancy she is in love with you?" insisted Sir William, in growing astonishment.

"No! no!" I said, hastily, for his question annoyed and irritated me. "But I only don't want her to marry Mr. Butler; I'd even be willing to marry her myself, though I once saw a maid in Albany—"

"What the devil is all this damned nonsense?" cried Sir William, testily. "What d'ye mean by this idiot's babble? Eh?"

The expression of my face at this outburst first disconcerted, then sent him into a roar of laughter. Such startled and injured innocence softened his impatience; he carefully explained to me that, as Felicity had no fortune, and I barely sufficient to sustain me, such a match could but prove a sorry and foolish one for Silver Heels and for me.

"If you were older," he said, "and if you loved each other, I should, perhaps, be weak enough not to interfere, though wisdom prompted. But it is best that Felicity should wed Mr. Butler, and that as soon as may be, for I am growing old very fast, older than I care to confess, older than I dare believe. This I say to you, for I have come to trust you and to lean on you, Michael; but you must never hint to others that I complain of age or feebleness. Do you understand?"

"Yes, sir," I answered, soberly.

"Besides," said Sir William, with a forced smile, "I have much to do yet; I mean to accomplish a deal of labour before I—well, before many weeks. Come, lad; we must not grope out here seeking unhappiness under these pretty stars. We are much to each other; we shall be much more—eh? Come, then; Quider will live, spite of those same slings and arrows of which you know not the totem marks."

As we descended the hill through shadowy drifts of spice-fern, Sir William looked long and hopefully at the candle burning in Quider's hut.

"Ho-no-we-eh-to," he murmured; "I have given him white belts—ho-way-ha-tah-koo!—they shall disinter him, though he lie dead. He came, bearing wampum; shall his spirit go out bearing a quiver—o-tat-sheh-te?—hoo-sah-ha-ho?"

"So-yone-wes; sa-tea-na-wat; he has a long wampum belt; he holds it fast, sir," I said, cheerfully mixing the tongues of the Six Nations to piece out my symbol.

So we went home, comforted and hopeful; but the morrow brought gravest tidings from Quider's lodge, for the Cayuga had fallen a-raving in his fever, and it was necessary to tie him down lest he break away.

Weighed down with anxiety concerning what Colonel Cresap might be doing on the Ohio, dreading an outbreak which must surely come if the Cayuga belts remained unanswered, Sir William, in his sore perplexity, turned once more to me and opened his brave heart.

"I know not what intrigues may be afoot, what double intrigues revolve within, what triple motives urge the men who have despatched Colonel Cresap on this adventure. But I know this, that should Cresap's colonials in their blindness attack my Cayugas, a thousand hatchets will sparkle in these hills, and the people of the Long House will never sit idle when these colonies and England draw the sword!"

Again that cold, despairing amazement crept into my heart, for I could no longer misunderstand Sir William that his sympathies were not with our King, but with the provinces.

He appeared to divine my troubled thoughts; I knew it by the painful smile which passed like a pale light from his eyes, fading in the shadowy hollows which care and grief had dug in his good, kind face.

"Learn from others, not from me, what acid chemistry is changing the heart of this broad land to stone," he said.

"I cannot understand, sir," I broke out, "why we should warn Colonel Cresap. Is it loyalty for us to do so?"

Sir William turned his sunken eyes on me.

"It is loyalty to God," he said.

The solemn peace in his eyes awed me; the ravage which care had left in his visage frightened me.

He spoke again:

"I may have to answer to Him soon, my boy. I have searched my heart; there is no dishonour in it."

We had been sitting on the bed in my little chamber. The window was open, the breeze fluttered the cotton curtains, a spicy breeze, laden with essence of the fern which covers our fields, and smells like bay-leaves crushed in one's palm.

The peace of Sabbath brooded over all, a cow-bell tinkled from the pasture, birds chirped. Sir William rose to stand by the window, and his gaze softened towards the sunlit meadows where buttercups swayed with daisies, and blue flower-de-luce quivered in the wind.

"God!" he muttered, under his breath. "That this sweet peace on earth should be assailed by men!"

Again into my breast came that strange uneasiness which this month of May had brought to us along with the robins and the new leaves, and which I began to breathe in with the summer wind itself—a vague unrest, a breathless waiting—for what?—I did not know.

And so it went on, Sir William and I walking sometimes alone together on the hill-sides, speaking soberly of that future which concerned our land and kin, I listening in silence with apprehension ever growing.

Often during that week came Mohawk sachems and chiefs of the Senecas and Onondagas to the Hall, pestering Sir William with petty disputes to judge between them. Sometimes it was complaint against drunken soldiers who annoyed them, sometimes a demand for justice, touching the old matters of the moonlight survey, in which one, Collins, did shamefully wrong the Mohawks by stealing land; and William Alexander, who is now Lord Sterling, and William Livingston did profit thereby—guiltily or innocently, I know not.

But these troubles Sir William settled impartially and with that simple justice which made fraud loathsome, even to frauds.

I do remember how he scourged and scored that villain German, Klock, for making the Mohawks drunk to rob them of their lands by cunning; and I recall how he summoned Counsellor John Chambers to witness justice between Mr. Livingston and the Mohawks:

"Billy Livingston," said Sir William, "bear this message to Billy Alexander, that the land belongs not to him or to you, but to my Mohawks! It is enough that I say this to you, for you are my old comrades and honoured friends, and I am assured you will relinquish all title to what is not your own. But, by God! Billy, if you do not, I shall spend every penny of my own on lawyers to drive you out—every farthing, though it beggars me!"

This was but one of many scenes at which I was present. Why Sir William always called me to bear him company in such private matters, I could not at once comprehend. Little by little, however, I saw that it was because of his trust in me, and his desire that I should know of such affairs; and his love and confidence made me proud. Was I not the only person in the world who knew his sentiments and his desire to stop Colonel Cresap on the Ohio, lest, in ignorance, he should turn the entire Six Nations against the colonies?

Had he not told me, sadly, that he could not speak of this plan even to his own son, Sir John Johnson, lest his son, placing loyalty to the King before obedience to his father, should thwart Sir William, and even aid Colonel Cresap to anger the Cayugas, and so injure the cause of the colonies?

He told me, too, that he could not confide in Mr. Butler or in his father, Colonel John Butler; neither dared he trust his sons-in-law, Colonel Claus or Colonel Guy Johnson, although they served as his deputies in Indian affairs.

All of these gentlemen were, first of all, loyal to our King, and all of them, clearly foreseeing a struggle between King and colonies, would not raise a finger to prevent Colonel Cresap from driving the Six Nations as allies into the King's arms.

"What I am striving for," said Sir William to me, again and again, "is to so conduct that these Indians on our frontiers shall take neither one side nor the other, but remain passive while the storm rages. To work openly for this is not possible. If it were possible to work openly, and if Quider should die, I would send such a message to my Lord Dunmore of Virginia as would make his bloodless ears burn! And they may burn yet!"

At my expression of horrified surprise Sir William hesitated, then struck his fist into the open palm of his left hand.

"Why should you not know it?" he cried. "You are the only one of all I can trust!"

He paused, eying me intently.

"Can I not trust you, dear lad?" he said, gently.

"Yes, sir," I cried, in an overwhelming rush of pity and love. "You are first in my heart, sir—and then the King."

Sir William smiled and thought awhile. Then he continued:

"You are to know, Michael, that Lord Dunmore, Governor of Virginia, is, in my opinion, at the bottom of this. He it is who, foreseeing the future, as do all thinking men, has sent the deluded Cresap to pick a quarrel with my Cayugas, knowing that he is making future allies for England. It is vile! It is a monstrous thing! It is not loyalty, it is treason!"

He struck his pinched forehead and strode up and down.

"Can Dunmore know what he is doing? God! The horror of it!—the horror of border war! Has Dunmore ever seen how savages fight? Has he seen raw scalps ripped from babies? Has he seen naked prisoners writhing at the stake, drenched in blood, eyeless sockets raised to the skies?"

He stood still in the middle of the room. There was a sweat on his cheekbones.

"If we must fight, let us fight like men," he muttered, "without fear or favour, without treachery! But, Michael, woe to the side that calls on these savages for aid! Woe to them! Woe! Woe! For the first scalp taken will turn this border into such a hell of blood and flame as the devil himself in his old hell never dreamed of!"

This outburst left me stunned. Save for Sir William, I knew not where now to anchor my faith. Our King already in these few days had become to my youthful mind a distant wavering shadow, no longer the rock to which loyal hearts must cling—unquestioning. And it is ever so; old faiths fall when hearts question, and I know not whether hearts be right or wrong to strive so hard for the answer which is their own undoing.

Still, however, in that distant England which I had never seen, the King, though fading to a phantom in my heart, yet loomed up still a vast and mighty shape, awful as the threatening majesty of a dim cloud on the world's edge, behind which lightning glimmers.

CHAPTER VII

Now the dark pages turning in the book of fate were flying faster than young eyes could mark. First to the Hall came Thayendanegea, brother to Mistress Molly, and embraced us all, eagerly admiring my uniform with an Indian's frank naïveté, caressing Silver Heels's curly pate and praising her beauty, and fondling Esk and Peter with Albany sweets till I forbade them to approach, for their stickiness did disgust me.

I had always been greatly attached to Thayendanegea, for he was a frank, affectionate youth, though a blooded Mohawk, and possessing the courtesy, gentleness, and graces of true quality.

Clothed like an English gentleman, bearing himself like a baronet, he conducted to the admiration and respect of all, and this though he was the great war-chief of the Mohawks, and already an honoured leader in the council of the Six Nations.

He never became a sachem, but remained always the most respected and powerful leader in the Long House. Even Huron and Delaware listened when he spoke. He never treated the Lenni-Lenape as women, and for this reason they listened always willingly to the voice of Joseph Brant, called Thayendanegea.

Now, though Sir William had hitherto trusted Brant in all things, I noticed he spoke not to Brant of Quider's mission, though Mr. Butler had already scented a mystery in the Cayuga's visit, and often asked why Quider had never spoken his message; for he was not aware that both message and answer had been delivered long ago.

That week there were three council fires at the Lower Castle, which Brant and Mr. Butler attended in company with a certain thin little Seneca chief called Red Jacket, a filthy, sly, and sullen creature, who was, perhaps, a great orator, but all the world knew him for a glutton and a coward.

Brant despised him, and it was Brant, too, who had given to Red Jacket that insulting title, "The Cow-Killer," which even the Mohawk children shouted when Red Jacket came to Johnson Hall after the council fires had been covered at the Lower Castle.

Our house had now been thronged with Indians for a week. Eleven hundred Mohawks, Cayugas, Senecas, Onondagas, and a few Tuscaroras lay encamped around us, holding long talks with Red Jacket, Mr. Butler, and Brant; but Sir William attended no fires, and very soon I discovered the reason. For suddenly Sir John Johnson arrived at the Hall, and with him

Colonel Daniel Claus and his lady from Albany, which abrupt advents began a stir and bustle among us that increased as, day by day, new guests arrived at our house. Johnson Hall, Colonel Guy Johnson's house, and the house of Colonel John Butler were now crowded to overflow with guests. Sachems and chiefs of the Oneidas arrived, officers from the Royal Americans and from the three regiments of militia which Tryon County maintained, officers from my own troop of irregular horse quartered at Albany, and whom I now met for the first time; and finally, in prodigious state, came our Governor Tryon from New York, with a troop of horse which, for beauty of clothing and impudence of deportment, I had never seen equalled.

The house rang with laughter and the tinkle of glasses from morning until night; on the stairs there swept a continuous rush and rustle of ladies' petticoats like the wind blowing through corn. Ladies filled the house; there were maids and lackeys and footmen and chair-bearers and slaves thronging porch and hallway, new faces everywhere, new uniforms, new gowns, new phrases, new dishes at table, new airs at the spinet, new songs.

"Tiddle tinkle" went our spinet all day and night, with some French ladies from Saint Sacrement a-singing la-la-la.

As by a magic touch the old homely life had vanished, old faces disappeared, old voices were silent. I looked in vain for Silver Heels, for Peter, for Esk. They were drowned in this silken sea.

And now, piling confusion on confusion, comes from the south my Lord Dunmore from Virginia, satin-coated, foppish, all powder and frill, and scented like a French lady. But oh, the gallant company he brought to Johnson Hall—those courtly Virginians with their graces and velvet voices, with their low bows and noiseless movements, elegant as panthers, suave as Jesuits, and proud as heirs to kingdoms all.

Some lodged at the inns in town, some with us, some with Sir John Johnson, and others with Colonel Butler. But they all thronged our house, day and night, till I was like to stifle with the perfumes and scented clothes of our white guests and the wild-animal aroma of the Indians.

For two days, indeed, I saw little of the company, for I lodged at the block-house with Mr. Duncan, keeping an eye on the pest-hut where lay the stricken Cayuga; this by Sir William's orders, though warning me to approach the hut no nearer than the sentries, and that with my hanker to my nose and a lump of sulphur in my mouth.

As for Silver Heels, I saw her but twice, and then she disappeared entirely. I was sorry for her, believing she had been cooped within the limits of nursery and play-room; but I had my pity for my pains, as it turned out.

It came about in this way: I had been relieved of duties at the block-house to receive reports of Quider's sickness, as it was now believed certain that the Cayuga must die; and I had been ordered to dress in my new uniform, to accompany Sir William to a review of our honest Tryon County militia, now assembling at Johnstown and Schenectady.

It was early morning, with the fields all dewy and a west wind blowing the daisies into furrows, when I left my chamber, booted, hair powdered in a club and tied with black, and my new silver gorget shining like the sun on my breast. I was in dress uniform, scarlet coat, buff smalls, sash and sword glittering, and I meant to cut a figure that day which people might remember. But Lord! Even on the staircase I found myself in a crowd of officers all laces and sashes and gold brocade, and buttons like yellow stars dancing on cuff and collar. My uniform was but a spark in the fire; I was obscured, nay snuffed out in the midst of the Virginians with their flame-colored scarfs and cockades, and the New York officers of the Governor's dragoon guard, gorgeous as the drummers of the French grenadiers.

Smothered by the hot air, the perfumes and pomatum on stock and queue, the warm cloying odour of dressed leather and new gloves of kid-skin, I made my way into the hall, but found it packed with ladies, all a-fanning and rustling, with maids tying on sun-masks and pinning plumes to rolls of hair that towered like the Adirondacks, all vegetation and birds.

Hat under arm, hand on hilt, I did bow and smile and beseech for a free passage to the fresh air, and it made me think of edging through the barn-yard with the feathered flock crowding and ruffling a thousand feathers. And as I threaded my way, minding my steps as well I might, it was: "Oh, la! My lady's skirt!" and "Lud! The lad's spur's in the lace!" "My mantua!" "Ah! my scarf's a-trail on the creature's sword!" "Grand dieu! et ma robe, monsieur!"

Standing at last in the portico with the fresh wind in my face, I perceived Sir William, attended by Sir John and Colonel Claus, inspecting the guard at the north block-house, and I made haste to join them, running fast, to the danger of my powdered hair, which scattered a small snowy cloud in the wind.

"Gad! The lad's powdered like a Virginian!" said Sir William, laughing and drawing me to him, pinching my ears and chin. Then he dusted the powder from my shoulders and turned me around, muttering to himself, "A proper officer, damme! a well-groomed lad; eh, Jack?"

"Yes," said Sir John, with his slow, reserved eyes shifting from my hat to my spurs. He gave me a damp finger to press, then his indifferent gaze wandered to the meadows below, where the brown and yellow uniforms of Colonel Butler's militia regiment spread out like furrows of autumn leaves.

I paid my respects to Colonel Claus, who honoured me with a careless nod, and passed before me to greet Colonel John Butler and his son, Captain Walter Butler.

The Butlers were of a stripe; there was the blank fixed eye of the night-bird in father and son, the deathly grimace to do duty as a smile, the mechanical observances of polite company, the compliments, the bows, the carriage of gentlemen, but back of it something lifeless, something slow and terrifying in voice and step—God knows what I mean! Yet often and often it came to me that inside their bodies something was lying dead—their souls, perhaps.

I stood behind Sir William, drawing on my gloves of kid-skin, observing the officers as they came up to join the staff, and stand and watch the two remaining regiments marching into the meadow below. These regiments were clothed in brown, green, and scarlet, one wearing green coats, t'other bright red with yellow facings, an over-gaudy effect and disturbing to my senses like the sounds of a spinet when Peter pounded on the keys.

They had built a gayly painted wooden pavilion in the meadow for the ladies and Governor Tryon and my Lord Dunmore, and now came the coaches and calashes burdened with beauty and tickled and tricked out in ribbons, and the Virginians all a-horse, caracoling beside the vehicles, a brave, bright company, by Heaven!—for they rode perfectly and with a gracious carelessness which contrasted favourably with the stiff, solid gallop of our Governor Tryon's dragoon guard.

Behind us the grooms were bringing up our mounts, and I slyly looked for Warlock, doubting lest he be 'portioned to some horseless guest. But there the dear fellow stood, ears pointed straight at me, and snorting for the caress of my hand on his muzzle.

"Mount, gentlemen!" said Sir William, briskly, setting toe to the stirrup held by young Bareshanks; and up into our saddles we popped, while the trumpet blew from the block-house, and down in the meadow the long painted drums boomed out the salute.

As we entered the meadow at a trot I caught a good, quick picture of the pavilion with its flags, its restless rows of ladies unmasking, fluttering kerchiefs and fans and scarfs; and my Lord Dunmore all over gold and blue, blinking like a cat in the sun, and the crimson of the Governor's mantle, clasped with gilt, falling from his solid epaulets. This I saw clearly, but as we broke into a gallop across the clover, the colours ran like tinted fires; the dull reds and blues of the Indians, the shimmer on gorgets and buckles, the rippling flags; yet it seemed as I flew past that I had seen a face up there which I knew well yet did not know, like those familiar eyes that look at us in dreams. Surely it was not Silver Heels. But there was no time for speculation now. Rub-a-dub-dub! Bang! Bang! Our brigade band was marching past with our head groom playing a French horn very badly, and old Norman McLeod a-fifing it, wrong foot foremost, which caused Sir William to mutter "damn!" and rub his nose in mortification.

"'SILVER HEELS!' I STAMMERED"

"Hay-foot! Straw-foot!" simpered a cornet of dragoons behind me, and I turned on him, and gave him a look.

"Did you say you were hungry?" I whispered, backing my horse gently against the horse of the insolent cornet.

"Hungry?" he stammered.

"You mentioned hay, sir," I said, fiercely.

He turned red as a pippin but did not reply.

Swallowing my anger and my shame for our militia yokels, I glared at the head of Colonel Butler's regiment, now passing, and was comforted, for the clod-hoppers marched like regulars with a solid double rank of fifers shrilling out "Down, Derry, down!" as smart as you please.

After them came the green-coated varlets, with a good round stench of the stables from their ranks, yet footing it proudly, and their fifes ringing a barbarous tune which is lately somewhat in vogue among us, the same being called "Yankee Doodle."

Followed our three companies of Royal Americans, drums beating "The Huron," a most warming march and loudly applauded by the long lines of country folk and Indians, sitting on the stone walls; and after them the inharmonious regiment in yellow and red, with two men drunk and a dog-fight in the rear, soberly observed by my Lord Dunmore, who laid a bet with our Governor, and lost on the spotted dog, they say.

There was a sham battle of the troops, too; half a gill to every fifth man, and fifty pounds for the cannon on the hill, which cost Sir William a pretty penny, our Governor refusing to allow for the powder burned. However, it was a fine pageant, and pleased all; and I was sorry when the last cartridge was spent and the brigade band played, "God Save the King."

We followed Sir William to the pavilion, dismounting there to ascend the stairs and pay our respects to the Governor and to Lord Dunmore.

"Come with me, Michael," said Sir William, wiping his face with his hanker till it glistened; and I followed the Baronet into the enclosure.

Lord Dunmore was tricked out like a painted actor, neither old nor young, but too white and pink and without any red blood in him, as far as I could see. He wore a wig—it was said he possessed twenty and valued at six thousand pounds—and his fingers, which I could see through the lace on his cuffs, were like white bird's claws loaded with jewels.

When Lord Dunmore saw Sir William he fell a-tapping his snuff-box and bobbing and smiling, nor did he rise until we had made our way to him.

"Lud! Lud!" he said, and fell a-simpering, with hands raised in feigned amazement at the magnificence of the review. "Lud! Lud! Sir William! A gallant fête! A brave defilé! Militia, not regulars, you say! Vive Dieu, Sir William, a most creditable entraining! Permettez—mes compliments le plus distinguée!"

"My aide-de-camp, Lord Dunmore," said Sir William, bluntly; "your Lordship will remember Captain Cardigan who died before Quebec? His son, my Lord!—and my dear kinsman, Michael Cardigan, cornet in the Borderers."

"Strike me!" simpered Lord Dunmore. "Strike me, now, Sir William! He has his father's eyes—Vrai Dieu! Curse me, if he has not his father's eyes, Sir William!"

At this remarkable discovery I bowed and said it was an honour to be considered like my father in any particular.

"Burn me!" murmured his Lordship, in an ecstasy at my natural response. "Burn me, Sir William, what a wit he has, now!" And he peeped at me, squeezing his eyes into two weak slits, and laid his snuff-box against his nose. Lord! What a false face he pulled at me!

Apparently surfeited with admiration, he invited Sir William to take snuff with him, then turning to Governor Tryon, who had just come into the stall, he fell to smirking and exclaiming and vapouring about God knows what, until I, weary and cloyed, glanced around me at the crowd on the seats above us.

There were a hundred pair of bright eyes fixed on us, and without vanity I perceived a few to meet mine, but the faces were not distinct, and I found it disconcerting.

Then a deep, pleasant voice sounded close beside me, and looking around, I saw our Governor Tryon smiling at me.

"I knew your father," he said; "it was a privilege, Mr. Cardigan, and one I take advantage of to address the son of so gallant a gentleman."

I replied warmly and gratefully, yet with military deference, and I saw Sir William observing me, well pleased at my bearing.

"In these times," said the Governor, clasping his cloak over his epaulets, "it is a pleasure to meet with modest loyalty in the younger generation. Loyal to parent, loyal to King! I predict we shall hear from you, Mr. Cardigan."

"Please God, sir," I replied, blushing scarlet; for into my mind crept that wavering doubt which, since Sir William had talked with me, haunted me like a shadow.

The Governor passed by with his clanking dragoons, among them the young jackanapes who had presumed to sneer at our yeomanry, and we delivered a pair of scornful glances at each other which crossed like broadswords.

And now my Lord Dunmore's boudoir on wheels drove up, and his purring Lordship minced off in the midst of his flame-coloured Virginians, for all the world like a white cat dancing through hell fire.

The ladies were rising, tying on sun-masks, standing in rows between the seats, and the officers loitered and whispered and played with their snuff-boxes, while the silent Mohawk chiefs looked on, standing like statues till the crowd gave them their liberty.

One lady there was, in a mask and silvery cloak, who looked at me so long through the eye-holes that I felt my heart begin a-beating; and another, too, in mask and rose mantle, who lifted the linen a trifle, displaying a fresh, sweet, smiling mouth. This one in rose turned twice to look at me, and it amused me to feel my heart go a-bumping at my ribs so loud, for she did truly resemble Marie Livingston.

Sir William and Colonel Claus had joined Lord Dunmore in his coach; Sir John and Colonel Butler attached themselves to our Governor Tryon. I, abandoned, rode back to the Hall with a company of Virginians and dragoons, wondering if ever I might acquire such horsemanship as the Southerners displayed.

Coming to the Hall, I met Sir William, whose smiling face grew haggard at sight of me, and he drew me apart, asking of news from Quider.

"He is not yet dead, sir," I replied, my heart aching for Sir William.

For a moment he stood staring at the ground, then bidding me report to Mr. Duncan at the block-house, walked away to disguise his anxious visage again with the oldest mask in the world—a smile.

That night Sir William provided two great banquets for our guests, one at the court-house in Johnstown, the other at Johnson Hall.

The splendid banquet at the court-house was given to all the visiting officers except Lord Dunmore, Governor Tryon, and their particular aides. To it were invited the Virginians, the New-Yorkers, the important Mohawk, Seneca, and Onondaga sachems, and chiefs of the Long House. Also were bidden the officers of our Royal Americans, such officers of the Border House as had come with Governor Tryon, and all gentlemen of distinction who had brought their ladies.

Colonel Claus and his lady presided as host and hostess, representing Sir William and Mistress Molly, and our brigade band played in the gallery during the banquet, and later on the portico of the court-house, where a great crowd of people had collected to cheer.

The other banquet was given at the same hour in our house, to honour Lord Dunmore and Governor Tryon.

There were gathered in the hallway and on the stairs a vast company of ladies and gentlemen when I came down from my little chamber to wait on Sir William. Here was the great Earl of Dunmore in a ring of fluttering ladies, peering, bobbing, tapping his snuff-box, preening the lace on his cuffs—and

I thought he resembled one of those irksome restless birds from the Canaries in a painted cage.

There was our Governor Tryon in purple silk from head to foot, with the broad sash and star on his breast, leaning over, hands clasped behind his back, to whisper jest or flattery to a young girl who tapped at him with her fan. There was my kinsman, Sir John Johnson, with his indifferent eyes and ungracious carriage, and old Colonel Butler watching the gay company as hawks, from sheer habit, watch peacocks, meaning no attack. There also strolled my impudent dragoon lad who had offended at the pavilion, and I will not deny he appeared to be an elegant and handsome officer, possessing those marked characteristics of fashion and assurance which one observes in all gentlemen from the city of New York.

Making my way carefully amid rustling petticoats and a forest of painted fans all waving like the wings of a swarm of moths drawn by the candle-light, I passed Mistress Molly on the arm of Sir William, touching my lips to her pretty fingers, which she held out to me behind her back.

Next I encountered Mr. Butler and honoured him with a scowl, which displayed my country breeding, it being the fashion among quality to greet one's enemy with more elaborate courtesy than one accords to friends.

People passed and repassed with laughter and whisper, and the scented wind from their fans swept my cheek.

Suddenly it seemed as though the voice of Silver Heels sounded in my ears, and for a moment I stared about me, astonished that she should be here. But I could not find her. Then her voice sounded again, clear as a pebbled spring in all that chatter, and turning, I saw it came from a young girl standing behind me. She was very delicate and pretty in her powder and patches, truly somewhat pale and lacking in plumpness, but with a pair of great hazel eyes like Silver Heels's, and the child's full lips. Certainly she had Silver Heels's voice, and her trick of widening her eyes, too, for now she perceived me, and—

"Why, Micky!" she cried.

"Silver Heels!" I stammered, striving to believe my eyes. What miracle of miracles had set her to grow tall and turn into a woman in a single week?

I stared almost piteously at her, trying to find my own familiar comrade in this whispering shower of silk and ribbon, this delicate stranger, smiling breathlessly at me with sparkling teeth set on the edge of her painted fan.

In her triumph she laughed that laugh of silver which sounded ever of woodlands and birds, the same laugh, the same gray eyes, and the same satin fingers laid on my wrist.

"Silly," she whispered, "I told you so. And it has come true; my gown is silk, my stockings silk, my shoes are Paddington's make and silken to the soles!"

"How did you grow?" I gasped.

"Have I grown? Oh, my gown and shoes count, too, and my hair rolled by Betty till I vowed she meant to scalp me! See my egrettes! Are they straight, Micky?"

Ere I could attempt to compose my thoughts, comes mincing my impudent dragoon, who seemed to know her, for he brought her a ribbon to tie above her elbow, explaining it was a new conceit from New York.

"It's this way," he explained, utterly ignoring my presence; "I tie this bow of blue above your elbow, so!—with your gracious consent. Now for a partner to lead you to the table I seek some gentleman and tie a blue bow to his sword-hilt."

"Pray tie it to Mr. Cardigan's," said Silver Heels, mischievously. "I have much to say to him for his peace of mind."

The dragoon and I, face to face, regarded each other with menacing composure.

"To deprive you of such an honour, sir," said he, coolly, "I protest reduces me to despair; but the light blue bows have already been awarded, Mr. Cardigan."

Instinctively I glanced at his own sword-hilt, and there fluttered a light blue ribbon. At the same moment I perceived that Silver Heels had been perfectly aware of this.

Mortified as I was, and stinging under the dragoon's impudence, I controlled myself sufficiently to congratulate him and courteously deplore my own ill fortune, without a grimace, though it stuck in my throat to say it.

"Let not your lady hear that!" said Silver Heels, with her fan hiding her lips. "How do you know, sir, which partner fate and Mr. Bevan may allot you?"

Mr. Bevan and I regarded each other in solemn hostility.

"May I have the honour of attaching this ribbon to your hilt, sir?" he asked, stiffly.

"You may, sir," said I, still more stiffly, "if it is necessary."

He tied a red bow-knot to my hilt; we bowed to each other, then with a smile and a word to Silver Heels which I did not catch, he saluted us again and strolled off with his nose in the air and his hands full of ribbons of every hue—the fop!

"Who is that pitiful ass?" I said, turning to Silver Heels.

"Why, Michael!" she protested, reproachfully, yet smiling, too.

"Oh, if he's one of your friends, I ask indulgence," said I, mad enough to pluck the blue knot from her arm.

"Truly, Michael," she sniffed, "you are still very young."

She seated herself by the big clock; I sat beside her, sullenly, and for a time I peered at her sideways. Verily, the impossible had overtaken us; she appeared to be fully as tall as half the ladies gathered around us; her self-possession and obvious indifference to me completed my growing discomfort. I looked at her small, silk-covered toes pushing out under her petticoat.

"Is the dandelion juice on them yet?" I asked, with piteous playfulness.

"Don't talk like that!" she said, sharply, drawing her feet in. And with that petulant movement the playmate I had so often bullied, slipped away from me forever, leaving in her place a dainty thing of airs and laces to flout me, whom I knew not, but whom I meant to be avenged on; for at moments, as I sat there, I could have yelled aloud in my vexation.

Lord! how they all ogled her, and came a-mincing, gentlemen and ladies, old and young, and I heard whispers around me that she was a beauty and would be rich one day. My Lord Dunmore, too, came a-dancing pit-pat! till I thought to hear his bones creak inside his white silk; and the dragoon jackanapes was there, having tied up everything with his ribbons save his own long ears, and it infuriated me to see him standing guard protector over Silver Heels, with jealous smiles for all who approached.

Now what the devil had seized all these gentlemen to set them smirking and vapouring over Silver Heels, I did not know, or rather, I knew perfectly well, because it was as plain as a Mohawk moccasin on a spotted trail that Silver Heels had suddenly become a beauty. Even I could see that. Granted her bosom lacked somewhat in fulness, granted a childish leanness of arm and neck, granted even a pallor which adorned her not, and which, to tell the truth, I knew came from fright, there was something in the frail moulding of her that drew eyes, something in the arm's slim contours that touched even me.

I might have taken a pride in her, had not all these bobbing pigeons come crowding about to share openly my unconfessed admiration. But they bowed and strutted and posed and flattered, pressing closer until she was shut from my sight by a circle of coat-skirts, tilted swords, and muscular calves in silken stockings.

Presently our fiddlers and bassoons started the "Huron;" there was a flutter to find ribbons that matched, and a world of bustle and laughter, with gentlemen and ladies comparing colours and bowing and curtseying without regard to neighbors' toes and petticoats—the tittering popinjays!

Truly, if this mode of choosing one's lady prevailed in New York, I at least found it smacked something of silliness and French frivolity.

I had now been crowded up against our tall clock in the hall, and stood there striving to get a glimpse of Silver Heels, completely forgetting that somewhere in the crush a lady with a scarlet ribbon on her arm might be waiting for me. And doubtless I should have remained there, gnawing my lip, till doomsday, had not Silver Heels espied me and come fluttering through the crowd with:

"Oh, Micky! Have you seen your lady? Your old friend Marie Livingston! But she is wedded now; she is that pretty Mrs. Hamilton from Saint Sacrement. Oh, you lucky boy! All the officers are raving over her! But I asked her if she remembered you, and she said she didn't, so there!"

"Silver Heels," I began, with the first appealing glance I had ever bestowed on a woman; "Silver Heels, I want to tell you something."

I do not believe she was listening, or perhaps the chatter around us drowned my voice, which was husky and over-fond, for she cried: "You must not detain me, Michael. Mr. Bevan is waiting for me."

And with that she was gone into the whirl, leaving me high and dry against my clock, and furious over I knew not what. For truly I myself did not know what it was I had been about to say to Silver Heels. As for this Mrs. Hamilton, it madded me to hear of her. I had long forgotten Marie Livingston—save as a name to goad Silver Heels withal.

Mrs. Hamilton, forsooth! What the foul fiend had I to do with another man's wife, whether Hamilton or Smith or Jones I cared not, while that ape of a New-Yorker had set himself in my rightful place beside Silver Heels! And what stabbed deepest was that Silver Heels found pleasure in his foolish company—ay, plainly preferred him to me—the ungrateful minx! I prayed fervently she might live to repent it. I pictured her remorse when she came to her senses. And in a moment more I had slipped into one of my waking dreams wherein justice was dealt out by the jugful all around, and I emerged from some scenes of carnage, calm, triumphant, gently forgiving Silver Heels the accumulated sins of her misspent life.

Sullenly dreaming there under the tall clock, and happening to lift my eyes towards heaven for some of its spare vengeance, I perceived on the stairs that same lady who had half raised her sun-mask at the review—I mean the one in the rose mantle, not the other in the silvery cloak, whom I now knew had been Silver Heels.

Down the stairs rustled my lady of the rose mantle, finger-tips playing a tattoo over the mahogany balustrade, and on her lips a smile, as I fancied, though later I came to know that it was only the natural expression of her mouth. Something in my memory stirred at that smiling face.

Now she was looking straight at me, with that delicate curve of her lips which sets men thinking, and at the same moment I perceived that she wore my colours. Marie Livingston! I should never have known her; so we were quits, the affected minx! This was Mrs. Hamilton!—this bright-eyed girl with her smooth rose-petal skin and her snowy hand on the balustrade. Could I be mistaken? Surely she wore my colours! I glanced at the knot on my sword-hilt, then pressed through the throng to the stairway. Now at last I could pay Silver Heels in her own wampum, and I meant to do it under her very nose.

I met Mrs. Hamilton at the foot of the stairs, but she did not appear to see me. Truly she was a miracle of innocence not to have perceived her colours on my hilt, or perhaps she was over-timid. So I addressed her reassuringly and made her a bow that I knew must be impressive. However, I found her less confused than I, for she insisted on matching ribbons very carefully, which hurt my pride somewhat. But when she could no longer doubt that our ribbons matched, she made me a whimsical reverence, and took my arm with a smile, and a cool: "Oh, I faintly recall you now, Mr. Cardigan. How you have grown!"

Out into the wilderness of silver and candle-light we passed, fiddle and bassoon a-playing with might and main, and we stood behind our chairs while my Lord Dunmore chattered a blessing, then seated ourselves amid a gale of whispers.

Through the flare of the candles I saw Brant and Sir John Johnson near us, and also that filthy Indian, Red Jacket, both hands already in a dish of jelly, a-gobbling and grunting to himself, which sent Lord Dunmore into peals of shrill laughter, though Sir William took no notice. Presently I perceived Silver Heels and Mr. Bevan, nearly opposite to us, and strove to catch her eye. But Silver Heels took small notice of me; her cheeks had gone red with her first sip of wine, and she sat there rosy and silent, head a little lowered, while that insufferable coxcomb whispered into her ear, and smirked, and played with his wine-glass till the very sight of the man sickened me.

Stung to the quick by her indifference to my presence, smarting in my fancied isolation, I resolved to show her that I cared not a whit for her or her dragoon. So I loosened my tongue and set it wagging so smartly that I think I astonished Mrs. Hamilton, who had been observing Mr. Bevan with her fixed smile. At any rate, she gave me a long, pleasant stare, and presently her fixed smile became very sweet and pretty, although I thought a trifle mocking.

"Is it not amusing?" she said, coolly; "here you sit with me, when you would give your tow-head to be prattling into Mistress Warren's ears; and here sit I at twiddle-thumbs, devising vengeance on Mr. Bevan, who belongs to me!"

Perplexed and disconcerted, I found no words to answer such an amazing sally. It shamed me, too. Perhaps my countenance had betrayed me, but her confession concerning Mr. Bevan was a bold one, and not at all to my taste.

"I thought you had a husband," said I, with boyish bluntness.

She coloured up like fire for a moment, and I was sorry I spoke, but I had my pity for my pains, for the next instant she was laughing at me as though I were a ninny, and I could discover no reason for her mirth.

"Please tell me your Christian name," she said, sweetly. "I really do desire to recall it."

"My name is Michael," said I, suspiciously.

"Was it not Saint Michael who so soundly spanked the devil?" she asked, with her innocent smile. "Truly, Mr. Cardigan, you were well named to chastise the wicked with such sturdy innocence!"

I fumed inwardly, for I had no mind to be considered a gaby among women.

"I am perfectly aware, madam, that it is the fashion for charming women to turn boys' heads," said I, "and I wish you might turn Mr. Bevan's head till you twisted it off his neck!"

"I'd rather twist yours," she said, looking up from her plate of broiled troutlings.

"Twist it off?" I asked, curiously.

"I—I don't know. Look at me, Mr. Cardigan."

I met her pretty eyes.

"No, not quite off," she said, thoughtfully. "You are a nice boy, but not very bright. If you were you would pay me compliments instead of admonition. Perhaps you will after the Madeira. Perhaps you will even make love to me."

"I will do it before the Madeira," said I. "You are certainly the prettiest woman in Johnson Hall to-night, and if you've a mind for vengeance on your faithless dragoon yonder, pray take me for the instrument, Mrs. Hamilton."

"Hush!" she said, with a startled smile. "I may take you at your word."

"I am taking you at yours," said I, recklessly, and loud enough for Silver Heels to hear.

In the dull din of voices around us I heard Silver Heels's laugh, but the laugh was strained, and I knew she was looking at me and listening.

"I don't know what you mean," said Mrs. Hamilton, reddening, "but I know you to be a somewhat indiscreet young man who handles a woman as he would a club to beat his rival to the earth withal."

"I mean," said I, in a low voice, "to make love to you and so serve us both. Look at me, Mrs. Hamilton."

"I will not," she said, between her teeth.

"Tell me," I pleaded, "what is your Christian name. I do really wish to know, Mrs. Hamilton."

Spite of the angry red in her cheeks she laughed outright, glanced sideways at me, and laughed again, so blithely that I thought I had truly never seen such careless ripened healthy beauty in any woman.

"My name is Marie Hamilton, of Saint Sacrement, please you, kind sir," she lisped, with an affected simper which set us both a-laughing again.

"If you ever had your heart stormed you had best prepare for no quarter now!" I said, coolly.

"Insolent!" she murmured, covering her bright cheeks with her hands, and giving me a glance in which amusement, contempt, curiosity, and invitation were not inharmoniously blended.

The Madeira had now turned my blood to little rivers of fire, I being but lately enfranchised from the children's pewters and small-beer; but yet I am so made that never then nor since have the delicate vapours of wines stifled such wits as I possess. It is my conscience only that wine dulls.

So amid the low tumult, the breezy gush of whispers, the laughter, and the crystal tinkle of silver and glass, I made indiscreet, clear-headed love to Mistress Marie Hamilton, retreating under her cruel satire, rallying in the bright battery of her eyes, charging the citadel of her heart with that insincere and gay abandon which harasses, disconcerts, and piques a woman who understands better how to repel true passion.

"In what school have you been taught to make love, sir?" she said, at last, breathless, amused, yet exasperated.

"In the school of necessity, madam," I replied.

"I pray you teach something of your art to Mr. Bevan," said she, spitefully, over her fan's silk edge.

"I am teaching him now," said I.

It was true. The dragoon was staring at Mrs. Hamilton in undisguised displeasure. As for Silver Heels, she observed us with a scornful amazement which roused all the cruelty in me, though I knew I was losing her innocent belief in me and tearing my respectability to shreds under her clear gray eyes.

For a bud from Mrs. Hamilton's caushet I threw away the pure faith of my little comrade; for a touch of her hand I blighted her trust; and laughed as I did it.

Only once was Mrs. Hamilton off her guard, when my earnest acting had suddenly become real to me—a danger, I have since found, that no actors are too clever to escape sometimes.

"If for one moment you could be in earnest," she ventured, with a smile.

I was on guard again before she finished, and she saw it, but was too wise to betray regret or anger for her mistake.

"Pray, cease," she said; "you weary me, Mr. Cardigan. The coldest among us reflect fire, even though it be as false as the dead fires of the moon. You are prettily revenged; let us have peace."

Now the healths flew thick and fast from Sir William and Lord Dunmore, the titled toast-masters, and we drank his Majesty George the Third in bumpers which set the Indians a-howling like timber wolves at Candlemas.

Indeed, our forest of lights might have served for the Romish feast itself.

Toast followed toast in a tempest of cheers, through which the yelps of the Indians sounded faintly. I saw Brant take a silver plate and a solid candle-stick from under Red Jacket's shirt, while that great orator, very drunk, sat a-hacking the cloth with a table-knife. I saw my Lord Dunmore, all in white silk and blazing with stars, rise to pledge the ladies, and stand swaying and leering and gumming his glass till it upset on his chin, and the jewels in his lace front dripped wine.

Mistress Molly we pledged with a shout, and she returned our courtesy with gentle gravity, but her eyes were for Sir William alone.

Then Lord Dunmore gave:

"Our lovely heiress, Mistress Warren!" ending in a hiccough, and poor Silver Heels, pale as a white blossom, half rose from her seat as though to fly to Mistress Molly.

Red Jacket was on his feet now, slavering and mouthing and hacking at the air, and Brant and I dragged him out into the garden where his squaw took charge, leading him lurching and howling down the hill. Before I returned, the ladies were in the hallway and the card-room, the gentlemen following in groups from the table, some shamefully unsteady of leg, and feebly scattering snuff in amiable invitation to their neighbours.

But Sir William had disappeared, and I hunted vainly for him until I encountered Mrs. Hamilton, who directed me to the library, whither, she averred, Sir William, Governor Tryon, and Lord Dunmore had retired.

"State secrets, Master Michael," she added, saucily. "You had best find Mr. Bevan and start those same lessons we have discussed."

"Let me instruct him by proxy," said I, drawing her under the stairs, and ere she could protest or escape, I kissed her lips three separate times.

She was in tears in an instant, which I had not counted on, and it needed my most earnest acting to subdue her indignation.

I had my arm around her, and my coat was all powder and rouge, when something made me look around. There was Silver Heels going towards the pantry with Betty, doubtless to pouch some sweets for her black nurse. Her head was steadily lowered, her lashes rested on her cheeks, but face and neck and bosom were glowing in a deep colour, and I knew she had perceived us, and that she despised us with all the strength of her innocent soul.

Stunned with the conviction that I had gone too far, I made out to play my miserable farce to an end and led Mrs. Hamilton out where Mr. Bevan could pounce upon her, which he did with an insolence that I had little spirit to notice or resent.

Then I hastened to the pantry where Silver Heels stood before the rifled dishes, hands to her face, and black Betty a-petting her. But at sight of me she turned scarlet and shrank back, nor would she listen to one word.

"What yoh done to mah li'l Miss Honey-bee?" exclaimed Betty, wrathfully, shaking her turban till the rings in her big ears jingled like sledge-bells in December. "I done 'spec' yoh, Mars Ca'digan, suh! Yaas, I 'spec' yoh is lak all de young gemmen!"

Then the old witch began a-crooning over Silver Heels with deadly glances at me:

"Doan yoh cyah, li'l Miss Honey-bee, doan yoh mind nuff'n! Huh! Had mah s'picions 'bout dat young Mars Ca'digan. Doan yoh mind him no moh'n a blue-tail fly!"

"Very well," said I, angrily, "you can do as you choose, and think what you like. As for your fool of a dragoon, Mrs. Hamilton will settle him, and if she doesn't I will."

My foolish outburst seemed to rouse a panther in Silver Heels, and for a moment I believed she meant to strike me. But the storm swept over, leaving her with limbs a-quiver and eyes wet.

"You have spoiled my first pleasure," she said, in a low, trembling voice. "You have conducted like a clown and a libertine where all beheld you making shameful love to a wedded woman! Oh, Betty, Betty, send him away!" she sobbed, burying her head in the black woman's breast.

"Silver Heels," I said, choking, "can you not understand that it is I who wish to wed you?"

Again the panther blazed in her gray eyes, but her lips were bloodless as she gasped: "Oh, the insult! Betty—do you hear? He would marry me out of pity! That is twice he has said it!"

"I said it before because I would not have you marry Mr. Butler," said I, wincing at her scorn. "But I say it now because—because—I love you, Silver Heels."

All her horror of me was in her eyes. I saw it and set my teeth hard, hopeless now forever, even of her careless affection.

And so I left her there, with Betty's arms around her, and the hot scorn in her eyes. But as I went away, chilled with self-contempt and mortification, heedless, utterly careless what I did to further degrade myself in her eyes, came black Betty a-waddling to pluck me by the sleeve and whisper:

"Doan yoh go to wed wif nobody, Mars Ca'digan, suh! Doan yoh go foh to co't nobody. Mah li'l chile—mah li'l Miss Honey-bee ain't done growed up yet, suh. Bime-by she'll know moh'n she 'specs 'bout gemmens, suh."

But my evil nature was uppermost, and I laughed and bade Betty mind her own affairs, leaving her there grumbling and mumbling about "fool boys" and "li'l fool Honey-bees," till the clatter and din from the card-room shut her voice from my ears.

CHAPTER VIII

When I came to the library the door stood partly open, and I could see a party of gentlemen lounging within, and somewhat boisterous over their wine and filberts; so thinking no harm to enter, I walked in and sat down on the arm of a leather chair by the window.

Nobody had observed me, however, and I was on the point of respectfully making known my presence to Sir William, when I saw Walter Butler rise and shut the door, taking the additional precaution to lock it. Turning to rejoin the company around the table, his dark golden eyes fell upon me, and he stood still, one hand tightening on the back of his chair.

"Well?" inquired Sir William, testily, looking up at Mr. Butler. "When you are seated, sir, I will continue, unless I weary the company."

"If Mr. Cardigan has been here all this time, I, for one, was not aware of it," observed Mr. Butler, coldly, never taking his unblinking eyes off me.

I began to explain to Sir William that I had but that moment came in, when he interrupted querulously, and motioned Mr. Butler to be seated.

"Tush! tush! Let be, let be, Captain Butler! My young kinsman has my confidence, and it is time he should know something of what passes in his own country."

"At sixteen," observed my Lord Dunmore, with a maudlin chuckle, "I knew a thing or two, I'll warrant you—curse me if I didn't, Sir William!"

Sir John Johnson regarded me without interest; Colonel Claus never even troubled to give me a glance, but I saw the hawk's eyes of Walter Butler watching me steadily.

"To resume," began Sir William, but Lord Dunmore broke out:

"At sixteen I had outlived you all—pierce me if I hadn't, now, Sir William! Scratch me raw! if I hadn't put a finger in the world's pudding, a-stirring the plums at sixteen, by God!"

"Doubtless, my Lord," said Sir William, dryly. "And now, gentlemen, concerning our show of force here, I have only to say—and I say it with all respect and submission to Governor Tryon—that I do not believe it will produce that salutary effect on the discontented in New York and Boston which Governor Tryon expects."

"Gad! I *do* expect it!" said Tryon, briskly. "Look you, Sir William, you and your militia dominate the county, and these rascals must be brought to understand it. Trust me, messires, the damned Yankees will know of this militia display before the post rides into Boston!"

"Add our Mohawks to the militia," observed Walter Butler, in a colourless voice.

Sir William's jaw was set hard, but he said nothing.

"Add the whole Six Nations," suggested Lord Dunmore, leering at Sir William; "come, now! curse me blind! but we shall have the whole Six Nations, and that filthy little Red Jacket to boot."

"My Lord," replied Sir William, "if it lay with your Lordship you would have Red Jacket against you."

This blunt rebuke almost sobered Lord Dunmore for a moment, and he asked Sir William what he meant.

"I mean," said the Baronet, "that you mocked this powerful chief, Red Jacket, at my table to-night, and he knew it. That is not the way to gain allies, my Lord."

"The drunken, guzzling son of a slut!" bawled Lord Dunmore, "d'ye think I care what the bandy-legged little beast thinks?"

"I only know," replied Sir William, curtly, "that if your Lordship has so conducted in Virginia, the King cannot look for any Indian support in that colony."

"Oh, choke me, Sir William, but that's too bad now!—pinch me blue if it isn't!" protested Lord Dunmore in a pet. Then a subtle smirk settled on his waxen cast of a face and he winked his weak eyes at Walter Butler, a proceeding observed by me and by Sir William.

Not for a moment now did I doubt that Lord Dunmore had set Colonel Cresap to drive the Cayugas into a hatred for the colonies, nor did I doubt but that Walter Butler knew of this plan, perhaps had even connived at it.

Sir William, too, had come to some quick conclusion, for I saw the crease deepen around his jaws, and his steady eyes strike fire. But he said nothing to interrupt Lord Dunmore, who had now launched into a gust of incoherent words and protestations and hiccoughs, to which all listened sneeringly until his voice ended with a hollow buzz inside his wine-glass.

There came a silence, broken by the clear sarcastic tones of Sir William.

"I beg permission to submit to Governor Tryon the opinion of a country Baronet—for what that opinion may be worth."

"With pleasure," said Governor Tryon, cordially, looking up from the plate of nuts he was picking.

"And this is my opinion," continued Sir William, "that, firstly, the disaffected classes in Boston and New York will not care a fig for our conference here, nor for our show of militia; that, secondly, if they should once entertain a suspicion that England, in the event of war, proposes to employ savages as allies to subdue rebellion, we would have to-morrow the thirteen colonies swarming like thirteen hives to sting us all to death—ay—and there would not be an Indian left twixt here and the Ohio!"

"What would become of them?" piped up Lord Dunmore, so innocently that I saw Governor Tryon pass his hand over his mouth to conceal a smile. But Walter Butler's passionless voice was sounding now, and I saw Sir William turn his head to lose no gesture or shade of meaning.

"It is come to the point where either the rebels are to win over the Indians, or where we must take measures to secure their services. I am not in a position to inform you, gentlemen, as to the actual existing conditions in the Indian Department. That, Sir William can do better than any one in America. Therefore, I beg Sir William to kindly make it clear to us what chances we have to win the support of the Six Nations—in the event of a rebel rising against the King's authority."

The tangled knot was cut, the cat had sprung from the bag. Yet nobody by glance or word or gesture appeared to be aware of it.

Sir William's manner was perfectly composed, though that deep crease binding his chin deepened, and his brows bent in towards his nose as he rested his chin on his hand and spoke, eyes fixed on his wine-glass:

"Captain Butler believes that it has come to this: that either those in authority or the disaffected must seek allies among these savage hordes which hang like thunder-clouds along our frontiers. Gentlemen, I am not of that opinion. I have said openly, and I care not who knows it, that if war must come between England and these colonies, let it be a white man's war; in mercy, let it be a war between two civilized peoples, and not a butchery of demons!

"I do believe—and I say so solemnly and before God—that it is possible to so conduct that these savages will remain neutral if war must come. Ay, more! *I* will answer for them!"

He lifted his eyes and looked straight at Lord Dunmore, raising his voice slightly, but betraying no passion.

"And, gentlemen, as I am his Majesty's intendant of Indian affairs in North America, I shall now do all that I can to pacify my wards, to keep them calm and orderly in the event of a war which I, for one, regard with horror. Were

I to do otherwise, I must account to my King for a trust betrayed, and I must answer also to Him whom King and subject alike account to."

On Walter Butler's lips a sneer twitched; my Lord Dunmore wiped his bleared eyes with a rag of lace and stared at everybody with drunken gravity.

"I know not," said Sir William, slowly, "what true loyalty may be if it be not to save the honour of our King, and rebuke those who seek to tarnish it. And if there are now those among his counsellors or deputies who urge him to seek these savages as allies, I say it is a monstrous thing and an inspiration from hell itself."

He swung on his elbow and fixed his eyes on Walter Butler.

"You, sir, know something of border war. How then can you propose to let loose these Indians on the people of our colonies?"

"Lest they let loose these same savages on us," replied Mr. Butler, calmly.

Sir William frowned.

"You do not know the colonists, Mr. Butler," he said. "What marvel then that my Lord North should misunderstand them, and think to buy their loyalty with tuppence worth o' tea?"

"Come, come, Sir William!" cried Governor Tryon, laughing, and plainly anxious to break the tension ere sharp words flew. "Did I not know you to the bone, sir, I should deem it my duty to catechise you concerning the six articles of loyalty!"

"I, too, i' faith!" squeaked Lord Dunmore. "Skewer me! Sir William, but you talk like a Boston preacher—ay—that you do, and—"

"Have done, sir!" cut in Sir William, with such bitter contempt that the faces of all present sobered quickly. Even Governor Tryon glanced uneasily at Lord Dunmore to see how he might swallow such a pill, but that nobleman only blinked stupidly and sucked his thin lips, too drunk to understand how like a lackey he had been silenced.

Sir John Johnson and Colonel Claus, deputies to Sir William in the Indian Department, exchanged puzzled glances. But I noticed that Mr. Butler never took his eyes from Sir William's darkening visage.

"There is one more matter," said the Baronet, "that I may be pardoned for introducing here amid all the perplexities of the times; but it is a matter touching on my own stewardship, and as that concerns my King, I deem it necessary to broach it."

He turned again deliberately on Lord Dunmore.

"It has come to my knowledge that certain unauthorized people are tampering with a distant tribe of my Cayuga Indians. I know not, nor do I care, what the motives of these men may be, but I protest against it, and I shall do all in my power—without infringing on the rights or laws of a sister colony—to protect my Cayugas from unlawful aggression!"

"Damme!" gurgled Lord Dunmore, passing his jewelled hand over his befuddled head. "Damme, Sir William, d'ye mean to accuse me? Curse me! Skewer me! Claw me raw! but it is not fair," he snivelled. "No, it is not fair! Take your hands off my sleeve and be done a-twitching it, Captain Butler! Damme! I never set Cresap on. Will ye have done a-pinching my arm, Captain Butler?"

The ghastly humour of the exposure, the ludicrous self-conviction of his tipsy Lordship—for nobody had mentioned Cresap—the startling disclosure, too, of Walter Butler's interest in the plot—for that it was a plot no longer could anybody doubt—cast a gloom over the company.

Every man present understood what Cresap's aggression meant; no man there dared acknowledge a desire for Cresap's success.

Then Sir William's sarcastic voice pierced the silence.

"I trust your Lordship would not believe that any gentleman present could harbour suspicions of a foul conspiracy between your Lordship and Captain Butler, to incite my Cayugas to attack white men!"

Walter Butler's slow eye rested on Lord Dunmore, on Sir William, and then on me. But his bloodless visage never changed.

"Gentlemen, gentlemen, let us have harmony here at any cost," protested Governor Tryon, half in jest, half in earnest. "God knows I have discord enough in New York town without seeking it among the loyalists of this county. Nobody believes that my Lord Dunmore is seeking trouble with your tame Indians, Sir William. If this fellow Cresap, who is a notorious malcontent, too, be imposing on the Cayugas, I doubt not that my Lord Dunmore will recall him and deal with him severely."

"No, I won't! Claw my vitals if I do!" snapped his Lordship, in the drunken sulks, and straightway fell a-squabbling with Walter Butler, who had again laid a hand on his arm.

For Captain Butler knew his treachery had been discovered, and his shameless impudence in openly attempting to muzzle his noble partner in conspiracy passed all bounds of decency.

I saw the angry light glimmer in Sir William's eyes, and I knew it boded no good to Walter Butler, as far as his hope of Silver Heels was concerned. A fierce happiness filled me. So now, at last, Sir William was discovering the fangs in his pet snake!

Lord Dunmore had succeeded in reversing a decanter of port over himself and Colonel Claus, and the latter, mad as a wet cat, left the room swearing audibly, while his playful Lordship threw a few glasses after him and then collapsed in a soiled heap of silk and jewels, feebly calling on "Billy Tryon" to try and "conduc like er—er—gen'l-m'n, b' God!"

Sir William was steadily staring at Walter Butler; I, too, had my eye on him; and, when he left the table to saunter towards the door, Sir William rose immediately to follow him, and I after Sir William.

He saw us coming as he opened the door, and surveyed us with cool effrontery as we joined him in the hallway.

"I shall not require your services hereafter as my secretary, Captain Butler," said Sir William. "Will you kindly hand your keys to me?"

"At your command, Sir William," replied Mr. Butler, drawing the keys from his pocket and presenting them with an ironical inclination.

The man's careless self-possession was marvellous considering he was facing the man he had so vilely betrayed.

"Mr. Butler," said Sir William, with reddening face, "I consider myself released from my consent to your union with my kinswoman, Miss Warren!"

"As to that, sir," observed Captain Butler, cynically, "I shall take my chances."

I heard what he said, but Sir William misunderstood him.

"It is your mischance, sir, to put no harsher interpretation on it. But my decision is irrevocable, Mr. Butler, for I have destined Miss Warren to a loyal man, my kinsman, Michael Cardigan!"

The spasm that jerked Mr. Butler's mouth into that ghastly grimace I knew so well, was not lost on Sir William.

"I'll take that chance, too," said Mr. Butler, bowing.

"What do you mean, sir?" demanded Sir William, steadying his voice with an effort.

But Walter Butler only replied with such glare at me that Sir William involuntarily turned to find me, rigid, behind him. The next moment Captain Butler passed noiselessly out into the starlight, wrapping his black cloak around him.

Sir William followed him mechanically to the door, and I at his heels, burning for a quarrel with Walter Butler, and awaiting only for Sir William to return to the library, and leave me free to follow and insult Mr. Butler for the treacherous villain he had proved himself.

But Sir William, seeing me slinking out, laid a hand on my shoulder and spun me sharply round on my heels to look into my eyes.

"Now what the devil are *you* up to?" he broke out, half divining the truth. "Michael! Michael! Don't be a fool! Are there not fools enough here to-night?"

"No, sir," I answered, sheepishly.

"That is not the way to serve me, lad," said Sir William, roughly. "Have I not sorrow enough without seeing you carried in here with a hole in your breast, you meddlesome ass?"

"I have a certain score to clean off," I muttered.

"Oh," observed Sir William, coldly, "a selfish quarrel—eh? I was a fond old fool to think I might count on you."

Tears started to my eyes; I could have bitten my tongue off.

"You can count on me, sir," I said, choking out the words. "I meant no harm; I am not selfish, sir; I care only for you."

"I know it, lad," he said, kindly. "And mind, I do not rebuke your spirit; I only ask you to learn discretion. This is no time to settle private matters. No man in America has that right now, because every man's life belongs to the country!"

"On which side, sir?" I faltered.

Sir William was silent for a while. Presently he took my arm and we walked out under the stars.

"My boy," he said, sadly, "I cannot answer you, but I can place matters in a clear light for you. The decision must remain with yourself."

Then he told me how the Boston people had been taxed without their consent, but I could not see why they should not cheerfully give their all to their King, and I said so.

"Very well," replied Sir William, gravely. "Let us approach the matter from your personal view. Here are you, young, vigorous, of good lineage, and sure to succeed to your uncle's title and estate some day. You are, at sixteen, an officer of his Majesty's border cavalry; you have every prospect of promotion; the King remembers your father, Governor Tryon is your friend. And I, Michael, have decided to leave you, in my testament, sufficient to maintain you handsomely should you desire to marry Felicity before your uncle's death. *That*, my boy, is the *King's side*.

"Now suppose, from a high motive of duty, you should suddenly resolve to embrace the cause of the plain people. Could you renounce your commission in the King's army to shoulder a firelock, perhaps a stable-fork, in the ranks of your countrymen? Could you give up ease, hopes, position? Could you give up your friends and kinsmen? Could you give up what sum I may leave you in my will? For Sir John would never let a penny of my money go to a rebel. Could you give up, if need be, the woman you loved? Think, and be not in haste to answer. For *that* is the *other* side to embrace, with perhaps a hangman's rope at the end."

"Am I to answer you to-night, sir?" I asked.

"God forbid!" he said, solemnly.

"I will say this," said I; "that where my heart is, I would follow in rags. And my heart is with you, sir."

He stood still, drawing me closer, but said nothing more, for there came running out of the darkness an officer with naked claymore shining in the starlight, and when he drew near we saw it was Mr. Duncan.

"The Indian is gone!" he panted. "Gone away crazed with fever! The doctor lies in the hut with a broken shoulder; Quider crushed it in his madness!"

Sir William swayed as though struck.

"The sentries chased him to the woods," continued poor Duncan, out of breath; "but he ran like a panther and—we had your orders not to fire. He will die, anyhow; the doctor says he will seek some creek or pond and die in the water like a poisoned rat. They are bringing the doctor now."

Up out of the shadow loomed two soldiers, forming a litter with their muskets, on which sat our doctor, Pierson, head hanging. And when Sir William came to him he looked up with a sick grimace and shook his head feebly.

"He broke those ropes as though they had been worsted," he said. "I tried to hold him down, but he had the strength of delirium, Sir William. I want that fat surgeon of the Royal Americans to set this bone," he added, weakly, and fell a-groaning.

Mr. Duncan started on a run for the barracks; the soldiers and the injured man passed on towards the guard-house, and Sir William stood staring after them.

Presently he said, aloud, "God's will be done on my poor country!"

We walked back to the house together. Some of the guests were leaving, but the card-room was still crowded, and in the library my Lord Dunmore lay on the carpet cursing and vomiting and shrieking that no man should put him to bed, and that he meant to crack another bottle or a dozen heads.

Here and there, out through the orchard, drunken Indians lurched lodgeward, followed by their patient squaws; here and there sedan-chairs passed, the grunting bearers stepping lively in the brisk night wind.

Below the hill, in Johnstown, the court-house windows were still twinkling with lights, and when the wind set our way, we could hear the distant strains of the brigade band playing for the dancers.

Sir William entered the hallway of his house and looked around. In a corner of one window sat Mrs. Hamilton and Mr. Bevan, somewhat close together; in another window were gathered Colonel Claus and his lady and Sir John Johnson, whispering. Brant, surrounded by a bevy of fine ladies, was turning over the pages of a book and answering questions in polite monosyllables, for he had a quiet contempt for those who regarded him as a curiosity, though susceptible enough to real homage.

"And out of all my house," murmured Sir William, in a bitter voice, "not one whom I can trust—not one!—not one!"

After a moment I plucked at his sleeve, reproachfully.

"Yes—I know—I know, my boy. But I need a man now—a man of experience, a man in bodily vigour, a man in devotion."

"You need a man to go to Colonel Cresap," I whispered. For the first and only time in my life I saw that I had startled Sir William.

"Let me go, sir?" I entreated, eagerly. "If I am keen enough to read your purpose, I am not too stupid to carry it out. I know what you wish. I know you cannot trust your message to paper, nor to a living soul except me. I know what to say to Colonel Cresap. Let me serve you, sir, for I do long so to help you?"

We had fallen back to the porch again while I was speaking, Sir William holding me so tightly by the elbow that his clutch numbed my arm.

"I cannot," he muttered, under his breath. "To-morrow Dunmore will set his spies to see that Cresap remains undisturbed. The Ohio trails will be watched for a messenger from me. Who knows what Dunmore's and Butler's men might do to carry out their designs on my Cayugas?"

"Dare they attack an officer in uniform?" I asked, astonished.

"What is there to prevent a shot in ambush? And are there no renegades in Johnstown to hire?" replied Sir William, bitterly. "Why, the town's full of them, lad; men as desperate as Jack Mount himself."

"But I know the woods! You, yourself, sir, say I am a very Mohawk in the woods!" I pleaded. "I fear no ambush, though the highwayman Jack Mount himself were after me. Have I not been twice to the Virginia line with Brant? Do you think I could fail to reach Cresap with the whole forest as plain to me as the Stony Way below this hill? And remember I carry no papers to be stolen. I could first go with belts to the Cayugas, and tell the truth about Quider and his party. Then I would deliver the belts as you delivered them to Quider. Then I would find Cresap and show him what a fool he is."

"And so serve the enemies of the King?" said Sir William, looking keenly at me.

"And so serve you, sir," I retorted, in a flash. "Are you an enemy to the King?"

"But, my boy," said Sir William, huskily, "do you understand that you must go alone on this mission?"

I sprang forward and threw my arms around him with a hug like a young bear.

"Then I'm going! I'm going!" I whispered, enchanted, while he murmured brokenly that he could not spare me and that I was all he had on earth.

But I would not be denied; I coaxed him to my little bedroom, lighted the candle, and made him sit down on my cot. Then I explained excitedly my purpose, and to prove that I knew the trails, I sharpened my treasured Faber pencil and made a drawing for him, noting every ford and carrying-place— which latter I proposed to avoid—and finally hazarded a guess as to the exact spot where Colonel Cresap might be found.

Also, in pantomime and whispers, I rehearsed the part I meant to play before the Cayugas, making the speeches that Sir William had made to Quider, as nearly as I could remember, and delivering each belt in dumb show and with all the dignity I could command, till I came to the last, which, by mistake, I spoke of as a *red* instead of *black* belt.

"Wait," interrupted Sir William, who had become deeply interested; "what is 'black' in the Mohawk tongue?"

"Kahonji," I replied, promptly.

"And in Onondaga?"

"Osuntah, sir."

"And in Cayuga?"

I hesitated, then blushed, for I did not know.

"Sweandaea," said Sir William, gravely; "how are you to bear my peace-belts if you know not the red of war from the black of good intent?"

"I should have said 'Hot-Kwah-Weyo'—*good*-red, not *war*-red," I replied, so naïvely that Sir William laughed outright.

"With such resourceful impudence," he said, "you cannot be misunderstood among the Six Nations. It eases my mind to find you quick and ingenious in a tight place, lad. But, Michael, have a care to use no Delaware words, for that would render my Cayugas suspicious."

I promised eagerly, and we sat down together to go over the trail, mile by mile, computing the circles I should be obliged to take to avoid the carrying-places where spies were most to be feared.

"Dunmore rides South in a week," said Sir William. "But he will not wait till he reaches Virginia before he sends out his emissaries to urge Cresap on. You must beat them, lad, and go afoot at that."

"I can go the faster," said I. "Horses are useless in the Pennsylvania bush until you reach Crown Gap. I take it that Lord Dunmore's men, being Virginians, will go mounted, and that gives me double time to reach Cresap."

And so we sat there together on the bed, planning, suggesting precautions, counting the dangers and mischances only to discount them with confidence in my knowledge of woodcraft, and the night wore on till my candle sank into a lake of wax, trailing a long, flaring flame.

"There is one thing I have thought of," said I, soberly. "It is this: if I am going out as an enemy to the King, I cannot for shame aid me by wearing the King's uniform. Therefore, with your approval, sir, I will go in my buckskins, unless you believe that, by this journey of mine, I will benefit our King."

"Then," said Sir William, slowly, "you must go in your buckskins, lad."

The moment had come; I was face to face with it now.

"Am—am I to resign my commission in the Border Horse, sir?" I faltered. The prospect of the sacrifice choked my speech, and my heart swelled with a grief that sent the water to my eyes in spite of me.

Sir William considered me in silence, then broke out: "No, no! Not yet. Who knows but what this war may never break over us! No, no, my boy! Your errand is an errand of justice and mercy. I send you as my own messenger. It is my duty to protect my Cayugas, and it is yours to obey me. You may, for the present at least, retain your commission and your sword with honour. It is Dunmore and Butler we are fighting now, not our King."

"I shall go in my buckskins, anyhow," I said, cheerfully, and thankful that the evil moment had been put off—that evil moment which I now understood was surely coming for us both. He knew it, too; his face was loose and seamed and gray and haggard; the light of the candle's smoky wick, swimming in wax, threw ghastly shadows over brow and cheeks.

As we sat there, my hand in his, staring at the phantoms of that ominous future, I heard Silver Heels come running up the stairs and stop at my door, calling out to Sir William.

When I opened the door she drew back scornfully, but, catching a glimpse of Sir William within, she marched past me and perched herself on Sir William's knees, both arms around his neck.

What she whispered to him I could not hear, but he promptly shook his head in refusal, and presently it came out that she was teasing to be allowed to go with a certain fat dame, Lady Shelton, and make a month's stay with her at Pittsburg.

"I do so long to go," pleaded Silver Heels. "I have never been anywhere, you know. And we are to have such rare pleasures at the June running races, and there will be horses from Virginia and Maryland and New York, and we are to have dancing every evening and a dinner given for me! Oh, dear! Oh, dear! I want to go so much! I truly do, sir, and I should be so happy and so thankful to you—"

"In Heaven's name, stop your chatter, Felicity!" cried Sir William, striving to undo her arms from his neck, but she only kissed him and clung so tightly and reproachfully that he gave up in sheer fatigue.

"Oh, go, then! Go, you little witch! And mind you take Betty with you! And mind that Aunt Mary provides for you ere you go!"

Silver Heels embraced him rapturously with a little shout of delight, and sped away to the nursery without a glance at me. What did I care? I had begun to dislike her cordially; I could afford to, now that she in her turn disliked Mr. Bevan.

I had also the savage satisfaction of remembering that she was free of Walter Butler forever, and I observed her departure grimly. As for Sir William's new desire to see us wedded, I had not at all made up my mind. Besides, Silver Heels despised me, and I would not endure that.

Presently Sir William rose and walked out into the hallway, saying, with affected carelessness: "Then you will start before dawn, Michael?"

"Yes, sir," said I, cheerfully.

"I shall be in the library when you go. Stop there a moment."

His voice was quivering, but he did not flinch, and I heard him descending the stairs towards the nursery where Mistress Molly was saying: "What is all this about Felicity's journeying to Pittsburg, Sir William? Why, the child has no clothes that befit her rank and station, dear, and the expense—"

"Tush! Who cares for the expense? If she's going she's got enough to start with, and I'll send to New York, my dear. Of course I know our little maid must outshine the rest o' them, Molly. Make a list for York, and I'll send it by Billy Tryon."

Their voices were shut out with the nursery door closing, and I stole back through the dark entry into my room and lighted another candle.

In the feverish delight of preparation, I gave little thought to Silver Heels. Excitement at the nearness of my departure proved a lively antidote for sorrow—nay, the fever of anticipation burnt out regret and seared with its caustic the frail unopened bud of romance.

Silver Heels? Silver Heels? What did I care now? Let her live to regret it all— after I had gone! Let her live to marvel at my mysterious disappearance, and vainly seek to solve it until I returned, loaded with glory and importance. Then I might see her at Fort Pitt. But what did I care? She couldn't marry Walter Butler; the dragoon Bevan belonged to Mrs. Hamilton; and now she was going to Pittsburg to see the races and be rid of both Butler and Bevan. So all was right everywhere; let the world spin on! As for me, I was off for glory and the green delight of the woodlands that I loved.

I made up my pack on the bed: a blanket, four pairs of Mohawk moccasins, a change of flannels, a spare shirt, and three pairs of knitted socks. Down in the store-room I found corn-meal, salt, and pork, and tied each in its sack. Powder and ball were to be had in the guard-house, so I ran across the grass and into the block-house where Wraxall, our sottish Johnstown barber, stood shaving Mr. Duncan.

"Better join me in a midnight shave!" he called out, as I darted past and unhooked the keys of the magazine from the brass nail over the fireplace.

When I returned with the powder and bullets I weighed them in the guard-house scales and gave Mr. Duncan a written receipt for them.

"Come! come! Mr. Cardigan," he said, "would you kill deer in May? What the deuce do you want of all this powder? Nobody has dug up any war-hatchets that I know of."

Wraxall, who was strapping his razor, looked at me curiously. I ignored Mr. Duncan's banter and plumped myself into the chair where he had been sitting.

"A close shave for Mr. Cardigan!" said Mr. Duncan, holding his dripping face over the barber's basin. "Unless," he added, politely, "the gentleman desires you to leave his mustachios à la Française."

My face being as smooth as a girl's, the barber sneered, but I bade him lather me deep and have a care to follow grain. I cared not a whit for Mr. Duncan's mirth, I was too happy, and when Wraxall had scraped me well, I ordered him to shear off my hair.

"Piteous Heaven!" exclaimed Mr. Duncan. "Nay, barber!—spare that queue!"

"Off it drops!" said I, briskly. "Now get the hair-powder out, and trim my hair to a crop, Wraxall! Whew! man, don't breathe on me, you malt-worm! I don't want to get drunk, I want a cropped head!"

"Shaved for a wig, sir?" demanded Wraxall, sulkily, fiddling with his shears.

"No, no," I replied, hastily, while Mr. Duncan roared with laughter; "I don't desire a shaved pate, my friend. Cut it à la coureur-de-bois!"

"Do you expect to take the King's highway with Jack Mount?" asked Mr. Duncan. But I refused to be drawn out, and finally he went away with his curiosity on tenter-hooks and none the wiser.

When Wraxall had shorn me and removed the powder from my hair, I gathered up my ammunition and provisions and hastened back to the house. The place was dark save for a light in the library. I felt my way up the stairs and into my chamber, where I first filled bullet-pouch and powder-horn, then rolled the spare ammunition and provisions into my pack and buckled the load tightly.

Now, rapidly undressing, I donned a new hunting-shirt and leggings, first making sure that the fringe had not been weakened by mice, to leave me without cords should I need them. Over my shoulders I slung powder-horn and bullet-pouch, slipped hatchet and hunting-knife into the clout pockets, and then took my rifle from the corner and unwrapped the deer-hide case.

Thrice I tested the flint, pouring a little powder into the pan, and thrice the pan flashed, and the ball of vapour shot up to the ceiling. So all was ready. I lingered only to buckle my money-belt under my shirt, pouch a dozen new flints and a case of wadding, then hoisted my pack to my shoulders, strapped it on the hips, blew out the candle, and stole into the hallway, trailing my rifle.

Passing the door of Silver Heels's chamber, my heart suddenly grew tender and I hesitated. But the memory of her many misdeeds hardened it immediately, and I went on, tasting contentedly of a perverse resentment which smacked pleasantly of martyrdom. All asses, they say, are born to martyrdom.

I crept past the nursery without accident, but barked my shins on the stocks in the hallway. Yet Mistress Molly did not awake—or was it that she knew what errand I was bound on? Perhaps. Still, to this day I do not know whether or not Sir William had confided in her. God rest her! I never saw her again.

I went softly through the lower hall, through the card-room, and tapped at the library door. It was opened without a sound.

We gazed silently at each other for a long time. I, for one, could not trust myself to speak. All the joy and exhilaration of adventure had suddenly left me; I felt the straps of my pack straining my shoulders, but the burden on my back was not as heavy as my heart's full load.

He seemed so old, so tired, so gray; his eyes had acquired that peering look which one notices in faces scored by care. What a blight had come upon him in these few weeks! Where was that ruddy glow, that full swell of muscle as he moved, that clear-eyed, full-fronted presence that I knew so well! How old his hands appeared under the cuff's limp lace; how old his loose face, all in ashy seams; how old his slow eyes—how old, old, old!

He rose as though his back, instead of mine, bore the burden, and together, without a word, we passed through the dark house and out to the porch. Dawn silvered the east, but the moon in its first quarter lay afloat in the western clouds, and a few stars looked down through a sky caked with frosted fleece.

He embraced me in silence, holding me a long time to his breast, yet never a word was said, and never a sound fell on the night air save my desperate gulps to crush back the sob that strained in my throat.

Presently I was conscious that I had left him, and was running fast through the darkness, blind as a bat for the tears, breathless, too, for, as I halted and turned to look back, far away against the dawn I saw our house as a black mass, with a single candle twinkling in the basement. So I knew Sir William still kept his vigil in the library.

The streets of Johnstown were dark, save for the rare lanthorns of the watchmen, but there seemed to be many people abroad, most of them noisy and quarrelsome. To tell the truth, I had never before seen so much swaggering and drunkenness in Johnstown, and I marvelled at it as I hastened on. Once, as I passed a tavern, two men, journeying in opposite directions, hailed each other with a new phrase: "Greeting, friend! God save our country!" At which a drunken soldier from the tavern bawled out: "God save our country—eh? That's the Boston rebels' password! God save the King and damn the country!—you yellow-bellied Whigs!"

A small crowd gathered, but I hastened on; yet behind me I heard oaths and blows and cries of: "Lobster! Tory! Kill the red-coat!" And everywhere along the street windows were raised and men looked out, some shouting: "Rebel!" "Traitor!" or "Bloody-back!" "Tea-sot—toss-pot!" and some called for the watch.

Many people began to rush hither and thither. A little peddler got under my feet and fell sprawling and squealing till I picked him up and set him on his legs. He was a small Hebrew man, Saul Shemuel, who came a-peddling often to our servants; but in his terror he did not know me, and he fled madly into Rideup's Tavern with a soldier after him, vowing he'd have one rebel scalp even though it were a Jewish one.

I had no time to linger, yet behind me I heard a sharp fight begin at Rideup's Tavern, which is another pot-house much frequented by Boston men. Presently as I climbed the hill I heard the drums at the guard-house beating the alarm, and I knew the fray would soon end with the patrol's arrival from their barracks.

But what had come over our staid towns-people and farmers and tenants that they should damn each other for rebels and Tories? It amazed me to see old neighbours shaking their fists out of windows and cursing one another with such extraordinary and unnecessary fury.

Truly, if in our village this question of tuppence worth o' tea drove men mad, what wonder Sir William and Governor Tryon should frown and shake their heads over a pinch o' snuff?

But I was to leave all this trouble behind me now. Already the misty wilderness loomed up in the south, vague as a ghostly vision in the moon's beams. Ah, my woods!—my dear, dear woods! One plunge into that dim, sweet shadow and what cared I for King or rebel or any woman who ever lived?

CHAPTER IX

My first three weeks in the woods were weeks of heaven. Never had I seen the forest so beautiful, never had the soft velvet lights clothed the wilderness with such exquisite mystery. Along the stony beds of lost ravines I passed and saw the frosty bowlders lie like silver mounds in the dawn, glimmering through steaming waters. I passed at eventide when the sunset turned the cliffs to crumbling crags of gold, and I saw massed mountain peaks reflected in pools where the shadows of great fish moved like clouds.

I ate and drank and slept in the dim wood stillness undisturbed; I waked when my guide, the sun, flamed through the forest, and I followed in his lead, resting when he hung circling in the noonday heavens, following again when he resumed the sky-trail towards the west, seeking my couch when he lay down below the world's blue edge to fold him in the blanket of the night.

Twice came the rain, delicately perfumed showers shaking down through a million leaves, leaving frail trails of vapour errant through the trees, and powdered jewels on every leaf.

And I lived well on that swift trail where the gray grouse scuttled through the saplings, and in every mossy streamlet the cold, dusky troutlings fought for the knot of scarlet yarn on my short hand-line. Once I saw bronzed turkeys, all huddled in a brood at twilight, craning and peering from their tree-perch; but let them go, as I had meat to spare. Once, too, at dawn, I heard a bull-moose lipping tree-buds, and lay still in my blanket while the huge beast wandered past, crack! crash! and slop! slop! through the creek, his hide all smeared with clay and a swarm of forest flies whirling over him. Lord, how rank he did smell, but for all that I was glad the wind set not the other way, for it is sometimes the toss of a coin what your bull-moose will do, run or fight at sight; nor is it even doubtful in September, when the moose-cow wallows and bawls across the marshes for her antlered gallant on the ridge.

I saw but one moose, for there are not many in our forests, though they say the Canadas do swarm with them, and also with elks and caribous.

There were few birds to be seen except near rivers: a blue-gray meat-bird here and there whining in the hemlocks, a great owl huddled on a limb, and sometimes a troop of black-cheeked chickadees that came cheerfully to hand for a crumb of corn. Squirrels were everywhere—that is, everywhere except through the pine belts, and there I had to make out with the bitter flesh of those villain partridges which feed on spruce-tips. I'd as soon eat a hawk in winter or dine on slices of fried spruce-gum, for truly there is more nourishment in a moccasin than in these ignoble birds dressed up like toothsome partridges.

I had not met a soul on the trail, nor had I found any fresh signs save once, and that was the print of a white man's moccasin on the edge of a sandy strip near the head-waters of the Ohio, which is called the Alleghany, north of Fort Pitt.

This foot-mark disturbed me, although it was three days old and pointing north. But that signified nothing, for the man who made it had come in a canoe, yet I could find no sign that a canoe had been beached there, nor, indeed, any further marks of moccasins, and I made moderate haste to get under cover, as I am timid about things I cannot account for.

Reason enough, moreover, for if there were no signs except that single imprint, it was clear that the man who left that mark was wading the river because he wished to leave no trail. And who is not suspicious of those who appear to be at pains to conceal their tracks?

There is something terrifying in the sudden apparition of a fellow-creature in the woods. When one has been living alone in the forest solitude, day after day, perhaps even craving company, I know nothing so shocking as the unexpected sight of another man in the wilderness.

Why this is so, why fear, caution, and anger are invariably the primal instincts, I do not fully understand.

Sometimes, lying perdu, I have seen the tasselled ears of a wild-cat flatten at first sight of a stranger cat; I have seen the wolverine snarl hideously as he winded a strange comrade; I have seen the solitary timber-wolf halt, hair on end and every hot fang bared, where a brother wolf had crossed his trail an hour before.

So I; for as I slunk away from that foot-mark in the sand-willows, I found myself priming my rifle and looking behind me with all the horror of a Robinson Crusoe, though I had miles of country to avoid the unknown man withal.

Early that morning, having crossed, as nearly as I could make out, the boundary between our Province of New York and the Province of Pennsylvania, I had approached, somewhat nearer than I meant to, the carrying-place on the Alleghany, which lies directly in the Fort Pitt trail.

Now, at mid-day, the sun heating the forest, I found my pack very heavy and my shirt wet with exertion, but dared not halt until I had circled around that carrying-place. So I toiled on, the very rifle in my hand heavy as lead, and my eyes nearly blinded with the sweat that poured from my hair and neck, bathing me in a sort of stinging coolness. My stomach, too, was asking the hour, and the green-eyed deer-flies whirled over me, fierce for blood, for I durst not lag even to wash my face in oil of pennyroyal.

It was only when at last above the trees in the east I perceived the blue peak of a mountain that I knew I was safe enough; for the peak in the east belonged to the Alleghany range, and I had steered a fine circle without losing a mile.

However, I jogged on along a runway made hard by the hoof of countless deer herds, until I came to a thread of water curving through the moss like a sword-blade on green velvet. Here I knelt, let go my pack, and rolled over on the moss, dog-tired.

Hands clasped on my empty stomach I lay looking up at the sky through the matted leaves that thatched my forest roof, too tired even to drink. But the accursed deer-flies drove me to water as they drive the deer, and I drank my fill and smeared me with pennyroyal and tallow, face and wrists.

For the first time since I had entered the wilderness I made no fire, but munched a cold breast of partridge and drove it into my stomach with bits of ash-cake, drinking a mouthful between bites to moisten the dry cheer. I ate very slowly, my eyes making their mechanical circuit of the silent trees, my ears ever flattened for a noise behind me.

Silence breeds silence; man's movements in the woods are soft and cat-like where caution is an instinct. I speak of true woodsmen—those who know the solitary life—not of loud and careless men who swagger into God's woodland mysteries as to a tavern tap-room.

Now, as I sat there, crumbs on my knees yet unbrushed, a sudden instinct arose in me that I had been followed; nay, not so sudden, either, for the vague idea had been slowly taking shape since I had seen that sign in the river-bed among the willows.

I had absolutely no reason for believing this; the foot-print was three days old and it pointed north. Yet, at the mere thought, the skin on my neck began to roughen and my nose gave little twitches. Unconsciously I had already risen, priming my rifle, and for a moment, I stood there, ankle deep in moss. Then, moved by no impulse of my own, I swear, I lifted my pack and passed swiftly along the little brook towards the main trail. Presently, through the willows to the right, I caught a glimpse of a shallow stream rushing noiselessly over a sand bottom, and on the other side of the stream I saw a notched tree, the Fort Pitt trail!

Now I deliberately made a string of plain foot-tracks along the sandy stream, pointing towards the shallowest spot. Here I forded, and made more tracks in the mud, entering the Fort Pitt trail. I ran down this trail till I came to a brier, and on the thorns of a spray which crossed the broad, hard trail, I left a few strings from my fringed hunting-shirt. Then I began to walk backward till I reached the spot where I had entered the trail from the sandy stream. I backed down this bank, forded the shallows, then, instead of coming out on the sand, I waded up stream to my little thread of a brook, and up that brook till I found a great log choking it. And behind this log I squatted, panting, and astonished at my own performance.

Yet, even now, I could not find reason to blush at my timid precautions, for that feeling of being followed still haunted me. It was neither a coward's panic nor a cool man's alarm; it was something that drove me to cover my tracks. The white hare does it when unpursued by hounds; the grouse do it when no pointer follows—why? I know no more than the white hare or the grouse.

From my form among the ferns, rabbit-like I huddled with palpitating flanks and nose atwitch in the wind. Nothing stirred save those sad, deformed leaves that drift earthward, dead ere spring is fled. Bubble! bubble! dripped the stream, its tiny waterfall full of voices, now clear, now indistinct, but always calling sweetly, "Michael! Michael! Michael!" And if your name be not Michael, nevertheless it will call you by your name. And the voice is ever the voice of the best beloved.

Alert, sniffing the air, I still could hear the voice of Silver Heels, down under the waterfall, and sometimes she called through laughter, "Michael!" and sometimes far away like a wind-blown cry, and sometimes like a whisper close to my face.

So rang her voice as an old song in my ears, the while my eyes scanned the dappled tree-trunks of a silvery beechwood, east and west, and through a long vista where, across a sunny streak of water, the Fort Pitt trail ran southwest.

The sun had spanned an hour's length on the blue dial of the sky, yet nothing moved in the woods. Still, strangely, I felt no impatience, no desire to chide myself for good time lost in groundless watchfulness. One by one the tall trees shed young leaves too early dead; the voices in the waterfall made low melody; the white sun-spots waned and glowed, mottling the silvered tree-trunks, lacing the water with a paler fretwork.

I sat now with my cheek on the cool, moist log, my rifle in my lap, watching the trees along the Fort Pitt trail. And, as I watched, I saw a man come out on the sandy bank of the stream and kneel down where my tracks crossed to the water's edge.

I was not astonished, but all over me my flesh moved, and without a sound I sank down behind my log into a soft ball of buckskin.

The man was Walter Butler. I knew him, though God alone knows how I could, for he wore the shirt of a Mohawk and beaded leggings to the hips, and at that distance might have been an Indian. He bore a rifle, and there was a hatchet in his beaded belt, and on his head he wore a round cap of moleskin under which his black, coarse hair, freed from the queue, fell to his chin.

He crouched there, examining my tracks with closest attention for full a minute, then rose gracefully and followed, tracing them up to the Fort Pitt trail.

Here I saw two other men come swiftly through the trees to meet him, but, though they gesticulated violently and pointed down the stream, they spoke too low for me to hear a single whisper.

Suddenly, to my horror, a canoe shot across my line of sight and stopped as suddenly, held by the setting-pole in midstream. It contained a white man, who leaned on the setting-pole, silently awaiting the result of the conference on the bank above.

The conference ended abruptly; I saw two of the men start south towards Fort Pitt, while Butler came hastily down to the water's edge and waded out to the canoe.

He boarded the frail craft from the bow, straddling it skilfully and working his way to his place. Then the two setting-poles flashed in the sunshine and the canoe shot out of sight.

My mind was working rapidly now, but, at first, anger succeeded blank perplexity. What did Captain Butler mean by following me through the forests? The answer came ere the question had been fully formed, and I knew he hated me and meant to kill me.

How he had learned of my mission, whether he had actually learned of it, or only suspected it from my disappearance, concerned me little. These things were certain: he was Lord Dunmore's emissary as I was the emissary of Sir William; he was bound for Cresap's camp as was I; and he intended to intercept me and kill me if that meant the winning of the race. Ay, he meant to kill me, anyhow, for how could he ever again appear in Johnstown if I lived to bear witness to his treachery?

I must give up my visit to the Cayugas for the present. It was to be a race now to Cresap's camp, and, though they had their canoe to speed withal, the advantage lay on my side; for I was seeking no man's life, whereas they must soon find that they had over-run their scent and would spend precious time in ambushes. Besides, they doubtless believed that somewhere I had a canoe hid, and that would keep them hanging around the carry-trails while I made time by circling them.

One thing disturbed me: two of them had gone by water and two by the Fort Pitt trail, and this threw me hopelessly into the wilderness without the ease of a trodden way.

Slowly I resumed my pack, reprimed my rifle, and turned my nose southward, bearing far enough west to keep out of earshot from the river and the trail.

At first I had looked upon Fort Pitt as a hospitable wayside refuge, marking nine-tenths of my journey towards Cresap's camp. But now I dared not present myself there, with Walter Butler hot on my trail, armed not only with hatchet and rifle, but also doubtless with some order of Lord Dunmore which might compel the officers at Fort Pitt to hand me over to Butler on his mere demand.

For, although Fort Pitt was rightfully on Pennsylvania soil, it had long been claimed by Virginia, and it was a Virginia garrison that now held it. Thus, should I stop there, I should be under the laws of Virginia and under the claw-thumb of Dunmore or anybody who might claim authority to represent him.

There is, I have been told, a vast region which lies between the Alleghany Mountains and the Mississippi, a desolate wilderness save for a few British garrisons at Natchez, at Vincennes, and at Detroit. These troops are placed there in order to establish the claim of our King to the region lately wrested from the French. Fort Pitt commanded the gateway to this wilderness, and the Ohio flowed through it; and for years Virginia and Pennsylvania had disputed for the right to control this gateway. Virginia held it by might, not right. Through it Daniel Boone had gone some years before; now Cresap had followed; and who could doubt that the Governor of Virginia had urged him on?

But the march of Cresap not only disturbed Sir William in his stewardship; it angered all Pennsylvania, and this is the reason:

The Virginians under Cresap went to settle, and to keep the Indians at a distance; the Pennsylvanians, on the other hand, went only to trade with the Cayugas, and they were furious to see Cresap's men spoil their trade. This I learned from Sir William on our evening walks about Quider's hut; and I learned, too, that Fort Pitt was a Virginia fortress on Pennsylvania soil, guarded not only against the savages, but also against the Pennsylvanians, who traded powder and shot and rifles with the Cayugas, and thus, according to my Lord Dunmore practically incited the savages to resist such philanthropists as himself.

Clearly then, no emissary of Sir William would be welcomed at Pittsburg fortress or town; and I saw nothing for it but to push on through the gateway of the west, avoiding Butler's men as best I could, and seeking the silly, deluded Cresap under the very nose of my Lord Dunmore.

My progress was slow; at times I sank between tree-roots, up to the thighs in moss; at times the little maidens of the flowering briers bade me tarry in their sharp, perfumed embrace. Now it was a wiry moose-bush snare that enlaced my ankles and sent me sprawling, pack and all; now the tough laurel bound me to the shoulders in slender ropes of blossoms which only my knife could sever. Tired out while yet the sun sent its reddening western rays deep into the forest, I knelt again, dropped my pack under a hemlock thicket, and crawled out to a heap of rocks which overhung a ravine.

The sunlight fell full in my face and warmed my body as I crept through a mat of blueberry bushes and peered over the edge of the crag down into the ravine.

A hundred feet below the Alleghany flowed, a glassy stream tinted with gold, reflecting forest and cliff and a tiny triangle of cobalt sky. Its surface was a mirror without a flaw, save where a solitary wild-duck floated, trailing a rippled wake, or steered hither and thither, craning its green neck after water-flies and gnats.

How still it was below; how quiet the whole world was—quieter for the hushed rumour of the winds on some far mountain spur.

The little blue caps which every baby peak had worn all day were now changed for night-caps of palest rose; the wild plum's bloom dusted every velvet mountain flank, the forest was robed in flowing purple to its roots, which the still river washed in sands of gold.

Below me a brown hawk wheeled, rising in narrowing spirals like a wind-blown leaf, higher, higher, till of a sudden its bright eye flashed level with mine and it sheered westward with a rush of whistling feathers. I watched it drifting away under the clouds into the sunset, with a silly prayer that wings might be fastened to my tired feet, as Minnomonedo, leaning out from the centre of heaven, dipped the first bird in Mon-o-ma, the Spirit Water, which was also I-ós-co, the Water of Light. "*Te-i-o! Te-i-o!*" I murmured, "*On-ti-o—I-é nia*, oh, *Mon-a-kee*!"

For God knows—and forgives—that, at sixteen, I was but an Algonquin in superstition, fearing Minnomonedo and seeking refuge in that God whom I did not dread.

In towns and cities the savage legends which I had imbibed with my first milk vanished from my mind completely, leaving no barriers to a calm worship of the Most High. But in the woods it was different; every leaf, every blossom represented links in those interminable chains of legends with which I had been nourished, and from which nothing but death can entirely wean me.

To me, the birds that passed, the shy, furry creatures that slipped back into the demi-light, the insects, the rocks, water, clouds, sun, moon, and stars were comrades with names and histories and purposes, exercising influences on each other and on me, and calling for an individual and intimate recognition which I cared not to disregard in the forest, though I might safely forget them amid the crowded wastes of civilization.

I do not mean to say that I credited the existence of such creatures as the wampum bird, nor did I believe that the first belt was made of a quill dropped to earth from the fearsome thing. This was nonsense; even at night I dared mock at it. But still every human being knows that, in the midnight wilderness, strange things do pass which no man can explain—strange beasts move, strange shapes dance by elf-fires, and trees talk aloud, one to another. If this be witchcraft, or if it be but part of a life which our vast black forests hide forever from the sun, I know not. Sir William holds that there are no witches, yet I once heard him curse a Huron hag for drying up his Devon cattle with a charm. We Christians know that a red belt lies ever between God and Satan. And I, as a woodsman, also know that, *if* there be demons in Biskoona, a thousand bloody belts lie for all time twixt *Minno* and *Mudjee*, call them what you will, and their voices are in the passing thunder and in the noises of the eight great winds.

Sprawling there on the warm rocks like a young panther in the sun, ears attuned to the faintest whisper of danger, I gnawed a strip of dried squirrel's flesh and sucked up the water from a dripping mossy cleft, sweet cheer to an empty belly.

As for fire, that was denied me by my sense, though I knew that the coming night would stiffen me. But I cared little for that: what occupied my thoughts was how to obtain food when a single shot might bring Butler and his trackers hot on the scent ere the rifle smoke had blown clear of the trees.

It was not always that one might knock down a stupid partridge with a stick, nor yet were there trout in every water-crack. I looked down at the darkening river, where the wild mallard still circled and darted its neck after unseen midges; and my mouth watered, for he was passing plump, this Southern lingerer, fresh from the great gulf.

"If he be there in the morning," thought I, "perhaps I may risk a shot and take to my heels." For had I not thrown Butler and his crew from my trail as easily as I brush a bunch of deer-flies from my hunting-shirt? And if I could do it once, I could repeat the trick in a dozen pretty ways of my own knowledge and of Thayendanegea's invention. Still I knew he was no forest blunderer, this Butler man; he had proved that in the Canadas; and I did not mean to be over-confident nor to rock caution to sleep in my first triumph.

And Lord!—how I hated him and wished him evil, waking, sleeping, in sickness and in health, ay, living or dead, I wished him evil and black mischance on his dark soul's flight to the last accounting. So, with thoughts of hatred and revenge, I saw the cinders of the sun go out behind the forest and the web of night settling over the world. Wrapped in my blanket, curled up in a bed of blueberry, I folded my hands over my body like a chipmunk and said a prayer to the God whom I did not fear. After that I reprimed my rifle, covering flint and pan to keep out the dew, settled the stock in a crevice near my head, and lay down again to watch for the full moon, whose yellow light was already soaring up behind a black peak in the east. And all night long I lay on that borderland of sleep which men in danger dare not traverse lest a sound find them unready. Slumbering, again and again I saw the moon through slitted lids, yet I rested and slept a sweet wholesome sleep which renewed my vigour by its very lightness.

Long before the sun had done painting the sky-scenes for his royal entry, I had brushed the dew from cap and blanket, primed my rifle afresh, and cautiously crawled to the cliff's brink.

Mist covered the river; I could not have seen a canoe had it been floating under my own crag; neither could I see my wild duck, though at times I heard his drowsy quack somewhere below, and the answering quack of his mate, now rejoining her lord and master. Perhaps a whole flock had come in by night.

Now, the intense stillness of early morn did not reassure me, nor did the careless quacking of the ducks convince me that the river and shore were untenanted save for them. Many a drowsing mallard has been caught by a lean fox or knocked on the head with a paddle. I had no mind to creep down and risk a shot at a shadow on the misty water, not knowing what else that mist might conceal. However, I was fiercely hungry, and I meant to have a duck. So, shivering, I undressed, and, stark naked, I picked my way down the clefts to the base of the cliff and slipped into the water like a mink.

The water was warmer than the air; I swam without a splash, straight towards the quacking sound, seeing nothing but the blank fog as yet, but meaning to seize the first duck by the legs if he were asleep, or by his neck if he dived.

Now, although I made no sound in the water, all around me I felt the presence of live creatures stirring, and soon there began a peevish sound of half-awakened water-fowl, so that I knew I was near to a flock of them.

Suddenly, right in my face, a duck squawked and flapped; I grasped at the bird, but held only a fistful o' feathers. In an instant the mist around me rang with strong wings beating the water, and with a whistling roar the flock drove past, dashing me with spray till I, smothered and choked, flung up my arm towards a floating tree-trunk. To my horror the log rolled completely over, and out of it two men fell, shrieking, on top of me, for the log I had grasped was a bark canoe, and I had spilled out my enemies on my own head.

We all went down, but I sank clear of the unseen men and rose again to swim for my life. They came to the surface behind me; I could see their shadowy heads over my shoulder, for the mist was lifting.

They were shouting now, evidently to others on the opposite bank, but my way led not thither, and I swam swiftly for the foot of my cliff, missing it again and again in the fog, until I found it at last, and ran panting and dripping up the cleft.

When I reached my rifle I leaned over the crag to look, but the river gorge remained choked with vapour, though here above all was bright gray dawn. The shouting below came clearly to my ears, also the splashing. I judged that the two men had thrown their arms over the capsized canoe, and thus, hands clasped, were making out to keep afloat; for in this manner only can a capsized canoe serve two men.

Drying my bruised feet and dripping skin in my blanket, I hastened to dress and strap on my pack, keeping a restless eye on the gulf below. When I was prepared, the sun, pushing up behind the peaks in the east, was already scattering the mist into long, thin clouds, and at intervals I made out the canoe floating bottom up, close inshore, and I heard the wrecked men paddling with their hands.

Presently Walter Butler's voice sounded from the bank, cautioning the swimming men to proceed slowly, and inquiring what was the cause for their upsetting.

They replied that a deer, swimming the river, had planted one foot in their bow while they slept, and so overturned the canoe. But I knew that Walter Butler would not be long in discovering the tracks of my naked feet in the shore-sands where I had landed while searching for my cliff, so I prepared to leave without further ado, though angrily tempted to make a target of the phantom group below.

So, with a stomach stayed with a mouthful of corn and water, I started silently westward, meaning to make a circle, and, hiding my tracks, recross the river to take advantage of their sure pursuit by travelling on the Fort Pitt trail until again hunted into the forest.

Munching my corn as I plodded on, I still kept a keen lookout behind, though in the forest one can seldom see but a rod or two, and sometimes not even a yard except down the vista of some woodland stream.

It was useless to attempt to cover my tracks, for I could neither avoid breaking branches in the tangle, nor keep from leaving foot-prints on the soft moss which even a Boston schoolmaster might read a-running. But I could trot along the tops of fallen logs like a partridge, and use every watercourse that wound my way, so breaking my trail for all save a hound or an Indian. And this I did to check the pursuit which I knew must begin sooner or later.

It began even sooner than I expected, and almost caught me napping, for, resting a moment to scrutinize a broad stretch of barren ground, around which I had just circled in order to keep cover, I saw a man creeping among the rocks and berry-scrub, doubtless nosing about for my trail. A moment later another man moved on the eastern edge of the mountain flank, and at the same time, far up the river, I saw the canoe floating.

That was enough for me, and I started on a dog-trot down the slope and along the river-bed, plunging through willows and alders till I came to a bend from which the naked shoulder of the mountain could not be seen.

Thayendanegea had taught me to do what people thought I would be likely to do, but to accomplish it so craftily that they would presently think I had done something else.

When at length those who pursued me should find my trail on the southern border of the open scrub-land, they would have no difficulty in following me down the long incline to the river where I now stood, ankle-deep in icy water. I had halted exactly opposite to the mouth of a rocky stream, and it was natural that I should ford the rapids here and continue, on the other bank, up that stream to hide my trail. They would expect me to do it, so this I did, and ran up the bed of the stream for a few rods, carelessly leaving a tiny dust line of corn-meal on the rocks as though in my headlong flight my sack had started a seam.

Then I turned around and waded down the brook again to the river, out to the shallow rapids, and so, knee-deep, hastened southward again to put the next bend between me and the canoe.

I was making but slow progress, for my sack galled me, the slippery, wet buckskin leggings chafed knee and ankle raw, and my soaked hunting-shirt glued its skirts to my thighs, impeding me at every stride. My drenched moccasins also left wet tracks on the Fort Pitt trail, which I knew the sun could not dry out for hours yet; but I did not believe that Butler and his crew would come up in time to see them.

I was mistaken; scarcely half an hour had passed ere their accursed canoe appeared bobbing down the rapids, paddles flashing in the sun; and I took to the forest again at a lively gait, somewhat disturbed, though my self-confidence permitted no actual anxiety to assail me.

I now played them one of Brant's tricks, which was to change moccasins for a brand-new pair of larger size, and soled with ridged bear-hide. I also reversed them, toe pointing to the rear, and they made a fine mark on the moss.

Every twenty paces I stooped to brush up the pile of the velvet moss and so obliterate my tracks for the next twenty paces.

In this manner I travelled for three hours without sign of pursuit, and had it not been for my pack I could have jogged on till night. But my galled shoulders creaked for mercy, and I struggled out once more into the Fort Pitt trail and stood panting and alert, drenched with sweat.

The trail had been trodden within the hour; I saw fresh sign of two different moccasins, and of a coarse boot of foreign style, all pointing southward. The moccasins were like one pair I had in my pack, of Albany make; the wearer of the boots toed in. These things I noticed quicker than I could relate them, and instinctively I changed my moccasins for the third time, and ran on, stepping carefully in the tracks of him who wore the Albany moccasins, and keeping a sharp eye ahead.

I had run nearly half a mile, and was beginning to look about for a vantage spot to rest on, when a turn in the trail brought me out along the river.

I scanned the stream thoroughly, and discovered nothing to balk at, but I could not see the opposite bank very plainly because the forest rose from the water's edge, and all was dusky where the low-arched branches screened the shore.

Under this a canoe might lie, or might not; there was no means of telling. I sniffed at the dusky screen of leaves, but had my sniffing for my trouble, as nothing moved there.

It was clear I could not remain in the Fort Pitt trail with at least two of the Butler crew behind me. Should I take to the tangled forest again? My shoulders begged me not to, but my senses jogged me to the prudent course. However, at certain times in men's careers, when body and mind clamour for different answers, a moment comes, even to the most cautious, when a risk smacks as sweet as a banquet.

One of those moments was coming now; I knew the risk of traversing that open bit of trail, but the hazard had a winy flavour withal, and besides it was such a few feet to safety—such a little risk. And I trotted out on the open trail.

Instantly a shot echoed in the gorge, and the pack on my back jerked. I never made such a jump in all my life before, for I had cleared the open like a scared fawn, and now stood glued to a tree, peering at the blue cloud of smoke which trailed along the opposite shore.

There it was!—there came their accursed canoe like a live creature poking its painted snout out of the leafy screen, and I cocked and primed my rifle and waited.

There were two men in the canoe; one paddled gingerly, the other had reloaded his rifle and was now squatting in the bow. But what astonished and enraged me was that I knew the men, Wraxall the barber, and Toby Tice, perfectly well. They were, moreover, tenants of Sir William, living with their families in Johnstown, and their murderous treachery horrified me.

I had never shot at a man; I raised my rifle and held them on the sights for a moment, but there was no fever of the chase in me now, only a heart-sick horror of taking a neighbour's life.

In a choked and shaky voice I hailed them, warning them back; my voice gave them a start, for I believe they thought me hard hit.

"Go back, you clowns!" I called. "Shame on you, Toby Tice! Shame on you, Wraxall! What devil's work is this? Are you turned Huron then with your knives and hatchets and your Seneca belts? Swing that canoe, I say! Au large! Au large!—or, by God, I'll drill you both with one ball!"

Suddenly Wraxall fired. Through the blue cloud I saw Tice sweep au large, and I stepped out to the shore and shot a ripping hole through their canoe as it heeled.

Wraxall was reloading desperately; Tice started to send the canoe towards me once more, but suddenly catching sight of the leaking bottom, dropped on his knees and tried to draw the ripped flaps together.

Behind my tree I tore a cartridge open, rammed in a palmful of buckshot, primed, and fired, tearing the whole bow out of their flimsy bark craft. The canoe stood up like a post, stern in the air, and Wraxall lay floundering, while Tice shrieked and fell sprawling into the river, head first, like a plunging frog, paddles, poles, and rifle following.

They were swimming my way now, but I shouted to them to sheer off, and at rifle point warned them across the river to land where they might and thank God I had not driven them to the bottom with an ounce of buck.

I was still watching them to see they landed safely, and had half turned to take the trail again, when, almost under my feet, a human hand shot up above the river-bank and seized my ankle, tripping me flat. The next moment a man leaped up from the shore where he had been crouching, but as I lay on my back I gave him a violent kick in the face and rolled over out of reach. Before I could grasp my rifle, his hatchet flew, pinning one flap of my hunting-shirt to the ground; and I wrenched the hatchet free and hurled it back at him, so that the flat of the blade smacked his face, and he dropped into the water with a scream.

Shaking all over, I rose and lifted my rifle, instinctively repriming. But the sight of the man in the mud, crawling about, gasping and blowing bloody bubbles, made me sick, and the next moment I turned tail and ran like a rabbit.

As I sped down the trail, over my shoulder I saw Walter Butler, planted out in the shoals of the river, taking steady aim at me, and I seized a tree and checked my course as his bullet sang past my face. Then I ran on, setting my teeth and vowing to repay that shot when my life was my own to risk again.

It was late in the afternoon when I turned once more from the trail and limped into the forest; and I was now close enough to exhaustion to feel for the first time in my life a touch of that desperation which makes a fury out of a cornered creature, be it panther or mouse.

For I had not been able to shake off pursuit, double and twist as I might. They were distant, it is true, but they plodded tirelessly, unerringly. Again and again I saw them on the rocks, on the vast arid reaches of the mountains, heads down to the trail, jogging along with horrid patience.

Once I doubled on them so close that I could see one of the band with his face tied up in a rag, doubtless the fellow who had tasted of his own toothsome hatchet. Walter Butler I could also distinguish, ever in the lead, rifle trailing. Only one among the others bore a rifle. I had certainly upset their canoe to good advantage. But now I began to repent me that I had not shot them in the water when I had the chance; for truly I was in a sorry condition to proceed farther, through forest or on trail; my limbs at times refused their service, and a twig tripped me when I needs must leap a log.

I fired my first long shot at them as they were entering a ravine below me, and I missed, for my hands were unsteady from my labouring breath. Yet I should have marked a deer where I pleased at that range.

This shot, however, delayed them, and they now advanced more slowly and cautiously, alert for another ambush. An hour later I gave them a second shot. My aim was wavering; my bullet only made one man duck his head.

I was fighting for time now. If I could keep on until dark I had no fear for the morrow. To tell the truth, I had no actual fear then; it seemed so impossible that these Johnstown yokels really meant to take my life, even if they caught me—this ass of a Toby Tice whom I had tipped for holding my stirrup more than once. And Wraxall, the red-headed barber sot, who had shaved me in the guard-house! How many times had he snatched off his greasy cap to me, as he loafed in tavern doors, sweating malt like a hop-vat!

But the nearness of Walter Butler was a very different affair. Even when I was but a toddling child at Mistress Molly's knee the sight of Walter Butler ever sent me fearfully hiding behind the first apron I could snatch at. Year by year my distrust and aversion deepened, until I had come to look forward serenely to that mortal struggle between us which I knew must come. But I had never expected it to come like this.

As I crept once more into the forest my hatred for this man gave me new strength, and I staggered on, searching for a vantage coign where I might take another shot at the grotesque crew. Up and up I crawled, faintly alarmed at my increasing weakness, for now, when a vine tripped me, I could scarce make out to rise again. In vain I whipped and spurred my lagging strength with stinging memories of all the scores I should wipe out with one clean bullet through Butler's head; it was nigh useless; I could barely move, and how was I to shoot with my brier-torn hands shaking so I could neither hold them still nor close my swollen fingers on the trigger? I needed rest; an hour would have sufficed to steady the palsy of exhaustion. If only the night would come quickly! But there were two hours of daylight yet, two long hours of light in which to track my every step.

I caught a distant glimpse of them far below me, searching the ravine and river-bank. How they had been lured off to the river I know not, but it gave me a brief chance for breath, though not for a shot; and I rested my face on my rifle-stock and closed my eyes.

I had been kneeling behind a granite rock in a bare waste of blueberry-scrub, close to the edge of the woods; and presently as I attempted to rise I fell down, and began to claw around like a blind kitten. Stand up I could not, and worst of all, I had little inclination to attempt it, the bed of rough bushes was so soothing, and the granite rock invited my heavy head. All over me a sweet numbness tingled; I tried to think, I strove to rouse. In vain I heard a sing-song drowsing in my ears: "They will kill you! They will kill you!" but there was no terror in it. What would it be, I wondered—a hatchet?—a knife at the throat like the deer's coup-de-grâce? Maybe a blow with a rifle-stock. What did I care? Sleep was sweet.

Then a quiver swept through me like an icy wind; with a pang I remembered my mission and the wampum pledges, the boast and the vow to Sir William.

Darkness crowded me down; my head reeled, yet I rose again to my knees, swaying and clutching at the rock which I could barely see. All around a thick night seemed to hem me in; I groped through a chilly void for my rifle; it was gone. Panic-stricken I staggered up, drenched with dew, and I saw the moon staring at me over a mountain's ghostly wall.

Slowly I realized that I had slept; that death had passed me where I lay unconscious in the open moorland. But how far had death gone?—and would he not return by moonlight, stealthily, casting no shadow? Ay, what was that under the tree there, that shape watching me?—moving, too,—a man!

As I shrank back my heel struck my rifle. In an instant I was down behind the rock to prime with dry powder, but to my horror I found flint missing, charge drawn, pan raised, and ramrod sticking helplessly out of the barrel. The shock stunned me for a moment; then I snatched at knife and hatchet only to find an empty belt dangling to my ankles.

In the impulse of fury and despair, I crouched flat with clinched fists, trembling for a spring; and at the same instant a tall figure rose from the bushes at my elbow, laughing coolly.

"Greeting, friend," he said; "God save our country!"

Speechless and dazed, I turned to face him, but he only leaned quietly on a long rifle and pinched his chin and chuckled.

"There are some gentlemen yonder looking for you, young man," he said. "I sent them south, for somehow I thought you might not be looking for them."

Weakness had dulled my wits, but I found speech presently to ask for my knife and hatchet.

He laid his head on one side and contemplated me in mock admiration.

"Now! Now! Let us go slow, friend," he said. "Let us converse on several subjects before you begin bawling for your playthings. In the first place your manners need polish. I said to you, 'Greeting, friend; God save our country!' and you make me no polite reply."

Something in the big fellow's impudence and careless good-humour struck me as familiar. I had heard that voice before, and under pleasant circumstances, it seemed to me; somewhere I had seen him standing as he was standing now, in his stringy buckskins and his coon-skin cap, with the fluffy tail falling like a queue.

"If you please," I said, weakly, "give me my hatchet and knife and receive my thanks. Come, my good fellow, you detain me, and I have far to travel."

"Well, of all impudence!" he sneered. "Wait a bit, my young cock o' the woods. I don't know you yet, but I mean to ere you go out strutting o' moonlight nights."

"Will you give me my hatchet?" I asked, sharply, edging towards him.

Before the words left my lips he snatched my rifle from me and stepped back, putting the rock between us.

"Now," he said, grimly, "you come into camp and take supper with me, or I'll knock your head off and drag you in by the heels!"

Aching with fatigue and mortification, I stood there so perfectly helpless that the great oaf fell a-laughing again, and, with a shrug of good-humoured contempt, handed me back my rifle as though I were an infant.

"Don't grind your teeth at me," he chuckled. "Come to the camp, lad. I mean no harm to you. If I did, there's men yonder who'd slit your pipes for the pleasure, I warrant."

He took a step up the slope, looked around in the moonlight encouragingly, then abruptly returned to my side and passed his great arm around me.

"I'm dog-tired," I said, weakly, making an effort to walk; but my knees had no strength in them, and I must have fallen except for his support.

Up, up, up we passed through the foggy moonlight, he almost dragging me, and my feet a-trail behind. However, when we reached the plateau, I made out to stumble along with his aid, though I let him relieve me of my rifle, which he shouldered with his own.

After a minute or two I smelled the camp-fire, but could not see it. Even in the darkest night a fire amid great trees is not visible at any considerable distance.

My big companion, striding along beside me, had been constantly muttering under his breath, and presently I distinguished the words he was singing:

—"One shoe off, one shoe on,

Diddle diddle dumpling, my son John—"

"I know you," I said, abruptly.

He dropped his song and glanced around at me.

"Oh, you do, eh? Well, I mean to know you, too, so don't worry, young man."

"I won't," said I, scarcely able to speak.

Presently I saw a single tree in the darkness, all gleaming red, and in a moment we entered a ruddy ring of light, in the centre of which great logs burned and crackled in a little sea of whistling flames.

I was prepared to encounter the other coureur-de-bois, and there he was, ferret-face peering and sniffing at us as we approached. However, beyond a grunt, he paid me no attention, and presently fell to stirring something in a camp-pot which hung from cross-sticks over a separate bed of coals.

There was a third figure there, seated at the base of a gigantic pine tree; a little Hebrew man, gathering his knees in his arms and peeping up at me with watery, red-rimmed eyes; Saul Shemuel!—though I was too weary to bother my head as to how he came there. As I passed him he looked up, but he did not appear to know me, though he came every spring to Sir William for his peddling license, and sometimes sold us children gaffs and ferret-muzzles and gilt chains for pet dogs.

He bade me good-evening in an uncertain voice, and peered up at me continually; and although I doubted that even Sir William could have recognized me now, I feared this Jew.

The big man brought me a bowl of broth and spread a blanket for me close to the blaze. I do not recollect drinking the broth, but I must have done so, for shortly a delicious warmth enveloped me within and without, and that is the last I remembered that night.

CHAPTER X

It was still dark when I awoke; the fire had become a pyramid of coals. By the dull glow I saw two figures moving; one of them presently crossed the dim, crimson circle and sat down beside me, fists clasped under his massive chin, rifle balanced on his knees.

"I am awake," I whispered. "Is there any trouble?"

Without moving a muscle of his huge frame, the forest runner said: "Don't come into the fire-ring. There's a man been prowling yonder, a-sniffing our fire, for the last four hours."

I drew myself farther into the darkness, looking about me, shivering and rubbing my stiffened limbs.

"How do you feel?" he asked, without turning his head.

I told him I felt rested, and thanked him so earnestly for his great kindness to me that he began to laugh and chuckle all to himself and drag his great chin to and fro across his knuckles.

"Consider yourself fortunate, eh?" he repeated, rising to come into the thicket and squat on his haunches beside me.

"Yes," said I, wondering what he found so droll in the situation.

"Ever hear of Catamount Jack?" he inquired, after a moment.

"Yes; you mean Jack Mount, the highwayman? But you are mistaken; the man who follows me is not Jack Mount," I replied, smiling.

"Sure?"

"Oh yes," I said, bitterly; "I ought to know."

"What do you know about Jack Mount?" he asked.

"I? Nothing—that is, nothing except what everybody knows."

"Well, what does Mister Everybody know?" he inquired, sneeringly.

"They say he takes the King's highway," I replied. "There's a book about him, printed in Boston."

"With a gibbet on the cover," interrupted the big fellow, impatiently. "Oh, I know all that. But don't they say he's a rebel?"

"Why, yes," I replied; "everybody knows he set fire to the King's ship, *Gaspee*, and started the rebels a-pitching tea overboard from Griffin's Wharf."

I stopped short and looked at him in amazement. *He* was Jack Mount! I did not doubt it for one moment. And there was the famous Weasel, too—that little, shrivelled comrade of his!—both corresponding exactly to their descriptions which I had read in the Boston book, ay, read to Silver Heels, while her gray eyes grew rounder and rounder at the exploits of these so-called "Minions of the Moon."

"Well," asked the forest runner, with a chuckle, "do you still think yourself lucky?"

I managed to say that I thought I was, but my lack of enthusiasm sent the big fellow into spasms of smothered laughter.

"Now, now, be sensible," he said. "You know you've a belt full of gold, a string of good wampum in your sack, and as pretty a rifle as ever I saw. And you still think yourself in luck? And you're supping with Jack Mount? And the Weasel's watching everything from yonder hazel-bunch? And Saul Shemuel's pretending to be asleep under that pine-tree? Why, Mr. Cardigan, you amaze me!" he lisped, mockingly.

So the little Hebrew had recognized me after all. I swallowed a lump in my throat and rose to my elbow. With Jack Mount beside me, Walter Butler prowling outside the fire-ring, and I alone, stripped of every weapon, what in Heaven's sight was left for me to do? Truly, I had jumped into that same fire which burns below all frying-pans, and presently must begin a-roasting, too.

"So they say I take the King's highway, eh?" observed Mount, twiddling his great thumbs over his ramrod and digging his heels into the pine-needles.

"They say so," I replied, sullenly.

He burst out petulantly: "I never take a *rebel* purse! The next fool you hear call me a cut-purse, tell him that to stop his mouth withal!" And he fell a-muttering to himself: "King's highway, eh? Not mine, not his, not yours—oh no!—but the King's. By God! I'd like to meet his Majesty of a moonlight on this same highway of his!"

He turned roughly on me, demanding what brought me into the forest; but I shook my head, lips obstinately compressed.

"Won't tell, eh?" he growled.

An ugly gleam came into his eyes, but died out again as quickly; and he shrugged his giant's shoulders and spat out a quid of spruce-gum he had been chewing.

"One thing's plain as Shemuel's nose yonder," he said, jerking a big thumb towards the sleeping peddler; "you're a King's man if I'm a King's highwayman, and I'll be cursed if you go free without a better accounting than a wag o' your head!"

Cade Renard, the Weasel, had come up while Mount was speaking, and his bright little eyes gleamed ruby red in the fire-glow as he scanned me warily from head to toe.

"What's his business?" he inquired of Mount. "I've searched his pack again, and I can't find anything except the wampum belts."

At this naïve avowal I jumped up angrily, forgetting fear, demanding to know by what right he dared search my pack; but the impassive Weasel only blinked at Mount and chewed a birch-leaf reflectively.

"What is he, Jack?" he asked again, turning towards me, as though I had been some new kind of bird.

"Don't know," replied Mount; "not worth the plucking, anyhow. Take his wampum belts, all the same," he added, with a terrific yawn.

"If you are a patriot," I said, desperately, "you will leave me my belts and meddle only with your own affairs."

Both men turned and looked at me curiously.

"*You* are no patriot," said Mount, after a silence.

"Why not?" I persisted.

"Ay—ay—why and why not?" yawned Mount. "I don't know, if you won't tell. The devil take you, for aught I care! But you won't get your belts," he added, slyly, watching me askance to note the effect of his words.

"Why not?" I repeated, choking down my despair.

"Because you'll talk with your belts to some of these damned Indians hereabouts," he grinned, "and I want to know what you've got to say to them first."

"I tell you that my belts mean no harm to patriots!" I repeated, firmly. "You say I am no patriot. I deny it; I am a better patriot than you, or I should not be in this forest to-day!"

"You are not a patriot," broke in Cade Renard; "you have proved it already!"

"You say that," I retorted, "because Jack Mount, the highwayman, gives me the Boston greeting—'God save our country!'—and I do not reply? What of it? I'm at least patriot enough not to pretend to be one. I am patriot enough not to rob my own countrymen. I can say 'God save our country!' as well as you, and I do say it, with better grace than either of you!"

The men exchanged sullen glances.

"That password is not fit for spies," said Mount, grimly.

"Spy? You take me for a spy?" I cried, in astonishment. "Well, if you are the famous Jack Mount, you've duller wits than people believe."

"I've wit enough left to keep an eye on you," he roared, starting towards me; but the Weasel laid his little, rough claw on the giant's arm, and at the same moment I saw a dark figure step just within the outer fire-ring, holding up one arm as a sign of peace. The man was Walter Butler. I dropped back softly into the shadow of the thicket.

Slowly Jack Mount strolled around the rim of the fire-circle, rifle lying in the hollow of his left arm. He halted a few paces from Butler and signed for him to remain where he stood. There was no mistaking that signal, for it was a Mohawk sign, and both men understood that it meant "Move and I shoot!"

"Well, Captain Butler," he drawled, "what can I do for you?"

"You know me, sir?" replied Butler, without the faintest trace of surprise in his colourless voice.

"Ay, we all know you," replied Mount, quickly; "even in your Iroquois dress."

"May I inquire your name, sir?" asked Butler, with that deathly grimace which was his smile.

"You may inquire, certainly you may inquire," said Mount, cordially. "You may inquire of my old friend, the moon. Gad, she knows me well, Captain Butler!"

After a silence Butler said: "You unintentionally misled me last evening, friend. The man I follow did not cross the river as you supposed."

"Really?" cried Mount, smiling.

There came another silence, then Butler spoke again:

"I am here on business of my Lord Dunmore; I am here to arrest a young man who is supposed to lie hidden in your camp. I call on you, sir, whoever you are, to aid me in execution of the law."

"The law! Gad, she's another acquaintance o' mine, the jade!" said Mount, laughing. "I suppose you bring that pretty valentine of hers—what some people call a warrant—do you not, Captain Butler?"

"I do," said Butler, moving forward and holding out a paper. Mount took it, and, while he read it, he deliberately shoved Butler back with his elbow to where he had been standing, crowded him back before his huge, outstretched arm, coolly scanning the warrant the while. And Butler could not avoid the giant save by retreating, step by step, beyond the dull red circle, and out against the sky-line, where a bullet could scarcely miss him.

Mount was now contemplating the warrant in deep admiration. He held it out at arm's-length, cocking his head on one side; he held it upside down; he turned it over; he scanned it sideways.

"Oh, Cade!" he called out, cheerily. "'Tis the same old valentine! Gad, Captain Butler, we have seen them in every one o' the thirteen colonies—my friend yonder, and I!"

"You are doubtless a sheriff, sir," observed Butler, patiently.

"No," said Mount; "no, not exactly what you could call a sheriff, Captain Butler; but I have had much business with sheriffs. I owe them more than I can ever repay," he added, sentimentally.

"Then you will understand, sir, the necessity of aiding the law," suggested Butler, holding out his hand for the warrant.

But Mount quietly pocketed the paper and began to whistle and reprime his rifle.

"May I trouble you for that paper?" asked Butler, with his chilling, sinister politeness.

There was a pause. Butler's eyes stole around the camp-fire, but only the little Hebrew was now visible, for I lay in the shadow and the Weasel had ominously vanished.

"You do not mean to retain this warrant, sir?" demanded Butler, raising his sneering voice, and searching the thickets for some sign of the ambushed Weasel.

"Oh, Captain Butler," said Mount, with a gigantic simper, "how can I resist you? Pray tell me who this bad young Michael Cardigan may be, and what he has done to get his name on this valentine?"

"It is a matter of treason," retorted Butler, sharply. "Come, my good man, have done with silly chatter and aid me to my duty in the King's name!"

Mount burst into a shout of laughter. "That's it! In the King's name! I've heard that, too,—oh yes, I've heard that o' moonlight nights!"

Butler observed him in astonishment, but Mount held his sides and roared in his mirth: "Comes friend Butler with his warrant, tripping it through the woods, and singing of the King like a titmouse on a stump. Ay, singing to me to help him take a stout fellow in the King's name! Ha! Ha! Ha! This funny Mr. Sheriff Butler!" Then, in a flash, he wheeled on Butler, snarling, every tooth bared: "Damn you, sir, do you take me for your lackey or the

King's hangman? To hell with you, sir! To hell with your King, sir! Did you hear me? I said, to hell with your King!"

Butler's face paled in the waning fire-light. Presently he said, in his slow, even tones: "I shall take care that your good wishes reach the King's ears. Pray, sir, honour me with your name and quality, though I may perhaps guess both."

"No need to guess," cut in the big fellow, cheerfully. "I'm Jack Mount; I burned the *Gaspee*, I helped dump his Majesty's tea into Boston harbour, and I should be pleased to do as much for the King himself. Tell him so, Captain Butler; tell my Lord Dunmore he can have a ducking, too, at his lordship's polite convenience."

Butler glared at him, but Mount raised his coon-skin cap and bowed mockingly. "Charmed, sir, charmed," he simpered. "Pray, permit me to present my comrade, Sir Cade Renard, of the backwood aristocracy, sometimes called the Weasel. He's so shy, sir. Friend Weasel, come out from behind that stump and bring your rifle; step up beside me and make a very fine bow to his Majesty's deputy-sheriff. Tell the kind gentleman what good men we are, Cade, and how proud we feel to entertain him."

The Weasel sauntered up and performed a slow, wriggling bow.

"Minions of the moon, sir," he said; "and so charmed to receive you, or anything you have of value. Your scalp, now, might bring five shillings at Baton Rouge, or is that but a scratch wig you wear, sir?"

"Will you deliver me my warrant and my prisoner?" demanded Butler, with a ghastly smile.

"No!" said Mount, abruptly changing his manner. "Make a new trail, you Tory hangman! March!" And he gave him a prod with his rifle.

Never had I seen such ferocity expressed on any human face as I saw now on Mr. Butler's.

He backed out into the brush, at the point of Mount's long rifle; then the red fire-glow left him, and he was gone into the darkness of early morning. Presently the Weasel stole after him.

Mount came swaggering back, pausing to drop the warrant on the hot coals as he passed. Renard returned in a few minutes, took his rifle, and squatted briskly down just beyond the fire-light.

As Mount came up to me, I rose and thanked him for the protection he had given so generously, and he laughed and laid one padded fist on my shoulder.

"Hark ye, friend," he said; "take your Indian belts and your pack and go in peace, for if Dunmore is after you, the sooner you start north the better. Go, lad; I'm not your enemy!"

"I go south," I replied, cautiously.

"Oh, you do, eh?" said Mount, fumbling in his pockets for the flint he had taken from my rifle. "Are you bound for Cresap's camp, too?"

"Are you?" I asked, reddening.

He rubbed his chin, watching me with sulky eyes.

"You answer ever with a question!" he complained, fretfully. "I ask you this and you ask me that—tom tiddle! tiddle tom!—and I be no wiser now for all I have heard your name."

"I know Michael Cardigan," observed the Weasel, quietly coming up, buckling on his pack.

"It's an honourable name," I began, in desperation, striving to stop him, but the Weasel ignored me and addressed himself to Mount.

"He's one of Sir William Johnson's household. That accounts for those peace-belts of wampum. Shemuel, yonder, knows the lad."

"Oho!" exclaimed Mount, staring at me. "So you come on Sir William's business to the Cayugas? Ha! Now I begin to grasp this pretty game. Sir William wishes his Cayugas to sit tight while Cresap builds forts—"

"Hush, for God's sake!" I pleaded, seeing that he had guessed all.

"Oh, I'll hush," he replied, eying me with frank curiosity. "I am no enemy to Sir William. A fairer and more honest gentleman lives not in these colonies, be he Tory or patriot! Oh, I'll hush, but every one knows Sir William will not have the Indians take sides in this same war that's coming so fast upon us. It's no secret, lad; every pot-house, every tavern tap-room is full o' gossip that Butler means to rouse the Indians against us, and that Sir William will not have it!"

"Since when have you come from Johnstown?" I asked, astonished.

"Oh, a week after you left," replied the Weasel. "We saw your tracks, but we went another way after the first week. You lost too much time."

Mount had now hoisted his pack to his shoulders and stood watching Shemuel, the Hebrew peddler, strapping up his dingy boxes, tucking in bits of lace and ribbon and cheap finery.

"Come on, Shemmy, you pigeon-toed woodchuck!" growled Mount, cracking a fresh lump of spruce-gum in his glistening teeth.

The little Jew looked up at me slyly, his grimy fists buried in the bowels of his gewgaws.

"Perhaps the gendleman cares to look at som goots?" he observed, interrogatively. "I haff chains, buckles, pins, needles, buttons, laces, knifes, ribbons for queue and gollarettes—"

Mount, with the toe of his moccasin, gently reversed Shemuel into one of his own boxes, then warning him to pack up if he valued his scalp, took my arm in friendly fashion and moved out into the gray woods.

"Touching this mission of yours to the Cayugas," he said, frankly, "I see no good to come of it, and I say this with all respect to Sir William. By-the-bye, Sir William has much to trouble him these days."

"I know that," said I, sadly.

"Oh no, you don't," smiled Mount. "There have been strange doings in Johnstown since you left: a change has come in a single week, lad; neighbours no longer speak; the town is three parts Tory to one part patriot; even brothers hate each other. Two taverns known to be the meeting-places of patriots have been set afire and shot into; and old John Butler is gone north, where, they say, he is raising a bloody crew of cut-throats, rangers, half-breeds, and young Mohawks. Sir William is holding long talks with Brant and Red Jacket at the upper castle. Oh, the sands begin to run faster now, and men must soon take one side or t'other, for there's more troops going to Boston, and that means the end of King George!"

I did not perhaps realize the importance of all he said; I had seen too little of the rebels themselves to credit the seriousness of the situation. But here was an opportunity to sound Mount on the Cresap affair, and I began earnestly.

"Can you not see that Colonel Cresap is driving the Cayugas into the King's ranks?"

"What do we care for the Cayugas?" replied Mount, contemptuously; and it was in vain I wasted argument on this man who had been born a woodsman, but who knew the savages only from the outside. I could not make him see the foolish uselessness of angering the Six Nations. He was one of that kind who detested all Indians, who professed to hold them in scorn, and who had passed his life in killing all he could.

"What are we to do?" he demanded, sarcastically. "Give up the frontier and go back to Virginia with tails between our legs?"

"Better that than serve as silly tools for Dunmore!" I retorted hotly.

"Dunmore!" sneered Mount. "We his tools, when the silly ass hasn't wits to twiddle his own thumbs?"

"He had the wit to send Butler to stop me!" I answered, bitterly.

Mount began to grin again and wink his eyes slyly.

"Butler came for something else, too," he said. "Dunmore's suite travelled south the day you left, and ought to be in Fortress Pitt by this hour to-morrow."

"What of it?" I asked.

"Ay, that's it, you see. Since you left Johnstown, all are talking of the new beauty who threw over Walter Butler—what's her name—a certain Miss Warren, ward of Sir William; and it is commonly reported that the dispute over the Indians and the quarrel betwixt Butler and Sir William stopped the match."

"What of it!" I broke out, hoarsely.

"Only that this beautiful Miss Warren came with Lord Dunmore's suite to Pittsburg, and Walter Butler has openly boasted he will marry her spite of Sir William or the devil himself. And here is the lady—and here comes her rash gallant tumbling after his jill!"

To hear her name in the southern wilderness, to hear these things in this place, told coarsely, told with a wink and a leer, raised such a black fury in me that I could scarce see the man before me. As for speaking, my throat closed and my breast heaved as though to burst the very straps on my pack. Oh, that I had killed Butler! I clutched my rifle and glared into the gray waste of misty trees. Somewhere out there that devil was lurking; and when I had fulfilled my trust I would seek him and end everything for good and all.

"Are you certain that Miss Warren is already in Pittsburg?" I managed to ask.

"We saw the ladies and the escort a week since," said Mount. "The trail is good for horses below Crown Gap, and they were well mounted, ay, nobly horsed, ladies and troopers, by Heaven! Was it not a splendid sight, Cade?"

"Gay and godless," replied the Weasel, buckling the straps on his pack more tightly and shifting the weight with a grunt. "Are you ready, Jack?"

Mount looked at me.

"Join us and welcome," he said, briefly. "It's safer than going alone. Our friend, Mr. Sheriff Butler, will be watching for us, and we mustn't keep the gentleman on tenter-hooks too long, eh, Cade?"

"Certainly not," said Cade; and we moved off due west, Mount leading, then Shemuel the peddler, then I, the Weasel trotting furtively in the rear.

At times the little peddler twisted his greasy neck to look back at me with an inscrutable expression that puzzled me; but he said nothing, so I only scowled at him, meaning to imply my disgust at his treachery. However, as we strung out through the forest, I quickened my pace and came up beside him, saying, "It was not very wise of you, Shemuel; the next time you come to our house you get no permit to peddle."

"Ach!" he said, spreading his fingers in deprecation, "don'd speag aboud it, Mr. Cardigan. Sir William he has giff me so many permids mitout a shilling to pay. Oh, sir, he iss a grand gendleman, Sir William, ain't he?"

"What made you betray my name and quality then, Shemuel?" I asked, curiously.

His small eyes sought mine, then dropped meekly, as he plodded on in silence. Nor could I get another word from him; so I fell back into my place, with a glance at the sun, which was still shining directly in my face.

"The Fort Pitt trail lies west by south," I suggested, over my shoulder, to the Weasel.

"There's a shorter cut to Cresap," he replied, cunningly.

"Shorter than the Pitt trail?" I asked, astonished.

"Shorter because healthier," he returned. And, answering my puzzled smile, he added, "A long life on a long trail, but there's ever a shorter cut to the gibbet!"

Mount, who had fallen back beside us, grinned at me and rubbed his nose.

"Butler will be sitting up like a bereaved catamount in the Pitt trail for us," he said. "I've no powder to waste on him and his crew. However, Mr. Cardigan, if you want to take a long shot, now's your chance to mark their hides."

He took me by the arm and led me cautiously a few rods to the left, then crouched down and parted the bushes with his hand. We were kneeling on the very edge of a precipice which I never should have seen, and over which I certainly should have walked had I been here alone. Deep down below us the Ohio flowed, a dark, slow stream, with jutting rocks on the eastern bank and a long flat sand-spit on the west.

At the point of this spit a man was standing, leaning on a rifle. It was not Butler.

"There's another fellow on that rock," whispered Mount, pointing. "Butler will be watching the slope below our camp."

"Let him watch it," observed the Weasel; "we'll be with Cresap by moonrise!"

"You can take a safe shot from here," smiled Mount, looking around at me; "but it's too far to go for the scalp."

I shook my head, shuddering, and we resumed our march, filing away into the west in perfect silence until the sun stood in mid-heaven and the heated air under the great pines drove us to the nearest water, which I had been sniffing for some time past.

Resting there to drink, I looked curiously at my three companions. Such a company I had never beheld. There was the notorious Mount, a giant in stringy buckskins, with a paw like a bear and a smooth, boyish face cut by the single, heavy crease of a scar below the right eye. With his regular features and indolent movements, he appeared to me like some overgrown village oaf, too stupid to work, too lazy to try.

Beside him squatted the little Jew, toes turned in, dirty thumbs joined pensively, musing in his red beard. His boots had left the foreign mark which I had seen the day before in the trail; the Weasel's moccasins were those of Albany make.

I examined the Weasel. Such a shrunken, serene, placid little creature, all hunting-shirt and cap, with two finely chiselled flat ears, which perhaps gave him that alert allure, as though eternally listening to some sound behind his back.

But the mouths of these three men were curiously well made, bespeaking a certain honesty which I began to believe they perhaps possessed after all. Even Shemuel's mouth, under his thin, red beard, was not the mouth of treachery, though the lips were shrewd enough, God wot!

"Well," cried Mount suddenly, "what do you think of us?"

Somewhat embarrassed, I replied politely, but Mount shook his head.

"You were thinking, what a row of gallows-birds for an honest man to flock with! Eh? Oh, don't deny it. You can't hurt my feelings, but you might hurt the Weasel's—eh, Cade?"

"I have sensitive feelings," said the Weasel dryly.

"I think you all stood by me when I was in distress," said I. "I ask no more of my friends than that."

"Well, you're a good lad," said Mount, getting to his feet and patting my shoulder as he passed me.

"Give him something to wreck his life and he'd make a rare ranger," observed the Weasel.

"Cade was in love," explained Mount soberly; "weren't you Cade?"

The weazened little man nodded his head and looked up at me sentimentally.

"Yes," went on Mount, "Cade was in love and got married. His wife ran away somewheres—didn't she Cade?"

Again the little creature nodded, looking soberly at me for sympathy.

"And then," continued Mount, "he just hunted around till he found me, and we went to hell together—didn't we, Cade, old friend?"

Two large tears stole down the Weasel's seamy cheeks. He rubbed them off with his smoky fists, leaving smears beside his nose.

"She took our baby, too," he sniffed; "you forgot that, Jack."

"So I did, so I did," said Mount, pityingly. "Come on, friends, the sun's sliding galley west, and it's a longer road to the devil than Boston preachers tell you. Come, Shemmy, old chuck, hoist that pretty nose up on both feet! Now, Mr. Cardigan!"

We marched on heavily, bearing southwest, descending the great slope of mountain and table-land which was but a vast roof, shedding a thousand streams into the slow Ohio, now curving out below us, red as blood in the kindling coals of sunset.

The river seemed but a mile distant, so clear was the air in the mountains, but we journeyed on, hour after hour, until the big yellow moon floated above the hills, and the river faded into the blue shadows of a splendid night.

Mount had thrown aside all caution now. He strode on ahead, singing a swinging air with full-chested lungs:

"Come, all you Tryon County men,

And never be dismayed,

But trust in the Lord,

And He will be your aid!"

And one by one we all took up the stirring song, singing cheerily as we marched in file, till the dark forest rang back word for word.

And I do remember Shemuel, his thumbs in his arm-pits, and cap over one eye, singing right lustily and footing it proudly beside Mount.

Suddenly a light twinkled on the edge of a clearing, then another broke out like a star in the bush, and soon all about us cabin-windows gleamed brightly and we were marching down a broad road, full of stones and stumps, and lined on either side by cultivated land and cabins enclosed in little stockades.

"Shoulder arms! Right wheel!" cried Mount; and we filed between two block-houses, and across a short bridge, and halted, grounding arms under the shadow of a squatty fort built with enormous logs.

The sentry had called out the guard, and the corporal in charge came up to us, lifting his lanthorn. He greeted Mount cheerfully, nodding and smiling at Renard also.

"Who the devil is this he-goat with red whiskers?" he demanded, illuminating Shemuel's cheerful features.

"Friend of liberty," said Mount, in a low voice. "Is Colonel Cresap in the fort, corporal?"

"No," said the corporal, looking hard at me; "he's off somewhere. Who is this gentleman, Jack?"

I looked at Mount, perhaps appealingly, wondering what he would say.

But he did not hesitate; he laid his great paw on my shoulder and said, "He's a good lad, corporal; give him a bed and a bowl o' porridge, and it's a kindness to Jack Mount you will do."

Then he held out his hand to me, and I took it.

"Good-night lad," he said, heartily. "We'll meet again to-morrow. I've a few friends to see to-night. Sleep tight to the bed and think not too much ill of this same Catamount Jack they write books about."

The Weasel sidled up and offered his small, dry hand.

"If you were ruined," he said, regretfully, "you'd make a rare wood-runner."

I thanked him uncertainly and returned Shemuel's low obeisance with an unforgiving nod.

"Pray, follow me, sir," said the corporal, with a civil bow, and I walked after him through the postern, out across the moonlit parade, and into the western barracks, where he lighted me to a tiny casemate and pointed to a door.

"We have messed, but there's some cold meat and a jug of cider for you," he said, affably. "Yonder's a bucket of water, and I'll leave this lanthorn for you. Open that door, and you'll find food and drink. Good-night, sir."

"Good-night," I said, "and pardon my importunity, but I have a message for Colonel Cresap."

"He returns to the fort to-morrow," said the soldier. Then, lingering, he asked the news from Boston and whether any more troops had been sent thither. But I did not know and he retired presently, whistling "The White Cockade," and making passes at the moonbeams with his bright bayonet.

As for me, I sat down on the bed, and slipping my sack from my shoulders, I rolled over on the blanket, meaning only to close my eyes for a minute. But dawn was shining in through the loopholes of the casemate ere I unclosed my eyes to the world again, and the drums and fifes were playing, the sun above the horizon.

Bang! went a cannon from the parapet, and, leaning out of the porthole, I saw the flag of England crawling up the halyards over my head.

I sprang out of bed, and without waiting for food, though I was half famished, I dressed hurriedly and ran out across the parade to the postern.

"How far is the Cayuga castle?" I asked the sentinel.

"About a mile up the river," he replied, adding: "It's not very safe to go there just now. The Indians have been restless these three weeks, and I guess there's deviltry hatching yonder."

"Don't they come in to the village at all?" I inquired, glancing around at half a dozen men who had gathered at the postern to watch the morning parade.

"There's a Cayuga, now," said the sentry, pointing to a short, blanketed figure squatting outside the drawbridge.

I walked across the bridge and approached the Indian, who immediately rose when he saw me, as though he expected ill-treatment, a kick perhaps. The movement was full of sad significance to me, like the cowering of a mistreated hound. Shame to those who inspire cringing in beasts! Double dishonour on those before whom men cower!

So this was the result of Cresap's coming! I saw it all in an instant; the bullying, overbearing pioneers were here to stay, backed by cannon and fort and a thousand long rifles, backed, too, by my Lord Dunmore, to play for a stake, the winning of which meant woe unspeakable to my native land.

The Indian was watching me sullenly. I held out my hand and said: "Peace, brother. I am a belt-bearer."

There was a silence. After a moment he took my hand.

"Peace, bearer of belts," he said, quietly.

"Our council fire is at Onondaga," I said.

"It burns on the Ohio, too," he replied, gravely.

"It burns at both doors of the Long House," I said. "Go to your sachems and wise men. Say to them that Quider is dead; that the three clans who mourn shall be raised up; that Sir William has sent six belts to the Cayuga. I bear them."

He stared at me for a full minute, then gravely turned north, across the cleared land, drawing his scarlet blanket over his face.

All that morning I waited patiently for Mount to come, believing that he might have some friend in the village who would give me a lodging where I could lie hid until Colonel Cresap returned to the fort.

Whether Butler had gone on to Pittsburg or whether he still lay in ambush for me below Crown Gap, I did not know.

One thing was clear: I could not remain at the fort without risk of arrest if Butler arrived in Cresap's camp with a new warrant. Every moment I tarried here in the barracks might bring danger nearer; yet, where was I to go?

Bitterly disappointed at the news that Cresap was in Pittsburg, I durst not, however, journey thither in search of him, for fear he might have started to return, and so risk passing him on the trails, of which there were seven that traversed the forest betwixt Pittsburg Fortress and Cresap's camp. And on the morrow, too, must I needs deliver my belts to the Cayugas at their castle. This was even more important than intercepting Colonel Cresap; for I might gain Cresap by argument, even though he returned here with fresh instructions from Lord Dunmore, and his mind poisoned against me by Walter Butler; but I, personally, could hope to wield no influence with the Cayugas save by what authority was invested in me through Sir William's wampum pledges.

However, spite of my dangerous predicament, I was ravenously hungry, and made out to clean my platter and bowl as many times as they cared to replenish it. Then I thanked my host, the corporal, and we shook hands in friendly fashion, he inquiring when I expected my friend Mount to return for me, and I replying that I did not know, but would make ready to join him at once.

The corporal, whose name was Paul Cloud, a New York man by birth, aided me to strap on my pack, conversing the while most agreeably, and finally, when I was prepared, he accompanied me to the parade-ground, where two companies of Virginia militia were drilling on the grass.

"My duties take me to the south stockade," he said, once more offering his hand. And again I thanked him for his hospitality so warmly that he seemed a trifle surprised.

"What friend of liberty could expect less?" he protested, smiling. "Are you a recent recruit, sir, that you marvel at the good-fellowship among us?"

"Are you, too, of that fellowship?" I exclaimed, amazed to find rebels in uniform.

He looked at me rather blankly.

"You'll scarce find a Tory in the regiment," he said, beginning to be amused at my ignorance. "As for Colonel Cresap's colonists yonder, I'll warrant them all save some two score malignants like Greathouse, the store-keeper, and the company he keeps."

His unsuspicious assumption that I was a rebel placed me in a most delicate and unhappy position. I knew not what to say nor how to explain the misunderstanding without, perhaps, seriously damaging Jack Mount, who had vouched for me—as a friend, I supposed, not as a rebel comrade.

"I am afraid I do not merit your confidence in matters touching the fellowship to which you and my friend Mount adhere," I said, stiffly, determined not to wear false colours. "I am not a patriot, corporal, and Jack Mount meant only a kindness to a brother man in distress."

Cloud cut me short with a hearty laugh.

"I guess Jack Mount knows what he is about," he said, clapping me on the shoulder. "Half our men are somewhat backward and distrustful, like you; but I'll warrant them when the time comes! Oh, I know them! It's your fawning, slavering, favour-currying Tory that I shy at! Ay, the man who snatches the very speech from between your teeth to agree with you. None o' that kind for me. I know them."

He stood there, serene, smiling, with folded arms, his kindly eyes void of all distrust; and I thought to myself that such a man must needs have at least an honest grievance to oppose his King withal.

"Well," he said, abruptly, "time is on the wing, friend. So fare you pleasantly, and—God save our country!"

"Amen," I replied, before I realized that I had acknowledged the famous patriots' greeting. He turned around to laugh significantly, then walked away towards the sallyport, swinging his hanger contentedly.

Ill-pleased with my bungling in such a delicate situation, and greatly disturbed at having implied my adherence to this fellowship of which I yet knew nothing, I stood on the parade, biting my lips in vexation and wondering where in the world to go.

The two companies of Virginia militia were marching and counter-marching at "support," halberdiers guiding, drummers and fifers leading off, and a long, lean major pacing to and fro, and watching the two captains with keen, wrinkled eyes.

The militia were mostly Virginians born, tall, stout fellows, smartly uniformed in drab and scarlet, and wearing the bugle on their cross-belts, indicating them to be light infantry. Truly, they wheeled and halted and marched and counter-marched most adroitly, carefully preserving distances and alignment; and I thought the major a martinet that he found nothing but fault with the officers and men. Certainly they paraded perfectly, their black knee-gaitered legs moving in unison, their muskets steady, their left arms swinging as one, which interested me because, in our militia of Tryon County, to swing the free arm is not allowed.

But I had no business to linger here; I felt that every minute redoubled my danger. Yet again I asked myself where under heaven I could go, and I thought bitterly of Mount for leaving me here neglected.

Plainly the first thing to be done was to get out of the fort. This I accomplished without the slightest trouble, nobody questioning me; and I shortly found myself in the road which appeared to be the main street of Cresap's village.

The fort, I now perceived, stood on a low hill in the centre of cleared ground. The road encircled the fort, then ran west through a roughly cultivated country, dotted with cabins of logs plastered over with blue clay. The circumference of the village itself appeared to be inconsiderable. Everywhere the dark circle of the forest seemed to crowd in the desolate hamlet; I say desolate, for indeed the scene was grim, even for the frontier. The whole country had a black appearance from the thousands of charred roots and stumps which choked the fields. Dead trees lay in heaps, stark patches of dead pines stood like gray spectres, blasted hemlocks, with foliage seared rusty, lined the landscape, marking the zones doomed to cultivation. These latter were girdled trees, but I saw no attempt to preserve any trees for shade around the cabins, or for shade along the fences, or for beauty.

We in Johnstown never girdled the bush without preserving rows of trees to ornament roads and fields, and this dismal destruction by fire and axe reacted on my sombre thoughts, depressing me dolefully.

Under a leaden sky, through which a pale sun peered fitfully, the blackened waste about me seemed horrible and ominous of horrors to come; the very soil in the fields was black with charcoal, through which the young corn struggled up into the fading sunshine as though strangling.

Cresap's Maryland colonists were busy everywhere with harrow and plough and axe and spade. The encircling woods echoed and re-echoed with their chopping; their voices rang out, guiding the slow ox-teams among the stumps. At intervals the crack of a rifle signalled the death of some partridge or squirrel close by.

There were men in the fields labouring half-naked at the unyielding roots; men in linen shirts and smalls, planting or weeding; men moving in distant fields, aimlessly perhaps, perhaps planning a rough home, perhaps a grave.

Women sometimes passed along the paths, urging gaunt cattle to gaunter pasture; children peered from high door-sills, hung from unpainted windows, quarrelled in bare door-yards, half seen through stockades; some chopped fire-wood, some carried water, some played in the ditches or sailed chips in the dark, slow stream that crawled out across the land towards the Ohio.

And here and there, on little knolls dotting the scene, tall riflemen stood, leaning on their weapons; sentinels mounting guard over flock and family below.

I looked at the flag on the fort; its dull folds hung dark and lifeless under a darkening sky. Below it paced a sentry to and fro, to and fro, with the gray light on his musket shining dimly.

I looked towards the black woods. They seemed to promise more protection than fort and flag; there was less gloom under their branches than under these sad cabin-roofs.

Unconsciously I began to walk towards the forest, yet with no idea what I should do there. A child here and there saluted me from stockade gates; now and then an anxious woman's face appeared at a window, watching me out of sight along the charred road. Presently I passed a double log-house, from the eaves of which dangled a green bush. The door bore a painted sign-board also, representing a large house with arms and legs like a man, at which I puzzled, but could not guess the significance.

I needed salt, having for the last week used white-wood ashes to savour my corn withal, so I entered the tavern and made known my needs to a coarse-featured, thick-set fellow, who lay in a chair smoking a clay pipe.

He rose instanter, all bows and smiles and cringing to my orders, begging me to be seated until he could find the salt sack in the cellar; and I sat down, after saluting the company, which consisted of half a dozen men playing cards by the window.

They all returned my salute, some leaning clear around to look at me; and although they resumed their game I noticed that they began talking in whispers, pausing sometimes in a shuffle to turn their eyes on me.

Presently the landlord came in with my small bag of salt, and set it on the scales with many a bow and smirk at me to beg indulgence for his delay.

"You have travelled far, sir," he said, pointedly; "there is northern mud on your hunting-shirt and southern burrs on your legging fringe. Ha! A stroke, sir! Touched, by your leave, sir! I have run the forests myself, sir, and I read as I run—I read as I run."

He was tying my sack up with grass, clumsily I thought for one who had lived as a forest-runner. But I waited patiently, he meanwhile conversing most politely. In fact, I could find no opportunity to courteously make an end to his garrulous chatter, and, ere I could refuse or prevent it, he had persuaded me to a pewter of home-brew and had set it before me, brimming with good stout foam.

"No water there, sir!" he observed, proudly; "body and froth hum like bee-hives in August! It is my own, sir, my own, barrel and malt and hops!"

I could do no less than taste the ale, and he picked up his pipe and begged the honour of sitting in my presence: all of which ceremony revealed to me that my language and bearing were not at all in concord with my buckskin and my pack, and that he was quite aware of the discrepancy.

"Perchance, sir, you have news from Boston?" he asked, with a jolly laugh.

I shook my head. The company at the table by the window had paused to listen.

"Well, well," he said, puffing his long clay into a glow, "these be parlous times, sir, the world over! And, between ourselves, sir, begging your pardon for the familiarity, sir, I have been wondering myself whether the King is wholly right."

The stillness in the room was intense.

"Doubt," said I, carelessly, "is no friend to loyalty."

I was drinking when I finished this choice philosophy, but through the glass bottom of my pewter I surprised a very cunning squint in his puffy eyes.

"Oho!" thought I, "you wish to know my politics, eh? Let us see how much you'll find out!" And I set down my pewter with a sigh of contentment and tossed him a shilling for my reckoning.

"But," he suggested, "cannot even the King be deceived by unscrupulous counsellors?"

"The King should know better than you whether his ministers be what you accuse them of being," I said, seriously.

"I meant no accusation," he said, hastily; "but I voiced the sentiments of many honest neighbours of mine."

"Sentiments which smack somewhat of treason," I interrupted, coldly.

Through the bottom of my mug again I saw he was still far from satisfied concerning my real sentiments. I listened as I drank: the card-players behind me were not playing.

"Landlord," I asked, carelessly, cutting short another argument, "what may your tavern sign mean with its house running loose on a pair o' legs?"

"It is my own name, sir," he laughed, "Greathouse! I flatter me there is some small wit in the conceit, sir, though I painted yon sign myself!"

So this was Greathouse, a notorious loyalist—this bloated lout who had been prying and picking at me to learn my sentiments? The slyness of the fellow disgusted me, and I could scarce control my open aversion, though I did succeed in leaving him with his suspicions lulled, and got out of the house without administering to him the kick which my leg was itching for.

From the corner of my eye I could see the card-players watching me from the window; it incensed me to be so spied upon, and I was glad when a turn in the scurvy, rutted road shut me out of their vision.

There were several houses just beyond me to the left; one displayed a holly-bush and wrinkled berries, a signal to me to avoid it, and I should have done so had I not perceived Jack Mount loafing in the doorway, and Shemuel seated on the horse-block, eating a dish of fish with his fingers.

From the blotched face and false smile of Greathouse to the filthy company of Shemuel was no advantage. If these two creatures were representatives of their respective causes, I had small stomach for either them or their parties. Tory and patriot, pot-licker and Jew, they disgusted me; and I returned Mount's cheery salute with a sullen nod, not pausing at the house as I passed by.

He came out into the road after me, asking what had gone amiss; and I told him he had left me at the fort without advice or counsel, and that I had quitted the barracks, not caring to be caught there by Butler and his warrant.

"Shame on you, lad, for the thought!" said Mount, angrily. "Do you think we do things by halves, Cade and I? The Weasel has been in touch with Butler's men all night, ready to warn you the moment they started for this camp! He's asleep in there, now," jerking his huge thumb towards the inn, "and I've just returned from seeing Butler well on the trail towards Pittsburg."

Mortified and ashamed at my complaint, and deeply touched by the quiet kindness of these two men who had, spite of fatigue, voluntarily set out to watch while I slept, I silently offered my hand to Mount. He took it fretfully, complaining that all the world had always misunderstood him as I had, and vowing he would never more do kindness to man or beast or good red herring!

"Small blame if the world requites your generosity as stupidly as I do," said I; whereat he fell a-laughing and drew me with him into the tavern, vowing we should wash out all bitterness in a draught of ale.

The inn, which was called "The Leather Bottle," appeared to be clean though rough. Tables and chairs were massive, hewn out of buckeye; horn instead of glass filled the tiny squares in the window frames, and a shelf ran around the tap-room just below the loopholes, whereon men could stand to fire in any direction.

Mount presented me to a young man in homespun who had been sitting by the chimney, reading a letter—a quiet, modest gentleman of thirty, perhaps, somewhat travel-stained and spotted with reddish mud, which proclaimed him an arrival from the south.

He gave me a firm, cool clasp of the hand and a curiously sharp yet not unkindly smile, promising to join us when he had finished the letter he was reading.

I had meant to tell Mount of my conversations with Corporal Cloud and with Greathouse, but hesitated because the smallness of the room would carry even a whisper to the stranger by the chimney.

Mount must have divined my intentions, for he said, in his hearty, deep-chested voice, "You may say what you please here, Mr. Cardigan, and trust this gentleman from Maryland as you trust me, I hope."

I had not caught the name of the young man from Maryland, and was diffident about asking. He looked up from his letter with a brief smile and nod at us, and we sat down beside one of the hewn buckeye tables and called upon the tap-boy for home-brew.

I began by telling Mount very frankly that he had put me in a false position as a rebel. I retailed my conversation with Corporal Cloud, how I had felt it dishonourable to accept hospitality under a misunderstanding, and how I had deemed it necessary to confess me. But this only appeared to amuse Mount, who laughed at me maliciously over his brown tankard and sucked in the frothy ale with unfeigned smacks of satisfaction.

"Tiddle—diddle—diddle! Who the devil cares!" he said. "I wish half of our patriots possessed your tender conscience, friend Michael."

I swallowed a draught in silence, not at all pleased to feel myself forced into a position whither it appeared everybody was conspiring to drive me.

"I'm loyal to the King," I said, bluntly; "and when I am ready to renounce him, I shall do so, not before."

"Certainly," observed Mount, complacently.

"Not that I care for Tory company, either," I added, in disgust, thinking of my encounter with Greathouse. And I related the affair to Mount.

The big fellow's eyes narrowed and he set his tankard down with a bang.

"A sneak!" he said. "A sly, mealy-mouthed sneak! Look out for this fellow Greathouse, my friend. By Heaven, I'm sorry he saw you! You can depend upon it the news of your arrival here will be carried to Butler. Why, this fellow, Greathouse, is a notorious creature of Lord Dunmore, set here to spy on Colonel Cresap and see that the militia have no commerce with rebel emissaries from Boston. Gad, had I not believed you trusted me, and that you would sit snug in the fort yonder instead of paying calls of state on all the Tories in town—"

He took a pull at the fresh tankard, set it down two-thirds empty, and lay back in his chair, licking his lips thoughtfully.

"How long do you stay here?" he asked.

"Until I deliver my belts—that will be to-morrow."

"I thought you wished to see Colonel Cresap, too?" he said.

"I do; he will return to-day they tell me."

Mount leaned over the table, folding his arms under his chest.

"Hark ye, friend Michael," he said. "Colonel Cresap, three-quarters of the militia, and all save a score or so of these villagers here are patriots. The Maryland pioneers mean to make a home here for themselves, Indians or no Indians, and it will be little use for you to plead with Colonel Cresap, who could not call off his people if he would."

"If he is a true patriot," I said, "how can he deliberately drive the Six Nations to take up arms against the colonies?"

"What you don't understand," replied Mount, "is that Colonel Cresap's people hold the Indians at small account. They are here and they mean to stay here, spite of Sir William Johnson and the Cayugas."

"But can't you see that it's Dunmore's policy to bring on a clash?" I exclaimed, in despair. "If Cresap is conciliatory towards the Cayugas, can't you see that Dunmore will stir up such men as Butler and Greathouse to commit some act of violence? I tell you, Dunmore means to have a war started here which will forever turn the Six Nations against us."

"Against *us*?" said Mount, meaningly.

"Yes—*us*!" I exclaimed. "If it be treason to oppose such a monstrous crime as that which Lord Dunmore contemplates, then I am guilty! If to be a patriot means to resist such men as Dunmore and Butler—ay, and our Governor Tryon, too, who knows what is being done and says nothing!—if to defend the land of one's birth against the plots of these men makes me an enemy to the King, why—why, then," I ended, violently, "I am the King's enemy to the last blood drop in my body!"

There was a silence. I sat there with clinched fist on the table, teeth set, realizing what I had said, glad that I had said it, grimly determined to stand by every word I had uttered.

"Lord Dunmore represents the King," said Mount, smiling.

"Prove it to me and I am a rebel from this moment!" I cried.

"But Lord Dunmore is only doing his duty," urged Mount. "His Majesty needs allies."

"Do you mean to say that Lord Dunmore is provoking war here at the King's command?" I asked, in horror.

The young man by the chimney stood up and bent his pleasant eyes on me.

"I have here," he said, tapping the letter in his hand, "my Lord Dunmore's commission as major-general of militia, and his Majesty's permission to enlist a thousand savages to serve under me in the event of rebellion in these colonies!"

I had risen to my feet at the sound of the stranger's voice; Mount, too, had risen, tankard in hand.

"I am further authorized," said the young stranger, coolly, "by command of my Lord Dunmore, to offer £12 sterling for every rebel scalp taken by these Indian allies of his most Christian Majesty."

At that I went cold and fell a-trembling.

"By God!" I stammered. "By the blood of man!—this is too much—this is too—"

Crash! went Mount's tankard on the table; and, turning to the young stranger with a bow, "I bring you a new recruit, Colonel Cresap," he said, quietly; "will you administer the oath, sir?"

Thunderstruck, I stared at the silent young man in his gray woollen hunting-shirt and cloth gaiters who stood there, grave eyes bent on me, tearing at the edge of his paper with his white teeth.

"Pray, be seated, Mr. Cardigan," he said, smiling. "I know you have a message for me from Sir William Johnson. I hold it an honour to receive commands from such an honourable and upright gentleman."

He drew up a heavy buckeye chair, motioning Mount and me to be seated; the tap-boy brought his tankard; he tasted it sparingly, and leaned back, waiting for me to speak.

If my speech was halting or ill-considered, my astonishment at the identity of the stranger was to blame; but I spoke earnestly and without reserve, and my very inexperience must have pleaded with him, for he listened patiently and kindly, even when I told him, with some heat, that the whole land would hold him responsible for an outbreak on the frontier.

When I had finished, he thanked me for coming, and begged me to convey his cordial gratitude to Sir William. Then he began his defence, very modestly and with frankest confession that he had been trapped by Dunmore into a pitfall, the existence of which he had never dreamed of.

"I am to-day," he said, "the Moses of these people, inasmuch as I have, at Lord Dunmore's command, led them into this promised land. God knows it was the blind who led the blind. And now, for months, I have been aware that Dunmore wishes a clash with the Cayugas yonder; but, until Sir William Johnson opened my eyes, I have never understood why Lord Dunmore desired war."

He looked at Mount as though to ask whether that notorious forest-runner had suspected Dunmore; and Mount shook his head with a sneer.

"He is a witless ass," he muttered. "I see nothing in Mr. Cardigan's fears that Dunmore means trouble here."

"*I* do," said Cresap, calmly. "Sir William is right; we have been tricked into this forest. Why, Jack, it's perfectly plain to me now. This very commission in my hands, here, proves the existence of every missing link in the chain of conspiracy. This commission is made out for the purpose of buying my loyalty to Dunmore. Can't you see?"

Mount shook his head.

Cresap flushed faintly and turned to me.

"What can I do, Mr. Cardigan? I have led these people here, but I cannot lead them back. Do you think they would follow me in a retreat? You do not know them. If I should argue with them every day for a year, I could not induce a single man to abandon the cabin he has built or the morsel of charred earth he has planted. And where should I lead them? I have nothing behind me to offer them. Virginia is over-populated. I have no land to give them except this, granted by the King—granted in spite of his royal oath, now broken to the Cayugas.

"You say the whole country will hold me responsible. I cannot help that, though God must know how unjust it would be.

"Were I to counsel the abandonment of this fort and village, Lord Dunmore would arrest me and clap me into Fort Pitt. Is it not better for me to stay here among these people who trust me? Is it not better that I remain and labour among my people in the cause of liberty?

"I can do nothing while a royal Governor governs Virginia. But if the time ever comes when our Boston brothers sound the call to arms, I can lead six hundred riflemen out of this forest, whose watchword will be, 'Liberty or Death!'"

He had grown pale while speaking; two bright scarlet patches flamed under his cheek-bones; he coughed painfully and rested his head on his hand.

"Go to your Cayugas," he said, catching his breath. "Tell them the truth, or as much of the truth as Sir William's wisdom permits. I am here to watch, to watch such crafty agents as Greathouse, and young Walter Butler, whom I met on the Pitt trail three hours since. Oh, I understand the situation now, Mr. Cardigan."

He tasted his ale once more, thoughtfully.

"Keep Sir William's Cayugas quiet if you can," he said. "I will watch Dunmore's agents that they do nothing to bring on war. I may fail, but I will do what I can. When do you speak to the Cayugas with belts?"

"At dawn," I replied, soberly.

"Poor devils," said Cresap, sadly, "poor, tricked, cheated, and plundered devils! This is their land. I should never have come had not Dunmore assured me the Cayugas had been paid for the country. And there is their great sachem, Logan, called 'The Friend of the White Man.' Greathouse has made a drunken sot of Logan, and all his family down to the tiny maid of ten. Ay, sir, I have seen Logan's children lying drunk in the road there by Greathouse's tavern—poor, little babies of twelve and ten, stark-naked, lying drunk in the rain!"

After a moment I asked why he had not expelled this fiend, Greathouse, and he replied that he had, but that Dunmore had sent him back under his special protection.

"What on earth can I do?" he repeated. "The Cayuga camp is rotten with whiskey. Their chiefs and sachems come to me and beg me to forbid the sale. I am powerless; for back of me stands Lord Dunmore in the shape of Greathouse. By God, sir, the man is a nightmare to me!"

"Why not twist his gullet?" observed Mount.

Cresap paid him no attention, and the big fellow pouted, muttering that it was a simple thing to exterminate vermin.

As we sat there, I heard the rain drumming against the horn panes in the window. The room had grown very dark.

Cresap rose, holding out his hand to me.

"Shall I administer the oath of fellowship, my friend?" he asked.

"Not yet," I replied, taking his hand.

"When you are ready, Mr. Cardigan," he said, simply. "Will you lodge here? That is well; the fort is not safe. And, if I mistake not, young Butler will be here to-morrow to search for you. He begged me to have you arrested should you be in my camp."

"I shall be at the Cayuga castle by dawn," I said.

"And after that?" inquired Mount. "You are not going to leave us, are you, lad?"

"I have my message to deliver to Sir William," I answered, earnestly; "and," I added, "truly, I do not believe there is anything on earth that can prevent my delivering my message, nor retard my returning and slaying this frightful enemy of mankind, Walter Butler."

CHAPTER XI

The rain fell thickly until midnight, and kept me listening to the double roll of the drops along the shingles. I lay in my blanket under the roof, and slept when the rain ceased, but awoke before dawn, listening to the wind roaring around the eaves. Pale clouds, scudding low, alternately hid and revealed the purple roof of sky on which stars hung trembling like drops of dew.

My landlord, Timothy Boyd, was already astir below, and presently he came up the ladder with a dish of porridge for me—a kindness, indeed, for I had thought to set out for the Cayuga castle on an empty stomach. He also brought me a bowl of coffee, the berries of which he said had been sent for my use by Colonel Cresap. I drank the coffee thankfully, sitting on my mattress of balsam tips. Then, by lanthorn-light, I dressed me, taking only bullet-pouch, powder-horn, and rifle, and bearing the six belts in the bosom of my shirt. I left my pack with Boyd, commending it to his care; and the rugged old man nodded placidly, bidding me rest assured of its safety.

"There is foul company at the 'Greathouse Inn,'" he said, as we descended the ladder to the tap-room below. "Greathouse received four guests an hour ago. Mount bade me warn you, sir. He said you would understand."

I understood at once. Butler, Wraxall, Toby Tice, and the fourth member of the band had arrived in Cresap's camp. But I cared not; I was about to accomplish my mission under their four noses, and live to balance my account with them later.

"Is Mount sleeping?" I asked.

The old man laughed.

"I have never seen him sleep," he said. "I know him well, but I have never seen him asleep. He is out yonder, somewhere, prowling."

"And Shemuel?—and Cade Renard?" I inquired.

"Shemuel is on his way to Pittsburg; Renard mouses with Mount. Is your rifle loaded, sir? There be foul company at the other inn. This night, too, did Greathouse make nine savages drunk with spirits. Have a care that they cross not your path, young man; for, drunk, your Indians go blind like rattlesnakes in September, and like those serpents, too, they strike without warning. Have a care, sir!"

"I wish you knew the Indians as well as I do," said I, smiling. "I fear none of them, save the Lenni-Lenape, and these I fear only because I have never known them. I think the whole world can be tamed with kindness."

Boyd shook his gray head, watching me in silence.

A brisk southwest wind was singing through the pines as I stepped out-of-doors and peered cautiously about. There was nothing stirring save the wind and the unseen leaves in the forest. I primed my rifle and sheltered the pan under the hollow of my arm, then stole forth into the starlit road.

To gain the river, whence the trail ran northward to the Cayuga camp, I was obliged to pass the fort, and consequently the "Greathouse Inn." But I had no fear at this hour o' morning, and I trotted on along the stump fence like a cub-fox in his proper runway, until the first curve in the road brought me to Greathouse's inn.

Shutters were drawn and bolted over every window, but candle-light streamed through loopholes in the tap-room, and I could hear men singing within and tapping on bowls with spoons:

"My true love is old Brown Bess."

Nosing the house delicately, I perceived odours of cooking, of rum toddy, and of tobacco smoke. Clearly Butler's company were supping after their long jog on the back trail from Fortress Pitt.

Satisfied that all was safe, I had silently begun skirting the road ditch shadowed by the fence, when a dark heap, which I had taken for a stump in the road, moved, rolled over, and moaned.

I stopped, frozen motionless. After a moment's wary reconnoitring, I crept forward again along the ditch, eyes fastened on the dim shape ahead, a human form lying in the black shadows of the road.

When I came closer I understood. At my feet, in a drunken stupor, sprawled a young Cayuga girl, limbs plastered with mud, body saturated and reeking with the stench of spirits. Her black hair floated in a pool of rain which spread out reflecting stars. One helpless hand clutched the mud.

I lifted the little thing and bore her to the shadow of the fence; but here, to my amazement, lay a drunken squaw, doubtless her mother, still clinging to an empty bottle; and, along the ditch and fence, flung in beastly, breathing heaps, I counted seven more barbarians, old and young, from the infant of ten to the young buck of twenty, all apparently of the same family, and all in a sodden swoon.

This was the work, then, done by a single agent of my Lord Dunmore, Royal Governor of Virginia!

Like torpid snakes they lay there, glistening in the grass, the children naked, the mother in rags, breathing out poison under the stars. The very air of morn sweated rum; candle-light from the loopholes fell across the bodies, flung limply on the grass.

There was nothing I could do for these victims of Greathouse; no aid within my power to give them. Heartsick, I turned away, and, quickening my steps, passed swiftly down the muddy trail, hastening to mend my pace ere dawn should find me missing at the council-fires burning for me on the dark Ohio.

There were no lights in the fort as I passed; the flag-staff stood out bare against the stars. On the epaulement above the outer trench something moved, probably a sentry.

But ere I reached the Ohio the eastern sky had turned saffron, through which stars still twinkled; and the drifted mist-banks lay heaped far out across the river, so I could not see the water, and must follow its course along the edge of this phantom stream, whose current was vapour and whose waves of piled-up clouds rolled noiselessly under the stars.

No birds fluted from the mist; even the winds had blown far away somewhere into the gray morning. But the Cayuga trail was broad and plain, and I took it at a wolf-trot, thoughtfully reading its countless signs by the yellow dawn as I went along, marks of white men, marks of moccasins, imprint of deer and cattle, trail of rabbit and following fox, and the hand-like traces of rambling raccoons. On, on, north upon the broad Cayuga trail, while through the brightening woods sleep fled with the mist and the world awoke around me. Land and river roused with breathing and sigh and scarce-heard stir; through earth and water the pulse of life fluttered and beat on, timed for the moment by the swift rhythm of my flying feet.

And now a thread of blue smoke, drawn far down the trail, set my nostrils wide and quivering; a flare of blinding yellow turned the world into gold; I had met the sun at the Cayuga camp; the tryst had been kept, thanks to the Lord!

Dark, uncertain forms loomed up in the eye of the sun, tall groups that never moved as I drew nigh; men who stood motionless as the pines where the council-fire smoked and flashed like a dull jewel in the sun.

"Peace!" I said, halting, with upraised hand. "Peace, you wise men and sachems!"

"Peace!" repeated a low voice. "Peace, bearer of belts!"

I moved nearer, head high, yet seeing in a blur, for the rising sun blinded me. And when I came to the edge of the fire, I drew a white belt of wampum from my bosom, and, passing it through the smoke, held it aloft, flashing in the sun, until every chief and sachem had sunk down into their blankets, forming a half-circle before me.

A miracle of speech came to me like the breath of my body; easy, sober, flowing words followed. I spoke as I had never dared hope I might speak. Forgotten phrases, caressing idioms, words long lost flew to aid me, yet not so fast that they crowded, stumbling and choking speech.

As I spoke, sight slowly returned to my dazzled eyes. I saw the sachems' painted masks, the totems of three tribes repeated on blanket and lodge, the Cayuga pipe-symbol hanging from the lodge posts, the witch-drum swinging under a bush, where ten stems had been peeled ivory white. Behind all this I saw the green amphitheatre of trees, blue films of smoke floating from unseen lodges, and over all the radiance of sunrise painting earth and sky with pale fire.

Belt after belt I passed through the fragrant birch-smoke; I spoke to them as Sir William had spoken to Quider with three belts, and my words were earnest and pitiful, for my heart was full of tenderness for Sir William and for these patient children of his, these lost ones, so far from the doors of the Long House.

The ceremony of condolence was more than a ceremony for me; with eager sympathy I raised up the three stricken tribes; I sweetened the ashes of the eternal fires; I cleared evil from the Cayuga trail, and laid the ghastly ghosts of those who stood in forest highways to confront the fifth nation of the great confederacy.

"Oonah! Oonah!" whimpered the wind in the pines, but I stilled the winds and purified them, and I cleansed the million needles of the pines with a belt and an enchanted word.

The last belt was passed, flashing through the smoke; the chief sachem of the Cayugas rose to receive it, a tall, withered man of the Wolf tribe, painted and draped in scarlet. His dim, wrinkled eyes peered at me through the smoke.

For a long time the silence was broken only by the rustling flames between us; then the old man placed the belt at his feet, straightened up, and spoke feebly:

"*Brother.* It is to be known that the Six Nations never meet in council when mourning, until some brother speaks as you have spoken.

"*Brother.* We mourn great men dead. Our Father, through you, our Elder Brother, has purified our fires, our throats, our eyes. Where the dead sat among us, three tribes have you raised up.

"*Brother.* Listen attentively!"

Behind him from the great painted lodge nine Indian boys entered the fire-circle and stood proudly with folded arms and heads erect. And the old sachem, in his scarlet robes, laid his shaking hand on each youth as he passed, always turning his aged eyes to peer at me as he repeated in his feeble, cracked voice of a child:

"We acquaint you that one of our sachems, called Quider, is dead; we raise up this boy in his place and give him the same name."

And, after each boy had been named from one of the dead Cayugas, he gave me a string of wampum to confirm it, while the chant of condolence rose from the seated chiefs and sachems, a never-ending repetition of brave histories, and prophecy of brave deeds from the beginning of all things through the stilled centuries into the far future locked in silence.

Hour after hour I stood with bent head and arms folded on my breast. Sometimes I prayed as I stood, that evil be averted from these wards of our King; sometimes I grew hot with anger at the men who could so vilely misuse them.

Dreaming there amid the scented birch-smoke, the chant intoning with the mourning pines, sombre visions took shape within my brain. I could not lay these ghosts, awful spectres of ruin and death crowding around a pallid, flabby, toothless creature of silks and laces, my Lord Dunmore, smirking at Terror wearing the merciless mask of Butler.

Around me the ceremony of condolence seemed to change to the sinister and grotesque Honnonouaroria or Dream Feast, with its naked demons hurling fire-brands; I swayed where I stood, then stumbled back out of the scented smoke which had nigh stupefied me. I opened my eyes dizzily. My ears were ringing with the interminable chant:

"Sah-e-ho-na,

Sah-e-ho-na."

I crossed my arms and waited, careful to keep out of the sweet smoke which had stolen away my senses and set me dreaming of horrors.

The sun hung above the pines; a slender purple cloud belted it, a celestial belt in pledge of promised storms, gathering somewhere beyond the world's green rim.

I watched the cloud growing; the sun died out through a golden smother from which plumes of vapour swept over the heavens, thickening till all the sky was covered with painted fleece. And, as I watched the storm's banners hanging from midheaven, the chant ended, and, in silence, three chiefs arose and moved towards me through the smoke. One by one they spoke to me, naming themselves: Yellow Hand, Tamarack, the ancient sachem robed in scarlet, and lastly the war-chief, Sowanowane.

It was Tamarack who continued:

"*Brother*. We have heard. The Three Ensigns of our nation have heard."

(*A belt.*)

"*Brother*. We all bear patiently this great wrong done us by Colonel Cresap. We are patient because Sir William asks it of us. But under these tall pines around us lie hatchets, buried deep among the pine-trees' roots. See, brother! Our hands are clean. We have not dug in the earth for hatchets."

(*A belt of seven.*)

"*Brother*. We pray that our elder cousin, Lord Dunmore, will remove from us his agent Greathouse. We pray that no more spirits be sold to the Cayugas. We pray this because we cannot resist an offered cup. We pray this because we drink—and die. It is death to us, death to our children, death to our nation."

(*A black belt.*)

"*Brother*. Bear our belts to our Father, Sir William Johnson, and to our elder cousin, Lord Dunmore. Intercede with them that they may heed our prayers."

(*A bunch of three.*)

"*Brother*. Depart in health and honour, bearing these sacred belts of peace—"

A frightful scream cut him short; scream after scream arose from the hidden lodges.

The assembly, gathered at the sanctuary of the council-fire, rose in a body, blankets falling to the ground, paralyzed, silent, while the horrid screaming rose to an awful, long-drawn shriek.

Somebody was coming—somebody plodding heavily, shrieking at every step, nearer, nearer—an old woman who staggered out into the circle of the council, dragging the limp body of a young girl.

"Nine!" she gasped. "Nine slain at dawn by Greathouse! Nine of the family of Logan! Look, you wise men and sachems! Look at Logan's child! Dead! Slain by Greathouse! Nine! Mother and children lie by the road, slain as they slept; slain, sleeping the poisoned sleep of Greathouse! Dead! Dead! Dead!"

Stupidly the sachems stared at the naked corpse, flung on the blankets at their feet. The scented smoke curled over the murdered child, blowing east and south.

Dry-eyed, sick with horror, I moved forward, and the stir seemed to arouse the sachems. One by one they looked down at the dead, then turned their flashing eyes on me. I strove to speak; I could not utter a sound.

The old sachem bent slowly and took a handful of ashes from the cold embers. Then, rubbing them on his face, he flung down every belt I had given him and signed to me to do the same with the belts delivered to me.

When I had dropped the last belt, Yellow Hand made a sign, and every chief, save Sowanowane, the war-chief, covered his head with his blanket. I fixed my eyes on the war-chief, dreading lest he hurl a red belt at my feet. But he only bent his head, bidding me depart with a gesture. And I went, stunned by the calamity that had come as lightning to blast the work I had done.

As I dragged myself back, heart-broken, leaden-footed, behind me I heard the death-wail rising in the forest, the horrid screaming of women, the fierce yelps of the young men, the thump! thump! thump! of the drum, dry and sharp as a squirrel's barking.

Utterly overwhelmed by the catastrophe, I wandered aimlessly into the forest and sat down. Hour after hour I sat there, and my shocked senses strove only to find some way to avert the consequences of the deed wrought by Greathouse. But the awful work had been done; the Gordian knot cut; my Lord Dunmore's war had begun at last, in deference to my Lord Dunmore's desires, and in accordance with his plans. Now, Cresap must fight; now, the Six Nations would rise to avenge the Cayugas on the colonies; now, the King of England would have the savage allies he desired so ardently, and the foul pact would be sealed with the blood of Logan's children!

"Never, by God's grace!" I cried out, in my agony; and I stumbled to my feet, my head burning and throbbing as though it would burst. The woods had grown dim; the day was already near its end—this bloody day! this sad day which had dawned so hopefully for all! Suddenly I began running through the forest, gnashing my teeth and cursing the King whom such servants as Dunmore served.

"Faster, oh, faster," I muttered, as I ran; "faster to slay this devil, Butler, who has counselled Greathouse to this deed!"

Again and again I stumbled and fell, but rose, not feeling the bruises, crazed to do vengeance on the wicked men who outraged God by living. But truly, vengeance is the Lord's, and He alone may repay, nor was I the instrument He chose for His wrath. Swiftly I ran, swifter ran His purpose; for, behold! a man rose up in my path and held me fast, a soldier, who shook me and shouted at me until my senses, which had sped before me with my vengeance, halted and returned. Presently I began to understand his words, and listened.

"Are ye mad?" he repeated. "Can't ye see the savages across the river following? The Cayugas are loose on the Ohio! It is war!"

Other men crept up and dropped into cover behind the trees around me; some were colonial soldiers, some farmers from the camp, some hunters in wool shirts and caps. All at once I saw Colonel Cresap come out into the trail close by, and, when he perceived me, he cried: "Logan's children have been murdered by Greathouse! The Cayugas are swarming on the Ohio!"

I hastened to his side and begged him to let me carry his promise to the Cayugas that Greathouse should be punished, and that his colonists would retire. He shook his head.

"Greathouse has fled to Pittsburg," he said. "I cannot retire with my people because they would not follow me. It is too late, Mr. Cardigan; Dunmore has sprung his trap. Ha! Look at that!" And he turned and shouted out an order to the soldiers around.

A dozen savages, naked to the waist, were fording the Ohio between us and the settlement. Already the soldiers were running through the woods along the river to head them off, and Cresap started after them, calling back for those who remained to guard the trail in the rear. Then a rifle went bang! among the trees; another report rang out, followed instantly by twenty more in a volley.

Down a low oak ridge, close by, I saw an Indian tumbling like a stone till he fell with a splash into a mossy hollow full of rain-water and dead leaves. After him bounded a hunter in buckskins, long knife flashing.

"Cresap!" I panted, "don't let him take that scalp! Have your men gone mad? You can stop this war! It is not too late yet, but a scalp taken means war— God in heaven! a scalp means war to the death!"

"Don't touch that scalp!" roared Cresap, hurrying towards the ranger, who was kneeling on one knee beside the dead Cayuga. "Nathan Giles! Do you hear me? Let that scalp alone, you bloody fool!"

It was too late; the ranger squatted, wrenching the scalp free with a ripping sound, just as Cresap ran up in a towering rage.

"They take ours," remonstrated the ranger, tying the ghastly trophy to his belt by its braided lock of hair; "I guess I have a right to scalp my own game!" he added, sullenly.

Cresap turned to me with a gesture of despair.

"You see," he said; and walked slowly away towards the river, where the rifles were ringing out shot on shot across the shoals below the shallow camp-ford on the edge of the roaring riffles.

So now, at last, Lord Dunmore's war had begun without hope of mediation. Too late now for embassy of peace, too late for truce or promises or the arbitration of fair speech. There is nothing on earth to compensate for a scalp taken, save a scalp taken in return. I had failed—failed totally, and without hope of retrieving failure. The first attempt must be the last. A scalp had been taken. My mission was at an end.

Ay, ended irrevocably now, for all around me firelocks and rifles were banging; the woods swam in smoke; the war-yelp sounded nearer and nearer; the white cross-belts of the soldiers glimmered through the trees.

Too miserable to shun danger, I sat down on a stone in the trail, my head in my hands, rifle across my knees. Presently a soldier who had been standing near me, firing across the river, fell down with a grunt and lay there flat on his back.

I stared at him stupidly, not realizing that the man was dead, though out of his head crawled a sluggish, dark red stream, dropping steadily onto the withered leaves. It was only when a swift, dusky shape came creeping out of the brush towards the dead man that I came to my senses and dropped behind the stone I had been resting on, barely in time, too, for a bullet came smack! against my rock, and after it, bounding and yelping, flew an Indian. He was on me ere I could fire, one sinewy fist twisted in my hair, but his knife snapped off short on my rifle-stock, and together, over and over we rolled, down a ravine among the willows, clawing, clutching, strangling each other, till of a sudden my head struck a tree, crack! And I knew nothing after that until the cool rain beating in my face awoke me. I lay very still, listening.

Somebody near by was trying to light a fire; I smelled the flint and the glowing tinder. Another odour hung heavily in the moist night air, the wild, rank scent of savage men, strong and unmistakable as the odour of a dog-fox in March.

I began to move noiselessly, working my head around so that I might see. My head was aching heavily; I could scarce stir it. At length I raised myself on my hands, and saw the spark from a flint fly into a ball of dry moss and hang there like a fire-fly until the tiny circle of light spread slowly into a glow, ringed with little flames that ate their way through the tinder-moss.

A tufted head bobbed down beside the flame; unseen lips blew the fire into a sudden blaze which brightened and flashed up, throwing ruddy shadows over bush and earth.

Then I saw that I lay on a hill-top in the rain, with dark, shaggy bushes hedging me. And under every bush crouched an Indian, whose dusky, half-naked body glistened with paint, over which rain-drops stood in brilliant beads.

Leggings, clouts, sporrans, and moccasins were soaked; the slippery, wet buckskins glistened like the hides of serpents; fringes, beaded belts, and sheaths shone as tinted frost sparkles at sunrise.

In the luminous shadow of the bushes I saw brilliant eyes watching me as I dragged myself nearer the fire. The red embers' glow fell on steel blades of hatchets, bathing them with blood-colour to the hilts.

Once, when I attempted to sit up, an arm shot out of the shadow, making the sign for silence; and mechanically I repeated the signal and laid my head down again on the cool, wet ground.

All night I lay, perfectly conscious, beside the Cayuga fire, yet not alarmed, although a prisoner.

The Cayugas knew me as a belt-bearer from Sir William; they could not ill-treat me. Tamarack, Yellow Hand, and Sowanowane would vouch for me to this party of young men who had taken me. I had harmed none of them; I had barely defended my life when attacked.

As I lay there on the windy hill-top, through the rain across the dim valley I could see the battle-lanthorns hanging on Cresap's fort, and I could hear the preparations for a siege, the hammering and chopping and cries of teamsters, the rumble of wagons over the drawbridge, the distant challenge of guards, the murmur and dulled tumult of many people hastening urgent business.

Beside me, on their haunches, crouched my captors, alert and curious, dressing their ears to the distant noises. There were eleven of them, young men with all their lives before them in which to win the eagle's plume; eleven lithe, muscular young savages, stripped to the belt, well oiled, crowns shaved save for the lock, and every man freshly painted for war. All wore the Wolf.

He who had taken me, now carried my pouch and powder-horn and bore my rifle. A scalp hung at his yellow girdle, doubtless the scalp of the soldier who had been shot beside me in the trail. I could smell the pomatum on the queue.

I spoke to them calmly, and at first they seemed inclined to listen, appearing surprised at my knowledge of their tongue. But they would reply to none of my questions, and finally they silenced me with sullen threats, which, however, did not disturb me, as I knew their sachems must set me free.

My head ached a great deal from the blow I had suffered; I was willing enough to lie quietly and watch the lights in the fort through the slow veil of falling rain; and presently I fell asleep.

The hot glare of a torch awoke me. All around me crowded masses of savages, young and old, women and youths and children. The woods vomited barbarians; they came in packs, moving swiftly, muttering to each other, and hastening as though on some pressing affair.

Women near me were digging a hole, and presently came a strong young girl, bearing a post of buckeye, and set it heavily in the hole, fitting it while the others stamped in the mud around it with naked feet.

The main crowd, however, had surged down into a hollow to the left, and, as I lay on the ground, watching the shadowy, retreating throng, of a sudden came three Indians driving before them a white man, arms tied, bloodless face stamped with horror indescribable.

As he passed the fire where I lay, I thought his starting eyes met mine, but he staggered on without speaking, down into the darkness of the hollow. I knew him. He was Nathan Giles, who had taken the first scalp in Lord Dunmore's war.

Shuddering, I sat up, turning my head towards the gloom below. There was not a sound. I waited, straining eyes and ears. My heart drummed on my ribs. I caught my breath and clinched my hands.

Without the slightest warning, the black pit below burst out in a sheet of light, shining on a thousand motionless savages; and in the centre of the glare I saw a naked figure, bound to a tree, twisting through smoke-shot flames.

For a second only the scene wavered before me; then I gripped my temples and pressed my face down into the cool, wet grass. Awful cries rang in my ears; the garrison at the fort heard them, too, for they fired a cannon, and I heard distant drums beating to arms.

"Thus you are to die," repeated the Indians beside me. "Thus you will die here on this hill at dawn. Thus you will suffer in plain view of the fort! This for the death of Logan's children!"

And one to another they said: "He is weeping. He is a woman. He will weep thus when he burns."

I heard them, but what they said left my mind numbed and cold. For me there was no meaning in their words; none at all. My ears shrank from the awful cries, now piercing the very clouds above me, hell's own solo accompanied by the ceaseless, solemn murmur of the rain.

Into my nostrils crept the stench of burnt flesh; it grew stronger and stronger. Silence fell, soothed by the whispering rain; then out of the night came the dull noise of many people stirring. They were coming!

As I rose, a Cayuga youth seized me and threw me heavily against the post I had seen the woman embed in the mud. I fought and strained and writhed, but they tied me, bracing me up stiff against the wet stake, trussed like a fowl for basting.

Around me the crowd was thickening; hundreds of tongues loaded me with insults; thrice a young girl reached out and struck me in the face.

They had begun piling wood around my feet, and stuffing the spaces full of dry moss, but before the heap reached my knees they decided to face me towards the fort, so the work accomplished had to be undone, my bonds loosened and retied, and my body shifted to breast the south.

Through the falling rain I saw morning lurking behind the eastern hills, and I cursed it, for the shock and terror had driven me out of my senses. I remember hearing a voice calling on God, but for a long time I did not know the voice was mine. It was only when the same young girl who had struck me lighted a splinter of yellow pine and thrust it through my arm that my senses returned. I opened my eyes as from a swoon, seeing clearly the faces around me, red under the torches. And foremost among those in front stood Tamarack in his scarlet robes, just as I had seen him at dawn through the smoke of the sacred fire. Now my voice came back, seeking my lips; my parched tongue moved, and I called on Tamarack to hear me, but he shook his head, though I adjured him by the belts I had borne and received, by the sanctuary of the council-fire whose smoke I had sweetened, and by the three tribes I had raised up.

"Lies," he said; "you come not from Johnstown! Your belts are lies; your words lie; your tongue is forked! You come from Cresap! Cresap shall see how you can die for him!"

"I speak the truth!" I cried out, in my agony. "I am a belt-bearer! I have laid the ghosts of your slain ones! Who dares send my spirit to teach your dead that you betray their ashes?"

There was a dead silence. Presently somebody in the throng said, distinctly: "If he speaks the truth, let him go. We honour our dead." And other voices repeated:

"We honour our dead."

"He lies," said Tamarack.

"I speak truth!" I groaned. "If you honour your dead, if you honour those whom I have raised up in their places, free me, brothers of the Cayugas!"

"Free him!" cried many.

For a space the throng was quiet, then a distant movement to my left made me turn hopefully. The throng wavered, parted, opened, and a white man came elbowing his way to the stake.

He whispered to Tamarack; the aged sachem stretched out his arm, making a mystic sign.

Eagerly the white man turned and looked at me, and I cried out with rage and horror, for I was face to face with Walter Butler.

He spoke, but I scarcely heard him urging my death.

Terror, which had gripped me, gave place to fury, and that in turn left me faint but calm.

I heard the merciless words in which he delivered me to the savages; I heard him denounce me as a spy of Cresap and an agent of rebels. Then I lost his voice.

I was very still for a while, trying to understand that I must die. The effort tired me; lassitude weighed on me like iron chains. To my stunned mind death was but a word, repeated vaguely in the dark chamber of life where my soul sat, listening. Thought was suspended; sight and hearing failed; there was a void about me, blank and formless as my mind.

"'THEY'VE HIT HIM,' SAID MOUNT, RELOADING HASTILY"

Presently I became conscious that things were changing around me. Lights moved, voices struggled into my ears; forms took shape, pressing closer to me. An undertone, which I had heard at moments through my stupor, grew, swelling into a steady whisper. It was the ceaseless rustle of the rain.

A torch blazed up crackling close in front. My eyes opened; a thrill of purest fear set every sense a-quiver. Amid the dull roar of voices, I heard women laughing and little children prattling. Faces became painfully distinct. I saw Sowanowane, the war-chief, thumb his hatchet; I saw Butler, beside him, catch an old woman by the arm. He told her to bring dry moss. It rained, rained, rained.

They were calling to me from the crowd now; everywhere voices were calling to me: "Show us how Cresap's men die!" Others repeated: "He is a woman; he will scream out! Logan's children died more bravely. Oonah! The children of Logan!"

Butler watched me coolly, leaning on his rifle.

"So this ends it," he said, with his deathly grimace. "Well, it was to be done in one way or another. I had meant to do it myself, but this will do."

I was too sick with fear, too close to death, to curse him. Pain often makes me weak; the fear of pain sickens me. It was that I dreaded, not death. Where my father had gone, I dared follow, but the flames—the thought of the fire—

I said, faintly, "Turn your back to me when I die; I have much pain to face, Mr. Butler; I may not bear it well."

"No, by God! I will not!" he burst out, ferociously. "I'm here to see you suffer, damn you!"

I turned my head from him, but he struck me in the face so that my mouth was bathed in blood; twice he struck me, crying: "Listen! Listen, I tell you!" And, planting himself before the stake, he cursed me, vowing that he could tear me with his bared teeth for hatred.

"Know this before they roast you," he snarled; "I shall possess your pretty baggage, Mistress Warren, spite of Sir William! I shall use her to my pleasure; I shall whip her to my feet. I may wed her, or I may choose to use her otherwise and leave her for Dunmore. Ah! Ah! Now you rage, eh?"

I had hurled my trussed body forward on the cords, struggling, convulsed with a fury so frantic that the blood sprayed me where the bonds cut.

Indians struck me and thrust me back with clubs, for the great post at my back had been partly dragged out of its socket by my frenzy, but I did not feel the blows; I fixed my maddened eyes on Butler and struggled.

But now the sachems were calling him sharply, and he backed away from me as the circle surged forward. Again the girl came out, bearing a flaming fagot. She looked up at me, laughed, and thrust the burning sticks into the moss and tinder which was stacked around me. A billow of black smoke rolled into my face, choking and blinding me, and the breath of the flames passed over me.

Twice the rain quenched the fire. They brought fresh heaps of moss, laughing and jeering. Through the smoke I saw the fort across the valley, its parapets crowded with people. Jets of flame and distant reports showed they were firing rifles, hoping perhaps to kill me ere the torture began. It was too far. The last glimpse of the fort faded through the downpour; a new pile of moss and birch-bark was heaped at my feet.

This time the girl was thrust aside and a young Indian advanced, waving a crackling branch of pitch-pine, roaring with flames. As he knelt to push it between my feet, a terrific shout burst from the throng—a yell of terror and amazement. Through the tumult I heard women screaming; in front of me the crowd shrank away, huddling in groups. Some backed into me, stumbling among the fagots; the young Indian let his blazing pine-branch fall hissing on the wet ground and stood trembling.

And now into the circle stalked a tall figure, coming straight towards me through the sheeted rain—a spectre so hideous that the cries of terror drowned his voice, for he was speaking as he came on, moving what had once been a mouth, this dreadful thing, all raw and festering to the bone.

Two blazing eyes met mine, then rolled around on the cringing throng; and a voice like the voice of the dead broke out:

"I am come to the judgment of this man whom you burn!"

"Quider!" moaned the throng. "He returns from the grave! Oonah! He returns!"

But the unearthly voice went on through the whimper of the crowd:

"From the dead I return. I return from the north. Madness drove me. I come without belts, though belts were given.

"Peace, you wise men and sachems! Set free this man, my brother!"

"Quider!" I gasped. "Bear witness."

And the dead voice echoed, hollow:

"Brother, I witness."

Trembling fingers picked and plucked and tugged at my cords; the bonds loosened; the sky spun round; down I fell, face splashing in the mud.

CHAPTER XII

How I managed to reach the fort, I never knew. I do not remember that the savages carried me; I have no recollection of walking. When the gate lanthorn was set that night, a sentry noticed me creeping in the weeds at the moat's edge. He shot at me and gave the alarm. Fortunately, he missed me.

All that evening I lay in a hot sickness on a cot in the casemates. They say I babbled and whimpered till the doctor had finished cupping me, but after that I rambled little, and, towards sunrise, was sleeping.

My own memories begin with an explosion, which shook my cot and brought me stumbling blindly out of bed, to find Jack Mount firing through a loophole and watching me, while he reloaded, with curious satisfaction.

He guided me back to my cot, and summoned the regiment's surgeon; between them they bathed me and fed me and got my shirt and leggings on me.

At first I could scarcely make out to stand on my legs. From crown to sole I ached and throbbed; my vision was strangely blurred, so that I saw things falling in all directions.

I think the regiment's surgeon, who appeared to be very young, was laying his plans to bleed me again, but I threatened him if he laid a finger on me, and Mount protested that I was fit to fight or feast with any man in Tryon County.

The surgeon, saying I should lie abed, mixed me a most filthy draught, which I swallowed. Had I been able, I should have chased him into the forest for that dose. As it was, I made towards him on wavering legs, to do him a harm, whereupon he went out hastily, calling me an ass. Mount linked his great arm in mine, and helped me up to the parapet, where the Virginia militia were firing by platoons into the forest.

The freshening morning was lovely and sweet; the west winds poured into me like wine. I lay on the platform for a while, peering up at the flag flapping above me on its pine staff, then raised up on my knees and looked about.

Bands of shadow and sunlight lay across the quiet forests; the calm hills sparkled. But the blackened clearing around the fort was alive with crawling forms, moving towards the woods, darting from cover to cover, yet always advancing. They were Cresap's Maryland riflemen, reconnoitring the pines along the river, into which the soldiers beside me on the parapet were showering bullets.

It was pretty to watch these Virginia militia fire by platoon under instructions of a tall, young captain, who lectured them as jealously as though they were training on the parade below.

"Too slow!" he said. "Try it again, lads, smartly! smartly! 'Tention! Handle—cartridge! Too slow, again! As you were—ho! When I say 'cartridge!' bring your right hand short 'round to your pouch, slapping it hard; seize the cartridge and bring it with a quick motion to your mouth; bite off the top down to the powder, covering it instantly with your thumb. Now! 'Tention! Handle—cartridge! Prime! Shut—pan! Charge with cartridge—ho! Draw—rammer! Ram—cartridge! Return—rammer! Shoulder—arms! Front rank—make ready! Take aim—fire!"

Bang! bang! went the rifles; the parapet swam in smoke. Bang! The second rank fired as one man, and the crash was echoed by the calm, clear voice: "Half-cock arms—ho! Handle—cartridge! Prime!"

And so it went on; volley after volley swept the still pines until a thundering report from the brass cannon ended the fusillade, and we leaned out on the epaulement, watching the riflemen who were now close to the lead-sprayed woods.

The banked cannon-smoke came driving back into our faces; all was a choking blank for a moment. Presently, through the whirling rifts, we caught glimpses of blue sky and tree-tops, and finally of the earth. But what was that?—what men were those running towards us?—what meant that distant crackle of rifles?—those silvery puffs of smoke fringing the entire amphitheatre of green, north, east, west—ay, and south, too, behind our very backs?

"Down with your drawbridge!" thundered the officer commanding the gun-squad. I saw Cresap come running along the parapet, signalling violently to the soldiers below at the sallyport. Clank! clank! went the chain-pulleys, and the bridge fell with a rush and a hollow report, raising a cloud of amber dust.

"My God!" shouted an officer. "See the savages!"

"See the riflemen," mimicked Mount, at my elbow. "I told Cresap to wait till dark."

Along the parapets the soldiers were firing frenziedly; the quick cannon-shots shook the fort, smothering us with smutty smoke. I had a glimpse, below me, of Cresap leading out a company of soldiers to cover the flight of his riflemen, and at intervals I saw single Indians, kneeling to fire, then springing forward, yelping and capering.

A tumult arose below. Back came the riflemen pell-mell, into the fort, followed by the militia company at quick time. The chains and pulleys clanked; the bridge rose, groaning on its hinges.

It was now almost impossible to perceive a single savage, not only because of the rifle-smoke, but also because they had taken cover like quail in a ploughed field. Every charred tree-root sheltered an Indian; the young oats were alive with them; they lay among the wheat, the bean-poles; they crouched behind manure-piles; they crawled in the beds of ditches.

"Are all the settlers in the fort?" I asked Mount, who was leaning over the epaulement, waiting patiently for a mark.

"Every man, woman, and child came in last night," he said. "If any have gone out it's against orders, and their own faults. Ho! Look yonder, lad! Oh, the devils! the devils!" And he fired, with an oath on his lips.

A house and barn were suddenly buried in a cloud of pitchy vapour; a yoke of oxen ran heavily across a field; puffs of smoke from every rut and gully and bush showed where the Indians were firing at the terrified beasts.

One ox went down, legs shot to pieces; the other stood bellowing pitifully. Then the tragedy darkened; a white man crept out of the burning barn and started running towards the fort.

"The fool!" said Mount. "He went back for his oxen! Oh, the fool!"

I could see him distinctly now; he was a short, fat man, bare-legged and bare-headed. As he ran he looked back over his shoulder frequently. Once, when he was climbing a fence, he fell, but got on his legs again and ran on, limping.

"They've hit him," said Mount, reloading hastily; "look! He's down! He's done for! God! They've got him!"

I turned my head aside; when I looked for the poor fellow again, I could only see a white patch lying in the field, and an Indian slinking away from it, shaking something at the fort, while the soldiers shot at him and cursed bitterly at every shot.

"It's Nathan Giles's brother," said a soldier, driving his cartridge down viciously. "Can't some o' you riflemen reach him with old Brown Bess?"

The report of Mount's rifle answered; the Indian staggered, turned to run, reeled off sideways, and fell across a manure-heap. After a moment he rose again and crawled behind it.

And now, house after house burst into black smoke and spouts of flame. Through the spreading haze we caught fleeting glimpses of dark figures running, and our firelocks banged out briskly, but could neither hinder nor stay the doom of those poor, rough homes. Fire leaped like lightning along the pine walls, twisting in an instant into a column of pitchy smoke tufted with tongues of flame. Over the whirling cinders distracted pigeons circled; fowls fluttered out of burning barns and ran headlong into the woods. Somewhere a frightened cow bellowed.

Under cover of the haze and smoke, unseen, the Indians had advanced near enough to send arrows into the parade below us, where the women and children and the cattle were packed together. One arrow struck a little girl in the head, killing her instantly; another buried itself in the neck of a bull, and a terrible panic followed, women and children fleeing to the casemates, while the maddened bull dashed about, knocking down horses, goring sheep and oxen, trampling through bundles of household goods until a rifleman shot him through the eye and cut his throat.

Soldiers and farmers were now hastening to the parapets, carrying buckets and jars of water, for Cresap feared the sparks from the burning village might fall even here. But there was worse danger than that: an arrow, tipped with blazing birch-bark, fell on the parapet between me and Mount, and, ere I could pick it up, another whizzed into the epaulement, setting fire to the logs. Faster and faster fell the flaming arrows; a farmer and three soldiers were wounded; a little boy was pierced in his mother's arms. No sooner did we soak out the fire in one spot than down rushed another arrow whistling with flames, and we all ran to extinguish the sparks which the breeze instantly blew into a glow.

I had forgotten my bruises, my weakness, and fatigue; aches and pains I no longer felt. The excitement cured me as no blood-letting popinjay of a surgeon could, and I found myself nimbly speeding after the fiery arrows and knocking out the sparks with an empty bucket.

Save for the occasional rifle-shots and the timorous whinny of horses, the fort was strangely quiet. If the women and children were weeping in the casemates, we on the ramparts could not hear them. And I do not think they uttered a complaint. We hurried silently about our work; no officers shouted; there was small need to urge us, and each man knew what to do when an arrow fell.

All at once the fiery shower ceased. A soldier climbed the flag-pole to look out over the smoke, and presently he called down to us that the savages were falling back to the forest. Then our cannon began to flash and thunder, and the militia fell in for volley-firing again, while, below, the drawbridge dropped once more, and our riflemen stole out into the haze.

I was sitting on the parapet, looking at Boyd's inn, "The Leather Bottle," which was on fire, when Mount and Cade Renard came up to me, carrying a sheaf of charred arrows which they had gathered on the parade.

"I just want you to look at these," began Mount, dumping the arrows into my lap. "The Weasel, he says you know more about Indians than we do, and I don't deny it, seeing you lived at Johnstown and seem so fond of the cursed hell-hounds—"

"He wants you to read these arrows," interrupted the Weasel, dryly; "no, not the totem signs. What tribes are they?"

"Cayuga," I replied, wondering. "Cayuga, of course—wait!—why, this is a Seneca war-arrow!—you can see by the shaft and nock and the quills set inside the fibres!"

"I told you!" observed the Weasel, grimly nudging Mount.

Mount stood silent and serious, watching me picking up arrow after arrow from the charred sheaf on my knees.

"Here is a Shawanese hunting-shaft," I said, startled, "and—and this—this is a strange arrow to me!"

I held up a slender, delicate arrow, beautifully made and tipped with steel.

"That," said Mount, gravely, "is a Delaware arrow."

"The Lenape!" I cried, astonished. Suddenly the terrible significance of these blackened arrows came to me like a blow. The Lenni-Lenape had risen, the Senecas and Shawanese had joined the Cayugas. The Long House was in revolt.

"Mount," I said, quietly, "does Colonel Cresap know this?"

The Weasel nodded.

"We abandon the fort to-night," he said. "We can't face the Six Nations—here."

"We make for Pittsburg," added Mount. "It will be a job to get the women and children through. Cresap wishes to see you, Mr. Cardigan. You will find him laying fuses to the magazine."

They piloted me to the casemates and around the barracks to the angle of the fort, where a stockade barred the passage to the magazine. The sentry refused us admittance, but Corporal Cloud heard us and opened the stockade gate, where we saw Cresap on his hands and knees, heaping up loose powder into a long train. He glanced up at us quietly; his thin, grave face was very pale.

"Am I right about those arrows?" he asked Mount.

"Mr. Cardigan says there's a Seneca war-arrow among 'em, too," replied Mount.

Cresap's keen eyes questioned me.

"It's true," I said. "The Senecas guard the western door of the Long House, and they have made the Cayugas' cause their own."

"And the eastern door?" demanded Cresap, quickly.

"The eastern door of the Long House is held by our Mohawks and Sir William Johnson," I said, proudly. "And, by God's grace! they will hold it in peace."

"Not while Walter Butler lives," said Cresap, bitterly, rising to his feet and turning the key of the magazine. "Throw that key into the moat, corporal," he said. "Mount, get some riflemen and roll these kegs of powder into the casemates."

"You know," he observed, turning to me, "that we abandon the fort to-night. It means the end of all for me. I shall receive all the blame for this war; the disgrace will be laid on me. But let Dunmore beware if he thinks to deprive me of command over my riflemen! I've made them what they are—not for my Lord Dunmore, but for my country, when the call to arms peals out of every steeple from Maine to Virginia."

Cloud lifted his hat. "Please God, those same bells will ring before I die," he said, serenely.

"They'll ring when the British fleet sights Boston," observed the Weasel.

"They'll ring loud enough for Harrod and Dan Boone to hear 'em on the Kentucky," added Mount.

I said nothing, but looked down at the powder trail, which led into the magazine through a hole under the heavy double door. Cresap pushed the heap of powder with his foot.

"Ah, well," he said, "it's liberty or death for all save human cattle—liberty or death, sure enough, as the Virginian puts it."

"Patrick Henry is in Pittsburg," began Mount; but Cresap went on without heeding him: "Patrick Henry has given my riflemen their watchword; and the day that sees them marching north will find that watchword lettered on the breast of every hunting-shirt—Liberty or Death."

Turning his clear eyes on me, he said, "You will be with us, will you not, sir?"

"My father fought at Quebec," I answered, slowly.

"And my father yonder at Fort Pitt, when it was Fort Duquesne, not under Braddock, but in '58, when the British razed the French works and built Fortress Pitt on the ruins. What of it? Your father and my father fought for England. They were Englishmen. Let us, who are Americans, imitate our fathers by fighting for America. We could do their memory no truer honour."

"I have not made up my mind to fight our King," I answered, slowly. "But I have determined to fight his deputy, Lord Dunmore."

"And all his agents?" added Mount, promptly.

"You mean Dunmore's?" I asked.

"The King's," said Cloud.

"Yes, the King's, too, if they interfere with my people!" I blurted out.

"Oh, I think you will march with us when the time comes," said Cresap, with one of his rare smiles; and he led the way out of the stockade, cautioning us to step clear of the powder.

"Cut a time-fuse for the train and bring it to me at the barracks," he said to Cloud; and, saluting us thoughtfully, he entered the casemates, where the women and children were gathered in tearful silence.

I heard him tell the poor creatures that their homes had gone up in smoke; that, for the moment, it was necessary to retire to Fort Pitt, and that each family might take only such household implements and extra clothing as they could carry in their arms.

There was not a whimper from the women, only quiet tears. Even the children, looking up solemnly at Cresap, bravely stifled the sobs of fear that crowded into every little throat.

The day wore away in preparation for the march. I had nothing to prepare; I had lost my rifle and ammunition when a prisoner among the Cayugas, and my spare clothing and provisions when Boyd's Inn was burned. Fortunately, Boyd had buckled on my money-belt for safe keeping, and the honest old man delivered it to me, condoling with me for the loss of my clothing and food; and never a word of complaint for his own loss of home and bed and everything he owned in the world, nor would he accept a shilling from me to aid him towards a new beginning in life.

"I am only seventy-three," he said, coolly; "when these arms of mine cannot build me a home, let them fashion my coffin!"

And he picked up his long rifle and walked away to help load the ox-teams with powder, ball, and provisions.

One thing that Mount told me aroused my anger and contempt: there was now not a Tory left among Cresap's people; all had fled when Greathouse fled, proving clearly that, if all had not aided in the slaughter of Logan's children, they at least had been informed of the plot and had probably been warned that the murderous deed would be laid at Tory doors.

Towards dusk our scouts began to come in, one by one, with sad stories concerning the outlying settlements and lonely farms. One had seen a charred doorway choked with dead children, all scalped; another, lying hid, saw a small war-party pass with eighteen fresh scalps, three of them taken from women and little girls; a third vowed that the Oneidas had joined in, and he exhibited a moccasin that he had found, as proof. But when I saw the moccasin, I knew it to be Mohawk, and it troubled me greatly, yet I did not inform Cresap, because I could not believe our Mohawks had risen.

At nine o'clock the postern was opened quietly, and the first detachment of riflemen left the fort, stealing out into the starlight, weapons at a trail. When the scouts returned to say that the coast was clear, the column started in perfect silence. First marched a company of Maryland riflemen; after them filed the ox-teams, loaded with old women and very small children, the wagons rolling on muffled wheels; then followed a company of Virginia militia, and after them came more ox-teams piled with ammunition and stores, and accompanied by young women and grown children. The rear was covered by the bulk of the militia and riflemen, with our brass cannon dragged by the only horse in the ill-fated town.

When the rear-guard had disappeared in the darkness, Cresap, Mount, Cade Renard, and I bolted the gates, drew up the drawbridge, locked it, and dropped the keys into the moat. Then Cresap and Mount ran across the parade towards the magazine, while we tied a knotted rope to the southern parapet and shook it free so that it hung to the edge of the counter-scarp below.

Presently Mount came hurrying back across the parade and up the scarp to where we stood, bidding us hasten, for the fuse was afire and might burn more quickly than we expected.

Down the rope, hand over hand, tumbled the Weasel, and then Mount motioned me to go. But just as I started, up above my head in the darkness I heard the flag flapping; I paused, then stepped towards the pole.

"The flag," I said. "You have forgotten it—"

"It's only the damned British flag!" said Mount. "Down the rope with you, lad! Do you want to keep us till the fort blows up?"

"I can't leave the flag," I said, doggedly.

"To hell with it!" retorted Mount, fiercely, and pushed me towards the rope.

"Let me alone!" I flashed out, backing towards the flag-pole.

"Oh, go to the devil your own way," growled Mount, but I saw he did not leave the rampart while I was lowering the flag and ripping it from the halyards.

Cresap came rushing up the scarp as I stuffed the flag into the breast of my hunting-shirt.

"Are you mad?" he cried. "Down the rope there, Cardigan! Follow him for your life, Jack Mount!"

And down I scrambled, followed by Mount and Cresap, and we all ran as though the Six Nations were at our heels.

In the dark we passed a rifleman who scampered on ahead to pilot us, and after ten minutes at top speed we joined the rear-guard and fell in with the major, panting.

"A slick trick you played," grunted Mount, "with that bloody British flag."

"It was mine, once," I retorted, hotly.

"Oh, you would blow us all up for it, eh?" asked the big fellow, pettishly. "Well, you be damned, and your flag, too!"

His voice was blotted out in a roar which shook the solid forest; a crimson flame shot up to the stars; then thunderous darkness buried us.

Half-smothered cries and shrieks came from the long convoy ahead, but these were quickly silenced, the frightened oxen subdued, and the column hastened on into the night.

"Now that the fort's exploded, look out for the Iroquois," said Mount, steadying his voice with an effort.

Cresap had given me a rifle. I halted to load it, then ran on to join Mount and Renard. We plodded on in silence for a while. Presently Mount asked me what I meant to do in Pittsburg.

"I mean to see Lord Dunmore," I replied, quietly.

Mount pretended to fear for his Lordship's scalp, but I was in no humour for jesting, and I said no more.

"What are you going to do to old Dunmore?" urged the big fellow, curiously.

"See here, my good man," said I, "you are impertinent. I am an accredited deputy of Sir William Johnson, and my business is his."

"You need not be so surly," grumbled Mount.

"You've hurt his feelings," observed the Weasel, trotting at my heels.

"Whose? Mount's?" I asked. "Well, I am sorry. I did not mean to hurt you, Mount."

"That's all very well, but you did," said Mount. "I've got feelings, too, just as much as the Weasel has."

"No, you haven't," said the Weasel, hastily. "I'm a ruined man, and you know it. Haven't I been through enough to give me sensitive feelings?"

Mount nudged me. "He's thinking of his wife and baby," he said. "Talk to him about them. He likes it. It harrows him, doesn't it, Cade?"

"It hurts fearful," replied the Weasel, looking up at me hopefully.

"You had a lovely wife, didn't you, Cade?" inquired Mount, sympathetically.

"Yes—oh yes. And a baby girl, Jack—don't forget the baby girl," sniffed the Weasel, trotting beside me.

"The baby must be nigh fifteen years old now, eh, Cade?" suggested Mount.

"Sixteen, nigh sixteen, Jack. The cunning little thing."

"What became of her?" I asked, gently.

"Nobody knows, nobody knows," murmured the Weasel. "My wife left me and took my baby girl. Some say she went with one of Sir Peter Warren's captains, some say it was an admiral who charmed her. I don't know. She was gone and the fleet was gone when they told me."

He laid his hard little hand on my arm and looked up with bright eyes.

"Since that," he said, "I've been a little queer in my head. You may have noticed it. Oh yes, I've been a little mad, haven't I, Jack?"

"A little," said Mount, tenderly.

"I have not noticed it," said I.

"Oh, but I have," he insisted. "I talk with my baby in the woods; don't I, Jack? And I see her, too," he added, triumphantly. "That proves me a little mad; doesn't it, Jack?"

"The Weasel was once a gentleman," said Mount, in my ear. "He had a fine mansion near Boston."

"I hear you!" piped the Weasel. "I hear you, Jack. You are quite right, too. I was a gentleman. I have ridden to hounds, Mr. Cardigan, many a covert I've drawn, many a brush fell to me. I was master of fox-hounds, Mr. Cardigan.

None rode harder than I. I kept a good cellar, too, and an open house—ah, yes, an open house, sir. And that was where ruin came in, finding the door open—and the fleet in the downs."

"And you came home and your dear wife had run away with an officer from Sir Peter Warren's ships—eh, Cade, old friend?" said Mount, affectionately.

"And took our baby—don't forget the baby, Jack," piped the Weasel.

"And if you could only find the man you'd slit his gullet, wouldn't you, Cade?" inquired Mount, dropping one great arm over the Weasel's shoulder.

"Oh, dear, yes," replied the Weasel, amiably.

I had been looking ahead along the line of wagons, where a lanthorn was glimmering. The convoy had halted, and presently Mount, Cade Renard, and I walked on along the ranks of resting troops and loaded wains until we came to where the light shone on a group of militia officers and riflemen. Cresap was there, wrapped in his heavy cloak; and when he perceived me he called me.

As I approached, followed naïvely by Mount and Renard, I was surprised to see a tall Indian standing beside Cresap, muffled to the chin in a dark blanket.

"Cardigan," said Cresap, "my scouts found this Indian walking ahead in the trail alone. He made no resistance, and they brought him in. He seems to be foolish or simple-minded. I can't make him out. You see he is unarmed. What is he?"

I glanced at the tall, silent Indian; a glance was enough.

"This man is a Cayuga and a chief," I said, in a low voice.

"Speak to him," said Cresap; "he appears not to understand me. I speak only Tuscarora, and that badly."

I looked at the silent Cayuga and made the sign of brotherhood. His dull eyes regarded me steadily.

"Brother," I said, "by the cinders on your brow you mourn for the dead."

"I mourn," he replied, simply.

"A son?"

"A family. I am Logan."

Shocked, I gazed in pity on the stern, noble visage. So this was Logan, the wretched man bereft of all his loved ones by Greathouse!

I turned quietly to Cresap.

"This is the great Cayuga chief, Logan, whose children were murdered," I said.

Cresap turned a troubled face on the mute savage.

"Ask him where he journeys."

"Where do you journey, brother?" I asked, gently.

"I go to Fort Pitt," he answered, without emotion.

"To ask justice?"

"To ask it."

"God grant you justice," I said, gravely.

To Cresap I said, "He seeks justice at Fort Pitt from Lord Dunmore."

"Bid him come with us," replied Cresap, soberly. "He may not get justice at Fort Pitt, but there is a higher Judge than the Earl of Dunmore. To Him I also look for the justice that men shall deny me on earth."

I took Logan by the hand and led him into a space behind the wagons. Here we waited in silence until the slow convoy moved, and then we followed as mourners follow a casket to the grave of all their hopes.

Hour after hour we journeyed unmolested; the stars faded, but it was not yet dawn when a far voice cried in the darkness and a light moved, and we knew that the warders of the fortress were hailing our vanguard at the gates of Pittsburg.

CHAPTER XIII

I awoke in a flood of brightest sunshine which poured over the walls of my chamber and bathed the sweet lavender-scented sheets on my bed.

The water in the washing-bowl reflected the sunlight, and the white ceiling above me wavered with golden-netted ripples. A gentle wind moved the curtains to and fro, a brisk breeze, yet saturated with the disquieting taint of unknown odours, odours of a town whose streets are thronged with strange people. Those bred within the strip which runs along the borders of a wilderness find the air of towns confusing, as a keen hound, running perdu, enters a vast runway where a thousand pungent trails recross.

Reconnoitring the room from my sunny couch, I poked my sun-warmed muzzle out of the sheets, sniffing and inspecting the unfamiliar surroundings. Then I cautiously stretched my limbs, and finding myself supple and sound, leaped lightly onto the rag-carpet in my bare feet and stood looking out of the window.

This lodging whither Mount and Renard had piloted me when our convoy passed the ramparts of Fortress Pitt, was an inn called the "Virginia Arms," a most clean and respectable hostelry, though sometimes suspected as a trysting-place for rebels. James Rolfe, a Boston man, was our host, a thin-edged, mottled, shrewd-eyed fellow, whose nasal voice sounded continually through the house from tap-room to garret, in sarcastic comment on his servants. I heard him now as I stood at the window:

"Oh, Hiram, yew dinged sack o' shucks, the gentleman in 27 is knocking on the floor! Jonas! A pot o' small-beer for the gentleman in 17! Land o' Goshen, yew run like a frost-nipped spider! The gentleman in 6 is waiting for his wig! What's that? Waal, yew go right 'round tew the hairdresser's and tell him tew bring that wig! Hey? Yes, the wig dressed a-lar-Francy! Don't set there rubbing yewr chin like a dumned chipimunk, Simon, while Mister Patrick Henry is waiting for them queue ribbons from Corwin's. Eh? You fetched 'em? Well, why in the name o' Virginy can't you say so? Clean them buckles for the gentleman in 20, yew darned clam!"

His penetrating, half-fretful, half-humorous voice died away towards the stables in the rear, and I parted the dainty curtains and peeped out into the streets of Pittsburg. Our inn stood on the corner of the town square, opposite the village green. Across the square rose some well-made barracks, painted white; I could see red-coated sentinels posted at the gates and walking their beats along the west stockade. A few handsome mansions faced the square, two churches and a public house completed the north side of the quadrangle. East and west shops and smaller houses lined the streets; the green bush hung in the sunshine, the barber's basin swung and glittered among a forest of gayly painted sign-boards.

But the people! Lord, how they trooped by, passing, repassing, threading the alleys, streaming across the green, soldiers in scarlet and buff, militia in brown and green, sober townsmen dressed as we dress in Johnstown, old gentlemen in snuffy smalls and big coats with broad cuffs and silver buttons, the butcher, bared of arm and head, with the wind fluttering his apron, the baker, white and sallow as his own muffins, ostlers, shop-keepers, chapmen, men in fustian shouldering pick or shovels, drovers in blue smocks carrying looped snake-whips. Now comes one in musty wig and steel spectacles, bulging umbrella under one arm, inquisitive nose buried in a Maryland newspaper—a schoolmaster!—or do I not know the breed. Anon, I see some tall, awkward riflemen, loitering idly before signs or gawking up at the county court-house, where a gilt fish swims in the sky.

Sometimes a horseman, in the uniform of Lord Dunmore's guards, trots by gracefully, with a smile and low salute for his friends and a stare at the fresh-cheeked maids who steal demurely along, basket on arm, to rifle the market for an early squash or a bunch o' green pease.

Many citizens I notice are reading the newspapers as they walk; many men meet and stop and converse eagerly, looking behind them at times as though an eavesdropper might be near. With bell and clapper the vender of ginger and cocoa-nut pushes his cart before him; peddlers, bending under Delaware baskets or leather trays, stand in the street, calling their wares: "Colours for the races!" "Tablets!" "Pencils!" "Chains!" "Cock-gaffs—steel or brass!" "Gentlemen's fancy!" "Dog-bells!" "Ferret-bits!"

A barefoot child in rags offers bills for the bull-baiting and for the Theatre Royal, crying in a thin, monotonous voice: "Race-week bills, my lords and gentlemen! Race-week bills for the Theatre Royal, my lady! Plays to be played—'The Beau's Stratagem,' 'Beggar's Opera,' 'The Devil to Pay,' 'The Fair Penitent,' 'The Virgin Unmasked!' and a variety of farces and merry pantomimes—and the bills are only a penny, my lady! The tickets to be had at Jamison's Coffee-House at four shillings—the bill to be had of me, Rosalie, child of Tanner Bridewell—only a penny!"

The pitiful voice in the sunshine touched me; I opened the window and tossed a shilling to the child, then hid behind the curtains while she kissed her palm at my window.

The winding of a brass horn brought me out of my concealment to peep again down into the street, where people were flocking around a public crier, who stood on a horse-block blowing his horn.

"Attention! Attention!" he cried, unfolding a paper, and presently commenced to read his news to the crowd:

"By permission of the Right Honourable Earl of Dunmore, Governor of Virginia! Four days' sport on Roanoke Plain. The Colonial Club offering prizes of £100 and £50; the Richmond Club offering two purses of £50. Attention! Sport on the Roanoke; an even and delightsome plain, most sweet and pleasant. To-day the Nobleman's and Gentleman's Purse of £50, free for any horse except Doctor Connolly's *Scimitar*, who won the plate last season. Second, a silver cup worth £12. Tuesday, County Subscription Purse of £50. No person will erect a booth or sell liquor without subscribing £2 to expenses of races.

"Gentlemen fond of fox-hunting will meet at the Buckeye Tavern by daybreak during the races.

"God save the King!"

He folded his paper, picked up his horn, and stepped down from the horse-block. After a little while I heard his horn again, sounding at the north angle of the square, and his strident voice, announcing the races, came fitfully on the wind.

I turned back into the room and began my toilet. How strange to find this town, undisturbed in its rural pleasures, busy about its own affairs, while scarce a night's journey to the north the frontier was in ashes, and the dead lay in the charred embers of their own door-sills!

How strange to look out on the peace of these sunny streets, with the cinders of Cresap's camp still clinging to my hunting-shirt; with my own blood caking the sore on my arm where a Cayuga child had thrust a lighted pine-splinter into my flesh! Strange!—ay, astonishing that these people here behind their fortress, their block-housen, their earthworks and stockades, should forget those who dwelt beyond the gates, wresting the dark soil, inch by inch, from the giant pines of the wilderness.

With a knife which Cresap had given me, I sat down to scrape the mud and filth from my hunting-shirt and to pick out the burrs and docks which clotted the fringe on my leggings.

Sombre thoughts filled me; I had a hard rôle to play before Lord Dunmore; I had a harder rôle to act before Silver Heels, if she were still here in Pittsburg.

It gave me no pleasure to find myself so near her. The attitude she had assumed towards me that last night in Johnstown had hurt enough to leave a scar. But when scars appear, wounds are healed; and so was mine. It was true, I had never loved her as men love sweethearts. Her sudden and amazing appearance as a woman had aroused my curiosity; her popularity and beauty my jealousy. It was hurt pride that tempered me when the playfellow I had tolerated and protected and tormented at my pleasure, tormented, tolerated, and finally ignored me.

I did not love her when I aroused her contempt with my courtship of Mrs. Hamilton. I did not love her when I followed her to the pantry to bully her into according me her respect once more. It was vanity: vanity when I sulked because young Bevan took her from me; vanity when I assailed the pretty ears of Mrs. Hamilton with callow cynicisms and foolish wit. I scorned myself for having deceived my own heart with the fancy that I had ever loved my cousin Silver Heels.

Now that the demon Butler had been exorcised by Sir William, and now that Sir William wished for my union with Silver Heels, and had promised me the means to maintain her as her rank required, I understood plainly that I did not love her in that way. She was only my playfellow; she had never been anything else. I meant to see her and tell her so; I meant to ask her forgiveness for offending her; I meant to seek her friendly confidence once more, to warn her that she should not tarry here in these troublous times, but return at once to Johnson Hall, where Sir William could protect her, not only from the savages, but also from that creature whose every breath of life was an offence to his Creator.

Doubtless, Silver Heels would go with me. Dunmore would be obliged to provide our escort; indeed, his Lordship would be glad enough to see me leave his town of Pittsburg ere I had finished with my business here.

I stood smoothing the thrums on sleeve and legging, somewhat ashamed to seek audience with anybody in such attire. I had money in my belt, enough to purchase clothing suitable to my station, but it was time that I lacked, not means or inclination.

I had laid my hand on the knob, intent on seeking breakfast below, and was about to open the door, when somebody knocked. It was Saul Shemuel, smiling and folding his hands over his belly—a greasy spectacle in sooth for a hungry stomach—and I scowled and bade him state his business quickly in the devil's name.

"Goot-day and greeding, sir," said the peddler, bowing and rubbing himself against the door like a cat. "Gott save our country, Mr. Cardigan. You are oxpected to join the gendlemens in 13, sir. Mr. Mount begs you will hold no gonversation mit strangers hereabouts, nor entertain no one until he sees you, sir."

"Who are you, anyway, Shemuel?" I asked, curiously.

"A peddler, Mr. Cardigan—only a poor peddler," he protested, spreading out his grimy fingers and peeping up cunningly. "Pray, do not look as if you knew me, sir, should you see me abroad in the streeds, sir. But if you wish to speag to me, please to buy a buckle; one buckle if I shall seek you here, two buckles if I am to follow you in the streed, sir, three buckles if you would seek me in my lodgings, Mr. Cardigan. I live at the 'Bear and Cubs Tavern,' sir, on the King's Road."

"Very well," I said, somewhat amused at the idea of my pining for Shemuel's company under any circumstances. "Where is room 13, Shemuel? Eh? Oh, you appear to know this inn. Here's sixpence for you, Shemmy. That's right, cut away now!"

"If I might speak von vort, sir," he began, hoisting his basket on his back and looking slyly up at me as I passed him.

"Well?" I said, impatiently.

"I haf often seen you, sir, at Johnson Hall."

"Well?"

"And I haf also sold gilt chains to Miss Warren."

"Well!" I demanded, sharply.

"Miss Warren iss here in Pittsburg, sir," he ventured.

"I supposed so," I said, coldly; "but that does not interest me."

"Maybe," he said, spitefully, "you don'd know somedings?"

"What things?"

"Miss Warren weds mit Lord Dunmore in July."

He was gone like a slippery lizard before I could seize him. He vanished around the corridor ere my thoughts assembled from the shock that had routed them. Now they began to rally pell-mell, and my cheeks burnt with scorn and anger, though I could not truly credit the preposterous news. That unformed child thrown into the arms of a thing like Dunmore! What possessed all these rakes and roués to go mad—stark, staring, March-mad—over my playfellow? What did an Earl want of her—even this bloodless Dunmore with his simper and his snuff and his laces and his bird's claws for fingers? What the devil had enchanted him to seek her for his wife; to make her Countess of Dunmore and the first lady in Virginia?

And Silver Heels, had she sold her beauty for the crest on this man's coach? Had she bargained her innocence for the rank that this toothless conspirator and assassin could give her? How in God's name could she endure him? How could she listen without scorn, look at him without loathing? An old man, at least a man who might be a rotten forty or a patched and mended sixty, with his painted face and his lipless line of a mouth—horror!—if she had seen him grinning and gumming his wine-glass as I had seen him—or sprawling on the carpet, too drunk to clean his own chin!

Agitated and furious I paced the hallway, resolving to seek out my lady Silver Heels without loss of time or ceremony, and conduct her back to the nursery where the little fool belonged.

Countess, indeed! I'd bring her to her senses! And wait!—only wait until Sir William should learn of this!

Somewhat comforted at the thought of the Baronet's anger and dismay, I pocketed my excitement and began to search for the door of room 13, where, according to Shemuel, I was expected. I had forgotten the peddler's directions; besides the house was unexplored ground for me, and I wandered about several corridors until I noticed a pleasant-faced gentleman watching me from the stairs.

He doubtless noticed my perplexity, for he bowed very courteously as I passed him and made some polite observation which required a civil answer; and before I was fully aware of it, he had invited me to a morning cup with him in the tap-room.

This was a trifle too friendly on short acquaintance; Shemuel's warning to hold my tongue and avoid strangers instantly occurred to me. On my guard, I prayed him to pardon my declining, with many compliments and excuses, which I heaped upon him to avoid the seeming discourtesy of refusing him my name.

He was truly a most pleasant gentleman, a stranger in Pittsburg, so he said, and bearing very gracefully the title of captain and the name of Murdy. He appeared most anxious to present me to his friend, Doctor Connolly, in the tap-room; but I begged permission to defer the honour and left him, somewhat nonplussed, on the stairway.

In a few moments I found room 13, and knocked. And, as I was ushered in, I glanced back at the stairway, and was annoyed to see my friendly Captain Murdy peering at me through the balustrade.

It was Corporal Paul Cloud who admitted me, greeting me respectfully, and immediately closing and locking the door. The room was large; a table stood in the centre, around which were gathered Jack Mount, Cade Renard, Jimmy Rolfe, the landlord of the "Virginia Arms"; my former host, Timothy Boyd; and another man whom I had never before seen. Cresap was not there, but, in a corner, wrapped to the eyes in his dark blanket, sat the bereaved Cayuga chief, Logan, staring at the floor.

The company were at breakfast, and when I approached to greet them, Mount jumped to his feet and gave me a warm handclasp, leading me to a chair beside the only man whom I did not know.

I saluted the stranger, and he bowed silently in return. He appeared to be a man of forty, elegantly yet soberly dressed, wearing his own dark hair, unpowdered, in a queue—a gentleman in bearing, in voice, in every movement—a thoroughbred to the tips of his smooth, well-ordered fingers. A pair of gold-rimmed spectacles which he wore had been pushed up over his forehead; now he lowered them to the bridge of his nose again, and looked at me gravely and searchingly, yet entirely without offence. The scrutiny of certain men sometimes conveys a delicate compliment.

Mount, in a very subdued voice, asked permission to present me, and the gentleman bowed, saying he knew my name from hearing of my father.

As for his name, I think anybody in the colonies—ay, in London, too—would know it. For the gentleman beside whom I had been placed was the famous Virginian, Patrick Henry, that fiery orator who had bade our King mark well the lives of Cæsar and Charles the First to profit by their sad examples: and when the cries of "Treason!" dinned in his ears, had faced a howling Tory Legislature with the contemptuous words: "If this be treason—make the most of it!"

Sideways I admired his delicate aquiline nose, his firm chin, the refinement of every muscle, every line.

He drank sparingly; once he raised his glass to me and I had the honour of drinking a draught of cinnamon cold-mulled with him.

There was little conversation at table. Mr. Henry asked Boyd about the burning of Cresap's village, and the brave old man told the story in a few, short phrases. Once he spoke to Cloud about the militia. Presently, however, he left the table and sat down by Logan; and for a long time we watched them together, this sensitive, high-bred orator, and the sombre savage, burying his grief in the dark ruins of a broken heart. Their blended voices sounded to us like the murmur of the deep thrilling chords of a harp, touched lightly.

Mount came over beside me, and, resting his massive head on his hands, spoke low, "Cresap was arrested last night by Doctor Connolly, Dunmore's deputy, and is to be relieved of his command."

"Is Doctor Connolly Dunmore's agent?" I asked, quietly. "Then he's here in the house now."

"I know it," said Mount. "He and his fawning agent, Murdy, are watching the inn to learn who is here. By-the-way, my name is anything you please, if they ask you. It won't do for the Weasel and me to flaunt our quality in Pittsburg town. There was once a fat Tory judge walking yonder on the highway, and—well, you know, moonlight and mischief are often abroad together. Curious, too, that this same fat judge should have come to grief; for he once issued some valentines to me and the Weasel."

I looked up sharply; Mount blinked mildly as a kitten who is filled with milk.

"Why did they arrest Cresap?" I asked.

"Why? Oh, Lord, the town is full o' people blaming Dunmore for this new war. There was like to be a riot yesterday when one of Cresap's runners came in with news of the rising. So Dunmore, frightened, called in Connolly and Murdy and they went about town swearing that Dunmore was innocent and that the wicked Cresap did it all. And now Connolly has had Cresap arrested, and he swears that Dunmore will make an example of Cresap for oppressing the poor Indians. There's your Tory Governor for you!"

Horrified at such hypocrisy, I could only gasp while Mount shrugged his broad shoulders and went on:

"But this rattlesnake, Dunmore, has bitten off more than he can poison. Logan's here to demand justice on Greathouse. And now you are here to protest in Sir William's name. Oh, it's a fine pickle Dunmore will find himself swimming in."

"When is Logan to have an audience with Dunmore?" I asked.

"To-night, in the fortress. And, Mr. Cardigan, I took the liberty of announcing to the Governor's secretary, Gibson, that an envoy from Sir William Johnson had arrived with a message for Lord Dunmore. So you also are to deliver your message to the Governor of Virginia in the hall to-night."

"But," said I, puzzled, "does Dunmore expect a messenger from Sir William?"

"Haven't you heard from Shemuel?" asked Mount. "I told him to tell you that Dunmore wants to marry the beautiful Miss Warren, who's cutting such a swath here. He sent his offer by runner to Sir William, and, being a Tory, an Earl, and Governor of Virginia, he naturally expects Sir William will throw the poor girl at his head!"

I took Mount's arm in my hand and tightened my grip till he groaned.

"Mark you, Mount," I said, choking back my passion, "this night my Lord Dunmore will learn some things of which he is ignorant. One of them is that my kinswoman, Miss Warren, is betrothed to me!"

The big fellow's eyes had grown wider and bluer as I spoke. When I finished he gaped at me like a dying fish. Suddenly he seized my hand and wrung it till the whole table shook, and Mr. Henry looked at us in displeasure.

"Tell the Weasel," said Mount, gently. "Tell him, lad. It will please him. He's full o' sentiment; he'll never breathe a word, Mr. Cardigan; the Weasel's a gentleman. He dotes on love and lovers."

Lovers! Love! The words fell harshly on my ear.

I did not love Silver Heels; I did not want to wed her. But something had to be done, and that quickly, if I was to take the silly, deluded girl back to Johnstown with me.

"Won't you tell the Weasel?" said Mount, anxiously.

"You tell him," I said. "You must stick by me now, Jack Mount, for the Lord knows what trouble lies before me ere I shake the Pittsburg dust off my moccasins!"

After a moment Mount said, "I suppose you don't know where Butler is?"

"You mean to say that Butler is back in Pittsburg?" I asked, faintly.

"He's in attendance on Dunmore, lad. Shemmy told me last night."

"Very well," said I, smacking my suddenly parched lips. "I will kill him before I leave Pittsburg."

Mr. Henry rose from his seat beside Logan and came over to where I was standing by the window.

"Mr. Cardigan," he said, "I know from Mount something concerning your mission here. I know you to be a patriot, and I believe that your honourable guardian, Sir William Johnson, will aid us with all his heart in whatever touches the good of our country. Am I not right?"

"Sir William's deeds are never secret, sir," I replied, cautiously. "All men may read his heart by that rule."

"Sir William has chosen in you a discreet deputy, to whom I beg to pay my sincerest compliments," said Mr. Henry, smiling.

"I can say this, sir," I replied, with a bow; "that I have heard him many times commend your speeches and the public course which you pursue."

"Sir William is too good," he replied, bowing.

"Ay, sir," I said, eagerly; "he is good! I do believe him to be the greatest and best of men, Mr. Henry. I am here as his deputy, though without orders, now that my mission to Colonel Cresap has failed. But, sir, I shall use my discretion, knowing Sir William's mind, and this night I shall present to my Lord Dunmore a reckoning which shall not be easily cancelled!"

"In the face of all his people?" asked Mr. Henry, curiously.

"In the face of the whole world, sir," I said, setting my teeth with a snap.

He held out his finely formed hand; I took it respectfully.

When he had gone away I drew Mount and Renard aside and asked them where Miss Warren was staying. They did not know.

"We'll make a tour of the town and find Shemuel; he knows," suggested Mount.

I assented, smiling bitterly to find myself so soon seeking Shemuel's company; and we three, clad in our soiled buckskins, descended the stairway and sallied forth into the sunlit streets of Pittsburg, arm in arm.

Riflemen, rangers, forest-runners, and the flotsam and jetsam from the wilderness were no rare spectacles in Pittsburg, so at first we attracted little attention. We would have attracted none at all had not Mount swaggered so, arms akimbo, fur cap over his left eye. He stopped at every tap-room, a sad habit of his in towns; and the oftener he stopped the more offensive became his swagger. The Weasel, too, strutted along, cap defiantly cocked, reaching up to tuck his arm under the elbow of his giant comrade, which at moments forced the little Weasel to march on tiptoe.

It was strange and ludicrous, the affection between these waifs of the wilderness; what Mount did the Weasel imitated most scrupulously, drinking whatever his companion drank, swaggering when he swaggered, singing whatever catch Mount sang. And the oftener they drank the more musical they became with their eternal:

"Diddle diddle dumpling,

My son John!—"

until I remonstrated so vigorously that they quieted their voices if not their deportment.

It was on Pitt Street that we found Shemuel, trudging towards the King's Road. A number of people gathered about him and followed him. Some bought ribbons or tablets for the races. The peddler saw us immediately, but made no sign as we approached until I asked the price of gilt buckles, and purchased three.

Then the little Jew fumbled in his pockets and whined and protested he could not make change, and I was uncertain what to say until he brightened up and begged us to follow to the "Bear and Cubs," just opposite, where change might be had in the tap-room.

The "Bear and Cubs" was a grizzly tavern, a squalid, unpainted house, swinging a grotesque sign which was meant to represent a she-bear suckling her young. The windows were dim with filth; the place reeked with the stale stench of malt and spirit dregs.

Into this grewsome hostelry I followed, perforce, to the tap-room, where Mount and Renard bawled for ale while I made known my business to Shemuel, who curiously enough appeared to suspect in advance what I wanted.

"If you hatt dold me this morning—ach!—bud I pelieved you care noddings, Mister Cardigan. She wass waiting to see you, sir, at Lady Shelton's in the Boundary—"

"Did you tell her I was here?" I asked, angrily.

"Ach—yess! I wass so sure you would see her—"

Exasperated, I shook my fist at the peddler.

"You miserable, tattling fool!" I said, fiercely. "Will you mind your own business hereafter? Who the devil are you, to pry into my affairs and spy upon your betters?"

"It wass to hellup you, sir," he protested, spreading his fingers and waving his hands excitedly. "I dold you she wass to marry Lord Dunmore; if you hatt asked me I could haff dold you somedings more—"

"What?"

"The bans will be published to-morrow from efery church in Pittsburg, Richmond, and Williamsburg!"

I glared at him, catching my breath and swallowing.

"Sir," he whined, "I ask your pardon, but I haff so often seen you in Johnstown, and Miss Warren, too, and—and—I would not haff harm come to her, or you, sir; and I pelieved you—you lofed her—"

I looked at him savagely.

"Ach!—I will mix me no more mit kindness to nobody!" he muttered. "Shemmy, you mint your peezeness and sell dem goots in dot pasket-box!"

"Shemuel," I said, "what did she say when you told her I was in Fort Pitt?"

"Miss Warren went white like you did, sir."

"And you said you would tell me where she was to be found?"

"Ach!—yess."

"What did she say?"

"Miss Warren wass crying, sir—"

"What?" I asked, astonished.

"Yess, sir; Miss Warren she only sat down under the drees, and she cry mit herselluf."

"And you came to get me? And my manner made you believe I did not care to see Miss Warren?"

"Miss Warren she knew I hatt come to fetch you. I dold her so. When I passed py dot Boundary again, she wass waiting under the drees—"

"How long since?"

"It is an hour, sir."

I fumbled in my belt and pulled out a gold piece.

"Thank you, Shemmy," I muttered, dropping it into his greasy cap; "tell Mount and Renard where I have gone."

"Ach—ach, Mister Cardigan," cried Shemuel, plucking me timidly by the sleeve, "von vort, if you please, sir. Remember, sir, I beg of you, that Miss Warren must not stay here. And if she will stay, and if she will not listen to you, sir, I beg you to gome to me at vonce."

"Why?" I asked, searching his agitated face.

"Pecause I haff a knowledge that will hellup you," he muttered.

"Very well," I said, calmly. "I will come to you, Shemmy, if I need you. Where is Lady Shelton's house?"

He led me to a back window and pointed out the Boundary, which was a tree-shaded road skirting the inner fortifications. Then he opened the rear door, pointed out the way through a filthy alley, across the market square, and then north until I came to a large, white-pillared house on a terrace, surrounded by an orchard.

As I walked swiftly towards the Boundary my irritation increased with every stride; it appeared to me that the world was most impudently concerning itself with my private affairs. First, Mount had coolly arranged for my reception by Dunmore without a word on the subject to me; and now the peddler, Shemuel, had without my knowledge or consent made a rendezvous for me with Silver Heels before I knew for certain that she still remained in Pittsburg. The free direction of my own affairs appeared to be slipping away from me; apparently people believed me to be incapable of either thinking or acting for myself. I meant to put an end to that.

As for Silver Heels, no wonder the announcement to her of my presence here had frightened her into tears. She knew well enough, the little hussy, that Sir William would not endure her to wed such a man as Dunmore: she knew it only too well, and, by the publishing of the bans, it was clear enough to me that she meant to wed Dunmore in spite of Sir William and before he could interfere or forbid the bans.

As I hastened on, biting my lip till it bled, I remembered her vow to wed rank and wealth and to be "my lady," come what might. And now the mad child believed she was in a fair way to fulfil her vow! I would teach her to try such tricks!

I found no great difficulty in discovering the house. Stone steps set in the hill-side led up to an orchard, through which, bordered by a garden, walks of gravel stretched to the veranda of the white-pillared house with its dormers and dignified portico.

There was a lady in the orchard, with her back turned towards me, leaning on a stone-wall and apparently contemplating the town below. My moccasins made no noise until I stepped on the gravel; but, at the craunch of the pebbles, the lady looked around and then came hastily towards me across the grass.

"Are you a runner from Johnstown?" she asked, sharply.

I stood still. The lady was Silver Heels. She did not know me.

She did not know me, nor I her, at first. It was only when she spoke. And this change had come to us both within four weeks' time!

That she did not recognize me was less to be wondered at. The dark mask of the sun, which I now wore, had changed me to an Indian; anxiety, fatigue, and my awful peril in the Cayuga camp had made haggard a youthful face, perhaps scored and hollowed it. In these weeks I had grown tall; I knew it, for my clothes no longer fitted in leg or sleeve. And I was thin as a kestrel, too; my added belt holes told me that.

But that I had not recognized her till she spoke distressed me. She, too, had grown tall; her face and body were shockingly frail; she had painted her cheeks and powdered her hair, and by her laces and frills and her petticoat of dentelle, she might have been a French noblewoman from Quebec. It were idle to deny her beauty, but it was the beauty of death itself.

"Silver Heels," I said.

Her hand flew to her bosom, then crept up on her throat, which I saw throbbing and whitening at every breath. Good cause for fear had she, the graceless witch!

After a moment she turned and walked into the orchard. 'Deed I scared her, too, for her dragging feet told of the shock I had given her, and her silk kirtle trembled to her knees. She leaned on the wall, looking out over the town as I had first seen her, and I followed her and rested against the wall beside her.

"Silver Heels," I asked, "are you afraid to see me?"

"No," she said, but the tears in her throat stopped her. Lord! how I had frightened her withal!

"Do you know why I am here?" I demanded, impressively, folding my arms in solemn satisfaction at the situation.

To my amazement she tossed her chin with a hateful laugh, and shrugged her shoulders without looking at me.

"Do you realize why I am here?" I repeated, in displeasure.

She half turned towards me with maddening indifference in voice and movement.

"Why you are here? Yes, I know why."

"Why, then?" I snapped.

"Because you believed that Marie Hamilton was here," she said, and laughed that odd, unpleasant laugh again. "But you come too late, Micky," she added, spitefully; "your bonnie Marie Hamilton is a widow, now, and already back in Albany to mourn poor Captain Hamilton."

My ears had been growing hot.

"Do you believe—" I began.

But she turned her back, saying, "Oh, Micky, don't lie."

"Lie!" I cried, exasperated.

"Fib, then. But you should have arrived in time, my poor friend. Last week came the news that Captain Hamilton had been shot on the Kentucky. Boone and Harrod sent a runner with the names of the dead. If you had only been here!—oh dear; poor boy! Pray, follow Mrs. Hamilton to Albany. She talked of nobody but you; she treated Mr. Bevan to one of her best silk mittens—"

"What nonsense is this?" I cried, alarmed. "Does Mrs. Hamilton believe I am in love with her?"

"Believe it? What could anybody believe after you had so coolly compromised her—"

"What?" I stammered.

"You kissed her, didn't you?"

"Who—I?"

"Perhaps I was mistaken; perhaps it was somebody else."

I fairly glared at my tormentor.

"Let me see," said Silver Heels, counting on her fingers. "There were three of us there—Marie Hamilton, I, and Black Betty. Now I'm sure it was not me you kissed, and if it was not Marie Hamilton—why—it was Betty!"

"Silver Heels," said I, angrily, "do you suppose I am in love with Mrs. Hamilton?"

"Why did you court her?" demanded Silver Heels, looking at me with bright eyes.

"Why? Oh, I—I fancied I was in love with you—and—and so I meant to make you jealous, Silver Heels. Upon my honour, that was all! I never dreamed she might think me serious."

The set smile on Silver Heels's lips did not relax.

"So you fancied you loved me?" she asked.

"I—oh—yes. Silver Heels, I was such a fool—"

"Indeed you were," she motioned with her lips.

How thin she had grown. Even the colour had left her lips now.

"There's one thing certain," I said. "I don't feel bound in honour to wed Mrs. Hamilton. I like her; she's pretty and sweet. I might easily fall in love with her, but I don't want to wed anybody. I could wed you if I chose, now, for Sir William wishes it, and he promised me means to maintain you."

"I thank Sir William—and you!" said Silver Heels, paler than ever.

"Oh, don't be frightened," I muttered. "I can't have you, and—and my country too. Silver Heels, I'm a rebel!"

She did not answer.

"Or, at least, I'm close to it," I went on. "I'm here to seek Lord Dunmore."

As I pronounced his name I suddenly remembered what I had come for, and stopped short, scowling at Silver Heels.

"Well, Micky?" she said, serenely. "What of Lord Dunmore?"

I bent my head, looking down at the grass, and in a shamed voice I told her what I had heard. She did not deny it. When I drew for her a portrait of the Earl of Dunmore in all his proper blazonry, she only smiled and set her lips tight to her teeth.

"What of it?" she asked. "I am to marry him; you and Sir William will not have him to endure."

"It's a disgraceful thing," I said, hotly. "If you are in your senses and cannot perceive the infamy of such a marriage, then I'll do your thinking for you and stop this shameful betrothal now!"

"You will not, I suppose, presume to interfere in my affairs?" she demanded, icily.

"Oh yes, I will," said I. "You shall not wed Dunmore. Do you hear me, Silver Heels?"

"I shall wed Dunmore in July."

"No, you won't!" I retorted, stung to fury. "Sir William has betrothed you to me. And, by Heaven! if it comes to that, I will wed you myself, you little fool!"

The old wild-cat light flickered in her eyes, and for a moment I thought she meant to strike me.

"You!" she stammered, clinching her slender hands. "Wed you! Not if I loved you dearer than hope of heaven, Michael Cardigan!"

"I do not ask you to love me," I retorted, sullenly. "I do not ask you to wed me, save as a last resort. But I tell you, I will not suffer the infamy of such a match as you mean to make. Renounce Dunmore and return with me to Johnstown, and I promise you I will not press my suit. But if you do not, by Heaven! I shall claim my prior right under our betrothal, and I shall take you with me to Johnstown. Will you come?"

"Lord Dunmore will give you your answer," she said, looking wicked and shaking in every limb.

"And I will give him his!" I cried. "Pray you attend to-night's ceremony in the fortress, and you will learn such truths as you never dreamed!"

I wiped my hot forehead with my sleeve, glaring at her.

"Doubtless," said I, sneeringly, "my attire may shock your would-be ladyship and your fashionable friends. But what I shall have to say will shock them more than my dirty clothes. True, I have not a bit of linen to clean my brow withal, and I use my sleeve as you see. But it's the sleeve of an honest man that dries the sweat of a guiltless body, and all the laces and fine linen of my Lord Dunmore cannot do the like for him!"

"I think," said she, coldly, "you had best go."

"I think so too," I sneered. "I ask your indulgence if I have detained you from the races, for which I perceive you are attired."

"It is true; I remained here for you, when I might have gone with the others."

Suddenly she broke down and laid her head in her arms.

Much disturbed I watched her, not knowing what to say. Anger died out; I leaned on the wall beside her, speaking gently and striving to draw her fingers from her face. In vain I begged for her confidence again; in vain I recalled our old comradeship and our thousand foolish quarrels, which had never broken the strong bond between us until that last night at Johnstown.

As I spoke all the old tenderness returned, the deep tenderness and affection for her that lay underneath all my tyranny and jealousy and vanity and bad temper, and which had hitherto survived all quarrels and violence and sullen resentment for real or imaginary offence.

I asked pardon for all wherein I had hurt her, I prayed for her trustful comradeship once more as few men pray for love from a cold mistress.

Presently she answered a question; other questions and other answers followed; she raised her tear-marred eyes and dried them with a rag of tightly fisted lace.

To soothe and gain her I told her bits of what I had been through since that last quarrel in Johnstown. I asked her if she remembered that sunset by the river, where she had spoken charms to the tiny red and black beetles, so that when they flew away the charm would one day save me from the stake.

But when I related the story of my great peril, she turned so sick and pallid that I ceased, and took her frail hands anxiously.

"What is the matter, Silver Heels?" I said. "Never have I seen you like this. Have you been ill long? What is it, little comrade?"

"Oh, I don't know—I don't know, truly," she sobbed. "It has come within the few weeks, Michael. I am so old, so tired, so strangely ill of I know not what."

"You *do* know," I said. "Tell me, Silver Heels."

She raised her eyes to me, then closed them. Neck and brow were reddening.

"You are not in love!" I demanded, aghast.

"Ay, sick with it," she said, slowly, with closed lids.

It was horrible, incredible! I attempted to picture Dunmore as an inspirer of love in any woman. The mere idea revolted me. What frightful spell had this shrunken nobleman cast over my little comrade that she should confess her love for him?

And all I could say was: "Oh, Silver Heels! Silver Heels! That man! It is madness!"

"What man?" she asked, opening her eyes.

"What man?" I repeated. "Do you not mean that you love Dunmore?"

She laughed a laugh that frightened me, so mirthless, so bitter, so wickedly bitter it rang in the summer air.

"Oh yes—Dunmore, if you wish—or any man—any man. I care not; I am sick, sick, sick! They have flattered and followed and sought me and importuned me—great and humble, young and old—and never a true man among them all—only things of powder and silks and painted smiles—and all wicked save one."

"And he?"

"Oh, he is a true man—the only one among them all—a true man, for he is stupid and vain and tyrannical and violent, eaten to the bone with self-assurance—and a fool to boot, Michael—a fool to boot. And as this man is, among them all, the only real man of bone and blood—why, I love him."

"Who is this man?" I asked, cautiously.

"Not Dunmore, Michael."

"Not Dunmore? And yet you wed Dunmore?"

"Because I love the other, Michael, who uses me like a pedigreed hound, scanning and planning his kennel-list to mate me with a blooded mate to his taste. Because I hate him as I love him, and shall place myself beyond his power to shame me. Because I am dying of the humiliation, Michael, and would wish to die so high in rank that even death cannot level me to him. Now, tell me who I love."

"God knows!" I said, in my amazement.

"True," she said, "God knows I love a fool."

"But who is this fellow?" I insisted. "What man dares attempt to mate you to his friends? The insolence, the presumption—why, I thought I was the only man who might do that!"

How she laughed at me as I stood perplexed and scowling and fingering the fringe on my leggings, and how her laughter cut, with its undertone ringing with tears. What on earth had changed her to a woman like this, talking a language that dealt in phrases which one heard and marked and found meant nothing, with a sting in their very emptiness?

"Very well," said I, "you shall not have Dunmore for spite of a fool unworthy of you; and as for that, you shall not have the fool either!"

"I am not likely to get him," she said.

"You could have him for the wish!" I cried, jealously. "I'd like to see the man who would not crawl from here to Johnstown to kiss your silken shoe!"

"Would *you*?"

"It pleases you to mock me," I said; "but I'll tell you this: If I loved you as a sweetheart I'd do it! I'll have the world know it is honoured wherever you touch it with your foot!"

"Do you mean it?" she asked, looking at me strangely.

"Mean it! Have you ever doubted it?"

The colour in her face surged to her hair.

"You speak like a lover," she said, with a catch in her breath.

"I speak like a man, proud of his kin!" said I, suspiciously, alert to repel ridicule. Lover! What did she mean by that? Had I not asked pardon for my foolishness in Johnson Hall? And must she still taunt me?

If she read my suspicions I do not know, but I think she did, for the colour died out in her face and she set her lips together as she always did when meaning mischief.

"I pray you, dear friend," she said, wearily, "concern yourself with your kin as little as I do. Bid me good-bye, now. I am tired, Michael—tired to the soul of me."

She held out her slim hand. I took it, then I bent to touch it with my lips.

"You will not wed Dunmore?" I asked.

She did not reply.

"And you will come with me to Johnstown on the morrow, Silver Heels?"

There was no answer.

"Silver Heels?"

"If you are strong enough to take me from Dunmore, take me," she said, in a dull, tired voice.

"And—and from the other—the one you love—the fool?"

"He will leave me—when you leave me," she answered.

"You mean to say this pitiful ass will follow you and me to Johnstown!" I cried, excited.

"Truly, he will!" she said, hysterically, and covered her face with her hands. But whether she was laughing or crying or doing both together I could not determine; and I stalked wrathfully away, determined to teach this same fool that his folly was neither to my taste nor fancy.

And as I passed swiftly southward through the darkening town I heard the monotonous call of the town watchman stumping his beat:

"Lanthorn, and a whole candle-light! Hang out your lights here! Light—ho! Maids, hang out your light, and see your lamp be clear and bright!"

CHAPTER XIV

I had learned from our host of the "Virginia Arms" that the so-called "Governor's Hall," which stood within the limits of the fortifications, had been built by the French in 1755. Poor Braddock's brief début before Fort Duquesne in that same year interrupted the building of "Governor's Hall," which was called by the French "La Fortresse de la Reine," and which, with the exception of our stone fort at Johnstown, was the only formidable and solidly fortified edifice of stone west of the Hudson.

When in '58 our troops seized Fort Duquesne and razed it, they not only spared La Fortresse de la Reine, but completed it—in exceeding poor taste—set the arms of Virginia over the portal, ran up their red, powder-stained flag, and saluted "Governor's Hall" with hurrahs of satisfaction, drums and fifes playing "The White Cockade."

Now the hall served sometimes as a court-house, sometimes as a temporary jail, often as a ballroom, occasionally as the Governor's residence when he came to Fort Pitt from Williamsburg.

In it he gave audiences to all plaintiffs, white or Indian; in it he received deputies from other colonies or from England.

The Governor of Virginia lived on the second floor while sojourning at Pittsburg; under his white and gold apartments stretched a long, blank, stone hall, around the walls of which ran a wooden balcony half way between the stone flagging and the ceiling of massive buckeye beams.

It was in this naked and gloomy hall, damp and rank with the penetrating odour of mortar and dropping, mouldy plaster, that my Lord Dunmore consented to receive the old Cayuga chief, Logan, of the clan of the Wolf, and by right of birth—which counts not with chiefs unless they be sachems, too—the chief also of the Oquacho of the Oneida nation.

Towards dusk a company of red-coated British infantry, with drummers leading, left the barracks opposite our inn, the "Virginia Arms," and marched away towards "Governor's Hall," drummers beating "The Huron." A crowd of men and boys trailed along on either flank of the column, drawn by curiosity to catch a glimpse of Logan, "The White Man's Friend," who was to ask justice this night of the most noble Governor of Virginia, the great Earl of Dunmore.

When the distant batter of the drums, echo and beat, had died away down the dark vista of the King's Road, I left my window in the "Virginia Arms" and descended the stairway into the street below, where Jack Mount and the Weasel ruffled it bravely and swaggered to and fro, awaiting my coming.

Mulled wine and sundry cups of cider, mixed rashly with long libations of James Rolfe's humming ale, had set their heads and tongues a-buzzing. They were glorious in their dingy buckskins, coon-skin caps cocked over their left ears, thumbs hooked jauntily under their arm-pits. They now occupied the middle of the street and patrolled it gayly, singing and shouting and interrupting traffic, returning a jest for a gibe, a laugh for a smile, or a terrible threat for any wayfarer who dared complain of being hustled or trodden on.

Men instinctively accorded them the room they seemed to desire; women understood them better, and took right of way, smiling the reproof which always brought the swaggerers up, cap-tails sweeping the street in extravagant salute. For there appeared, in those two graceless bibbers of wines, that gravity and politeness of intoxication which so grotesquely parodies the dignity of gallantry, and with which it is almost hopeless for sober people to contend.

However, I spoke to them so cuttingly that they relapsed into injured silence and ambled along on either side of me without serious offence to passing citizens.

We soon found ourselves in a crowd, the current of which swept down the King's Road towards the fortress; and we followed in the wake, while past us rode companies of officers, gentlemen, and sometimes squads of the Governor's horse—those same gay, flame-coloured Virginians whom I had so admired at Johnstown a month ago.

Coaches passed us, too, rolling towards the fortress, and through the glass windows we caught glimpses of ladies in cloaks of swan's-down, with their plumes and jewels shining in the rays of the coach-lamps. Gilded sedan-chairs began to appear, gayer and more painted and polished than our chairs in Johnstown, and the bearers often in handsome liveries, with a major-domo leading the way and footmen to heel, and my lady peeping out at us shabby foot-farers plodding along in the street beside her.

Cresap's men were plentiful among the crowd, some of them sullen and muttering, others loud in their demands for Cresap's release, threatening trouble for those who had jailed their leader, and careless who heard them. There were a few forest-runners dressed as we were, numbers of riflemen in green capes and gray wool shirts, and rangers in brown and yellow deer-skins, with thrums dyed scarlet or purple.

A short, thick-set fellow, wearing a baldrick fringed with scalps, was pointed out by people as one of Boone's and Harrod's dare-devils; and truly he looked his part, though the scalp-belt pleased me not.

I heard him boasting that the trophies were Wyandotte scalps, which news, if true, meant one more ally for the Cayuga and one more enemy for the colonies when the breach with England came. It sickened me to hear the great fool boast.

The bulk of the throng, however, was made up of sober, peaceful citizens, men of the quiet classes, in homespun and snuffy hats, guiltless of the silver buckle on knee or shoe, silent, reserved, thoughtful men of moderate gesture and earnest eyes, whose rare voices disturbed no one and whose inoffensive conduct rebuked the rufflers as no words could do.

Jack Mount, who at first appeared inclined to play the rôle of a marching orator and distribute morsels of his wit and learning to all who would pay him the fee of their attention, subsided of his own accord among the quiet company wherein we now found ourselves and contented himself and the Weasel with a series of prodigious yawns, at which they both never seemed to tire of laughing.

They also sang in a subdued chorus:

"Quak'ress, Quak'ress, whither away?

Pray thee stay thee, Quak'ress gray.

I thy Quaker fain would be,

Yet dare not swear I care for thee!"

However, the few Quakers in the throng took no offence, and I presently nudged my mannerless comrades into a snickering silence.

The people ahead of us had now stopped, and, looking over their heads, I saw the dark shape of the "Governor's Hall," partly illuminated by two great lanthorns set in iron sockets flanking the portal. Shining in the feeble light moved the bayonets of the guards above the darkly massed crowd, while coach after coach rolled up and chair after chair deposited its burden of bejewelled beauty at the gateway. And all these people, all these dainty dames and gallants, had come to see the famous Logan—to hear the great Cayuga orator, "The Friend of the White Man," ask why his little children had been slain by the white men, whose faithful friend he had been so long. Truly, there might be here something newer than the stale play at the Theatre Royal. It was not every day that my lady might hear and see an old man asking why his children had been murdered.

The crowd in front of us was compact, yet when Mount set his broad chest against it, the people hastily made a lane for him. The Weasel and I followed our big companion, elbowing our way to the portal, where Mr. Patrick Henry awaited us and passed us through the sentries and guards and pompous big-bellied tip-staves who turned up their vinous noses at the three shabby men from the forest.

Candle-light softened the bare walls and benches; candle-light set silks and jewels in a blaze where the ladies, banked up like beds of rustling roses, choked the wooden balcony above our heads, murmuring, whispering, fluttering fans and scarfs till the perfumed breeze from their stirrings fanned my cheeks. And more of them were arriving every moment; the wooden stairway leading to the gallery was ablaze with starred sashes and petticoats, and twinkling satin shoon, with now and then the sparkle of a hilt as some scented gallant ascended with his fluttering and gorgeous convoy.

The scarlet coats of colonial and British officers spotted the galleries; here and there a silver gorget caught the light, blinding the eyes with brilliancy, only to turn and sink to a cinder as the wearer moved.

I looked for Silver Heels, but, from the floor below, all faces were vague and delicate as massed blossoms in a garden, and eyes sparkled as faintly as dew on velvet petals all unfolded.

At the end of the hall two carpeted steps led to a stone platform hung with a flag and the arms of Virginia. This was the Governor's audience-seat; the gilded chair in the centre was for him; the tables that flanked it for his secretaries.

For envoys, deputies, and for all plaintiffs, red benches faced the platform; behind these stretched rank on rank of plain, unpainted seats for the public, or as much of it as the soldiers and tip-staves thought proper to admit.

This same public was now clamouring at the gate for right of entrance without favour or discrimination, and I could hear them protesting and shuffling at the portal behind us, while the soldiers disputed and the tip-staves tapped furiously on the stones with their long, tasselled wands.

"Why should not the public enter freely a public place?" I asked of Patrick Henry.

"They will, one day," he said, with his grave smile.

"Drums beating," added Mount, loudly, but withered at once under the sharp stare of displeasure with which Mr. Henry favoured him.

We now took seats on the last of the red benches, which stood near the centre of the hall, and in one corner of which I perceived Logan sitting bolt upright, eyes fixed on space, brooding, unconscious of the thronged beauty in the galleries above him or of the restless public now pouring into the hall behind his back.

Mr. Henry took his seat beside the stricken chief; next followed Jack Mount, lumbering to his place; and I heard a stir pass around the gallery with whispers of wonder and admiration for the giant, followed by a titter as the little Weasel trotted to his seat next to Mount. I sat down beside the Weasel, closing the row on our bench, and turned around to watch the people filling up the hall behind me. They were serious, sober-eyed people, and, unlike the gay world in the galleries, had apparently not come to seek amusement in the clothes of three shabby rangers or in the dumb grief of a savage.

"They are mostly patriots," whispered the Weasel, "peppered with Tories and sprinkled with Dunmore's spies. But they don't blab what they know—trust them for that, Mr. Cardigan."

"I can see Paul Cloud and Timothy Boyd sitting together, and our host of the 'Virginia Arms,' Rolfe," I said, leaning to search the audience. Then I caught a glimpse of a face I knew better, the scarred, patched-up visage of the man whom I had made to taste his own hatchet. Startled, and realizing for the first time the proximity of Walter Butler, I hunted the hall for him with hopeful eyes, for I meant to seek him and kill him without ceremony when the first chance came. I could not find him, however, but in a corner near the door, whispering together and peeping about, I discovered his other two creatures, Wraxall, the Johnstown barber, and Toby Tice, the treacherous tenant of Sir William. Where the cubs were the old wolf was not far away, that was certain. But search as I might I could find nothing but the wolf's stale trail.

One circumstance impressed me: behind Wraxall and Tice sat Saul Shemuel, hands folded on his stomach, apparently dozing while waiting for the spectacle to begin. But he was not asleep, for now and again, between his lids, I caught a sparkle of open eyes, and I knew that his large, soft ears were listening hard.

While I was still watching Shemuel, the Weasel nudged me, and I turned to see the platform before me alive with gentlemen, moving about and chatting, seating themselves in groups, while behind them half a dozen British officers in full uniform lounged or stared curiously up at the packed balconies.

Some of the gentlemen on the platform exchanged salutes with ladies in the balconies, some smiled or waved their hands to friends. But that soon ceased, and the commotion on the platform was stilled as a gorgeous tip-staff advanced, banging his great stave on the stones and announcing the coming of his Lordship the Earl of Dunmore, Royal Governor of his Majesty's colony of Virginia. God save the King!

Swish! swish! went the silken petticoats as the gallery rose; the people on the floor rose too, with clatter and shuffle and scrape of benches shoved over the stones.

Ah! There he was!—painted cheeks, pale eyes, smirk, laces, bird-claws and all—with a splendid order blazing on his flame-coloured sash and his fleshless legs mincing towards the gilded chair under the canopy which bore the arms of Virginia and the British flag.

Before he was pleased to seat himself, he peered up into the balcony and kissed his finger-tips; and I, following his eyes by instinct, saw Silver Heels sitting in the candle-flare, scarlet and silent, with her sad eyes fixed, not on my Lord Dunmore, but on me.

Before I met her eyes I had been sullenly frightened, dreading to speak aloud in such a company, scarcely hoping to find my tongue when the time came to voice my demands so that the whole town could hear. Now, with her deep, steady eyes meeting mine, fear fell from me like a cloak, and the blood began to race through every limb and my heart beat "To arms!" so fearlessly and so gayly that I smiled up at her; and she smiled at me in turn.

Again the Weasel began twitching at my sleeve, and I bent beside him, listening and watching the gentlemen on the platform.

"That's John Gibson, Dunmore's secretary—the man in black on the Governor's left! That loud, bustling fellow on his right is Doctor Connolly, Dunmore's deputy for Indian affairs. He arrested Cresap to clear his own skirts of blame for the war. Behind him sits Connolly's agent, Captain Murdy. Murdy's agent was Greathouse. You see the links in the chain?"

"Perfectly," I replied, calmly; "and I mean to shatter them if my voice is not scared out of my body."

"Scourge me that ramshackle Dunmore!" whispered Mount, thickly, leaning across the Weasel. "Give him hell-fire and a—hic!—black eye—"

Mr. Henry jerked the giant's arm and he relapsed into a wise silence, nodding his thanks as though Mr. Henry had imparted to him an acceptable secret instead of a reproof.

We were near enough to the platform to hear the Governor chattering with Gibson and Doctor Connolly, and sniffing his snuff as he peeped about with his lack-lustre eyes.

"Que dieu me damne!" he said, spitefully. "But you have a mauvais quart d'heure ahead, Connolly!—curse me if you have not! Faith, I wash my hands of you, and you had best make your sulky savage yonder some good excuse for the war."

Connolly's deep voice replied evasively, but Dunmore clipped him short:

"Oh no! Oh no! The people won't have that, Connolly!—skewer me if they will! Body o' Judas, Connolly, you can't make them believe Cresap started this war!"

Connolly whispered something.

"Eh? What? I say I wash my hands o' ye! Didn't you hear me say I washed my hands? And mind you clear me when you answer your filthy savage. I'll none of it, d'ye hear?"

Connolly flushed darkly and leaned back. Gibson appeared nervous and dispirited, but Captain Murdy smiled cheerfully on everybody and took snuff with a zest.

"And, Connolly," observed Dunmore, settling himself in his gilded chair, "you had best announce the restoration to rank and command of Cresap. Ged!—that ought to put the clodhoppers yonder in good humour, to keep them from snivelling while your dirty savage speaks."

Presently Connolly arose, and, making a motion for silence, briefly announced the restoration of Cresap to command. There was no sound, no demonstration. Those in the balconies cared nothing for Cresap, those on the floor cared too much to compromise him with applause.

I heard Dunmore complaining to Gibson that the first part of Connolly's programme had fallen flat and that he, Dunmore, wanted to know what Gibson thought of refusing Logan the right of speech.

Gibson nervously shook his head and signalled to the interpreter, a grizzled sergeant of the Virginia militia, to take his station; and when the interpreter advanced, announcing in English and in the Cayuga language that the Governor of Virginia welcomed his brother, Logan, chief of the Cayugas, warrior of the clan of the Wolf, and "The White Man's Friend," I saw Patrick Henry touch Logan on the shoulder.

Slowly the Indian looked up, then rose like a spectre from his sombre blanket and fixed his sad eyes on Dunmore.

There was a faint movement, a rustle from the throng on floor and gallery, then dead silence, as from the old warrior's throat burst the first hollow, heart-sick word:

"*Brother!*"

Oh, the grim sadness of that word!—the mockery of its bitterness!—the desolate irony of despair ringing through it! *Brother!* That single word cursed the silence with an accusation so merciless that I saw Connolly's heavy visage grow purple, and Gibson turn his eyes away. Only my Lord Dunmore sat immovable, with the shadow of a sneer freezing on his painted face.

Logan slowly raised his arm:—

"Through that thick night which darkens the history of our subjugation, through all the degradation and reproach which has been heaped upon us, there runs one thread of light revealing our former greatness, pleading the causes of our decay, illuminating the pit of our downfall, promising that our dead shall live again! Not in the endless darkness whither priests and men consign us is that thread of light to be lost; but from the shadowy past it shall break out in brilliancy, redeeming a people's downfall, and wringing from you, our subjugators, the greeting—*Brothers!*

"*Fathers*: For Logan, that light comes too late. Death darkens my lodge; my door is closed to sun and moon and stars. Death darkens my lodge. All within lie dead. Logan is alone. He, too, is blind and sightless; like the quiet dead his ears are stopped, he hears not; nor can he see darkness or light.

"For Logan, light or darkness comes too late."

The old man paused; the silence was dreadful.

Suddenly he turned and looked straight at Dunmore.

"I appeal to any white man if he ever entered Logan's lodge hungry and he gave him not meat; if he ever came cold and naked and he clothed him not!"

The visage of the Earl of Dunmore seemed to be growing smaller and more corpse-like. Not a feature on his ghastly mask moved, yet the face was dwindling.

Logan's voice grew gentler.

"Such was my love," he said, slowly. "Such was my great love for the white men! My brothers pointed at me as they passed, and said, 'He is the friend of white men.' And I had even thought to live with you, but for the injuries of my brothers, the white men.

"Unprovoked, in cold blood, they have slain my kin—all!—all!—not sparing woman or child. There runs not a drop of my blood in the veins of any living creature!

"Hearken, *Brothers*! I have withstood the storms of many winters. Leaves and branches have been stripped from me. My eyes are dim, my limbs totter, I must soon fall. I, who could make the dry leaf turn green again; I, who could take the rattlesnake in my palm; I, who had communion with the dead, dreaming and waking; I am powerless. The wind blows hard! The old tree trembles! Its branches are gone! Its sap is frozen! It bends! It falls! Peace! Peace!

"Who is there to mourn for Logan? Not one!"

The old man bent his withered head and covered his face with his blanket. Through the frightful stillness the painful breathing of the people swept like a smothered cry; women in the balcony were sobbing; somewhere a child wept uncomforted.

Patrick Henry leaned across to me; his eyes were dim, his voice choked in his throat.

"The great orator!" he whispered. "Oh, the great man!—greatest of all! The last word has been said for Logan! I shall not speak, Mr. Cardigan—it were sacrilege—now."

He rose and laid one arm about the motionless chief, then very gently he drew him out into the aisle. There was not a sound in the hall as they passed slowly out together, those great men who had both struck to the hilt for the honour of their kindred and of their native land.

Now, when at last he had disappeared, a living spectre of reproach, which the guilt of men had raised to confound the lords of the New World, those gathered there to listen breathed again, and hastened to forget that glimpse which they had caught of the raw heart of all tragedy—man's inhumanity to man.

Dunmore came slowly from his trance, mechanically preening his silken plumage and ruffling like a meagre bird; Connolly rose from his seat and shook himself, and, finding nothing better to do, went about the platform, snuffing the candles, a duty pertaining to servants, but which he was doubtless thankful to perform as it brought his back to the spectators and gave his heavy, burning face a respite from the pillory of eyes. Gibson leaned heavily on his writing-table, wan, loose-jawed, and vacant-eyed. As for Captain Murdy, he sat serenely in his chair, shapely legs crossed, examining the lid of his snuff-box with ever-freshening interest.

Above us in the galleries some people had risen and were about to leave. The rustle of silks and satins seemed to break the heavy quiet; people breathed deeply, shifted in their seats, and turned around. Some stood up to go; chairs and benches grated on the stones; shoes shuffled and tapped sharply.

I had already determined to defer my interview with Lord Dunmore, because, after the great chief's speech, my poor words must fall stale on ears attuned to the majestic music of a mighty soul. So, in the stir and noise around us, I rose and touched Jack Mount, motioning him to follow. But before he could find his feet and summon his wits to set them in motion, and ere I myself had edged half-way to the aisle, I heard Doctor Connolly speaking in that loud, hectoring tone, and I caught the name of Sir William Johnson shouted from the platform.

"If the messenger from Johnstown be present," continued Doctor Connolly, "let him be assured of a warm welcome from his Lordship, the Earl of Dunmore, Governor of Virginia."

So the infatuated Dunmore, grasping at a straw to dam the current of public sentiment, thought to fill empty minds with the news of his betrothal, trusting that as all the world loves a lover, this same planet might find an opportunity to take him to its sentimental bosom.

His purpose was plain to me and perfectly loathsome; and as I stood there, watching him, I could see the rouge crack when he simpered. But I would not speak now.

Presently, looking around, I found that all those who had risen had again seated themselves, and that I, fascinated by the repulsive visage of Dunmore, stood there all alone.

My first impulse was to sit down hastily; my next to keep my feet, for it was too late to seek cover now, and Connolly was smiling at me, and Gibson nodded like a dazed mandarin. Dunmore, too, was peering at me and tapping his snuff-box complacently, and the sight of him brought the blood to my head and opened my mouth. But no sound issued. A woman in the gallery laughed outright.

"Are you not a messenger from Sir William Johnson?" prompted Connolly, with his domineering smile of patronage.

"Yes, Doctor Connolly," I replied, slowly. As I spoke, fright vanished.

There was a pause. Dunmore tapped on his box and moistened his slitted mouth with a tongue which looked perfectly blue to me, and he fell a-smirking and bridling, with sly, rheumy glances at the gallery.

"Lord Dunmore," I said, steadily, "ere I inform you why I am here, you shall know me better than you think you do.

"I am not here to tell you of that chain which links the Governor of Virginia with the corpse of Logan's youngest child!—nor to count the links of that chain backward, from Greathouse to Murdy, to Gibson, to Connolly, to—"

"Stop!" burst out Connolly, springing to his feet. "Who are you? What are you? How dare you address such language to the Earl of Dunmore?"

Astonished, furious, eyes injected with blood, he stood shaking his mottled red fists at me; Dunmore sat in a heap, horrified, with the simper on his face stamped into a grin of terror. The interruption stirred up my blood to the boiling; I clutched the back of the bench in front of me, and fixed my eyes on Connolly.

"I do not reply to servants," I said; "my business here is not with Lord Dunmore's lackeys. If the Earl of Dunmore knows not my name and title, he shall know it now! I am Michael Cardigan, cornet in the Border Horse, and deputy of Sir William Johnson, Baronet, his Majesty's Superintendent of Indian Affairs for North America!

"Who dares deny me right of speech?"

Dunmore lay in his chair, a shrunken mess of lace and ribbon; Connolly appeared paralyzed; Gibson stared at me over his table.

"I am not here," I said, coolly, "to ask your Lordship why this war, falsely called Cresap's war, should be known to honest men as 'Dunmore's war.' Nor do I come to ask you why England should seek the savage allies of the Six Nations, which this war, so cunningly devised, has given her—"

"Treason! Treason!" bawled a voice behind me. It was Wraxall; I recognized his whine.

"But," I resumed, pointing my finger straight at the staring Governor, "I am here to demand an account of your stewardship! Where are those Cayugas whom you have sworn to protect from the greed of white men? Where are they? Answer, sir! Where are Sir William Johnson's wards of the Long House? Where are the Shawanese, the Wyandottes, the Lenape, the Senecas, who keep the western portals of the Long House? Answer, sir! for this is my mission from Sir William Johnson. Answer! lest the King say to him, 'O thou unfaithful steward!'"

Hubbub and outcry and tumult rose around me. Dunmore was getting on his feet; Connolly flew to his aid, but the Governor snarled at him and pushed him, and went shambling out of the door behind the platform, while, in the hall, the uproar swelled into an angry shout: "Shame on Dunmore! God save Virginia!"

An officer in the gallery leaned over the edge, waving his gold-laced hat.

"God save the King!" he roared, and many answered, "God save the King!" but that shout was drowned by a thundering outburst of cheers: "God save our country! Hurrah! Hurrah! Hurrah!"

"Three cheers for Boston!" bawled Jack Mount, jumping up on his bench; and the rolling cheers echoed from balcony to pavement till the throng went wild and even the sober Quakers flung up their broad-brimmed hats. In the gallery ladies were cheering, waving scarfs and mantles; the British soldiers at the door looked in at the astounding scene, some with sheepish grins, some gaping, some scowling under their mitred head-gear.

Mount had caught me up in his arms and was shouldering his way towards the door, yelping like a Mohawk at a corn feast; and presently others crowded around, patting my legs and cheering, bearing me onward and out past the sentinels, where, for a moment, I thought soldiers and people would come to blows.

But Mount waved his cap and shouted an ear-splitting watchword: "The ladies! Honour the ladies!" and the crowd fell back as the excited dames and maidens from the balcony issued in silken procession from the hall, filing between the soldiers and the crowd, to enter coaches and chairs and disappear into the depths of the starlight.

I could not find Silver Heels, and presently I gave up that hope, for the throng, hustled by the soldiers, began shoving and scuffling and pressing, now forward, now backward, until the breath was near squeezed from my body and I made out to slip back with Mount and Renard to the open air.

Mount was enthusiastic. "Look sharp!" he said eagerly. "There will be heads to break anon. Ha! See them running yonder! Hark! Do you not hear that, Cade? Clink—whack! Bayonet against cudgel! They're at it, lad! Come on! Come on! Give it to the damned Tories!"

The next instant we were enveloped in the crowd, buffeted, pushed, trodden, hurled about like shuttle-cocks, yet ever retreating before the line of gun-stocks which rose and fell along the outer edge of the mob.

The fight was desperate and silent, save for the whipping swish of ramrods whistling, the dull shocks of blows, or the ringing crack of a cudgel on some luckless pate. Under foot our moccasins moved and trampled among fallen hats and wigs, and sometimes we stumbled over an insensible form, victim of gun-stock or club or a buffet from some swinging fist.

Once, forced to the front where the soldiers were jabbing and lashing the mob with gun-butt, ramrod, and leather belt, a drummer boy ran at me and fell to thumping me with his drum, while a soldier cuffed my ears till I reeled. Astonished and enraged by such scurvy treatment I made out to wrest the drum from the boy and jam it violently upon the head of the soldier, so that his head and mitre-cap stuck out through the bursted parchment.

A roar of laughter greeted the unfortunate man, who backed away, distracted, clawing at the drum like a cat with its head in a bag. Then the battle was renewed with fury afresh; a citizen wrested a firelock from a soldier, drove the butt into the pit of his stomach, and struck out sturdily in all directions, shouting, "Long live our country!" Another knocked a soldier senseless and tore off his white leggings for trophies—an operation that savoured of barbarism.

"Scalp their legs! Skin 'em!" bawled the man, waving the leggings in triumph; and I saw he was that same ranger of Boone and Harrod who wore a baldrick of Wyandotte scalps.

It began to go hard with the King's soldiers, but they stuck to the mob like bulldogs, giving blow for blow so stanchly and so heartily that my blood tingled with pleasure and pride, and I called out to Jack Mount: "Look at them, Jack! What very gluttons for punishment! Nobody but British could stand up to us like that!"

A crack on the sconce from a belt transformed my admiration into fury, and I drove my right fist into the eye of one of these same British soldiers, and followed it with a swinging blow which sent him spinning, receiving at the same moment such a jolt in the body that I, too, went sprawling and gasping about until Mount pulled me out of the crush.

When I had found my breath again, and had mastered that sick faintness which comes from a blow in the stomach, I prepared to return to the fray, which had now taken on a more sinister aspect. Bayonets had already been used, not as clubs but as daggers; a man was leaning against a tree near me, bleeding from a wound in the neck, and another reeled past, tugging at a bayonet which had transfixed his shoulder. But the end came suddenly now; horsemen were galloping up behind the jaded soldiers; I saw Shemuel dart out of the swaying throng and take to his heels, not even stopping to gather up hats, handkerchiefs, and wigs, of which the sack on his back was full to the top.

When Shemuel left a stricken field it was time for others to think of flight; this I perceived at once when the Weasel came scurrying past and called out to me. Mount followed, lumbering on at full speed; the throng melted and scattered in every direction, and I with them. Trust me, there was fine running done that night in Pittsburg streets, and many a tall fellow worked his legs as legs are seldom worked, for the gentlemen of the Governor's horse-guards were riding us hard, and we legged it for cover, each fox to his own spinny, each rabbit to the first unstopped earth. Tally-ho! Stole away! Faith, it was merry hunting that night in Pittsburg town, with the townspeople at every window and the town-watch bawling at our heels, and the gentlemen riders pelting down the King's Road till those who could double back doubled, and walked panting to cover, with as innocent mien as they could muster.

Mount, Renard, Shemuel, and I had crossed the Boundary at respectable speed, and were now headed for the dirty alley which conducted to the rear door of Shemuel's den, the "Bear and Cubs." We were about to enter this lane, no longer fearing pursuit—and I remember that Mount was laughing, poking the Weasel in his short-ribs—when, without warning, five men rushed at us in a body, overturning us all save Jack Mount. The next moment we were locked in a struggle; there was not a cry, not an oath, not a sound but the strained gasp and heavy breathing, at first; but presently a piercing yell echoed through the alley, and Shemuel ran squattering into the inn. He had stuck a handful of needles into his assailant's leg, and the man bounded madly about, while the alley re-echoed with his howls of dismay.

As for me, I found myself clutched by that villain, Wraxall, and I would have shouted with joy had he not held me by the windpipe until I was nigh past all shouting. The creature was powerful; he held me while Toby Tice tried to tie my wrists; but the Weasel fell upon them both and kicked them so heartily that they left me and took to their heels perdu.

And now came the host of the "Bear and Cubs," lanthorn in one hand, a meat-knife in the other, and after him a tap-boy, an hostler, a frowzy maid, and finally Shemuel, white with fear. But reinforcements had arrived too late—too late to help us take the impudent band, which had fled—too late to bring to life that dark mass lying at the foot of the wall in the filth of the alley.

Mount seized the lanthorn and lowered it beside the shape on the ground.

"His neck is broken," he said, briefly. It was his quarry; he ought to know.

One by one we took the lanthorn and looked in turn on the dead.

"Greathouse," whispered Mount, moving the body with his foot.

"Greathouse, eh?" grumbled the host of the "Bear and Cubs." "Well, he can't lie here behind *my* house." And he caught him by the heels and dragged him to a black spot under a rotten shed. There was a cistern there. I moved away, feeling strangely faint. Mount linked his arm in mine.

Presently there sounded a dull noise under the ground, a shock and thick splashing.

"Greathouse, eh?" muttered the shaggy innkeeper, winking at us. "Well, Greathouse is in a small house behind a pot-house now, and the devil, no doubt, will see that he lands in a hot-house!"

Mount shrugged his shoulders and turned away indifferently. He had done his part; he had no slur for the dead. The Weasel and I followed, and together we traversed the market-square unmolested, and headed for the "Virginia Arms," discussing the utterly unprovoked attack on us by Butler's band.

There had been five of them; I had recognized Wraxall and Tice, the Weasel identified Murdy, Shemuel had thrust half his stock of needles into one fellow's leg, whom I knew to be the man who had supped on his own hatchet, and Mount had sternly accounted for his assailant.

"So Greathouse is dead," muttered the Weasel.

"One thing is clear: they were after you," observed Mount, turning on me.

"It is strange," I said, "that Butler was not there. He must know what it means for him unless he can strike me from behind, because I shall never miss him, face to face."

I spoke not in boast, nor in angry heat; I meant what I said, and devoutly believed that nothing on earth could shield such a man from the man he had so foully misused.

Coming into Pitt Street we found all empty and dark save for the lanthorn hanging on its pole from every seventh house, and a lone watchman who lifted his light to scan us, but durst not question or stop us, though we bore marks enough of the fray to satisfy any friendly jury of our guilt.

As for Mount, his shirt and leggings were in rags, for he had played Orlando Furioso to his simple heart's satisfaction, and now one naked arm peeped coyly from a flapping sleeve, and his great legs twinkled white under the tattered nether-garments. The Weasel, who had a genius for keeping himself neat under distressing circumstances, appeared to be none the worse for wear, but guiltless he could not be, for he carried a soldier's mitre-cap in his hand and obstinately refused to part with the proof of his valour. As for me, there were some seams which needed a thread, and somebody's blood on my shirt which water would wash away.

"I went this noon to a tailor-woman on the Buckeye Road, and did command me new deer-skins," said Mount. "I will borrow their cost of you," he added, naïvely.

I felt for my money-belt and luckily found it safe. Mount accepted the money cheerfully, promising to show me on the morrow how fine he could be in new clothes, and mourning the fact that his greasy garments had cost him a cruel epithet that day from a maid he had attempted to kiss behind a barn on three minutes' acquaintance.

"Faith, she mocked me for a tankard-tip and called me pottle-pot," he said, sadly. "God knows I drink little for my height, and so I told her, too!"

We were already at the "Virginia Arms," and I took him by the elbow and drew him firmly past the tap-room.

"Are we not to sniff a posset?" he demanded, in injured surprise. But he surrendered without a scene, for the late fighting had cleared his head of alcohol, and we mounted to my chamber, bidding a servant to fetch inkhorn, wax, sand, quill, and three sheets of good, clean paper.

When I had lighted my candle, and the materials for writing had been brought, I sat down on the bed and drew the table up before me.

"What are we to do while you write?" asked Mount, sulkily.

"Keep out o' mischief and the tap-room," said I, mending the quill with my hunting-knife.

They stood around rather blankly for a spell while I was composing the first letter, but presently I noticed they had squatted on the floor and were playing at jack-straws with pine splinters from the boards.

My three letters cost me great labour; writing and composition do ever rack me, mind and body, for I know that I spell not as others spell, nor write as I ought to write in the Boston style, and, moreover, those little dots which warn the wise reader that a phrase is ended mean little to me; so I pepper my sheet well with them and trust to God that they fall not on barren soil.

Thus armed with my quill, and doubly armed in the innocence of my ignorance, I made out to accomplish my three letters. The first was this:

"*Sir William Johnson, Bart.*

"HONOURED AND BELOVED SIR,—My mission I have discharged and It hath come to naut. i return to johnsonhall Tomorrow, setting out with Felicity. i, will explane all. War is brocken out, ye Senecas, Lenape, Wyandot, and Showanese dugg up ye hatchett Cresap is fled ye fort and camp burnt Logans family foully murderd with my duties and respects to Ant Molly and my duties and respectfull affections for you. I have the honnour to subscribe myself your dutyfull deputy and kinsman

"MICHAEL CARDIGAN
"Cornet, Border Horse."

My second letter read thus:

"*My deer Kinswoman Mistress Warren.*

"DEER COZZEN,—I write to say that I write to acquaint you that it Is my determination to set out for johnsonhall tomorrow morning therefore Pray be prepared to accompanie me with Black Betty and Your boxes i will command a post-chaise, escort, and horses for such is my right as deputy of Sir William. if I ketch enny fools who seek to mate you I will harm them. i will find a suitable husband for you never fear cozzen i sign myself your affectnate cozzen

MICHAEL CARDIGAN
"Cornet of Border Horse."

My third letter was brief:

"*To the Hon: the Earl of Dunmore,
Royal Governor of Virginia, etc.*

"MY LORD,—My kinswoman Misstress Felicity Warren is my betrothed and She will leave Pitt tomorrow with me and under the escort which it is my right to demand and your lordship's dutie to furnish, with post-chaise, forage, and provisions. Escort and conveyance should be at the Virginia Arms by noon.

"I have, sir, the honour
to subscribe myself y'r
ob't servant

"MICHAEL CARDIGAN

"Special deputy of Sir Wm. Johnson, Bart.,
and cornet in the Royal American Legion of
Border Horse."

CHAPTER XV

I was awakened shortly after daylight by a hubbub and stirring in the street outside, and I lay in bed, listening, half asleep. About six o'clock the Weasel opened my chamber door, saying that Pittsburg was filling with refugees from the frontier, and that a battalion of militia under Cresap had just left to scout on the Monongahela.

I asked him whether messengers had brought me answers to my letters from Lord Dunmore and Miss Warren, and he replied in the negative and shut the door.

About seven I arose and dressed, standing by the window and looking out over the square. The streets of Fort Pitt were lively enough at this early hour; apparently since daybreak hundreds of refugees, men, women, and toddling infants, fleeing from the red scourge on the outer frontiers, had been coming into Pittsburg town. Many were almost naked, proving their dire peril and hasty night retreat, some drove a few sheep or calves, some carried geese or chickens in their arms, others, more fortunate, guided oxen yoked to wagons, on which were piled bedding, kettles, dishes, and what poor household furniture they dared linger to gather before leaving their homes to the Cayugas and their fields to the timber wolf.

At dawn, when the vanguard of this wretched procession had first appeared, straggling through Pittsburg streets, the town-watch took charge of the dazed fugitives and found shelter for them in the fortress; but, as the town awoke and rubbed its eyes to find the streets swarming with exhausted strangers dragging their numbed limbs or sitting on steps and porches, the people threw open their doors and took the outcasts to their firesides. But the houses of the Samaritans were filled to overflow ere the cloaked watchman had called his last hour:

"Four o'clock! A sweet June morning and sad tidings from the frontier!"

And, as the fugitive creatures still came creeping in past the fortress, the double guard was called out and squads told off to conduct the unfortunates to the barracks, court-house, "Governor's Hall," market-sheds, and finally into the churches. And it was pitiful to see them making their way painfully into the square, where many sat down on the turf, and some fell down in the street, and others slept, leaning upright against fences and trees, clasping some poor household relic to their breasts.

Bareheaded children lay slumbering on stone steps; young women, with infants at suck, sat dumb and vacant-eyed on the ground, too weak to reply to those who offered aid. Haggard men, dragging their rifles, turned sunken, perplexed eyes, slowly answering in monosyllables, as though stunned by the swift ruin which had overwhelmed them.

And the story repeated was always the same: burning and butchery everywhere; the frontier a charred, blood-soaked desert; homes, crops, cattle, the very soil itself had gone roaring up in smoke, and all behind was blackness—hopeless, unutterable devastation.

The living fled, the dead lay where they had fallen—and the dead were many. Scarcely a family but had lost a child or a father; few of the aged escaped; neighbours had fallen under hatchet and knife; friends had disappeared.

To and fro the good people of Pitt hastened on their errands of pity; others, having done their part, gathered in groups discussing openly the riot of the previous evening and the scenes in "Governor's Hall."

It was, truly enough, not the first time that Pittsburg streets had been filled with fugitives from the far frontiers; but last night's riot was the first which had ever disturbed the little town, although there had been a disturbance when, early in the week, a runner from Cresap came in to announce the fate of Logan's children and the rising of the Cayugas.

But this new outbreak was very different: people and soldiers had come to blows; blood had flowed, although nobody exactly understood for what reason it had been shed. Patched pates and plastered cheeks were plentiful about the streets; there were rumours, too, of tragedies, but these rumours proved baseless when the morning wore away. As for the death of Greathouse, nobody suspected it, because nobody, except Dunmore and his followers, was aware that Greathouse had fled to Fort Pitt. It is probable that even Wraxall and Murdy and Tice supposed that Greathouse had escaped from us, and that he was somewhere in close cover, waiting an opportunity to rejoin them.

There appeared to be no effort on the part of the town-watch or of the soldiers to arrest any citizen whose body or apparel bore marks of the conflict. Citizens and soldiers eyed each other askance, but apparently without rancour or malice, like generous adversaries who appreciate a fight for its own sake, and respect each other for stout blows given and returned.

Certainly neither could complain of the scarcity of knocks. Scores of noddles had been laid open by citizens' cudgels or by the brass buckles on the soldiers' belts; scores of pates bore brave bumps and pretty protuberances, coyly hiding under patches that exhaled the aroma of vinegar. Many a respectable wig knew its rightful owner no longer; many a pair of spectacles had been gathered into Shemuel's basket; many, many hats had vanished into memory, probably, however, to reappear, peddled by this same Shemuel, when safe opportunity offered and peace once more smiled her commercial smile.

That morning I had reckoned with my host of the "Virginia Arms." As he appeared somewhat uneasy about the reckoning of Jack Mount and the Weasel, I settled that, too, my means permitting me.

However, I observed to Rolfe that the friends of liberty ought to trust each other implicitly, and he answered that they did, especially when cash payments were made.

"Is that the Boston creed?" I asked, scornfully.

"I guess it is," said he, with a shrewd wink.

I began to detest the fellow, and was curt with him as he left my room; but, when Cade Renard strolled in a few moments later, I was astonished to learn that this same James Rolfe had aided Mount to throw the tea-chests into the sea, and had beggared himself in contributing to every secret patriotic society in Boston.

That was my first lesson in ethics. I began to understand why it was that generous people turned niggards when it came to paying tuppence tax on tea; how a man might exact what was his due and yet be no miser; and how he might beggar himself nor stain his name as a spendthrift.

"He'll lend me what he has," said the Weasel, sitting down to lace his hunting-shirt; "but he would be unpleasant if I attempted to escape from here without a reckoning. I am glad you paid; we have no money. We were speaking of tapping our fat Tory magistrate again—"

"Taking the road?" I exclaimed.

"No, taking the judge's purse. He is so fat, positively he disgusts us."

I looked at the little man in horror. He returned my gaze mildly, and tied the leather laces under his chin.

"If," said I, stiffly, "you or Mount require money, I beg you will borrow it from me, as long as we travel together. Also," I continued, angrily, "you may as well know that I do not care to figure with you and Jack Mount in any book or ballad or pamphlet decorated with a picture of a gallows!"

"Do you suppose we like that picture either?" asked the Weasel, in astonishment. "Why, Mr. Cardigan, that picture is perfectly repulsive to us."

"Then why do you take the King's highway?" I asked, blankly.

"You are hurting my feelings," said the Weasel. "Why do you use such terms? Besides, we discriminate; we only offer ourselves some slight recompense for the disgust which overpowers us when we meet with fat Tory magistrates on a moonlit highway."

I stared at him, indignant at the levity with which he used me; but after a moment I was obliged to believe that he intended no levity, for never had I seen such guileless innocence in any features. Clearly the man's past sorrows had been too much for his mind. He was simple.

There was little profit in continuing the subject; if Renard and Mount chose to justify their reputations I could not prevent them. As far as I was concerned they had proved kindly and loyal, and, now that I was so soon to part with them, I desired to do so in gratitude and friendship.

It was already past eight o'clock by the Weasel's large silver watch, and still no reply came to me from either Dunmore or Silver Heels. Renard and I looked out of the window, watching the soldiers conducting the homeless frontier families to the barracks. We spoke of last night's riot, computing the casualties suffered by the soldiers and wondering what proclamation Dunmore would issue, or if he would have the courage to issue any, considering how the people had shown their detestation of him.

"If you were not a deputy of Sir William Johnson, Dunmore would have jailed you for what you said," observed the Weasel. "You have cast the last grain into the scales and they have tipped him out, repudiated and dishonoured. *Hic jacet Dunmoreus, in articulo mortis.* But Walter Butler lives, friend Michael. Beware, sir! *Latet anguis in herba!*—there lies the snake perdu!"

"Who are you, Weasel?" I asked, curiously. "Truly, you are smoother in Latin than am I; but I confess myself disguised in this hunting-shirt, whereas you wear it to the manner born. Yet, I swear you are no forest-runner withal."

"I was born a gentleman," said the Weasel, simply. "I read the classics for my pleasure—but I am forgetting, Mr. Cardigan, I am forgetting so many, many things. It is sixteen years now since I met with my trouble—sixteen years to forget in—and that with a mind which is not quite clear, sir, not quite clear. However, I have remembered enough Latin to entertain you, and that is something, after all, if it is not an answer to your question."

He spoke gently, but there was a sting in the tail of his speech which I certainly deserved for my impertinent prying into his past, and I very promptly asked his pardon for my thoughtlessness.

"I am certain it was nothing more than that," he said, cheerfully; "pray you, my dear sir, believe me that I took no offence. Sometimes my tongue is sharp; my infirmity is my poor apology. I do not wonder at your amusement to hear a shabby forest-runner stammer Latin. But I shall forget my Latin, too; I shall forget all save what I pray to forget."

With his forefinger he quietly obliterated a tear in each eye.

"You know I had a wife?" he asked.

"And baby," I added, mechanically.

"Exactly, sir; a wife and baby girl—the sweetest little maid—"

And, following his mania, to which I lent myself out of pity, he repeated the fragments of the tale I had come to know so well, adding nothing new, nor casting any light on anything he said.

Mount came in noisily while the Weasel was speaking, but, though the big fellow was impatient and burning to exhibit the new clothes which he wore, he sat down quietly until Renard had finished the familiar tale. Heaven alone knows how many times Mount had heard it, but his sympathy never failed, and now he looked so tenderly and lovingly at the Weasel that I almost loved him for it, swaggering, tippling, graceless purse-taker that he was.

However, after maintaining for a full minute that sober silence which decency as well as his loyal affection for the Weasel required, he ventured to call our attention to his new buckskins, fitted, cut, and stitched in twenty-four hours by four tailor-women, whom he described as modest and yet no bigots, as they had appreciated the kiss apiece which he had joyously bestowed upon them.

"No saucy maid durst call me pottle-pot now!" he said, triumphantly, smoothing his soft, new garments with his fingers, and regarding his deeply fringed legs with naïve delight. "Which brings to mind that I have drunk no morning draught this day," he added, clacking his tongue and winking at the Weasel.

"Mr. Cardigan is in some trouble," observed the Weasel, hesitating.

"Oh, then we won't drink while a friend is in trouble," said Mount, sitting down on the bed.

"It is only that I have no letter from Dunmore or from Miss Warren," I muttered, looking out into the street to spy if a messenger were coming our way.

We sat there in silence, gnawing our knuckles, and it did not please me to wait Lord Dunmore's pleasure like a servant.

That Silver Heels had not yet written also displeased me, for I was not then habituated to the ways of a maid.

"Do you think the runner I hired to carry my letter to Sir William will be scalped?" I asked, turning to look at Mount.

"He *has* been scalped," said Mount, quietly.

Thunderstruck, I sprang to my feet, and finally found tongue to ask how he had heard such news.

"Why, lad," he said, modestly, "I followed your runner last night when he left you abed here, and he had not gone ten paces from this inn ere a man left the shadow of the trees yonder to dog us both. It was what I feared; but, Lord!—I caught the fellow by the market yonder, and trounced him till he could neither stand nor sit. I was a fool; I should have followed your runner and brought him back. I did follow, but he had struck a fast pace, and besides they delayed me at the fortress gate with questions about my business. When I cleared the sentries I started to run; but my journey was short enough, God knows!"

He paused, looking down at the fur cap he was slowly twirling on his thumb.

"Your messenger lay dead by the wood's edge," he added, abruptly.

"I had not dreamed the savages were so near," said I, horrified.

"*Some* savages are," he observed.

"Was he scalped?" I asked.

"In Mohawk style, lad."

"Impossible!" I cried.

"Not at all. I say he was scalped in Mohawk fashion, leaving the raw strip over the forehead, but I did not say that Mohawks scalped him."

"What do you mean?" I asked, huskily.

"I mean that Walter Butler's men did this, and that your letter is now in Dunmore's hands."

Rage blinded me. Doubtless I made some noise and talked wildly of seeking Dunmore, and I know I found myself struggling with Mount to leave the room. But I was an infant in his grasp, and presently I sat down again, perforce, while Mount and Renard reasoned with me somewhat sternly.

"The sooner you leave Pitt the safer for you," said Mount. "The town talks of little but your accusation of Dunmore last night. You may think yourself safe because you are Sir William Johnson's deputy, but I know that Dunmore and Butler will treat you as they did your messenger if you give them half a chance. What's to prove that the Cayugas be not your murderers? Tush, lad! This is no time for boyish fury. Get your kinswoman, Miss Warren, out of this town. Get her out to-night. Are you waiting for Dunmore's escort and horses? You will see neither, save perhaps in pursuit of you. Why, lad, the Governor is crazed with the disgrace you have brought upon him! Trust me, he will stop at nothing where he can strike unseen."

"You mean he will not answer my letter or accord me escort?" I asked, astonished.

"If he furnished you escort, it would be an escort of murderers who would take care you never saw Johnstown," said the Weasel.

"Can't you feel that you are in a trap?" asked Mount. "Gad! it should pinch you ere this!"

"And you leave it to us to open it for you," added the Weasel, sagely. "We are none too safe here ourselves. Mayhap some of those same pamphlets and ballads and books may be sold hereabouts to our discredit."

"I also think that Cade and I have outstayed our welcome," said Mount, with a grin. "If we meet your friend Butler, run we must."

At that moment Rolfe came up from below, bearing in his hand a letter for me, and saying that it had been brought hither by a servant in Lady Shelton's livery.

I took the letter; the seal had already been broken, and I glared at Rolfe and pointed to it.

"Ay," he observed, shaking his head; "the slavering servant fetched it so. It may be accident; it may be design, Mr. Cardigan. You best know, sir, who may be your foes in Pittsburg town, and what they might gain by a knowledge of your letters."

"The inn, here, is closely spied," observed Mount, coolly. "Doubtless my lady Shelton's lackeys can be bribed as well as the King's ministers."

"The sooner we leave the happier we shall be," said the Weasel, cheerfully. "Jimmy Rolfe, that stout post-chaise, well provisioned, and four strong horses might help us to-night—eh, friend?"

"I cannot pay for that," I said, blankly, looking up from my letter.

"The chaise is yours," said Rolfe, resentfully. "Pay when you can, sir; I trade not with friends in need." And he went out, disrespectfully slamming the door.

"A rare man," said Mount, "but touchy, lad, touchy. Give the devil his due and Jim Rolfe would wear shillings on his coat-tails."

"He is a loyal friend," I said, reddening. "I have much to learn of men."

"And men have much to learn of you, lad!" said Mount, heartily. "Come, sir, read your nosegay, and may it bring you happiness! Weasel, turn thy back and make pretence to catch flies."

I went over to the window, and, leaning against the bars, opened the violated letter and read it carefully:

"Dear Cozzen Michael,—I am not permitted to accompany you today to Johnstown it being a racing day and I pledged to attend with Lady Shelton and divers respectable ladies and gentlemen.

"And oh Micky why did you say such things to Lord Dunmore last night? I have been ill of it all night and in a fever for fear they may harm you, though Lady Shelton assures me your person is safe, being a deputy of Sir William, and further says that you are an unmannerly and bold rebel and desires not your presence in her house, and desires me to inform you. Oh Micky what have you done? I do not desire any longer to wed Lord Dunmore and be a Countess, but I had not thought to have you speak so to Lord Dunmore. He came here last evening in a white fury and showed me the letter you had written to him. He says that you are not the messenger he expected, though you may be a deputy, and he vows he will not be so vilely used, and he will not give me up but will publish the banns to-day in Pitt, come what may. Which has frightened me so I write to you that I do not wish to be a countess any more and would be glad to go to Aunt Molly and Sir William.

"I will rise from bed at eleven o'clock to-night and go out into the orchard with Black Betty. Pray you cozzen, greet me with a post-chaise and take me away from these dreadful, dreadful people.

"Your cozzen,

"Felicity.

"Postscriptum

"To witt, I will not wed you though we be affianced, and I will wed no man upon your recommendation. With your own affairs I pray you be dilligently active and concern yourself not with mine hereafter."

When I had again read the letter I examined the wax. The paper had been carelessly folded and more carelessly sealed; and I called to Mount and the Weasel, pointing out that, though the letter was unsealed, the wax itself had not been broken.

"I do not think," said I, "that this letter has deliberately been tampered with. This is only carelessness."

"It was certainly sealed and folded in haste," remarked the Weasel, poking at the wax with his forefinger.

Mount also pretended to believe that negligence or haste accounted for the open letter, and, satisfied, we sat down to discuss the measures to be taken for a fortnight flight.

I had a mind to follow Silver Heels to the races, trusting that I might find a moment to warn her most solemnly not to fail us. Mount thought the idea most wise, offering to bear me company, and the Weasel agreed to remain and assist Rolfe to equip and furnish our post-chaise with the necessaries for a long journey.

It was understood between us that Silver Heels and Black Betty were to ride in the chaise, and I with them; that Mount and the Weasel would sit the horses as postilions, and that Shemuel should ride atop. It was further decided that, as the northern and western frontier were impassable in view of the border war, we should take the post-road to the Virginia border, make for Williamsburg, and from there turn north across Maryland and the Jerseys, reaching Johnstown through New York and Albany.

I gave the Weasel money to purchase powder and ball, which we all lacked, and to buy for me a silver watch and a rifle or firelock to replace the loss of my own. Also, I charged him to purchase pistols for me and for Shemuel, with flint and ball for the same, and to sharpen our knives and hatchets against need.

"You waste breath," observed Mount, yawning. "The Weasel never neglects to file his claws for battle."

"Very well," said I, wincing; "it seems that of us all I alone know nothing of my own affairs."

"You will learn," said the Weasel, kindly, and I was obliged to swallow their well-meant patronage and follow Mount to the street.

"If I had my way," said I, resentfully, "I would take Miss Warren from the races and set out by noon."

"If I had my way," observed Mount, "I should not try to escape to-night at all."

"Why not?" I asked, in surprise.

"Because of that unsealed letter."

"But we agreed it was accident!"

"Ay, *we* agree, but mayhap there are others yet to disagree."

"Nonsense!" I said.

"Doubtless," said Mount, with the faintest trace of irony, enough to flavour his mild smile with that mockery which hurts the pride of very young men.

Offended, I strode on beside him, and neither he nor I offered to speak again until Mount suddenly stopped in the middle of the King's Road and looked back.

"What's amiss?" I asked, forgetting my sulks.

"Oh, we are followed again," said Mount, wearily.

I stared about but could see nobody who appeared to be observing us. There were numbers of people on the King's Road, trudging through the dust as were we, and doubtless also bound for the races on Roanoke Plain. I saw no vehicles or horsemen: the quality in their chairs and coaches would go by the fashionable Boundary; the fox-hunting horsemen met at the "Buckeye Tavern," a resort for British officers and gentlemen; unpretentious folk must foot it by the shortest route, which was to pass the fortress by the King's Road.

"Are you sure we are followed?" I asked.

"Not quite," said Mount, simply. "I shall know anon. Trust me in this, lad, and take pains to do instantly what I do. Perhaps my life may pay for this day's pleasure."

"I will take care to imitate you," said I, anxiously. "You know how deeply in your debt I stand confessed."

"Good lad," he said, gravely; "I do not doubt you, friend Michael. As for any debt, your courtesy has long cancelled it."

The quaint compliment had a pretty savour, coming from one whose world was not my own.

We were now passing that angle of the fortified works through which the King's Road passes between two block-housen. The sentries, standing in the shadow of the stockade, watched us without visible interest, turning their idle heads to scan the next comer, and stare impudently if it were some petticoat.

So, unquestioned, we passed out into the country, where a few heavily stockaded farms flanked the road, always built on heights, and always free from trees or any cover that might shelter an attacking enemy. Beyond these farms the road became a turnpike, and we stopped at the toll-gate to pay tuppence to the keeper's wife, who sat nursing a baby, one hand on a rifle, which she never let go until the evening brought her husband to keep his perilous vigil there all night.

"No," she said, listlessly, "no Indians have troubled us. Yet, God knows I sleep not while my man is out here in the night, though they send a patrol from the fortress every hour."

Mount earnestly advised her to give up the toll-gate until the border had quieted; but she only stared, saying, "How, then, are we to live?" And we passed on in silence, side by side.

Beyond the toll-gate a broad road curved out from the turnpike, running south, and Mount pointed it out as the road we were to travel that night.

"It crosses the Virginia border by that blue hill yonder," he said, then suddenly jerked his head over his shoulder.

"I think I am right; I think I know the jade," he said, calmly.

"Is it a woman who follows us?" I asked, amazed.

"Ay, a bit of a lass, maybe eighteen or thereabouts."

"You know her?"

"And she me," said Mount, grimly. "Harkee, friend Michael, if you must needs know the truth, her father is—Gad! I can scarce say it to you, but—well—her father is what they call a thief-taker."

"What has that to do with us?" I asked.

Mount spoke with an effort: "Because I have stopped some few purse-proud magistrates upon the highway, they say evil things o' me. That lass behind us means to follow me and tell her lout of a father where I may be found."

I was horrified, and he saw it and stopped short in his tracks.

"You are right," he said, simply; "a gentleman cannot be found in such company. Go on alone, lad; it is right, and I shall bear no malice."

"Jack!" I said, hotly; "do you believe I would cry quits now? Damnation! Come on, sir! I would as soon take the King's highway myself!"

His firm mouth relaxed and quivered a little; he hesitated, then walked forward beside me with a touch of that old swagger, muttering something about gentle blood and what's bred in the bone.

"It's all very well," he said; "it's all very well for some of our people to say that we men are created equal. There's no truth in it. A broodhound never cast whippets, let them say what they will!"

We were now in sight of the flag-covered pavilion on Roanoke Plain, and on either side of us the road was lined with those drinking-booths and peddler-stands and cheap-jack tents which had pitched camps here for the day rather than pay the tax required to sell their wares within the racing-grounds.

Around them the townspeople clustered, some munching gingerbread and pies, some watching the gilded wheel of fortune spin their pennies into another man's pockets, some paying for a peep into a dark shed where doubtless wonders were to be seen for a penny. Ragged children sold colours and cards for the races; peddlers assailed our ears at every step; fortune-tellers followed us, predicting unexpected blessings, which turned to curses when we passed along unheeding; acrobats, tumblers, jugglers, strong men, and merry-andrews hailed us as their proper prey. And, in sooth, had it not been for the sickening knowledge of Mount's peril, I should have found keen pleasure in spending all I had, to see everybody and everything at this show; for I do dearly love strange sights, and in Johnstown I have always viewed them all, with Silver Heels and Esk and Peter, when the season of racing brought these gay folk to our town.

But now I had no stomach for pleasure, nor had Mount, for he scarcely glanced at the booths as we passed, though there was ale there, and sweet Virginia wines, which drew the very honey-bees themselves.

Suddenly Mount said, "This will not do; I have been hunted long enough!"

"What are you going to do?" I asked.

"Hunt in my turn," he said, grimly.

"Hunt—what?"

"The lass who hunts me. Follow, lad. On your life, do as I do. Now, then! Gay! Gay! Ruffle it, lad! Cut a swagger, cock your cap, and woe to the maid who is beguiled by us!"

The change in him was amazing; his airs, his patronage, his chaff, his lightening wit!—it was the old Mount again, quaffing a great cup of ale, pledging every pretty face that passed, hammering his pewter to emphasize his words, talking with all who would answer him; glorious in his self-esteem, amusing in his folly, a dandy, a ruffler, a careless, wine-bibbing, wench-bussing coureur-de-bois, and king of them all without an effort.

Peddler and gypsy were no match for him; his banter silenced the most garrulous, his teasing pleased the wenches, his gay gallantries made many a girl look back at him, and many a smile was returned to him with delicate surplus of interest.

"Which is the maid?" I asked, under my breath.

"Yonder, stopping to stare at gingerbread as though she had never beheld such a sweet before. Now she turns; mark! It is she with the pink print and chip hat on her hair, tied with rose ribbons under the chin."

"I see her," said I.

She was a healthy, red-cheeked, blue-eyed girl, with lips a trifle over-full and bosom to match withal. She appeared uneasy and uncertain, watching Mount when he raised a laugh, and laughing herself as excuse, though her mirth appeared to me uneasy, now that I understood her purpose.

She had been edging nearer, and now stood close to us, at the entrance to an arbour wherein were set benches in little corners, hidden from prying eyes by strips of painted cloth.

"Will no maid pity me!" exclaimed Mount. "I am far, far too young to drink my wine alone in yonder arbour!"

"I have not been invited," cried a saucy wench, laughing at us over the shoulder of her companion, who backed away, half laughing, half frightened.

"God helps those who help themselves," said Mount, turning to find her who had followed him close to his elbow.

He smiled in her face and made her a very slow and very low bow, drawing a furrow through the dust with the fluffy tail on his coon-skin cap.

"If I knew your name," he said, "I might die contented. Otherwise I shall content myself with a life of ignorance."

She seemed startled and abashed, fingering her gown and looking at her shoe-buckles, while Mount bent beside her to whisper and smile and swagger until he entreated her to taste a glass of currant wine with us in the arbour.

I do not know to this day why she consented. Perhaps she thought to confirm her suspicions and entrap some admission from Mount; perhaps, in the light of later events, her purpose was very different. However, we three sat in the arbour behind our screens of painted cloth, and Mount did set such a pace for us that ere I was aware there remained not a drop of currant in the decanter, no more cakes on the plate, and he had his arm around the silly maid.

Intensely embarrassed and ill at ease with this pot-house gallantry, which was ever offensive to my tastes, I regarded them sideways in silence, impatient for Mount to end it all.

The end had already begun; Mount rose lightly to his feet and drew the girl with him, turning her quietly by the shoulders and looking straight into her eyes.

"Why do you follow me?" he asked, coolly.

The colour left her face; her eyes flew wide open with fright.

"I shall not hurt you, little fool," he said; "I had rather your father, the thief-taker, took me, than harm you. Yes, I am that same Jack Mount. You are poor; they will pay you for compassing my arrest. Come, shall we seek your father, Billy Bishop, the taker of thieves?"

He drew her towards the gate, but she fell a-whimpering and caught his arm, hiding her face in his buckskin sleeve.

Disgusted, I waited a moment, then turned my back and walked out into the sunshine, where I paced to and fro, until at last Mount joined me, wearing a scowl.

As we turned away together I glanced into the arbour and saw our lass of the ribbons still sitting at the table with her head buried in her arms and her pink shell-hat on the grass.

As for Mount, he said nothing except that, though he no longer feared the girl, he meant, hereafter, to trust to his heels in similar situations.

"It might be less irksome," said I, curling my lip.

"Ay; yet she has a pretty face, and a plump neck, too."

"The daughter of a thief-taker!" I added, contemptuously.

"Pooh!" said he. "She has thirty sound teeth and ten fingers; the Queen of Spain has no more."

CHAPTER XVI

As we came to the high stockade which surrounded the Roanoke Racing Plain, a bell struck somewhere inside; there was a moment's silence, then a roar, "They're off!" and the confused shouting of a crowd: "Greensleeves leads! Heather-Bee! Heather-Bee!" which suddenly died out, ceased, then swelled into a sharp yell: "Orange and Black! Orange wins! Baltimore! Baltimore! Baltimore! No! No! The Jersey colt! The Jersey colt! Crimson! Crimson!" A hush; the dull, double thud of galloping; a scramble, a rush, and a hurricane of wild cheers: "Heather-Bee! Heather-Bee! Good Greensleeves! Hi—yi—yi! Hooray!"

"I would I had a sovereign laid on this same Heather-Bee," said Mount, mechanically fumbling in his empty pockets.

I glanced at him in surprise. Had the novelty of our present peril already grown so stale that the shouting of a rabble over a winning horse could blot it out?

He observed my disapproval and took his hands from his pocket-flaps, muttering something about a passion for betting; and I paid the gate-keepers the fee they demanded for us both, which included a card giving us entry to the paddock.

When I entered I expected to see a "sweet and delightsome plain," as the public crier had advertised so loudly with his horn, but truly I was not prepared for the beauty which was now revealed. Bowered in trees the lovely pale green meadow lay, all starred with buttercups and cut by the bronzed oval of the course. Pavilion and field glowed in the colours of fluttering gowns; white and scarlet and green marked the line where half a dozen mounted jockeys walked their lean horses under the starter's tower. The sun blazed down, gilding the chestnut necks of the horses; a cool breeze bellied the bright sleeves of the jockeys, and blew the petticoats and ribbons till they flapped like rainbow flags.

Mount was nudging me, sulkily demanding to be informed where bets were placed, and adding that he knew a horse as well as the next man. However, when he proposed that I allow him to double my capital for me, I flatly refused, and reproached him for wishing to risk anything now.

"Well, then," he muttered, "lay a sovereign yourself for luck;" but I paid no attention, and fixed my eyes on the pavilion to search it through and through for Silver Heels.

The longer I searched the more hopeless I felt my task to be; I could see a score of maids in that vast bouquet, any one of which might have been Silver Heels, but was not.

I then sought to discover Lady Shelton, a large, sluggish lady whom I had noticed at Johnstown—not attracted by her beauty, but to observe her how she did eat a barrel of oysters in pickle, when visiting our guard-house with her kinsman, Colonel Guy Johnson.

I could not find her, though there were many ladies in the pavilion who appeared to resemble her in largeness and girth, and in fatness of hand and foot.

With my arm on Mount's, who had fallen a-pouting, I paced the sward, searching the pavilion through and through, unmindful of the battery of bright eyes which swept and raked us with indolent contempt. Where was Silver Heels? Ay, where in the devil's name had the little baggage hid herself? Many ladies and their consorts in the pavilion were rising and passing under a yellow canopy to the right, where there appeared to be a luncheon spread on tables; and I did see and smell large bowls of sweetened punch, Mount smelling the same and thoughtfully clacking his tongue.

"The quality," he observed, "have punch and French wines. Yet I dare wager a pocketful o' sixpences that they have not my depth, and God knows I would cheerfully prove it."

"Nobody is like to challenge you," I said, coldly. "Come, we must find my cousin, Miss Warren, or our journey here fails."

The fox-hunting gentry in pink were coming across the field in a body, spurs glistening and curly horns striking fire in the sunshine. As they passed us, clink! clink! over the turf, a strangely familiar eye met mine and held it—the puzzled eye of a young man, dressed in red coat and tops and wearing a black velvet cap. Where had I seen him before? He, too, appeared perplexed, and, as he passed, involuntarily touched the peak of his cap with his hunting-whip. Suddenly I knew him, and at the same moment he left the company and came hastily up to me, offering his hand. The fox-hunter was my old acquaintance, Mr. Bevan, the dragoon, and he had actually recognized me under my sunburn and buckskins. Rivals never forget.

However, there was no mistaking his cordiality, and I should have been an oaf and a churl not to have met him fairly by the hand he offered.

"*Sans arrière pensée, sans rancune!*" he said, heartily, the French not pleasing me; but I returned his straightforward clasp and told him I bore no more malice than did he.

"I heard you speak in 'Governor's Hall,'" he said, and I saw his eyes twinkle, though his mouth betrayed no mirth, so I only bowed seriously and told him I was honoured by his presence.

"Was not that gentleman Patrick Henry—the one in black who led the poor savage out?" he asked.

"Doubtless you know Patrick Henry better than I do," I answered, cautiously.

He laughed outright.

"Pray, believe me, Mr. Cardigan, I am not prying. It is rumoured that Patrick Henry has been at some rebel tavern in town. A few thought they recognized him in 'Governor's Hall,' and many claim that he wrote that great speech for Logan."

"If he did he is the greatest orator of our times," I said.

"Do you believe he did?"

"No," said I, bluntly.

He looked at me with curious, friendly eyes.

"You have become famous, Mr. Cardigan, since we last met."

"You would say 'notorious,'" I rejoined, smiling.

He protested vigorously:

"No! no! I understand you are not of our party, but, believe me, were I a— a—patriot, as they say, I should be proud to hear a comrade utter the words you uttered in 'Governor's Hall'!"

"Did I say I was a rebel?" I asked, laughing.

"Well," he rejoined, "if that speech did not commit you, we are but a dull company here in Pittsburg."

He glanced after his comrades, who were now entering the canopied space where refreshments lay piled between the bottles and punch-bowls; and he straightway invited me, turning with a bow to include Jack Mount, whom I had not dared present under his proper name.

Mount began to accept with a flourish, but I cut him short with excuses, which Mr. Bevan accepted politely, expressing his regret. Then again he offered me his hand so frankly that I drew him aside, and begged his indulgence and forgetfulness for my boorish behaviour at Johnson Hall.

"The fault was mine," he said, instantly; "I sneered at your militia and deserved your rebuke. Had I not deserved it, I should have called you out, Mr. Cardigan."

"You conducted properly," said I; "on the contrary, I must blush for my churlishness when you favoured my hilt with a ribbon."

His friendly eyes grew grave, and he began bending his hunting-whip into a bow, thoughtfully studying the buttercups at his feet.

After a moment he looked up, saying, "Do you know that this morning the banns were published for the wedding of Lord Dunmore and your kinswoman, Miss Warren?"

So, after all, and in spite of my letter, Dunmore had done this shameful thing! I think my scowling face gave Bevan his answer, for he laid his hand on my arm and looked at me earnestly.

"It is no shame," he said, "for me to tell you that Miss Warren has refused me. How can a heart be humbled which has loved such a woman?"

"She is not a woman yet," I said, harshly; "she is a child, and a wilful one at that! Damnation! sir, it maddens me to see men after her, and she but fifteen!"

"Miss Warren celebrated her sixteenth birthday with a dinner at Lady Shelton's a week since," said Bevan, colouring up.

I thought a moment, frowning and counting on my fingers. Yes, that was true; Silver Heels was sixteen now. But that only increased my irritation, for the danger suddenly assumed menacing proportions, which must increase every moment now that the barriers of childhood no longer barred the men who hunted her.

"I have told you this," said Bevan, stiffly, "because I believed you were in love with Miss Warren, and must suffer great pain to learn of her betrothal to Lord Dunmore."

"And—what then, sir?" I asked, angry and perplexed.

"This, Mr. Cardigan! That my own ill fortune has not left me less devoted to her happiness; that this marriage is a monstrous thing and will one day drive her to despair; that I do most earnestly believe that Miss Warren loves a man more worthy of her."

"What man?" I demanded, sharply.

"You should not ask me that!" he retorted, more sharply still.

"But I do! Confound it, I know from her own lips that she dotes on some conceited, meddling ass! And if I can but lay my hand on his collar—"

Bevan was staring at me in such frank amazement that I bit my words short.

"Did Miss Warren confess that she loved?" he asked.

I assented in silence.

"A—a fool?"

I nodded.

Bevan burst into a bitter laugh.

"Then let me tell you, sir, that I have heard her praise this same meddling fool and laud his every word as Heaven's own wisdom! Ay, sir, and boast of his bravery and his wit and his glorious person till I thought this fool a very god from Olympus, and marvelled at my own blindness in not earlier perceiving it."

"You know him?" I cried.

"Indeed, he is now well known in Pittsburg town, Mr. Cardigan."

"But you—"

"Yes, I know him."

After a moment's silence I said, "Is he worthy of her?"

"What man is?" he answered, quietly.

"Oh, many men; pardon, but you are in love, and so are blinded. I see clearly. I know my cousin, and I know that she is a wilful maid who has raised the devil out o' bounds, and is ready to run to cover now."

Bevan was red in the face.

"It is a kinsman's privilege to criticise," he said.

"A kinsman's duty!" I added. "Were I not jealous for her honour and happiness, I would cry Dunmore *merci!* and think my cousin a fortunate maid! Curse him! When I think of that man I can scarce look at my hands so guiltless of the creature's blood. But they will not stay clean long if he pushes me. God help the man who bars our way northward!"

"If you mean to take her," said Bevan, in a low voice, "I wish you godspeed. But how can you pass the fort, Mr. Cardigan?"

"Do you believe Dunmore would detain us?" I asked, blankly.

"I know he would if he heard of it in time."

I thought a moment, then laid my hand on Bevan's shoulder, and, on the impulse, told him what our plans were. He listened in silent sympathy, nodding at times, turning to glance at Mount, who sat under a tree chewing grass-blades and sniffing at the distant punch-bowls.

When I had told him all, he reflected, slowly switching the sod with his whip. Presently he said: "I am glad you told me this. I will be at the King's Road gate to-night. If there is trouble with the sentries I will vouch for you."

His quiet generosity touched me deeply, and I told him so.

"Could a gentleman do less?" he asked, gravely. Then a sudden smile lighted his eyes, and he added: "She will never give up her Olympian god, though she thought to fling him away for his indifference. And, Mr. Cardigan, though this man she loves is truly all she claims, he is, as she told you, the greatest fool on earth!"

"Then he can never have her!" I said, contemptuously.

"Ah—wait!" he replied, with a curiously sad smile. "A fool and his folly are soon parted when in the company of Miss Warren."

"You believe he will follow her? That's what she said, too!" I exclaimed, hotly.

Again he burst into a laugh which was quite free from bitterness.

"Yes, he is certain to follow you," he said. "Black Care rides behind the horseman, but this man will stick closer than your own shadow."

"We'll see," I muttered.

He offered me his hand, pressing mine firmly.

"You know Miss Warren is here?" he asked, cautiously.

"I am seeking her," said I.

"She walked to the hill, yonder, with Lady Shelton, after the last race," he said, pointing with his whip to a wooded knoll which I could just see rising behind the paddocks.

"Dunmore is searching everywhere for her," he added, significantly.

So we parted, I warm with gratitude, he quietly cordial, yet still wearing that singular smile which I could not quite understand.

As for pity, I had none for him, nor did I believe his sorrow could be very profound over his dismissal by Silver Heels. But then I knew nothing of such matters, having never been in love. As for the gentleman-god who had turned Silver Heels's silly head, I meant to deal with him the instant he made his appearance.

Mount, tired of cropping the herbage under his tree, rejoined me fretfully, demanding to know why I had not accepted the invitation to refreshment; and I told him quite plainly that I had no intention to further test his sobriety, in view of the work we had before us.

Together we entered the paddock, where hostlers and jockeys were grooming the beautiful, slender horses, and though I longed to linger, I dared not stay longer than to hug one splendid mare and whisper in her listening, silky ears that she was a beauty without peer.

The boy who was washing her sourly warned me off, doubtless fearing the touch of a stranger, lest he prove one of those miscreants who harm horses. So I passed on, nodding good-bye to the lovely mare, Heather-Bee, as she was called by the name stitched on her blanket.

In the rear of the paddock a path led through a gate and up the wooded knoll. I looked around for Mount; he was plaintively helping himself to a cup of water from the horse-trough spring, so I waited. And, as I stood there, down the path came two fat people, a lady and her escort, picking their way with all the majesty of elephants. I knew Lady Shelton at once; none could mistake that faded and moon-like face with the little selfish under-lip and the folded creases beside a mouth which was made only for feeding. None could mistake those little fat feet, trotting under the daintily raised petticoat.

She scarcely deigned to glance at me; the gentleman beside her paid me no attention; and I was thankful enough that Lady Shelton had not recognized me.

They were waddling down the paddock some distance away when Mount rejoined me, complaining of the cheerless draught which my obstinacy had compelled him to swallow, and we passed the gate and ascended the pretty slope.

We were, perhaps, half-way up the slope, when I heard a footstep behind us and glanced back. What was my astonishment to behold the Weasel trotting along at our heels.

"Where on earth did you come from?" I asked.

"From the 'Virginia Arms,'" he replied, seriously. "I like to be near Jack."

Mount, in pleased surprise, had already laid his great paw on the Weasel's shoulder. Now he smiled at the little careworn man with wonderful tenderness. It was strange, the affection between these two roaming men, the naïve fidelity of the Weasel, the fostering care of the younger giant, whose attitude was sometimes fatherly, sometimes filial.

The Weasel looked back at the course where, already, the bell was striking to warn the jockeys, and where, one after another, the horses cantered out to the judges' stand and stood restively, or backed and pirouetted and reared in the sunshine.

"Have you ever before seen a race?" I asked.

"I? A race?" He waved his hand with a peculiarly sad gesture. "Many a noble horse has carried my colours on Cambridge Downs," he said, simply. "Many a plate have my youngsters won for me, Mr. Cardigan."

He looked out over the green meadow, folding his small, dry hands meekly.

"Lord, Lord," he murmured, "the world has changed since then! The world has changed!"

"Friends have not," murmured Mount.

"No, no, you are quite right, Jack," said Renard, hastily.

"Then who the devil cares how the world may change," snapped Mount. "Come, Cade, old friend, sit you here in the sweet grass and you and I will wager straws on the jockeys' colours yonder, while our young gentleman here lightly goes a-courting!"

I did not choose to notice Mount's remark, knowing that he meant no offence, so I left the pair sitting on the sod and climbed the remaining half of the slope alone.

Now, no sooner had I reached the top of the knoll than I perceived Silver Heels, sitting upon a rock, reading a letter; and when I drew near, my moccasins making no sound, I could not help but see that it was my letter she perused so diligently. It gratified me to observe that she apparently valued the instructions in my letter, and I trusted she intended to profit by them, for Heaven knew she needed admonition and the judicious counsel of a mature intellect.

"Silver Heels," I began, kindly.

She started, then crushed the letter to a ball, thrusting it into her bosom.

"Oh, Michael, you are insufferable!" she cried.

"What!" I exclaimed, astonished.

Her eyes filled and she sprang up.

"I know not whether to laugh or cry, so vexed am I!" she stammered, and called me booby and Paul Pry, drying her eyes the while her tongue upbraided me.

"I am not spying," said I, hotly; "don't pretend that scrawl was a love-letter, for I know it to be my own!"

"Ah—you *did* come spying!" she flashed out, stamping her foot furiously.

"Lord! was there ever such a spiteful maid!" I cried. "I came here to have a word with you concerning our journey this night. I care not a penny whistle for your love-letters. Can you not understand that?"

She turned somewhat pale and stood still. Her under-lip quivered between her teeth.

"Yes," she said, slowly, "I understand."

I had not meant to speak harshly, and I told her so. She nodded, scarcely listening. Then I spoke of our coming journey, which, though it galled me to say so, I explained to her was nothing less than a flight.

She acquiesced, saying she was ready, and that she only longed to leave the town forever. She said that she had known nothing but unhappiness here, and that the memory of it would always be abhorrent, which surprised me, as I had understood that the gentleman-god dwelt hereabouts. However, I said nothing to disturb her or endanger her docility, and we discussed our plans reasonably and with perfect calmness.

I was pleased to see that she already appeared to be in better health. Rouge and patch had disappeared; her colour was better; her eyes brighter; her lips redder. Also, her gown was simpler and more pleasing to me, and her hair bore no extravagant towers, but was sweetly puffed and rolled from her white forehead. Still, her arms were more frail than I liked to see, and there rested a faint bluish shadow under each eye.

"How came you to find me out, here in my retreat?" she asked, slowly.

"Mr. Bevan told me," I replied, watching her.

"Poor Mr. Bevan," she murmured; "how jealous you were of him."

"He is a splendid fellow," I declared, much ashamed.

"So you are already friends," she observed, in a musing way.

"I trust so," I replied, fervently.

"Is it not sudden?" she asked.

But I would not commit myself.

"Silver Heels," I said, "does it not seem good to be together again here in the sunshine?"

"Ah, yes!" she cried, impetuously, then stopped.

Doubtless she was thinking of the gentleman-god.

I sat down on the grass beside her and began pulling buttercups. One I held under her white chin to see if she still loved butter.

"I love all that I ever loved," she said, leaning forward over her knees to pluck a tiny blue bud in the grass.

"Do you remember that day you bit me in the school-room?" I asked, with youthful brutality.

The crimson flooded her temples. She involuntarily glanced at my left hand; the scar was still there, and she covered her eyes tightly with her hands.

"Oh! Oh! *Oh!*" she murmured, in horror. "What a savage I was! No wonder you hated me—"

"Only at moments," I said, magnanimously; "I always liked you, Silver Heels."

Presently she drew her hands from her eyes and touched her flushed cheeks with the blue blossom thoughtfully.

"Michael," she said, "I—I never told you, but I was very glad when you came to explain to me that night in the pantry."

"Well," said I, stiffly, "you certainly concealed your pleasure. Lord, child, how you scorned me!"

"I know it," she muttered, in quick vexation; "I was a perfect fool. You see, I—I was hurt so deeply that it frightened me—"

"You ought to have known that I meant nothing," said I. "Mrs. Hamilton tormented me till I—I—well, whatever I did was harmless. Anyway, it was done because I thought I loved you—I mean like a lover, you know—"

"I know," said Silver Heels.

"After that," said I, smiling, "I knew my own mind."

"And I knew mine," said Silver Heels.

"And now I know the difference between hurt vanity and love," I added, complacently.

"I, too," said Silver Heels.

"You can't know such things; you are scarcely sixteen," I insisted.

"My mother was wedded at sixteen; she wedded for love."

After a silence I asked her how she knew that, as she had never seen her mother.

"Sir Peter Warren has told me in his letters," she said, simply. "Besides, you are wrong when you say I never saw my mother. I did, but I was too young to remember. She died when I was a year old."

"But you never saw your father," I said.

"Oh no. He was killed at sea by the French."

That was news to me, although I had always been aware that he had died at sea on board his Majesty's ship *Leda*, one of Sir Peter's squadron.

"Who told you he was killed by the French?" I asked, soberly.

"Sir Peter. A few days after you left Johnstown I received a packet from Sir Peter. It came on a war-ship which put in at New York, and the express brought it. Sir Peter also wrote to Sir William. I don't know what he said. Sir William was very silent with me after that, but just before I left with Lady Shelton to come here, he had a long talk with me—"

She stopped abruptly.

"Well?" I asked.

Silver Heels twirled the blue bud in her fingers.

"He said—to—to tell you if I saw you in Pittsburg—to—to—I mean that I was to say to you that Sir William had changed his mind—"

"About what?" I demanded, irritably.

"Our betrothal."

"Our betrothal?"

"Yes. I am not to wed you."

"Of course not," I said, rather blankly; "but I thought Sir William desired it. He said that he did. He said it to me!"

"He no longer wishes it," said Silver Heels.

"Why?"

"I don't know," she answered, faintly.

I was hurt.

"Oh, very well," I observed, resentfully, "doubtless Sir William has chosen a wealthy gentleman of rank and distinction for you. He is quite right. I am only a cornet of horse, and won't be that long. All the same, I cannot see why he forbids me to wed you. He told me he wished it! I cannot see why he should so slight me! Why should he forbid me to wed you?"

"Do you care?" asked Silver Heels.

"Who—I? Care? Why—why, I don't know. It is not very pleasant to be told you are too poor and humble to wed your own kin if you wish to. Suppose I wished to?"

After a moment she said: "Well—it's too late now."

"How do you know?" I said, sharply. "I do not see why I should be driven away from you! It is unfair! It is unkind! It is mortifying and I don't like it! See here, Silver Heels, why should Sir William drive me away from you?"

"You have never needed driving," said Silver Heels.

"Yes, I have!" I retorted. "Didn't you drive me away for Bevan?"

After a silence she stole a glance at me.

"Would you come back—now?"

Something in her voice startled me.

"Why—yes," I stammered, not knowing exactly what she meant; "I cannot see that there is such difference in rank between us that Sir William should forbid me to wed you. Of course you would not wed beneath you, and, as for me, I'd sooner cut my head off!"

"I was afraid," she ventured, "that perhaps—perhaps Sir William thought you had become too fine for me. I could not endure to wed you if that were true."

This was a new idea. Was it true that my quality unfitted me to mate with Silver Heels? The idea did not gratify me now.

"I'll tell you this," said I, "that if I loved you in that way—you know what I mean!—I'd wed you anyhow!"

"But I would not wed you!" she said, haughtily.

"You would not refuse me?" I asked, in amazement.

"I should hate you—if you were above me—in rank!"

"Even if you loved me before?"

"Ah, yes—even if I loved you—as I love—him whom I love."

Her clear eyes were looking straight into mine now. Again her voice had stirred some new and untouched chord which curiously thrilled, sounding stealthily within me.

She lowered her eyes to the blue blossom in her fingers, and I saw her crush it. What soft, white fingers she had! The flushed tips, crushing the blossom, fascinated me.

Again, suddenly, my heart began to beat heavily, thumping in my throat so strangely that I shivered and passed my hand over my breast.

Silver Heels bent lower over her idle hands; her fingers, so exquisite, were still now.

Presently I said, "Who is this fool whom you love?"

I had not thought to fright or hurt her, but she flushed and burned until all her face was surging scarlet to her hair.

"Silver Heels," I stammered, catching her fingers.

At the touch the strange thrill struck through my body and I choked, unable to utter a word; but the desire for her hands set me quivering, and I caught her fingers and drew them, interlocked, from her eyes. Her eyes! Their beauty amazed me; their frightened, perilous sweetness drew my head down to them. Breathless, her mouth touched mine; against me her heart was beating; then suddenly she had gone, and I sprang to my feet to find her standing tearful, quivering, with her hands on her throbbing throat. I leaned against a sapling, dazed, content to meet her eyes and strive to think. Useless! In my whirling thoughts I could but repeat her name, endlessly. Other thoughts crept in, but flew scattering to the four winds, while every pulse within me throbbed out her name, repeating, ceaselessly repeating, in my beating heart.

We were so poor in years, so utterly untried in love, that the strangeness of it set us watching one another. Passion, shaking frail bodies, startles, till pain, always creeping near, intrudes, dismaying maid and youth to love's confusion.

With a sort of curious terror she watched me leaning there, and I saw her trembling fingers presently busied with the silken hat ribbons under her chin, tying and retying as though she knew not what she did. Then of a sudden she dropped on the rock and fell a-weeping without a sound; and I knelt beside her, crushing her shoulders close to me, and kissing her neck and hands, nay, the very damask on her knees, and the silken tongue of her buckled shoon among the buttercups.

Why she wept I knew not, nor did she—nor did I ask her why. Her frail hands fell listlessly, scarcely moving under my lips. Once she laid her arm about my neck, then dropped it as though repelled. And never a word could we find to break the silence.

I heard the wind blowing somewhere in the world, but where, I cared not. I heard blossoms discreetly stirring, and dusky branches interlacing, taking counsel together behind their leafy, secret screens. My ears were filled with voiceless whisperings, delicate and noiseless words were forming in the silence, "I love you"; and my dumb tongue and lips, unstirring, understood, and listened. Then, when my sweetheart had also heard, she turned and put both arms around my neck, linking her fingers, and her gray eyes looked down at me, beside her knees.

"Now you must go," she was repeating, touching her little French hat with tentative fingers to straighten it, but eyes and lips tenderly smiling at me. "My Lady Shelton and Sir Timerson Chank will surely return to catch you here if you hasten not—dear heart."

"But will you not tell me when you first loved me, Silver Heels?" I persisted.

"Well, then—if you must be told—it was on the day when you first wore your uniform, and I saw you were truly a man!"

"That day! When you scarcely spoke to me?"

"Ay, that was the reason. Yet now I think of it, I know I have always loved you dearly; else why should I have been so hurt when you misused me; why should I have cried abed so many, many nights, vowing to my heart that I did hate you as I hated no man! Ah—dear friend, you will never know—"

"But," I insisted, "you grew cool enough to wed Lord Dunmore—"

"Horror! Why must you ever hark back to him when I tell you it was not I who did that, but a cruelly used and foolish child, stung with the pain of your indifference, maddened to hear you talk of mating me as though I were your hound!—and my only thought was to put myself above you and beyond your reach to shame me—"

"Oh, Silver Heels!" I murmured, aghast at my own wickedness.

But she was already smiling again, with her slender hands laid on my shoulders.

"All that tastes sweetly—now," she said.

"It is ashes in my mouth," I said, bitterly, and upbraided myself aloud, until she placed her fingers on my face and silently signed me to turn around.

At the same instant a wheezy noise came to my ears, and the next moment, over the edge of the slope, a large, round face rose like the full moon.

Fascinated, I watched it; the wheezing grew louder and more laboured.

"Lady Shelton! Oh, go! go!" whispered Silver Heels. But it was too late for flight had I been so minded.

Suddenly my Lady Shelton's fat feet began to trot as though of their own notion, for her cold, flabby features expressed no emotion, although, from the moment her moon-like face had risen behind the hill, I saw that her eyes were fixed on me.

After her puffed the fat gentleman, Sir Timerson Chank, and behind him came mincing Lord Dunmore, fanning his face with a lace handkerchief, his little gold-edged French hat under his arm. Faith, he was in a rare temper.

Lady Shelton paddled up to Silver Heels, halted, and panted at her. Then she turned on me and panted at me until her voice returned. With her voice, her features assumed a most extraordinary change; billows of fat agitated the expanse of chin and cheek, and her voice, babyish in fury, made me jump, for it sounded as though some tiny, pixy creature, buried inside of her, was scolding me.

Sir Timerson Chank now bore down on my left and presently rounded to, delivering his broadside at short range; but I turned on him savagely, bidding him hold his tongue, which so astonished him that he obeyed me.

As for Dunmore, his shrill prattle never ceased, and he danced and vapoured and fingered his small-sword, till my hands itched to throw him into the blackberry thicket.

"If," said I, to Lady Shelton, "you are pleased to forbid me your door, pray remember, madam, that your authority extends no farther! I shall not ask your permission to address my cousin, Miss Warren—nor yours!" I added, wheeling on Sir Timerson Chank.

"Sir Timerson! Sir Timerson! Arrest him! You are a magistrate. Sir Timerson! Arrest him! Oh, I'm all of a twitter!" panted Lady Shelton.

But Sir Timerson Chank made no sign of compliance.

"Lord Dunmore," I said, "by what privilege do you assume to vapour and handle the hilt of your small-sword in Miss Warren's presence?"

"Sink me!" cried Lord Dunmore. "Sink me now, Mr. Cardigan; you should know that I have privileges, sir. I will have you to know that I have privileges, sir! Crib me! but I will assert my rights!"

"Your—what?" I replied, contemptuously.

"My rights! My privilege to defend Miss Warren—my rights, sir! I stand upon them, crib me, if I don't!"

"Shame on you!" cried Lady Shelton, panting angrily at me. "Shame on you—you mannerless, roving, blustering, hectoring rebel!—you—you *boy*! Oh, I'm all of a twitter! Sir Timerson, I'm all of a twitter!—"

"Oh tally!" broke in Dunmore, peeping at me through his quizzing-glass. "The lad's moon-mad! A guinea to a china orange that the lad's moon-mad. You may see it in his eyes, Sir Timerson. You may see he's non compos—eh, Sir Timerson? Sink me if he isn't!"

How I controlled myself I scarcely know, but I strove to remember that a hand raised to Lord Dunmore, Governor of Virginia, meant the ruin of my plans for the night. As I stood staring at the wizened macaroni, aching to take his sword, break it, and spank him with the fragments, I saw Jack Mount and the Weasel cautiously reconnoitring the situation from the hill's edge.

Ere I could motion them away they had made up their minds that I was in distress, and now they came swaggering into our circle, thumbs hooked in their shirts, saluting poor Silver Heels with a flourish that drew a thin scream from Lady Shelton.

"Trouble with this old scratch-wig?" inquired Mount, nodding his head sideways towards Lord Dunmore.

"Damme!" gasped Dunmore. "Do you know who I am, you beast?"

"I know you're a ruddled old hunks," said Mount, carelessly. "Who may the other guinea wig-stand be, Mr. Cardigan?"

As he spoke he looked across at Sir Timerson Chank, then suddenly his eyes grew big as saucers and a low whistle escaped his lips.

"Gad!" he exclaimed. "It's the magistrate or I'm a codfish!"

"Fellow!" roared Sir Timerson, his face purpling with passion. "Fellow! Thunder and Mars! Lord Dunmore, this is Jack Mount, the highwayman!"

For an instant Dunmore stood transfixed, then he screamed out: "Close the gates! Close the gates, Sir Timerson! He shall not escape, damme! No, he shall not escape! Call the constables, Sir Timerson; call the constables!"

Mount had paled a little, but now as Sir Timerson began to bellow for a constable, his colour came back and he stepped forward, laying a heavy hand on the horrified magistrate's shoulder.

"Come now; come now," he said; "stop that bawling, or I'll put your head between your knees and truss you up like a basted capon!" And he gave him a slight shake which dislodged Sir Timerson's forty-guinea wig.

"You Tory hangman," said Mount, scowling, "if I ever took a penny from you it was to help drive you and your thieving crew out of the land! Do you hear that? Now go and howl for your thief-takers, and take his Lordship, here, with you to squall for his precious constables!" And he gave Sir Timerson a shove over the grassy slope.

Lady Shelton shrieked as Sir Timerson went wabbling down the hill, but Mount turned fiercely on Dunmore and shook his huge fist under his nose.

"Hunt me down if you dare!" he growled. "Move a finger to molest me and the people shall know how you stop public runners and scalp them, too! Oho! Now you scare, eh? Out o' my way, you toothless toad!"

Dunmore shrank back, almost toppling down the hill, which he hurriedly descended and made off after Sir Timerson towards the pavilion.

"Come," said I, "that will do for the present, Jack. Look yonder! Your friend, the magistrate, is toddling fast to trap you. You should be starting if you mean to get out of this scrape a free man."

"Pooh!" replied Mount, swaggering. "I've time to dine if I chose, but I'm not hungry. Come, Cade; we needs must kick some planks out of that stockade below us, if they guard the gates. But we have time to stroll."

The Weasel did not appear to hear him, and stood staring at Silver Heels with an expression so strange that it was almost terrifying. For a moment I feared he had gone stark mad.

"Cade!" repeated Mount. "What is the matter, Cade? What do you see? Not another fat magistrate? Cade! What on earth troubles you, old friend?" And he stepped quickly to the Weasel's side, I following.

"Cade!" he cried, shaking his comrade's arm.

The Weasel turned a ghastly face.

"Who is she?" he motioned, with his lips.

"Do you mean Miss Warren?" I asked, astonished.

"A ghost," he muttered, shivering in every limb.

Presently he began to move towards Silver Heels, and Mount and I drew him back by the shoulders.

"Cade! Cade!" cried Mount, anxiously. "Don't look like that, for God's sake!"

"For God's sake," repeated Renard, trembling.

His eyes were dim with tears. Mount leaned over to me and whispered: "He is mad!" But the Weasel heard him and looked up slowly.

"No, no," he said; "a little wrong in the head, Jack, only a little wrong. I thought I saw my wife, Jack, or her ghost—ay, her ghost—the ghost of her youth and mine—"

A spasm shook him; he hid his face in his hands a moment, then scoured out the tears with his withered fingers.

"Ask the young lady's pardon for me," he muttered; "I have frightened her."

I walked over to Silver Heels, who stood beside Lady Shelton, amazed at the scenes which had passed so swiftly before her eyes, and I drew her aside, mechanically asking pardon from the petrified dowager.

"He is a little mad," I said; "he thought he saw in you the ghost of his lost wife. Sorrow has touched his brain, I think, but he is very gentle and means no harm. Speak to him, Silver Heels. I owe my life to those two men."

She stood looking at them a moment, then, laying her hand on my arm, she went slowly across to Mount and Renard.

They uncovered as she came up; the Weasel's face grew dead and fixed, but the pathos in his eyes was indescribable.

"If you are Mr. Cardigan's friends, you must be mine, too," said Silver Heels, sweetly. "All you have done for him, you have done for me."

Fascinated, Mount gaped at her, tongue-tied, clutching his coon-skin cap to his breast. But the fibre of the two men showed the difference of their grain in a startling form, for, into Renard's shrunken frame came something that straightened him and changed him; he lifted his head with a peculiar dignity almost venerable, and, stepping forward, took Silver Heels's small hand in his with a delicate grace that any man might envy. Then he bent and touched her fingers with his lips.

"An old man's devotion, my child," he said. "You have your mother's eyes."

"My—my mother's eyes?" faltered Silver Heels, glancing fearfully at me.

"Yes—your mother's eyes—and all of her. I knew her, child."

"My—mother?"

He touched her hand with his lips again, slowly.

"I am a little troubled in my head sometimes," he said, gravely. "Do you fear me?"

"N—no," murmured Silver Heels.

Their eyes met in silence.

Presently I took Silver Heels by the hand and led her back to Lady Shelton.

"Madam," I said, "if aught of harm comes to these two men, through Lord Dunmore, betwixt this hour and the same hour to-morrow, there is not a hole on earth into which he can creep for mercy. Tell this to my Lord Dunmore, and bid him stay away. I speak in no heat, madam; I mean what I say. For as surely as I stand here now, that hour in which Lord Dunmore and Sir Timerson start to hunt us down, they die. Pray you, madam, so inform those gentlemen."

Then I turned to Silver Heels, who impulsively stretched out both hands. The next moment I rejoined Mount and Renard, and we passed rapidly through the grove and down the hill to the stockade, where Mount drove out a plank with his huge shoulder, and we were free of Roanoke Plain.

CHAPTER XVII

At ten o'clock that night I sat in the coffee-room of the "Virginia Arms," outwardly cool enough, I trust, but terribly excited nevertheless, and scarce able to touch the food on my plate.

Heretofore, although I have always dreaded physical pain, I may truthfully say that the prospect of it had never deterred me from facing necessary danger; and I can also maintain that, until the present moment, the possibility of disaster to me or mine had never terrified me beforehand.

Now it was different; I seemed to be utterly unable to contemplate with philosophy the chance of misfortune to Silver Heels, through failure of my plans or accident to my proper person. It was, I think, responsibility and not cowardice that frightened me; for who was there to take care of Silver Heels if anything happened to me?

One by one I counted and discounted the dangers I ran: first, arrest at any moment as an accomplice of the notorious Jack Mount; second, assassination by Dunmore's agents; third, assassination by Butler's company; fourth, arrest and imprisonment as a suspected rebel and open advocate of sedition; fifth, danger from the Cayugas after our escape from Fort Pitt.

Should any of these things befall me, as well they might, what in the world would become of Silver Heels? Small wonder I found no heart to eat, though this totally new condition of mind parched me with a thirst so persistent that my host, James Rolfe, was obliged to caution me and bring me to my senses ere I had dulled them hopelessly in his brown home-brew.

The post-chaise, loaded and ready for a three weeks' journey, stood in the mews with the four strong horses harnessed, and Jack Mount at their heads. He and the Weasel were to ride as post-boys, with Shemuel and I in front.

It lacked an hour yet of the time appointed, and it was the suspense of that hour's waiting which set every nerve in my body aching. If we could only have gone somewhere else to wait!—but where could we go and find safety from warrants in this little town where every patriot inn was known? Certainly it was better for us to endure the strain here among sympathizers, where we could count on our host and on his guests and on every servant from stable to kitchen.

The arms and ammunition which the Weasel had purchased were now properly stowed in the post-chaise. Rifles and pistols had been primed and loaded, powder-horns replenished, flint and ball fitted, and pans oiled.

Again and again I went out into the mews, leaving my food untasted, only to find Mount standing quietly at the horses' heads and the Weasel pacing up and down, plunged in reverie.

At last Shemuel appeared, slinking past the lighted inn windows and into the mews, where we waited in the starlight, rubbing his hands and peering about with alert obsequiousness and an apparent inability to appreciate the tension that I, for one, quivered under.

"I haff sold all my goots," he remarked, cheerfully; "my packets I haff stored mit my friends at dose 'Bear and Cubs.' I puy me Delaware paskets in Baltimore—eh, Jack?"

"Here are your pistols," I said; "do you know how to use them?"

"Ach yess," he replied, with a sly smile at Mount, who grunted, and said:

"Shemmy is just as handy with pistols as he is with his needles. No fear, Mr. Cardigan," and looking around, he motioned the peddler to his side.

"I hear that the Monongahela is in flood," he said. "Is the wooden bridge all right, Shemmy?"

Shemuel did not know and went away to inquire, returning presently from the stables with the information that heavy storms had swept the southern mountains and the Monongahela was over its banks, but the dam below the bridge had gone out, leaving the wooden structure safe.

"Then there won't be a ford for twenty miles," muttered Mount, "and I'm glad of it. Shemmy, just borrow four new axes of Rolfe, will you? And, say, just shove them into the boot!"

Again Shemuel disappeared, and after a short absence came trotting back with the bundle of brand-new axes on his shoulder.

"Are they ground?" asked Mount.

"You can shave mit them," said Shemuel, running his dirty thumb along the edges. Then he shoved them into the boot and looked cunningly up at me.

The slow minutes dragged on. Hands clasped behind me, I walked up and down the muddy alley, twisting my interlocked fingers until every nail throbbed. Mount smoked a cob-pipe and watched me; Renard stood apart, staring up at the stars, immersed in thought; Shemuel pattered silently among the restive horses, thumbing the harness and poking his prying fingers into axle and unlighted coach-lamp.

Up and down I walked, heart beating heavily, watching the mouth of the alley for a lurking spy, or a file of soldiers, or Heaven knows what phantoms, which fancy conjured in my excited brain. But I saw nothing to alarm us, and was about to recommence an examination of the new rifle which Renard had bought me, when we were all startled by a rattle of hoofs filling the square with quick echoes.

Instantly every man there reached for his rifle; the alley itself suddenly resounded with the clattering hoof-strokes of a hard-ridden horse. There was a rush, a shadow, and a breathless shout from the horseman: "Express—ho! Stand back! I pass! I pass!"

"It's an express," muttered Mount, lowering his long rifle to lean on it and watch the dark rider pull his frantic horse to its haunches and fling the bridle on the snorting creature's neck, while he turned in his stirrups and searched his wallet by the glow of the opening kitchen door.

Rolfe, in his shirt-sleeves and apron, came out of the door, holding his hands up for the packets.

"Three for you, Jimmy," said the bareheaded express-rider, passing the letters over. "Draw me a pot o' beer, for Heaven's sake."

"Where is your mate?" asked Rolfe, anxiously.

"Hiram? Full of war-arrows t'other side o' Crown Gap. Here's his pouch."

"Scalped?" asked Rolfe, in a low voice.

"I reckon he is. He never knowed nothing after the third arrow. Them Wyandottes done it."

A tap-boy hurried out with the brimming pewter, and the shadowy rider emptied it at a gulp.

"'Nother, Jim," he said, stolidly.

"There's blood onto your jaw," said Rolfe, gloomily.

"Ay, they drew blood. I lost my hat"—here he swore fiercely—"and it ain't even paid for, Jim!"

"You orter be glad you got through, Ben Prince," said Rolfe, grimly.

"I am—drat that boy! where's my beer? Oh, there you are, are you? Gimme the pot and quit gaping. Hain't you never seed a express before?"

An admiring circle of hostlers and kitchen wenches laughed hysterically. The post-rider swaggered in his saddle and stretched out his feet contentedly.

"Life ain't all skittles," he observed; "but beer is beer the round world round!" and he drained the pot and tossed it dripping to an honoured scullion.

"News o' Boston?" asked Rolfe, meaningly.

"Plenty! Plenty! Port Bill in force; Tommy Gage on top; Sam Adams lying low; more redcoats landed, more on the way, more to come; rich poorer; poor starving; that's all!"

He gathered his bridle and winked at a coy kitchen-maid.

"Your beau has went to Johnstown, Sairy," he said; "I seen him a-training hay-foot, straw-foot, with old Sir Billy's Tryon County milish. That reminds me, Jim"—turning to Rolfe—"I've a packet for a certain Michael Cardigan, somewhere to be hunted up south o' Crown Gap—"

"Right here!" said Rolfe, promptly, and the express passed the letter to him. Then, with a careless, "See you later!" he wheeled his horse short and galloped back along the alley, which rang with shouts of "Good luck! Good luck! There's bed and bait for you here, Benny!"

The crowd on the steps flocked back into the kitchen, the door closed, then opened to let out Rolfe, who advanced towards me, letter in one hand, flaring candle in the other.

"Light the coach-lamps," I whispered, and, taking the candle and letter, sat down on a pile of pine timber to read what Sir William had sent me:

"DEAR LAD,—By runners from the Cayuga, I know how gallantly you have conducted. Dearer than son you are to me, prouder am I than any parent. If what we had hoped and prayed for has failed—as I can no longer doubt—it is so ordained, and we struggle in vain. *Nitor in adversum; nisi Dominus, frustra!*

"I am holding the Mohawks back by their very throats, but mischief brews at the Upper Castle, whither Joseph (Thayendanegea) has gone with the belts from me.

"Red Jacket's conduct condemns me to uneasiness. He is an orator; the foul murder of Logan is his text. I need say no more, save that I still hold the Mohawks back.

"Colonel John Butler, his conduct concerns me, and I needs must view it with grief and alarm. His dishonoured son, Walter Butler, is still absent; the elder Butler has retired to the lakes, where I am informed he is gathering Tory malecontents and foolish young Onondagas, for what ultimate purpose I can only imagine.

"A most deadly and bitter feeling runs flood in Johnstown; nightly outrages are reported to me, and I fear that the so-called patriots are quite as blameworthy as are the loyalists. Whig and Tory hate and wait.

"Dear lad, the sands of my life are running very swiftly. I am so tired, so tired! Come when you can; I have much to talk over ere these same sands run out, leaving a voided glass in the sunlight. If you, by hazard, pass through

Fort Pitt, you will accompany Felicity on her return hither, which return I have instantly commanded her by this express. I have received a singular letter from my Lord Dunmore, which has astonished me. My answer to him I delay until Felicity returns. Doubtless she will travel hither by way of Richmond. The escort, which Lord Dunmore must furnish, will, on their return journey, take with them my reply to his Lordship.

"If this letter reaches you in time, come back with Felicity; if not, come by the safe route through Richmond. Overtake her if you can do so.

"Your Aunt Molly is well and sweetly anxious to see you safe home. Esk and Peter do flourish—yet I like not Peter's haunting the public houses where things are uttered to poison young minds. I have trounced him soundly seven times, and mean to continue.

"The news from Boston is ominous. More ships are about to sail, bearing more troops and cannon. I know not how it will end! Ay—but I *do* know, and so must every thinking man. *Praemonitus praemunitus!*

"Michael, I have had a most strange and unpleasant letter from Sir Peter Warren, who encloses with it certain amazing documents which he has carefully perused, to his great mortification and discontent. These papers were lately sent to him from Chatham dockyard, having been discovered under the cabin flooring of the war-ship *Leda*, which his brother lately commanded and which is now repairing at Chatham.

"The documents concern Felicity—and us all—and I wish you to know that I no longer approve of your union with her, at least not until both she and you are fully acquainted with the contents of these documents.

"And now, dear son, I can but wait for you to come. The house is dull without you. I have sometimes sought to drown care in the river, whither I go with gillie Bareshanks to fly-fish for trouts. But I am growing sad and old, and nothing pleases, though I do throw my flies as I did at thirty, looping each cast without a splash.

"Always y^r affectionate

"WM. JOHNSON, BART.

"Post Scriptum.—On y^r return I have planned a fishing-trip to the Kennyetto at Fonda's Bush, where, report is, a monstrous trout hath been seen to jump frequently in that bend of the stream due east from the sugar bush on the hill.

"W. J."

My eyes were swimming when I lifted them from the sheets of paper, now damp with dew. For a moment I rested my head on my hands, feeling the rising tide of homesickness choking me. Then that subtle courage, which a word from Sir William ever infused, warmed my blood and calmed my beating heart.

I rose serenely, and laid the letter to the candle's flame, watching it burn and crisp and fall in flakes which no prying spy might decipher. Then I looked at my new watch, and was amazed to find that it lacked but a few moments to the time set for our departure from the "Virginia Arms."

Rolfe had already lighted the chaise-lamps; Shemuel had crawled inside with our weapons, and Renard sat his post-saddle, adjusting the stirrups; while Mount was preparing to climb into the saddle of the nigh leader.

"Is it dark out there in the square?" I asked of Rolfe.

"I guess the lanthorns swing a-light on every seventh," he said. "I darkened mine, but the watchman came battering and bawling tew the door and made me light up again."

Mount was now in his saddle; I held my ticking time-piece under the coach-lamp, eyes following the slow pointers travelling towards the hour.

And, as I stood there, there came creeping a woman into the alley, cloaked and bareheaded, halting and crouching to scan our chaise-lamps under her inverted hand. Ere Rolfe or I could stop her she ran to the horse on which Mount was sitting and caught the forest-runner by the fringe on his sleeve. Then, in the rays of the chaise-lamp, I knew her for the thief-taker's child.

"Hoity-toity, what the devil's tew pay?" said Rolfe. "Darn the ruddled vixens who come a-drabbing into my mews, with a hussy tew hail you afoot and a baggage tew boot on the boot—"

"Keep quiet!" I said, sharply. "There's trouble abroad somewhere!"

"Oh, Mr. Cardigan," called Mount, softly, "Sir Timerson and a gang o' cudgels is coming up Pitt Street and Bully Bishop's with them!"

The girl turned her frightened face to me:

"They came for father to take Jack Mount; I ran out the back door, sir. Oh, hasten! hasten!" she wailed, looking at Mount and wringing her hands.

The big fellow stooped from his saddle and deliberately kissed her.

"Thank you, my dear," he said; "I'll come back for another before I die. Au large, Jimmy! Up with you, Mr. Cardigan!"

"Turn those horses! Take their heads!" whispered Rolfe. "There's one back way tew every mews, and half a dozen to this!"

The next moment I had wheeled the chaise-and-four back into the darkness and around a rambling row of sheds and stables, following Rolfe, then to the left, then a demi-tour to the right, which brought us up against a heavy stockade. But already Rolfe had set a creaking gate swinging loosely, and we bumped out into a field, hub-deep in buttercups.

"I'll keep the scratch-wigs amused," whispered Rolfe, as I climbed to the forward seat and picked up my rifle; and away we jolted across the star-lit pasture and out into a narrow, unlighted cattle lane, which we followed to the bars. These Shemuel let down, popping back into the chaise like a jack-o'-box, and Mount rode our horses out into the dark Boundary Road.

There was not a soul to be seen, not a light, not a sound but the hum of our turning wheels and the slapping trot of our horses.

Presently, on a dark hillock to our right, I saw lighted windows glimmering among trees, and I called in a low voice to Mount and sprang noiselessly to the road. A lane led around the hillock to the right; up this dim path I conducted the chaise-and-four until I found room to turn them back, facing the Boundary Road again. Here our chaise might lie concealed from passing folk on the highway, and here I quietly bade Mount and Renard await me, while Shemuel held the horses' heads.

The night was warm and fragrant under the great June stars as I passed silently along the lane, climbed the hillock and entered the orchard. Through the dim trees I stole towards the house, where two windows on the ground floor were lighted up.

Then, as I leaned breathless against a tree, in the distant gloom the fortress bell struck slowly, eleven times.

Second after second passed, minute followed minute, and my eyes never left the closed door under the pillared porch. Presently I looked at my watch; a quarter of an hour had passed. The seconds began to drag, the minutes loitered. Time seemed to stand still in the world.

Far away in the fortress the bell struck the half-hour, and on the west breeze came the dull cry of sentinels calling from post to post under the summer stars.

Suddenly the dark door opened; a heavy figure appeared in silhouette against the light. My heart stood still; it was Black Betty.

The negress peered out into the darkness, north, west, south, and finally looked up at the stars. Then, as though summoned from within, she turned quickly and entered the house, leaving the door wide open behind her.

Impatience was racking me now; I waited until I could wait no longer; then, in the shadow of the trellis-vines, I stole up to the porch. The hallway was empty; I stepped to the sill, crossed it, and surveyed the empty stairway and the gallery above. There was not a soul in sight. Now alarm seized me, a swift, overpowering dread which drove me on to seek and face whatever was in store for me. A door on my right stood open; I looked in, then entered the smaller of two rooms, which were partly separated from each other by folding doors. Candles burned in gilt sconces; glass cabinets glittered; mirrors reflected my full length so abruptly that I started at the apparitions and clutched my hunting-knife.

Treading on the velvet carpet I passed into the farther apartment which, by a little gallery and waxed floor, I knew to be the ballroom. Not a soul to be seen anywhere. Glancing hurriedly at the empty ranks of gilded chairs, I strove to crush out the fear which was laying icy fingers on my breast, and I had already turned to re-enter the smaller room when I heard the front door close and voices sounding along the outer hallway. I stepped behind a gilt cabinet and drew my heavy knife, perfectly aware that I was trapped like a fox in a snap-box.

Through the carved foliage of the cabinet I saw three people enter the room. The skin all over my body roughened at the sight of them; and what held me back I do not know—perhaps that kind Providence which watches over fools—for I began to tremble in every contracting muscle as do cats in ambush when their quarry passes unsuspecting.

There they stood in low-voiced consultation—Lady Shelton, my Lord Dunmore, and my mortal enemy, Walter Butler, tricked out in lace and velvet. He stood so near to me that my hot hand could have fastened on his throat-strings where I crouched. He turned towards Dunmore with a gesture.

"Sir Timerson should find them to-night," he said; "your thief-taker, Bully Bishop, is with them, I understand."

"They are to search every rebel rat-hole in town," cried Dunmore, eagerly; "they should claw them ere dawn, Captain Butler. *Vive Dieu, nous allons les clouer en terrain bouché!*"

Lord Dunmore leered at Lady Shelton, and then contemplated his small French hat as though seeking countenance for his halting tongue.

"If I am to conduct Miss Warren," said Butler, gloomily, "you had best see her without delay, my Lord."

His round, amber eyes of a bird were fixed on Dunmore.

"Come now," said Dunmore, slyly, "I am half minded to conduct her myself, Captain Butler, curse me if I am not. I hear you once vowed to wed her in spite of Sir William and me too! Damme, I've a notion you mean me ill, you rogue!"

"Your Lordship is merry," sneered Butler, but I saw his blank eyes contracting as he spoke.

"Faith, I am not over-merry," said Dunmore, plaintively, drawing a diamond pin from his wig and contemplating it. "I like not this night journey to Williamsburg, that's flat!—and I care not if you know it, Captain Butler."

"Then I pray you to release me from this duty," sneered Butler.

Dunmore eyed him askance, twirling his jewelled pin.

"If I merit your suspicions," added Butler, icily, "I beg to wish you good fortune and good-night!" And he bowed very low and turned curtly towards the door.

"No! Damme if I suspect you!" cried Dunmore, hastily. "Come back, Captain Butler! Oh tally, man!—is there no wit in you that you freeze at a jest from an over-fond suitor? You shall conduct Miss Warren to Williamsburg. I say it! I mean it! Body o' Judas! am I not to follow as soon as I hang this fellow Mount and his rabble o' ragged pottle-pots?"

Butler came back, and—oh, the evil in his fixed stare as his kindling eyes fastened on Dunmore again!

"Will you be pleased—to—to receive Miss Warren immediately?" asked Lady Shelton, in a flutter of jellyfied excitement. "I have her closely watched wherever she takes a step. She has her boxes packed, the wilful child! Lud! she would have been gone these two hours had not Captain Butler's man caught my footman with a guinea!"

"I have a copy of her letter," squeaked Dunmore, angrily. "Faith, I could scratch her raw for what she wrote to that dirty forest-running fellow, Cardigan!"

"Fie! Fie!" tittered Lady Shelton, hysterically, shaking a fat finger at the painted beau. "Over-fond lovers should forgive!"

"Curse me if I forget, though," muttered his Lordship. "If I have to wait till Innocents' day, I'll birch the little baggage yet!"

He turned nervously to Butler:

"You had best attend in the ballroom, Captain Butler. Gad! I can persuade her, I think, within the half-hour. Lady Shelton, you will be in one of your cursed twitters if you remain here, and those same twitters set me dancing. Damme, madam! you are twittering now! I sha'n't endure it! I can't endure it! Pluck me bald if I can!"

"I—I will send her to you," stammered the dowager, curtseying in a panic.

"And stay away until you're wanted," added Dunmore, brutally.

Lady Shelton stared at him with frightened eyes; then her little fat feet set themselves in motion, and she pattered hastily out of the room. The men exchanged sneers.

"I'll be rid o' that ruddled sack o' lollypops now," observed Lord Dunmore, complacently. "Will you not take your turn, Captain Butler? No? Well, I owe thanks to Sir Timerson then. Pst! There's some one on the stairs! Give me joy, Captain Butler, and mind you keep closed eyes, you rogue!"

Butler gave him a contemptuous stare, then swung on his heel, and balancing his thin hand on the hilt of his small-sword, walked noiselessly into the dim ballroom.

Dunmore stood listening, passing the diamond pin back through his wig, and shaking out the long, delicate lace on his cuffs.

Nobody came. He raised his spy-glass and tiptoed over to the mirror, primping, preening, smirking, and ogling himself, occasionally turning his good ear to the door to listen.

Presently he began to pace the velvet, fanning his nose with a lace handkerchief, and simpering all to himself.

The extravagance of his dress might have amused me had not my mind been filled with deadly thoughts. He was all in yellow, silk coat, and silver-shot waistcoat, with breeches of gold brocade and white silk stockings. Lace tumbled in soft cascades over his claw-like fingers; a white sash and star, set with brilliants, covered his breast; a gorgeous stock glittered under the fluffy lace at his withered throat.

I noted these features, one by one, but my thoughts had flown up-stairs to seek throughout this shameful house for the dear maid who had given herself to me.

Suddenly she appeared at the door, so suddenly that Lord Dunmore started from the mirror with a suppressed squeal of surprise. As for me, I quivered in my lurking-place, and for a moment could scarce see her for the mist in my eyes.

Yet there she stood, hesitating, smiling, her hands busy with the buckle of a travelling-coat adorned with row on row of dainty capes. Under the silvery gray coat I could see her little doe-skin shoon peeping out. Now, with gloved hands, she began widening the hood on her head, to tie it beneath her chin, with a sidelong glance at the mirror and a faint smile for her mirrored face.

Never, never had I seen her so lovely, never had her eyes so thrilled me, nor her sweet, dumb lips called to me more clearly. For a moment I thought she had perceived me through the cabinet's gilded foliage; but my presence was still all unsuspected.

At first sight of her hood and travelling-coat, Lord Dunmore had scowled. Then, fascinated, he pretended to a trance and clasped his hands, rolling his rheumy eyes towards heaven. Seeing her face fall, however, he recovered quickly enough and leered at her from head to toe.

"Cruel one," he piped out in ecstasy, mincing towards her. "Cruel one, what do you ask that I may adore?"

"Your Lordship's pardon," she said, gravely; "I am here to ask forgiveness."

"Granted! You have it," protested Dunmore, eagerly, leading her to a chair and bowing above her as she was seated. "You have grieved me, but man was made to grieve. I forgive, and give my love as guerdon."

"You are too generous," said Silver Heels, sorrowfully; "I may keep only your forgiveness, my Lord."

She would have spoken again, but Dunmore bent his stiff joints and dropped on both knees, ogling her with watery eyes.

She half rose and drew back with a pleading gesture, but the infatuated fool drowned her protests with his shrill prattle, and clasping his transparent hands together under the lace, pleaded his suit so passionately that my gorge rose and I could scarce contain myself.

At last his chatter died away in miscellaneous noises, sniffs, gulps, and senile sounds; and he tried to seize her gloved hand, making a clacking smack with his thin, dry lips.

Silver Heels shrank deep into her chair, hiding her hands from him under her chin, and begging him to rise, which he did at last, scowling his displeasure.

Then, very gravely and pitifully, she told him that she did not love him, that she had given her love to another, and that she could now only ask his forgiveness, yet never forgive herself for the wickedness she had so wilfully practised.

He stood listening in silence at first, then his faded eyes narrowed with fury, and in his worn cheeks, under the rouge, a sickly colour stained the flesh. The change in the man was frightful.

"D'ye mean to throw me over for that wood-running whelp, Cardigan?" he burst out. "Oh no, my lady, that cock won't fight, d'ye hear?"

The startling coarseness of the outbreak brought Silver Heels to her feet in frightened astonishment. Horror mantled throat and cheeks with crimson; she shrank back, catching support on a marble table beside her.

All over Dunmore's scowling visage the enamel was cracking; he paced the carpet like one demented, chattering and scratching at the air.

"I will not be so used! Curse me if I will!" he snarled, biting his polished nails. "Hell's fury! madam; do you think to throw me over for a hind of buckskin? Damn me if you shall!—and Lady Shelton saw him kiss you on the knoll at that! Fine sport, madam! Fine sport! So you think to make me the laughing-stock o' Virginia? So you write letters to your buckskin lout and plan to run off with him in a post-chaise—eh? Damned if you shall! Damned if you do!"

"Pray—pray let me pass," gasped Silver Heels, choking with fright.

He caught the door in his hand, closing it, and planted himself with his back against it. Then he fumbled behind him for the key, but it was in the other side of the door.

"Oh no, not yet," he said.

"I must pass that door," repeated Silver Heels, breathlessly.

"By God, you shall not!" he cried. "You shall stay here all night, d'ye hear? Ay, and folk shall hear of it and gossip, too, and the whole world shall know how the Governor of Virginia bundled to win a worthless wife! I tell you I mean to have you, and if you wed me not fair you shall wed me compromised, and thank me, too, for my name to cloak your shame withal!"

His voice ended in a shriek; the door behind him burst open, flinging him forward, and Black Betty appeared, eyes ablaze and teeth bared. The next instant Silver Heels sprang through the portal, the door banged, and I heard the key turn on the other side with a click.

Dumfounded, I looked stupidly through the window behind me, then my heart leaped up, for there, at the foot of the garden, stood a post-chaise and four, lamps lighted, and postilions sitting their horses. There, too, were Silver Heels and Betty, setting foot to the chaise step. Dark figures aided them, the chaise door shut. I thanked God silently and turned to deal with these wicked men whom He had given into my hands.

Dunmore, insane with fury, was clawing at the window to raise it; Butler came swiftly from the ballroom and tried the door. Finding it locked, he looked at Dunmore with a ghastly laugh.

"She's gone!" shrieked Dunmore. "Gone in a chaise! That black slut of hers did it! Let me out! Let me out! I'll claw them raw! I'll pinch them to death! I *won't* stay here, d'ye hear?"

His voice soared into a falsetto screech, and he tore at his gums with his nails and stamped his feet.

"Give place there!" said Butler, brutally elbowing the frantic man aside. "Let me through that window, you doddering fool! You're done for; it's my turn now."

"What!" gasped Dunmore. Then terror blanched his face, and he began to scream: "That was *your* chaise! You mean to cheat me! You mean to steal her! That was your chaise, and it's gone! No! No! Damme, you shall not catch them at the gates!" And he flung himself on Butler to drag him from the open window.

"Drive on!" shouted Butler, leaning out and calling to the people in the chaise.

Startled, I turned and stared through the window behind me. To my horror the horses started and the chaise began to move off. Even yet I did not comprehend that the chaise was not my own, but to see it slowly rolling away in the night terrified me, and I bounded out into the room—barely in time, for Butler had already forced Dunmore from the open window and had laid his hand on the wall to hoist himself out. Quick as the thought, I balanced my heavy knife, hilt to palm, swung forward and let it fly like lightning. The blade whistled true and struck, pinning Butler's arm to the wall. God! how he shrieked and shrank, twisting and turning to tear the blade loose. Dunmore ran around like a crazed rat, but I knocked him senseless with a chair, and sprang at Butler, who, writhing and ghastly pale, had just freed his left hand of the knife. He ran at me with his sword, but I shattered my heavy chair across his face, and seized him, meaning to cut his throat. Twist and tear and clutch as he would, he could not escape or hurt me; the coolness of murder was in my heart; I strangled him with one hand and hunted around the floor for my knife. It was gone, I could not find it. Then a wave of fury blazed in my brain; I lifted the struggling wretch with both hands above my head and brought him down on the floor, where he crashed as though every bone in him were shattered to the marrow.

As I reeled, panting, towards the window, the key turned in the locked door and Lady Shelton's frightened face appeared. When she saw me she rushed at me and screamed, but I thrust the harridan out of my path, vaulted through the open window, and ran down the orchard slope. Then, as I sprang into the lane, I almost dropped, for there, where I had left it, stood my post-chaise, awaiting me.

"Mount!" I shouted in terror. "Is she here?"

"Here?" he cried. "You are mad! Have you lost her?"

Through my whirling senses the awful truth broke like a living ray of fire.

"Out o' the saddle!" I shouted. "She has taken another chaise. It's Butler's men! Ride for her! Ride!"

"Gone?" thundered Mount, leaping to the seat, while I sprang to his vacant saddle. But I only lashed at the horses, and set my teeth while the dust flew and the pebbles showered through the flying wheels.

It seemed hours, yet it was scarcely five minutes, ere the gate-house lights broke out ahead, dots of dim yellow dancing through the dust. Now we were galloping straight into the eye of the great brass lanthorn set above the guard-house; there came a far call in the darkness, a shadow crossed the lamplit glare, then I turned in my saddle and shouted: "Draw bridle!"—and our four horses came clashing in a huddle with a hollow volley of hoof-beats.

"Road closed for the night!" said a sentinel, walking towards us from the darkness ahead, cap, buckle, and buttons glittering in the lamplight.

"A post-chaise passed five minutes ahead of us," began Mount, angrily.

"Tut! tut! my good fellow," said the sentry; "that's none o' your business. Back up there!"

"I wish to see Mr. Bevan," said I, scarce able to speak.

"Mr. Bevan's gone home to bed," said the soldier, impatiently. "He passed that other post-chaise at a gallop, or it would have been here yet, I warrant you. Come, come, now! You know the law. Clear the road, now!—turn your leaders, post-boy—back up, d'ye hear!"

"I tell you I've got to pass!" I persisted.

"Oh, you have, have you? And who are you, my important friend?" he sneered, barring our way with firelock balanced.

"I am deputy of Sir William Johnson!" I roared, losing all self-control. "Stand clear, there!"

"If you move I'll shoot!" he retorted; then without turning his head he bawled out: "Ho, sergeant o' the quarter-guard! Post number seven!—"

"Drive over him!" I shouted, lashing at the horses. There was a jolt, an uproar, a rush of frantic horses, a bright flash and report. Then a wheel caught the soldier and pitched him reeling into the darkness. I turned in my stirrups, glancing fearfully at Renard, who was recovering his balance in the saddle behind me and lifting a firelock to the pommel.

"Shot?" I asked, breathlessly.

"No; I caught his firelock; it exploded in my hand."

"Look out!" called Mount, from his front seat on the chaise. "The toll-gate's right ahead! There's a camp-guard due there at midnight! Out with your coach-lamps!"

Shemuel jerked open each lanthorn and blew out the lights; darkness hid even the horses from our sight.

A camp-guard! Suppose the gate was closed! Thirty men and a drummer ahead of us!

"Cut the pike!" cried Mount, suddenly. "We save six miles by the old Williamsburg post-road! Turn out! Turn out!"

Far ahead the toll-gate lamp twinkled through the dust; I signalled to Renard and dragged the horses into a trot, straining my eyes for the branch road we had seen that morning. I could see nothing.

"By Heaven! the guard is gone; there's only a sentry there!" said Mount, suddenly.

"Pst!" muttered Renard. "We are the grand rounds, mind you. Answer, Jack!"

"Halt!" cried a distant sentry. "Who goes there?"

"Grand rounds!" sang out Mount.

"Stand, grand rounds! Advance, sergeant, with the countersign!" came the distant challenge again.

"Now," muttered Mount, leaping softly to the turf, "when I call, ride up to me. Hark for a whippoorwill!"

He vanished in the darkness. I waited, scarcely breathing.

"He won't kill him," whispered the Weasel; "you will see, Mr. Cardigan, how it's done. He'll get behind him—patience, patience—pst!—there!"

A stifled cry, suddenly choked, came out of the night; the lanthorn at the toll-gate went out and the toll-house door slammed.

"It's the keeper barricading himself," whispered Renard; "he thinks the sentry has been surprised and scalped. Hush! Mount is calling."

"Whippoorwill! Whippoorwill!" throbbed the whimpering, breathless call across the meadow; the Weasel answered it, and we trotted on until a dark shape rose up in the road and caught at the leaders, drawing them to a standstill.

"'Nother firelock," said Mount, shoving the weapon into the chaise and going back to the horses. "Here's the post-road; I'll guide you into it." And he started east through a wall of shadow.

"Where's the sentry?" whispered Renard.

"In the ditch with his coat tied over his head and my new hanker in his mouth. The frightened fool bit me so I scalped him—"

"What!" cried the Weasel.

"Oh, only his wig. Here it is!" And he flung the wig at Renard, who caught it and tossed it into the chaise for Shemuel.

Mount halted the horses; Shemuel struck flint to tinder, and came around to light the coach-lamps. Under their kindling radiance a dusty road spread away in front of us. Mount unlocked a lighted coach-lamp and went forward, holding the light close to the road surface. Several times he squatted to look close into the dust.

Presently he turned and ran back to us, set the lamp in its socket, locked the clamp, and sprang into his seat. Shemuel hastily scrambled into the chaise, stuffing the wig into his pocket.

"They've taken the turnpike!" cried Mount, cheerily. "Now, lads! Whip and spur and axle-grease! Ride, Cade! Look sharp, Shemmy, you weasel-bellied rascal! We've got them by half an hour, or I'll eat my coon-skin cap!"

"Freshen all primings!" I called out to Shemuel, and sent my whip whistling among the horses.

Away we bolted, chaise swaying, lamps sweeping the dusty roadside bushes, and the gallop increased to a dead run as we whirled down an incline and out along a broad, flat, marshy road, where the jolting lamps flashed on the surface of a swift stream keeping pace with us through the night.

"We catch them where the pike swings south into this road," called Mount; but through the whistling wind I could barely hear him. Louder and louder blew the wind across the flats, shrieking in my ears; wetter and wetter grew the road, until the splash of the horses grew to a churning, trampling roar. Like a flash the stream turned across the road; the shallow water boiled under our rush—a moment only—then into the wet road again, with the stream scurrying on our right.

Through the pelting storm of mud I clutched bridle and whip with one hand and pushed my pistol under my shirt with the other, calling out to Renard to do the same.

"Get my axe loose from the boot, Shemmy!" cried Mount. "Draw rein, Cade! Now, Mr. Cardigan!" And he leaped to the ground and ran splashing through the road, calling out for us to follow at a walk.

Suddenly our horses' hoofs sounded hollow on a wooden bridge; the muddy planks glimmered under the coach-lamps, and, as he walked the horses over, far below us we heard the dull roar of water pouring through the solid rock. Now came the echoing cracks of Mount's axe, biting the supports of the bridge, and presently Shemuel joined him, chopping like a demon.

"We lose time!" I groaned, turning to the Weasel. "Call Mount to let the bridge go."

"We'll lose time if the bridge stands," said Renard, coolly. "Dunmore's horse will take our trail sooner or later, and we may have to wait an hour for the chaise we are chasing."

Minute after minute dragged, timed by the interminable axe-strokes. Presently the Weasel wriggled out of his saddle, ran to the boot, and hurried away, axe on shoulder, and I sat there alone in the lamplight, gnawing my lips and groaning.

But now, above the sharp axe-strokes and the deep roar of the torrent, I caught the sound of creaking timbers. Crack! Crack! Then a long-drawn crackle of settling beams, ending in a crash which set the blowing horses on their hind legs. Ere I could pull them down, Mount came running back, followed by Renard and Shemuel.

"No need to gallop now," observed Mount, shoving the axes into the boot and brushing the mud from his face. He climbed into his seat; Shemuel sought the body of the chaise, and Renard mounted the horse behind me.

"Walk the horses," said Mount; "we are an hour ahead yet. The roads cross just below here. Cheer up, Mr. Cardigan; we'll sight them over our rifles yet. And when Dunmore's horsemen come to the bridge yonder, they'll have some twenty miles to wander ere they can cross the Monongahela to-night."

"The river is in flood; you can hear it," added Renard. "There's no ford for twenty miles where a horse could live to-night."

"Lord! Won't Dunmore rage!" muttered Mount.

I had not thought of pursuit, but there was probably no doubt that Dunmore's horse were already hunting our trail somewhere between the stockade and the toll-gate. If that were so our plans must be changed, for we could not traverse Virginia with the Governor's dragoons at our heels.

Distracted with anxiety, cold and feverish by turns, I strove to regain self-command, and in a measure succeeded. Mount was of my opinion that we must take a forest road over the mountains and make straight for Philadelphia—on foot, if our chaise could not take us. He asked me about the Indians we might encounter, and I told him we had nothing as yet to fear from the Lenape, who could not be bound by clan ties to take up the Cayugas' quarrel until the Mohawks rose.

"Well," said Mount, "curse them all, I say. One moccasin looks like another, and all redskins smell like foxes. I take your word for it that the Lenape are afraid to breathe unless the Mohawks give them leave, so I hope we get through without a war-yelp in our ears."

"There's the Tuscaroras," said Renard, gloomily.

It was true. In my misery and torturing fear for Silver Heels, I had forgotten the Sixth Nation, bands of whom roamed the forests north of the Virginia line. But reflection quieted apprehensions concerning the Tuscaroras, who also must first take council with our Mohawks before drawing their hatchets in a Cayuga quarrel.

I explained this to Mount, who swore a great deal and shrugged his shoulders, but nevertheless I knew he was greatly relieved.

"There's a wood road over the mountains," he said. "Cade knows it. He came that way hunting his wife at Annapolis when the British fleet put in. Didn't you, Cade?"

The Weasel turned in his saddle.

"Jack," he said, gently, "I know my wife is dead. We will never speak of her any more."

Mount was silent. Presently he jumped to the ground and came walking along beside my horse, one hand on my stirrup.

"I don't know," he muttered, under his breath—"I don't know whether that's a healthy sign or not. Ever since Cade saw your lady—Miss Warren—he keeps telling me that his wife is dead, and that God has forgiven her and has told him to do so, too. Somehow he has changed. Do you note it? His voice, now, is different—like a gentleman's. Somehow, he makes me feel lonely."

I was scarcely listening, for, just ahead, I fancied I could see a signpost which must mark cross-roads. After a moment I called excitedly to Mount, pointing out to him the tall post in the middle of the road. Behind it the moon was setting.

"Ay," he said, coolly, "that's our runway. The game will cross here in an hour or so. Sit your saddle, Mr. Cardigan; there's time to whistle the devil's jig to an end yet."

But I was out of my saddle and priming my rifle afresh before he could finish.

"Poor lad," he said, pityingly. "Lord, but you're white as a cross-roads ghost. Shemmy, take the chaise south till you come to a spring brook that crosses the road; it's a hundred yards or so. Cover the coach-lamps with blankets and look to the horses a bit. Cade, I guess you had better take this side of the road with me. We want to be sure o' the post-boys. Mr. Cardigan, try to shoot the driver through the head. There's too much risk in a low shot."

"For God's sake, be careful!" I begged them. "Remember the lady is in the chaise. Can't you kill the leading horses—wouldn't that be safer?"

They were silent for a while. Presently Mount looked guiltily at me, muttering something about "highwayman style," but Renard shook his head.

"Well," began Mount, combatively, "it's the safest. I can stop the chaise all alone without a shot fired if you wish."

He looked at me; there was a joyously evil light in his sparkling eyes.

"This is familiar ground to me," he said, impudently. "Cade and I stopped Sir Timerson Chank by that signpost."

After a moment he added: "Coach and six; post-boys, coachman, footmen, and guards—all armed—eh, Cade, old spark? Lord, how they gaped when I took off my hat and invited Sir Timerson to a stroll! Do you mind that fat coachman, Cade?—and all the post-boys agape and cross-eyed with looking into your rifle-barrel?"

"Jack," I groaned, "I cannot endure delay. Post us, for Heaven's sake. I'm nigh spent with fright and grief."

"There, there!" said Mount, affectionately clapping me on the shoulder. "You will see your dear lady in half an hour, lad. No fear that we will miss—eh, Cade? We shoot straighter for our friends' than for our own lives."

Then he bade the Weasel take his stand to the left, and posted me to the right; he himself sat down cross-legged under the signpost—a strange, monstrous shape squatting in the light of the setting moon.

I heard the click, click, of the closing rifle-pans in the darkness, and for the twentieth time I renewed my priming, fearing the night air might flash the powder in the pan.

The silence weighed me down; awful fear shot through and through me, stabbing my swelling heart till I quivered from head to toe. Try as I might I could scarcely crush back the dread which sometimes chained my limbs, sometimes set them trembling. Suppose that after all they had gone north, risking the war-belt for a dash through to Crown Gap? This was foolish, and I knew it, for they were bound for Williamsburg. Yet the dreadful chance of their mistaking the route and plunging into a Cayuga ambuscade drove me almost frantic.

I thought of Silver Heels, while straining my ears for the sound of the chaise that bore her. Strange, but in my excitement I found myself utterly unable to recall her face to mind. Other faces crowded it out, and I could see them plainly, God wot!—Dunmore, falling under my heavy blow; Butler, his ghastly visage shattered, writhing with my clutch at his throat; Greathouse, as he lay in the alley with the lanthorn's light on his bloated face—enough! Ay, enough now, for in my ears I seemed to hear the crash of Butler's bones as I had dashed his accursed body to the floor, and I trembled and wondered what God did to punish those who had slain.

Punish? Perhaps this was my punishment now—perhaps I was never to see Silver Heels again! Terrible thoughts gathered like devils and clamoured at my ears for a hearing, and I lay on the wet grass, listening and staring into the night, while my dry lips burnt with the fever that consumed me. Around me the darkness seemed to be rocking like water; my head swam as if invisible tides were ebbing through it. Again and again I seemed to be falling, and I started to find my eyes wide open and burning like fire.

Suddenly a faint, far sound in the night stilled every pulse. I saw Mount slowly rise to his feet and step into the shadow of the signpost. The whispering call of a whippoorwill broke out from the bushes where Renard lurked, and I stood up, icy cold but calm, eyes fixed on the darkness which engulfed the road ahead.

Again the distant sound broke out in the stillness; it came again, clear and unmistakable. Now the noise of rapidly galloping horses sounded plainly; wheels striking stones rang out sharp and clear; two lights sparkled in the distance, growing yellower and bigger, while the road beneath flashed into sight in the advancing radiance.

On, on they came, horses at a heavy gallop, chaise swinging and lurching, right into the cross-roads. Then a blinding flash and crash split the gloom, echoed by another, and then a third. I leaped from my cover into a frantic mass of struggling horses which Renard was dragging violently into the road-ditch, while Mount, swinging his rifle, knocked down a man who fired at him and beat him till he lay still.

A shadowy form leaped from the seat in front and ran across my path, doubling and disappearing into the darkness; another slid from his horse, sinking to the ground without a sound, though the crazed animal kicked and trampled him into the mud.

As I sprang to the chaise, I saw the driver lurch towards me, and I aimed a blow at him with my rifle, but he pitched off heavily, landing in a heap at my feet, face downward in the grass. Now the horses swung in front of me, plunging furiously in the smashed harness; crash! went a wheel; the chaise sank forward; a horse fell.

"Look out! Look out!" shouted Mount, behind me, as I ran to the swaying vehicle.

"Silver Heels!" I cried, tearing at the door of the chaise.

For a second I saw her terrified face at the window; her cry rang in my ears; then the door burst open and Wraxall sprang out, burying his knife in my neck.

Down we went together, down, down into a smothering darkness that had no end, yet I remember, after a long, long time, looking up at the stars—or perhaps into her eyes.

Then my body seemed to sink again, silently as a feather, and my soul dropped out, falling like a lost star into an endless night.

CHAPTER XVIII

I knew afterwards—long, long afterwards—that I had been stabbed repeatedly; how many times is now of little consequence, although I have sometimes counted the white cicatrices on my body, tracing each with wonder that I had not long ago done with this life.

For that matter, I was regarded as already ended when they tore my assailant from my body and shattered him to death with their hatchets and knives, pistoling him again and again while he still quivered in the long grass.

As for me, I appeared to be quite dead, and whether to bury me there or in some kinder spot, none could determine, while the dear maid I loved lay senseless in Black Betty's arms.

As it was afterwards told to me in the saddest days of my life, so I tell what now befell the rescued, the rescuers, and that scarcely palpitating body o' mine, the soul of which floated on the dark borderland of Death. For it came to happen that dawn, lurking behind the eastern hills, set dull signals of fire on every western peak, warning Mount and Renard that day was on their trail to bare it for all who chose to follow.

My senseless sweetheart they bore to the waiting chaise, and, my body still retaining some warmth, they bore that, too, because they dared not bury me before she had seen me dead with her own eyes.

All that day they rode west by north, climbing the vast divide, halting to lie perdu when their keen ears heard movements all unseen, pushing on to tear the path free while their axes rang out among the windfalls. Then, when the western sun sank beyond the Ohio into the sea of trees, the winds of the east filled their nostrils and the long divide had been passed at last.

That night my dear love opened her eyes, and the darkness that enchained her fell, so that she crept to my feet as I lay in a corner of the chaise and laid her head on my knees.

Whether she thought me alive or dead none knew. Betty had bared my body to the waist and washed it. For a corpse they do as much. Later, without hope, Mount brought a pannikinful of blue-balsam gum, pricked from the globules on the trunk, and when Betty had once more washed me, they filled the long gashes with the balsam and closed them decently, strip on strip, with the fine cambric shift which my sweetheart tore from her own body.

Later, when the moon was coming up, they carried me lying in a blanket, my sweetheart walking beside me, and her silken shoon in tatters till her feet bled at every step, but refused to go back to the chaise. That night they thought me surely dead and watched without sleep lest the rigidity of dissolution surprise me ere my limbs had been laid straight. But the morning found me as I was, and the first shadow of night revealed no change, nor was I dead on the next morning, nor on the next, nor yet the next.

A still Sabbath in the forest, passed amid the sad twilight of the trees, gave them hope; for I had opened my eyes, though I saw nothing. But that night Death sat at my right hand, and the next night Death cradled my head; and my dear love lay at my feet and looked Death steadily in the eyes.

The fever which loosened every muscle burned fiercely all night long, and my voice broke out from my body like a demon mocking within me. A few of the Lenape, roaming near, followed and shot at us towards dawn, driving us north into the forest, where the chaise was abandoned, the traces cut, and the horses loaded with corn.

North and south the runways of the Long House pierced the wilderness, and these were the trails they followed, the men on foot, bearing me on their litter of blankets and balsam-boughs, the women crouching on the sack-laden horses.

As for me, I lived on through cold and heat, storm and stress, seeing nothing, hearing nothing, dumb, save when the demon hidden in my body mocked and laughed between my blackened lips. That demon was always watching things which I could not see, peeping out through my eyes into hell. Hours came when there was no water, and the demon knew it and mouthed and cursed between my shrinking lips. Then he would turn on me and tear at my throat and gnaw me and thrust his claws into my brain. Sometimes I heard his low laughter, for though I could neither see nor hear aught in the world, I could hear the demon sometimes, and feel him in my body, setting fire to the blood till it boiled like the water he craved.

At night he often stole my body and carried it where the darkness burnt and charred. There he would take out my bones, one by one, and break them for the marrow to dry hard.

These things no one has told me. I remember them in sleep sometimes, sometimes waking.

What I have heard from others is vague, and to me unreal as a painted scene in a picture where a film has settled under cobwebs. I hear that I breathed through days which I never saw, that I opened my eyes on lands which are strange to me, that my babble broke primeval silences which God himself had sealed. Nay, not I, but the demon mocked through those voiceless voids and lost ravines, through the still twilight of the noonday forest, through midnight summits muffled in the clouds. But only I know that, or dream it sometimes when I ponder on my end and on that fair salvation which my father finds lately in Christ.

Now, my dark soul, to hidden realms addressed, returned to me one night, and, listening, heard the demon scratching at my bones. Then, weary and perplexed, inside my body crept my soul and drew the lids of both eyes down, so that we might sleep together before the busy demon knew.

Yet I, having my soul again, opened my eyes to find a star was watching me; then, content, lay closer to my soul and slept. And thus the demon found us, and so fled back to the sleepless hell from whence he came.

Sleeping, I smelled lavender in the forest, and I thought the wood had windows where a sweet wind blew. Truly, there was a window somewhere near me, for I found my eyes had opened and could see it where the curtains swayed in the sun.

Hours later I looked again; the window was still there, and the moon beyond, low among pines whose shapes I knew.

Hours came and faded into sunshine; days brought bright spots on the curtains; night brought the moon and the tall pines. Sweet-fern, too, I smelled sometimes, and I heard a soothing monotone of familiar sound below me.

One day a cock crew and I fell a-trembling all alone, I knew not why. That night a new sound woke me, and I felt the presence of another person. Moonlight silvered the window of a room which I knew; but I was very quiet and waited for the sun, lest the phantoms I divined should trick me.

Then came a morning—perhaps the next, but I am not sure—when I knew I was in a bed and very tired, too tired to see aught but the sheets and the sunlit curtains beyond. That night, however, I heard rain falling on a roof and fell asleep, watching the window for the hidden moon.

When I first recognized the room, my memory served me a trick, and I thought of the school-room below where the others were imprisoned—Silver Heels, Peter, and Esk. Slyly content to doze abed here in Sir William's room, I understood that I must have been lying sick a long, long time, but could not remember when I had fallen ill. One thing sure: I did not mean they should know that I was better; I closed my eyes when I felt a presence near, lying still as a mouse until alone again.

Sometimes my thoughts wandered to the others in the school-room with Mr. Yost, for I did not remember he had been scalped by the Lenape, and I pitied Silver Heels and Esk and fat Peter a-thumbing their copy-books and breathing chalk-dust. Faith, I was well off in the great white bed, here in Sir William's room.

I could see his fish-rods on the wall, looped with silk lines and scarlet feather-flies; his hunting-horn, too, and his whip and spurs hanging from hooks beneath a fox's-mask and brush. There hung his fowling-pieces above the mantel, pouch and horn dangling from crossed ramrods; there rose his bookcase with the eared-owl atop and the Chinese jar full o' pipes, long as my arm and twice as strong—a conceit which sent a weak wave of mirth through my body I could not move.

Soft! They are coming to watch me now. So I slyly close my eyes till they go away or give me the drinks they brew to make me sleep. I know them; were I minded I might gather strength to spit out their sense-stealing stuffs. But I swallow and dream and wake to a new sun or to mark the waxing moon, now near its full.

Our Doctor Pierson was here to-day and caught me watching him. They'll soon have me in the school-room now, though I do still play possum all I can, eating my gruel, which a strange servant brings, and pretending not to see her. Yet I am wondering why the maid is so silent and that her gown is so dark and stiff.

Later that day I saw Colonel Guy Johnson come into the room and look at me, but I did not mean he should think me awake, and so closed my eyes and lay quiet. When Sir William should come, however, I would open my eyes, for I had been desiring to see him since I saw his rods and guns. It fretted me at times that he neglected me, knowing my love for him.

Once, as I lay dozing, Peter crept into the room and stared at me. He had grown tall and gross and heavy-eyed, so that I scarce knew him, nor had he a trace of Sir William in his slinking carriage, which was all Mohawk, and the worst Mohawk at that. I was glad when he ceased thumbing the bedposts and left me.

The next day I saw Doctor Pierson beside me and asked for Sir William. He said that Sir William was away and that I was doing well. We often spoke after that, and he was ever busy with my head, which no longer ached save when he fingered it.

Then one night I awoke with a cry of terror and found myself sitting upright, bathed in chilly sweat, shouting that the Cayugas were abroad and that I must hold them back by the throat till Sir William could arrive and restrain them.

Lights soon moved into the room; I saw Doctor Pierson and Guy Johnson, but the dammed-up floods of memory had broken loose like an old wound, and the past came crowding upon me till I fell back on the pillows, convulsed and gasping, while the strong hands of the doctor began their silent work, tapping head and body, till somebody gave me a draught and I drowsed perdu.

Day broke—the bitterest day of life I was to know. I felt it, listening to the rain; I felt it, in the footsteps that passed my door—footsteps I did not know. Why was the house so silent? Why did all go about so quietly, dressed in black? Was there some one dead in the house below? Where was Silver Heels? Why had she never come to me? How came I here? Where was Jack Mount and Cade Renard? And Sir William, where was he that he came not near me—me who had lain sick unto death in his service and for his sake?

Dread numbed me; I strove to call, but my dumb lips froze; I strove to rise, and found my body wrecked in bed without power, without sense, a helpless, inert thing between two sheets.

Why was I here? Why was I alive if aught had harmed Silver Heels? God! And I safe here in bed? Where was she? *Where was she?* Dead? Why do they not tell me? Why do they not kill me as I lie here if I have returned without her?

I must have cried aloud in my agony, for the doctor came running and leaned over me.

"Tell me! Tell me!" I stammered. "Why don't you tell me?" and strove to strike him, but could not use my arms.

"Quiet, quiet," he said, watching me; "I will tell you what you wish to know. What is it then, my poor boy?"

"I—want—Felicity," I blurted out.

"Felicity?" he repeated, blankly. "Oh—Miss—ahem!—Miss Warren?"

I glared at him.

"Miss Warren has gone with Sir John Johnson to Boston," he said, dryly.

My eyes never left him.

"Is that why you cried out?" he asked, curiously. "Miss Warren left us a week ago. Had you only known her she would have been happy, for she has slept for weeks on the couch yonder."

"Why—why did she go?"

"I cannot tell you the reasons," he said, gravely.

"When will she return?"

"I do not know."

With a strength that came from God knows where, I dragged myself upright and caught him by the hand.

"She is dead!" I whispered. "She is dead, and all in this house know it save I who love her!"

A strange light passed over the doctor's face; he took both my hands and looked at me carefully. Then he smiled and gently forced me back to the pillows.

"She is alive and well," he said. "On my honour as a man, lad, I set your heart at rest. She is in Boston, and I do know why, but I may not meddle with what concerns this family, save in sickness—or death."

I watched his lips. They were solemn as the solemn word he uttered. I knew death had been in the house; I had felt that for days. I waited, watching him.

"Poor lad," he said, holding my hands.

My eyes never left his.

"Ay," he said, softly, "his last word was your name. He loved you dearly, lad."

And so I knew that Sir William was dead.

CHAPTER XIX

Day after day I lay in my bed, staring at the ceiling till night blotted it out. Then, stunned and exhausted, I would lie in the dark, crying in my weakness, whimpering for those I loved who had left me here alone. There was no strength left in me, body or mind; and, perhaps for that reason, my suffering was too feeble to waste what was left of me, for I had not even the strength of the fretful who do damage themselves with every grimace.

Certain it was that my thinned blood was growing gradually warmer, and its currents flowed with slightly increasing vigour day by day. The fever, which had come only partly from my wounds, had doubtless been long in me, and had fermented my blood as the opportunity offered when Wraxall nigh drained my every vein with his butcher's blade.

The emaciation of my body was extreme, my limbs were pithless reeds, my skull grinned through the tensely stretched skin, and my eyes were enormous.

Yet, such sturdy fibre have I inherited from my soldier father that grief itself could not retard the mending of me, and in the little French mirror I could almost see my sunken muscles harden and grow slowly fuller. Like a pear in a hot-frame, I was plump long before my strength could aid me or my shocked senses gather to take counsel for the future.

The dreadful anguish of my bereavement came only at intervals, succeeded by an apathy which served as a merciful relief. But most I thought of Silver Heels, and why she had left me here, and when she might return. Keen fear lurked near to stab me when, rousing from blank slumber, my first thought was of her. Then I would lie and wonder why she had gone, and tell myself I loved her above all else, or whimper and deem her cruel to leave me.

One late afternoon the doctor came with a dish of China oranges, which I found relief in sucking, my gums being as yet somewhat hot and painful. He made a hole in an orange and I sucked it awhile, watching him meditatively. He wore crape on his arm—the arm that Quider had broken, and which now he could not bend as formerly.

"Why does not my Aunt Molly come to see me?" I asked, quietly.

"Dear lad," said the doctor, raising his eyebrows, "did you not know she had gone to Montreal?"

"How should I know it," I asked, "when you tell me nothing?"

"I will tell you what I am permitted," he answered, gently.

"Then tell me when my cousin Felicity is coming back? Have you not heard from Sir John Johnson?"

"Yes—I have heard," replied the doctor, cautiously.

I waited, my eyes searching his face.

"Sir John returns to-morrow," he said.

A thrill set my blood leaping. I felt the warm colour staining my pinched face.

"To-morrow!" I repeated.

The doctor regarded me very gravely.

"Miss Warren will remain in Boston," he said.

The light died out before my eyes; presently I closed them.

"How long?" I asked.

"I do not know."

The orange, scarcely tasted, rolled over the bed and fell on the floor. I heard him rise to pick it up.

I opened my eyes and looked at the distant pines through the window.

"Doctor," I muttered, "I am heartsick for a familiar face. Where are the people who have lived in this house? It is scarce four months that I have been away, yet all is changed and strange—new servants everywhere, no old, friendly faces—nay, even Peter has grown so gross and sullen that I scarce knew him. Where is Esk? Is there not one soul unchanged?"

"Have I changed?" he asked.

"Yes—you are gray! gray!—and smaller; and you stoop when you sit."

After a moment he said: "These are times to age all men. Have you yourself not aged in these five months? You went away a fresh-faced lad, scarce weaned from your alley-taws and the chalky ring! You return a man, singed already by the first breath of a fire which will scorch this land to the bedded rock!"

Presently I asked, "Is war certain?"

He nodded, looking at the floor.

"And—and the Six Nations?" I asked again.

"On our side surely," he said, in a low voice.

"On our side?" I repeated.

He looked at me suddenly, stern mouth tightly shut. A cold light touched his gray eyes and seemed to harden every feature.

"When I say 'our side' I assume you to be loyal, Mr. Cardigan," he said, curtly.

The change in his shrewd, kindly face amazed me. Was it possible for old friends to turn so quickly? Was this coming strife to poison the world with its impending passions?

"If you have become tainted with rebel heresy since you left us, thank God you have returned in time to purge your mind," he said, sternly. "Sir William has gone—Heaven rest his brave soul!—but Sir John is alive to take no uncertain stand in the face of this wicked rebellion which all true loyal hearts must face."

I looked at him serenely. Who but I should know what Sir William had thought about the coming strife. Those sacred confidences of the past had cleared my mind, and made it up long since. Had I not, in Sir William's service, braved death for the sake of these same rebels? I understood my mission better now. I had gone in the cause of humanity—a cause which was not embraced by the loyal subjects of our King. I had failed, but failure had brought wisdom. Never could I set my back against the firm rock of loyalty to fight for a name that now meant nothing to me. I had quenched my thirst at bitter waters; I had learned that men could beggar themselves for principle and die for a tuppenny tax with pockets full.

"Lad," said the doctor, kindly, "the two rough woodsmen who brought you home did what their rude skill permitted to save your life. They washed your wounds and bound them with balsam and linen; they bore you faithfully for miles and miles through the valley of death itself. But, lad, they could not have saved you had not something intervened between you and that keen blade which searched your life to slay it!"

He rose and took something from the chest of drawers in the corner. It was a British flag, all torn and hacked and covered with black stains.

"It was found rolled up beneath your hunting-shirt," he said, solemnly. "Look on it, lad! For this torn flag, which your father died defending, held back that deadly knife, shielding the vital spark beneath its folds. A hair's-breadth more and you had died at the first stab. The flag was your strength and shield: let it become your salvation! It was your father's flag: exalt it!"

He spread the flag reverently upon the bed. I touched its folds, stiff with my own blood. It was the flag of Cresap's fort which I had taken, seeing it abandoned by all.

"I shall always honour it," I said, half unconsciously.

"And the men who bear it!" he added.

"That is very different," I said, wearily, and turned my head on the pillow.

When I looked again he was folding the flag and placing it in the chest of drawers, smiling quietly to himself. Doubtless he thought me loyal to the King whose armies bore the flag my father died for. But I was too tired to argue further.

"There is one man I would like to see," I said, "and that is Mr. Duncan. Will you send to the guard-house and beg him to come to me, doctor?"

"Ay, that I will, lad," he said, cheerily, picking up his hat and case of drugs. "And, by-the-way, your regiment of Border Horse will be here in a month. You will doubtless be content to see the gallant troopers in whose ranks you will one day serve, please God."

"Perhaps," I said, closing my eyes.

I must have fallen into a light sleep, for when I unclosed my eyes I saw Mr. Duncan beside me, looking down into my face. I smiled and raised one hand, and he took it gently in both of his strong, sun-browned hands.

"Well, well, well," he muttered, smiling, while the tears stood in his pleasant eyes; "here is our soldier home again—that same soldier whom I last saw in the guard-house, having his poll clipped by honest Wraxall, à la coureur-de-bois—eh?"

I motioned feebly for him to find a chair beside my bed, and he sat down, still holding my hand in his.

"Now," I said, "explain to me all that has happened. The doctor tells me what I ask, but I have had little inclination to hear much. I like you, Mr. Duncan. Tell me everything."

"You mean—about Sir William?" he asked, gently.

"Yes—but that last of all," I muttered, choking.

After a silence he straightened up, unhooked his sword, and laid it against the wall. Then, settling comfortably back in his chair, he clasped his hands over his white gaiters and looked at me.

"You must know," he said, "that Colonel Guy Johnson is now superintendent of Indian affairs in North America for his Majesty. He has appointed as deputies Colonel Claus and Colonel John Butler—"

"Who?" I exclaimed.

"Colonel Butler," repeated Mr. Duncan; "you remember him, don't you?"

"Yes, I remember him," I replied; "where is he?"

"He and Joseph Brant are organizing the loyalists and Indians north of us," said Mr. Duncan, innocently. "This border war in Virginia has set the Six Nations afire. Many of our Mohawks have slipped away to join Logan and Sowanowane against this fellow Cresap who murdered Logan's children; the others are restless and sullen. There was but one man in the world who could have controlled them—"

He paused.

"I know it," said I. "You mean Sir William."

"Ay, Mr. Cardigan, I mean Sir William. Well, well, there is no help now. It is Sir John Johnson's policy to win over the savages to our side; but I often think Sir William knew best how to manage them. It will be dreadful, dreadful! I for one wish no such allies as are gathering north of us under Joseph Brant and Colonel Butler."

"Why do you not say as much to Sir John?" I asked.

"I? What weight would my opinion carry? I have said often to those who ask me that I would give all I possess to see the savages remain neutral in this coming strife."

"Do you also believe it is coming?"

"Surely, surely," he said, lifting his hand solemnly. "Mr. Cardigan, you have been away, and have also been too ill to know what passes at our very doors. You are ignorant of the passion which has divided every town, village, and hamlet in Tryon County—ay, the passion which has turned neighbours to bitterest foes—the passion which has turned kinship to hatred—which sets brother against brother, son against father!

"Our village of Johnstown yonder seethes and simmers with Tory against Whig, loyalist against rebel. Houses are barricaded; arms stored, stolen, and smuggled; seditious words uttered, traitorous songs sung, insults flung in the faces of the King's soldiers. We of the Royal Americans receive the grossest epithets; curses and threats are flung in our teeth; sentries on guard are mocked and reviled; officers jeered at in tavern and street.

"I do not believe such fierceness would betray itself if the question here were but the old Boston grievance—the ancient protest against taxing people without the people's consent. No, it is not the wrangle between Parliament and colonies that has brought the devil's own confusion into Tryon County; it is the terrible possibility that one or the other side may let loose the savages. We of Tryon County know what that means. Small wonder then, I say, that the rebels curse us for swine and dogs and devils incarnate because we are slowly gaining the good-will of the Six Nations."

He wiped his face with a laced hanker and pressed his temples, frowning.

"Yet," he said, "the rebels, too, would doubtless use the savages against us if they could win them over. Sir John says so. That is why he sent Thayendanegea and Colonel Butler to recruit in the north. They say that Captain Walter Butler is with Cresap. I don't know; I have not seen him in months."

"I know," said I, quietly.

"Doubtless you met him then at Cresap's camp?"

"Doubtless."

Mr. Duncan waited a moment, then laughed.

"You were ever a man to keep your own counsel," he said.

"What have you heard from Cresap's men?" I asked.

"Nothing save that the war is a fierce one. An express came in yesterday with news that the Cayugas had been terribly whipped by the backwoodsmen under Andy Lewis, somewhere near the Great Kanawha. The express rider got it from some of Cresap's men, but it may not be true."

After a silence I asked him what month of the year it now was. I had noticed yellow leaves outside.

"October," he said, pityingly; "did you not know it?"

I tried to realize the space of time which had been wiped out from my memory.

"When did Sir William—die?" I muttered, painfully.

Mr. Duncan looked at me with tears in his eyes.

"On Monday, the 11th of July."

"Tell me—all," I motioned, with quivering lips.

"It is history," he said, simply. "I will tell you what I heard and what I witnessed.

"On the 1st of July we received news of the murder of Bald Eagle, a friendly Delaware chief. Rumour had it that one of my Lord Dunmore's agents had slain the old man, but that, of course, is preposterous. It is hard to sift truth out of rumours. Why, the wildest statements were openly made in some taverns that young Walter Butler had murdered the old man. What reason could Walter Butler have to slay a friendly chief in Pennsylvania?"

"Go on," I said, grimly.

"Well, then, this murder was committed while the poor old man was sitting in his canoe on one of the streams near Fort Pitt. After tearing the scalp from the old man the murderer set him afloat in his canoe. The ghastly progress of the dead was seen by Indians and whites, and the news, following the report of the outrage on Logan by that creature Daniel Greathouse, roused the Six Nations to fury.

"You know that even after the Logan outrage Sir William had held back the warriors of the Long House; but this fresh crime drove them frantic. They might still have held off had not Bald Eagle been scalped, but you know, Mr. Cardigan, that the Six Nations *always* regard the scalping of a murdered person as a *national* act, not an individual one, and *always* accept it as a declaration of war."

"I know," I said.

"The sachems of the Long House," continued Mr. Duncan, "immediately notified Sir William that they desired to see him without delay. When you think, Mr. Cardigan, that the murders of Logan's children and of Bald Eagle touched every clan tie in the Six Nations, nothing could prove more clearly the marvellous influence of Sir William over the savages than the fact that their first impulse was not to seize hatchet and knife and begin an indiscriminate butchery of our people, but to solicit a conference with Sir William, so that they might state their wrongs calmly and ask his advice. Lord! Lord! A great man died in last July; and who can take his place?"

Again he wiped his brow and clasped his gaitered knees with his hands.

"In two days," he resumed, "two hundred Onondagas came here, with intelligence that four hundred more were on their way. Then they came in hordes—Mohawks, Senecas, Cayugas, and Oneidas. From morning till night Sir William was engaged in talking with them, persuading and promising and exerting himself tirelessly to hold the gathering tempest in check.

"He was even then far from well; his old trouble had returned; he could scarcely drag himself up here to this room when night came. Yet he said to me, after an exhausting conference with the Oneidas, 'Mr. Duncan, I have daily to combat with thousands of white men who, by their avarice, cruelty, or indiscretions, are constantly counteracting all my judicious measures with the Indians. It is not the Indians I blame. I shall persevere: the occasion requires it; and I shall never be without hope till I find myself without that influence which has never yet forsaken me.'

"'That influence is built up on your personal honour,' I said; 'it can never forsake you.'

"He smiled—you know his rare smile, Mr. Cardigan—"

Mr. Duncan almost broke down; my eyes were dry and throbbing.

"On the 7th of July," he resumed, "we had a thousand Indians assembled here at the Hall. The sachems and chiefs were earnestly pleading for the congress. Sir William was sick abed and suffering pitifully, but he rose and refused to listen to Doctor Pierson, saying that the congress should never be delayed by anything but his own death.

"The weather was frightfully hot; nearly the whole of the first day was occupied by the speech of Senhowane, a Seneca chief, who made out a bitter case against the white people of Cresap's command. A Cayuga war-chief followed the Seneca, speaking until the moon rose.

"The next day was the Sabbath. Sir William lay abed all day, unable to see for the frightful pains in his head. Yet the next day, at half-past nine in the morning, Sir William was at the fire, belts in hand.

"Never, never, Mr. Cardigan, had any one heard him speak with such eloquence. Sick unto death as he was, he stood there in the burning July sun, hour after hour, in the cause of peace. He spoke with all the fire and vivacity of youth; his words held the savages' grave and strained attention until the end."

Mr. Duncan paused, staring at space as though to fix that last scene in his mind forever.

"I was commanding the escort," he said. "My men saluted as the Indians left the congress. When the last chief had disappeared, I saw that Sir William was in distress, and ran to him. He lurched forward into my arms. I held him a moment. He tried to speak, but all he could say was, 'Tell Michael I am proud—of—him,' and then fell back full weight. We got him to the Hall and laid him on the library couch. A gillie rode breakneck for Sir John, who was at the old fort nine miles away. Mistress Molly had gone to Schenectady; there remained no one of his own kin here."

Mr. Duncan leaned forward, with his face in his hands.

"Sir John came too late," he said; "Sir William died utterly alone."

As I lay there I could hear the robins chirping outside, just as I had so often heard them from the school-room. Could this still be the same summer? Years and years seemed to have slipped away in these brief months between May and October.

"Where is he buried?" I asked.

"In the vault under the stone church he built in the village. When you can walk—we will go."

"I shall walk very soon now," said I.

After a moment I asked who had succeeded Sir William.

"In title and estate Sir John succeeds him," said Mr. Duncan, "but the King has conferred the intendancy of Indian affairs on Colonel Guy Johnson."

"Is he as close a friend as ever of Colonel Butler and Joseph?"

"Quite. Joseph Brant is a special deputy, too."

"Then God save our country," I replied, calmly, and closed my eyes.

Lying there, thinking, I saw for a moment into that red horror called the future—which now, thank God, is already the past.

"When Sir John returns from Boston you will hear the will read," said Mr. Duncan.

"When does he return?" I asked, opening my eyes.

"To-morrow, we hope."

"Why did he go?"

"I do not know," said Mr. Duncan, frankly.

"Why did he take Miss Warren?"

"I'm sure I do not know," he answered.

"Will she return with him?"

"I cannot say—but I suppose she will," replied Mr. Duncan, looking curiously at me.

"The doctor says she will not return with Sir John."

"Ah!"

"Why?"

"Lord, lad, I don't know!" he exclaimed, amused.

"Did Miss Warren see me while I was ill?"

"Ay, that she did," he cried. "She never left you; they could not drag her away to eat enough to keep a bird alive. She hung over you, she followed the doctor, holding to his sleeve and asking questions till the good man nigh lost his senses. And all the time Sir John was fuming and impatient to be off to

Boston, but Miss Warren would not go until the doctor was able to promise on his sacred honour that you were not only out of danger, but that you would recover completely in mind and body."

"And then?" I muttered.

"Why, then Sir John would no longer be denied, and she must needs journey with him to Boston. I know that she herself did not understand why she was going, except that some legal affairs required her presence."

"And she left no word for me?"

"None with me. I heard her ask Sir John how soon you would be able to read if she wrote you, but Sir John shook his head without reply. Then she asked the doctor, and I think he told Miss Warren she might write in October if she remained in Boston as long as that. So, doubtless, the express is already galloping up the old post-road with your letter, Mr. Cardigan."

Presently—for I was becoming very tired—I asked about the two forest-runners who had brought me hither, not mentioning their names for prudence sake.

"I don't know where they are," said Mr. Duncan, rising to buckle on his sword. "The little, mild-spoken man disappeared the day that Sir John and Miss Warren left for Boston. The other, the big, swaggering fellow, abandoned by his running-mate, seemed astonished, and hunted about the village for a week, swearing that there was foul play somewhere, and that his comrade would never willingly have deserted him. Then our magistrate, Squire Bullock, was stopped and robbed on the King's highway—ay, and roundly cursed for a Tory thief—by this same graceless giant in buckskin who brought you here. They sought for him, but you know how those fellows travel. He may be in Quebec now, for aught I know—the impudent rascal."

After a moment I said, "Miss Warren, you say, cared for me while I lay ill?"

"Like a mother—or fond sister."

I closed my eyes partly.

He looked down at me and pressed my hand.

"I have tired you," he said, gently.

"No, you have given me life," I answered, smiling.

CHAPTER XX

Long before Sir John returned, or, indeed, long before we had any word from him, I was dressed and making hourly essays at walking, first in the house, then through the door-yard to the guard-house, where I would sit in the hot sun and breathe the full-throated October winds. Keen and sweet as apple-wine, the air I drank warmed and excited me; my eyes grew clear and strong, my lean cheeks filled, my wasted limbs once more began to bear me with the old-time lightness and delight.

Too, I found myself at times nosing the wind with half-closed eyes, like a young hound too long kennelled, or sometimes listening, yet lost in reverie, as hounds listen on winter nights, drowsing by the dull fire.

A hundred little zephyrs that knew me whispered to me through open windows. At night I caught the faint echo of the breezes' laughter under the eaves; sometimes I heard the big wind stirring the dark pines, so far away that none but I could hear it playing with the baby breezes.

They were little friendly breezes, the spirits of spirits, with dainty, familiar voices, too delicate to frighten the birds they sometimes gossiped with. Even the slate-gray deer-mouse, with his white belly, feared not my little friends, the winds; for oft I heard him, in the creamy October moonlight, tuning his tiny elfin song to the night wind's fluting.

On warm, spicy days Mr. Duncan and I would seek the stone church, sitting silent for hours in the purple and crimson rays of the stained window, watching the golden dust-bands slanting on the tomb.

The resentment of bitter grief had died out in my heart; sorrow had been purged of selfishness; I felt the calm presence of the dead at my elbow where'er I went. Strength and quiet came to me in voiceless communion; high resolve, patience, and hope were bred within me under the serene glow of those jewelled panes. On the gray-stone slab at my feet, dreaming, I read the story of a noble life, "Keep faith with all men," and here, in silence, I sought to read and understand the changeless laws which shelter souls and mark the mile-stones of a blameless life.

When the southwest sun hung gilding the clover, over miles of upland I passed, as I had roamed with him, twisting the bronzing sweet-fern from its woody stem, touching the silken milk-weed to set free its floss, halting, breast-deep in crimsoning sumach, to mark the headlong, whirling covey drive through the thorns into the purple dusk.

His hounds bayed from their kennels; there was no one to cast them free; and the red fox throttled the fowls by moonlight; and the lynx squalled in the swamp. His horses trampled the stables till the oak floors, reverberating, hummed thunder; there was no one to bit and bridle them; the moorland clover swayed untrodden in the wind, and the dun stag stamped the crag.

Night and day the river rushed to the sea; night and day the brooks prattled to their pebbles, the slim salmon lay in the pools, the lithe trout stemmed the gravel-rifts; but never a line whistled in the silence, and never a scarlet feather-fly sailed on the waters among the autumn leaves.

Yet, though land and water were lonely without him, I was not lonely, for he walked with me always over the land he had known, and his voice was in the soft, mild winds he loved so well.

With the memory of Silver Heels it was different. Every scented stem of sweet-fern was redolent of her; every grass-blade quivered for her; the winds called her all day long; the brooks whispered, "Where is Silver Heels?"

Through our old play-grounds, in the orchard, on the stairs, through the darkened school-room I followed, haunting the vanished footsteps—gay, light, flying feet of the child I had loved so long, unknowing.

Her stocks stood outside the nursery door; the brass key was on the nail. In her dim chamber hung the scent of lavender, while through the half-closed shutters a faint freshness crept, stirring the ghostly curtains of her bed.

Wistfulness, doubt, tenderness, and sadness came and went like sun-spots on an April day. I waited with delicious dread for her return; I fretted, doubted, hoped, all in the same quick heart-beat, which was not all pain. Only that ghost of happiness which men call hope I knew in those long autumn days alone among the haunts of varied yesterdays.

When the golden month drew near its end, amid the dropping glory of the maple-leaves, one sun-drenched morning I awoke to hear the drums and pipes skirling the march of "Tryon County Men":

"Hark to the horn in the dawn o' the morn!

Rally, whoever ye be;

For it's down Derry Down, and it's over the lea,

And it's saddle and bridle as sure as you're born!

Scattered and trampled and torn is the corn

As we ride to the war in the morning;

Down Derry Down!

Down Derry Down!

For we ride to the war in the morning!"

"Officer o' the guard! Turn out the guard!" bawled the sentry under my window. As I looked out the drums came crashing past, and behind them tramped the Highlanders, kilts and sporrans swinging, firelocks aslant and claymore blades shining in the sun.

It was the new regiment organized by Sir John, picked men all, and fierce partisans of the King, weeded from the militia regiment lately disbanded at Johnstown by order of Governor Tryon.

Behind them, fifes squealing the "Huron," came the reorganized battalion of yeomanry, now stripped clean of rebel suspects, and rechristened "Johnson's Greens;" stout, brawny yokels with hats askew and the green cockade veiled in crape, their hunting-shirts caped triple and fringed deep in green wool, their powder-horns tasselled and chased in silver gilt.

I watched them swinging north into the purple hills for their month's training, the new order having arrived some eight days since from Governor Tryon.

Leaning there in the casement, wrapped in my dressing-gown, I saw Colonel Guy Johnson ride up to the block-house, dismount, and call out Mr. Duncan. Then began a great bustle among the soldiers, for what reason I did not understand, until a knocking at my door brought a gillie with Colonel Guy Johnson's compliments, and would I dress in my uniform to receive Sir John, who was expected for breakfast.

My heart began to beat madly; could it be possible that Sir John had brought Silver Heels, after all? Doctor Pierson had said that she would remain for the present in Boston; but perhaps Doctor Pierson did not know everything that went on in the world.

To crush back hope from sheer dread of disappointment was a thankless task and too much for me. I dressed in my red uniform, tied my silver gorget, hung my sword, and drew on my spurred boots. Standing by the mirror, pensive, I thought of my delight in these same clothes when first I wore them for Sir William. Alas! alas! The gilt lace dulled under my eyes as I looked; the gorget tarnished; the spurs rang sadly in the silence. I twisted a strip of crape in my hilt, shook out the black badge on my sleeve, and went down-stairs, very soberly, in the livery of the King I must one day desert. Perhaps I was now wearing it for the last time. Well, such things matter nothing now; true hearts can beat as freely under a buckskin shirt as beneath the jewelled sashes of the great.

As I reached the porch Mr. Duncan came hurrying past, buttoning his gloves.

"Sir John is in the village," he said, returning my salute, "and he has an escort of your regiment at his back. My varlets yonder need pipe-clay, but I dare not risk delay."

"Where is Colonel Guy?" I asked, but at that moment he came out of the stable in full uniform, and Mr. Duncan and I joined him at salute. He barely noticed me, as usual, but gave his orders to Mr. Duncan and then looked across the fields towards the village.

"Is Felicity with Sir John?" I inquired.

"No," he answered, without turning.

My throat swelled and my mouth quivered. Where was she, then? What did all this mean?

"By-the-by," observed Colonel Guy, carelessly, "Sir John has chosen another aide-de-camp in your place. You, of course, will join your regiment at Albany."

I looked at him calmly, but he was again gazing out across the fields. So Sir John, who had never cared about me, had rid himself of me. This brought matters to a climax. Truly enough, I was now wearing my red uniform for the last time.

I looked across the yellowing fields where, on the highway, a troop of horse had come up over the hill and were now galloping hither in a veil of sparkling dust. I watched them indifferently; the drums at the guard-house were sounding, beating the major-general's salute of two ruffles; the horsemen swept up past the ranks of presented firelocks and halted before the Hall.

And now I saw Sir John in full uniform of his rank, badged with mourning, yet all a-glitter with medals and orders, slowly dismount, while gillie Bareshanks held his stirrup. Alas! alas! that he must be known by men as the son of his great father!—this cold, slow man, with distrustful eyes and a mouth which to see was to watch. His very voice seemed to sound a warning in its emotionless monotony; his lips said, "On guard, lest we trick you unawares."

Sir John greeted Colonel Guy, holding his hand and dropping into low conversation for a few moments. Then, as I gave him the officers' salute, he rendered it and offered his hand, asking me how I did.

I had the honour to report myself quite recovered, and in turn inquired concerning his own health, the health of Aunt Molly, and of Silver Heels; to which he replied that Mistress Molly with Esk and Peter was in Quebec; that

Felicity was well; that he himself suffered somewhat from indigestion, but was otherwise in possession of perfect health.

He then presented me to several officers of my own regiment, among them a very young cornet, who smiled at me in such friendly fashion that my lonely heart was warm towards him. His name was Rodman Girdwood, and he swaggered when he walked; but so frankly did he ruffle it that I could not choose but like him and smile indulgence on his guileless self-satisfaction.

"They don't like me," he said, confidentially, as I took him to my own chamber so that he might remove the stains of travel. "They don't like me because I talk too much at mess. I say what I think, and I say it loud, sir."

"What do you say—loud?" I asked, smiling.

"Oh, everything. I say it's a damned shame to send British troops into Boston; I say it's a doubly damned shame to close the port and starve the poor; I say that Tommy Gage is in a dirty business, and I, for one, hope the Boston people will hold on until the British Parliament find their senses. Oh, I don't care who hears me!" he said, throwing off his coat and sword and plunging into the water-basin.

His servant came to the door for orders, but Girdwood bade him let him alone and seek a pot o' beer in the kitchen.

"I trust I have not shocked your loyalty, Mr. Cardigan," he said, using a towel vigorously.

"Oh no," I laughed.

"I don't mean to be discourteous," he added, smoothing his ruffled lace; "but sometimes I feel as though I must stand up on a hill and shout across the ocean to Parliament, 'Don't make fools of yourselves'!"

I was laughing so heartily that he turned around in humorous surprise.

"I'm afraid you are one of those disrespectful patriots," he said. "I never heard a Tory laugh at anything I said. Come, sir, pray repeat 'God save the King'!"

"God save"—we began together, then ended—"our country!"

I looked at him gravely. He, too, had grown serious. Presently he held out his hand. I took it in silence.

"Well, well," he said, "I had little thought of finding a comrade in our new cornet."

"Nor I in the Border Horse," said I, quietly.

He turned to the mirror and began retying his queue ribbon. After a twist or two the smile came back to his lips and the jauntiness to his carriage.

"It's all in a lifetime," he said. "Lord, but I'm hungry, Cardigan! Honest Abraham, I haven't broken a crust since we left Schenectady!"

"Come on, then," I said; "we subalterns must not keep our superiors, you know."

"They wouldn't wait for us, anyway," he said, following me down-stairs to the breakfast-room, into which already Sir John and his suite were crowding.

The breakfast was short and dreary. Sir John's unsympathetic presence had never yet warmed even his familiars to gayety. Those who were under his orders found him severe and unbending; his equals, I think, distrusted him; but his superiors saw in him a latent energy which they believed might be worth their control some day, and so studied him carefully, prepared for anything from fidelity to indifference, and even, perhaps, treachery.

Benning, major in the Border Horse, strove indeed to liven the breakfast with liberal libations and jests, neither of which were particularly encouraged by Sir John. As for Colonel Guy Johnson, he brooded in his dish, a strange, dark, silent man who had never, to my knowledge, shown a single human impulse for either good or evil. He was a faultless executor of duty intrusted, obeying to the letter, yet never offering suggestions; a scrupulously clean man in speech and habit; a blameless husband, and an inoffensive neighbour. But that was all, and I had sooner had a stone idol as neighbour than Colonel Guy Johnson.

The living Johnsons seemed to be alike in nature. I do not even now understand why I thought so, but I sometimes believed that they had, deep in them, something of that sombre ferocity which burned in the Butlers. Yet to me they had exhibited nothing but the most passionless reserve.

When the gloomy breakfast was ended, Colonel Guy Johnson conducted his guests to the porch, where they made ready for the inspection of our two stone block-houses and the new artillery in the barracks, sent recently by Governor Tryon at Sir John's request.

Supposing I was to follow, as I no longer remained aide-de-camp to the major-general, I started off with Rodman Girdwood, but was recalled by a soldier, who reported that Sir John awaited me in the library.

Sir John was sitting at the great oak table as I entered, and he motioned me to a seat opposite. He held in his hands a bundle of papers, which he slowly turned over and over in his fingers.

He first informed me that he had selected another aide-de camp, not because he expected to find me unsatisfactory, but because it was most desirable that young, inexperienced officers should join the colours as soon as possible. He said that the times were troublous and uncertain; that sedition was abroad in the land; that young men needed the counsel of loyal authority, and the example and discipline of military life. He expected me, he said, to return to Albany with the squadron which had served him as escort.

To which I made no reply.

He then spoke of the death of his father, of the responsibilities of his own position, and of his claim on me for obedience. He spoke of my mission to Cresap and the Cayugas as a mistake in policy; and I burned to hear him criticise Sir William's acts. He asked me for my report, and I gave it to him, relating every circumstance of my meeting with the Cayugas, my peril, my rescue, the fight at Cresap's fort, the treachery of Dunmore, Greathouse, Connolly, and the others.

He frowned, listening with lowered eyes.

I told him of the insult offered our family by Dunmore; I told how Silver Heels escaped. Then I related every circumstance in my relations with Walter Butler, from my first open quarrel with him here at the Hall to his deadly assault on me while in discharge of my mission, and finally how he had fallen under my fury in Dunmore's presence.

Sir John's face was expressionless. He deplored the matters mentioned, saying that loyal men must stand together and not exterminate each other. He pointed out that Dunmore was the royal Governor of Virginia; that an alliance with Felicity was an honour we were most unwise to refuse; he regretted the quarrel between such a zealous loyalist as Walter Butler and myself, but coolly informed me that he had heard from Butler, and that he was recovering slowly from the breaking of an arm, collar-bone, and many ribs.

This calm acknowledgment that Sir John and my deadly enemy were in such intimacy set my blood boiling. His amazing complacency towards these men after the insults offered his own kin took my breath.

He said that his policy in regard to the Cayuga rising was not the policy of Sir William. His efforts were directed towards the solid assembling of all men, so that the loyal might in the hour of danger present an unbroken front to rebellion and discontent. It was, he said, my duty to lay aside all rancour against Lord Dunmore and Captain Butler. This was not the time to settle personal differences. Later, he could see no objection to my calling out Walter Butler or demanding reparation from Lord Dunmore, if I found it necessary.

I was slowly beginning to hate Sir John.

I therefore told him how we had done to death the wretch Greathouse; how I had shot the driver of the coach, who was the unknown man who had tasted his own hatchet in the forest.

Sir John informed me that I and my party had also slain Wraxall and Toby Tice, and that Captain Murdy alone had escaped our fury.

I was contented to hear it; contented to hear, too, that Walter Butler lived; for, though no man on earth deserved death more than he, I had not wished to slay any man in such a manner. I could wait, for I never doubted that he must one day die by my hand, though not the kind of death that he had escaped so narrowly.

Sir John now spoke of the will left by Sir William. He held a copy in his hand and opened it.

"You know," he said, "that your fortune is not considerable, though my father has invested it most fortunately. The income is ample for a young man, and on the decease of your uncle, Sir Terence, you will come into his title and estate in Ireland. This should make you wealthy. However, Sir William saw fit to provide for you further."

He turned the pages of the document slowly, frowning.

"Where is my own money?" I asked.

Sir John passed me a letter, sealed, which he said would recommend me to the lawyer in Albany who administered my fortune until I became of legal age. Then he resumed his study of the will.

"Read from the beginning," I said. I had a curious feeling that it was indecent to ignore anything Sir William had written, in order to hurry to that clause relating only to my own selfish profit.

Sir John glanced at me across the table, then read aloud, in his cold, passionless voice:

"In the name of God, Amen! I, Sir William Johnson, of Johnson Hall, in the County of Tryon and Province of New York, Bart., being of sound and disposing mind, memory, and understanding, do make, publish, and declare this to be my last Will and Testament in manner and form following:

"First and principally, I resign my soul to the great and merciful God who made it, in hopes, through the merits alone of my blessed Lord and Saviour Jesus Christ, to have a joyful resurrection to life eternal—"

He stopped abruptly, saying that he saw no necessity for reading all that, and turned directly to the clause concerning me. Then he read:

"And as to the worldly and temporal estate which God was pleased to endow me with, I devise, bequeath, and dispose of in the following manner: Imprimis. I will, order and direct that all such just debts as I may owe, at the time of my decease, to be paid by my son Sir John Johnson, Baronet....

"Item. To my dearly beloved kinsman and ward, Michael Cardigan, I give and bequeath the sum of three thousand pounds, York currency, to him or the survivor of him. Also my own horse Warlock."

Sir John turned several pages, found another clause, and read:

"To the aforesaid Michael Cardigan I devise and bequeath that lot of land which I purchased from Jelles Fonda, in the Kennyetto Patent; also two hundred acres of land adjoining thereto, being part of the Perth Patent, to be laid out in a compact body between the sugar bush and the Kennyetto Creek; also four thousand acres in the Royal Grant, now called Kingsland, next to the Mohawk River, where is the best place for salmon fishing; also that strip of land from the falls or carrying-place to Lot No. 1, opposite to the hunting-lodge of Colonel John Butler, where woodcocks, snipes, and wild ducks are accustomed to be shot by me, within the limits and including all the game-land I bought from Peter Weaver."

Sir John folded the paper and handed it to me, saying, "It is strange that Sir William thought fit to bequeath you such a vast property."

"What provision was made for Felicity?" I asked, quietly.

"She might have had three thousand pounds and a thousand acres adjoining yours in the Kennyetto Patent," replied Sir John, coldly. "But under present circumstances—ahem—she receives nothing."

I thought a moment. In the hallway I heard the officers returning with Colonel Guy Johnson from their inspection.

"Where is Felicity?" I asked, suddenly.

He looked up in displeasure at my brusqueness, but did not reply. I repeated the question.

"She is near Boston," he said, with a frown of annoyance. "Her lawyer is Thomas Foxcroft in Queen Street."

"When will she return here?"

"She will not return."

"What!" I cried, springing to my feet.

Sir John eyed me sullenly.

"I beg you will conduct in moderation," he said.

"Then tell me what you have done with my cousin Felicity!"

"She is not your cousin, or any kin to you or to us," he said, coldly. "I have had some correspondence with Sir Peter Warren, which, I may say, does not concern you. Enough that Felicity is not his niece, nor the daughter of his dead brother, nor any kin whatever to him, to us, or to you. Further than that I have nothing to say, except that the young woman is now with her own kin, and will remain there, because it is her proper legal residence. Better for you," he added, grimly, "and better for us if you had not meddled with what did not concern you, and had allowed Lord Dunmore to take her—"

"Dunmore! Wed Felicity!" I burst out.

"Wed? Who said he meant to wed her? He did not; he knew from Sir Peter Warren who Felicity is; he knew it before we did, and informed Sir Peter. Wed her? Ay, with the left hand, perhaps."

I rose, trembling in every limb.

"The damned scoundrel!" I stammered. "The damned, foul-fleshed scoundrel! God! Had I known—had I dreamed—"

"You will control your temper here at least," he said, pointing to the card-room, where Colonel Guy Johnson and the Border officers were staring at us through the open doors.

"No, I will not!" I cried. "I care not who hears me! And I say shame on you for your indecency! Shame on you for your callous, merciless judgment, when you, God knows, require the mercy you refuse to others, you damned hypocrite!"

"Silence!" he said, turning livid. "You leave this house to-night for your regiment."

"I leave it in no service which tolerates such blackguards as Dunmore or such bloodless criminals as you!" I retorted, tearing my sword from my belt. Then I stepped forward, and, looking him straight in the eyes, slammed my sheathed sword down on the table before him.

"You, your Governors, and your King are too poor to buy the sword I would wear," I said, between my teeth.

"Are you mad?" he muttered, staring.

I laughed.

"Not I," I said, gayly, "but the pack o' fools who curse my country with their folly, like that withered, half-witted Governor of Virginia, like that pompous ass in Boston, like you yourself, sir, though God knows it chokes to say it of your father's son!"

"Major Benning," cried Sir John, "you will place that lunatic under arrest!"

My major started, then took a step towards me.

"Try it!" said I, all the evil in me on fire. "Go to the devil, sir!—where your own business is doubtless stewing. Hands off, sir!—or I throw you through the window!"

"Good Gad!" muttered Benning. "The lad's gone stark!"

"But I still shoot straight," I said, picking up Sir William's favourite rifle and handling it most carelessly.

"Mind what you are about!" cried Sir John, furiously. "That piece is charged!"

"I am happy to know it," I replied, dropping it into the hollow of my arm so he could look down the black muzzle.

And I walked out of the room and up the stairs to my own little chamber, there to remove from my body the livery of my King, never again to resume it.

I spent the day in packing together all articles which were rightly mine, bought with my own money or given me by Sir William: my books, my prints, some flutes which I could not play, my rods and fowling-pieces, all my clothing, my paper and Faber pencil—all gifts from Sir William.

I wished also for a memento from his room, something the more valuable to me because valueless to others, and I found his ivory cane to take and his leather book, the same being a treatise on fishing by a certain Isaac Walton, who, if he tells the truth, knew little about the habits of trout and salmon, and did write much foolishness in a pretty manner.

However, Sir William loved to read from Isaac Walton his book, and I have oft heard him singing lustily the catches and ballads which do abound in that same book—and to its detriment, in my opinion.

Laden with these, and also with a scrap of sleeve-ribbon, all I could find in Silver Heels's chamber, I did make two bundles of my property, done neatly in blankets. Then, to empty my purse and strong-box and fill my money-belt, placing there also my letter of recommendation to the lawyer, Peter Weaver, Esquire, who administered my investments.

Gillie Bareshanks I hailed from the orchard, bidding him saddle Warlock with a dragoon's saddle, and place forage for three days in the saddle-bags, dropping at the same time my riding-coat from the window, to be rolled and buckled across the pommel.

I dressed me once more in new buckskins, with Mohawk moccasins and leggings, this to save the wear of travel on my better clothing, of which I did take but one suit, the same being my silver-gray velvet, cut with French elegance, and hat to match.

Now, as I looked from the windows, I could see Sir John, Colonel Guy, and their guests, mounting to ride to the village, doubtless in order that they should be shown Sir William's last resting-place. So I, being free of the house, wandered through it from cellar to attic, because it was to be my last hour in the only home I had ever known.

Mercifully, though the heart be full to breaking, youth can never fully realize that the old order has ended forever; else why, even in bitterest sorrow, glimmers that thread of light through darkness which we call the last ray of hope? It never leaves us; men say it flees, but it goes out only with the life that nourished it.

Deep, deep in my heart I felt that I should look upon these familiar walls once more, when, in happier days, my dear love and I should return to the hills we must always love for Sir William's sake.

And so I strayed through the silent, sunny rooms, touching the walls with aching heart, and bidding each threshold adieu. Ghosts walked with me through the dimmed sunbeams; far in the house, faintest familiar sounds seemed to stir, half-heard whispers, the echo of laughter, a dear voice calling from above. Over these floors Silver Heels's light feet had passed, brushing every plank, perhaps the very spot I stood on. Hark! Over and over again that fading echo filled my ears for an instant, as though somebody had just spoken in a distant room.

Passing the stocks where Silver Heels had so often sat to pout and embroider, or battle with us to protect her helpless feet from torment, I came to the school-room once more.

Apparently nobody had entered it since I had written my verses on Eurydice—so long, so long ago. There were traces of the verses still—smeared from my struggle with Silver Heels when I had written:

"Silver Heels toes in like ducks."

Heaven save the libel!

And here on a bench was my tattered mythology, thumbed and bitten, and the fly-leaf soaked with ink where Peter had made a scene of battle in Indian fashion, the English being scalped on all sides by himself, Esk, and Joseph Brant, all labelled.

I took the book, turning to where I had written my bequest to Silver Heels on the inside cover, and then carried it to my chamber, there to add this last link of childhood to the others in my packets.

I do not exactly understand why, but I also carried with me the flag I had taken from Cresap's fort, and rolled it up in my uniform which was given me by Sir William.

Neither flag nor uniform were any longer mine, yet I ever have found it impossible to neglect that which I once loved. So I rolled the bunting and my scarlet clothes with my best silver-gray velvet, and tied all together.

When young Bareshanks came to announce that Warlock waited, I bade him carry my two packets down, following, myself, with Sir William's long rifle, and otherwise completely equipped with hatchet, knife, powder and ball, flint and tinder, and a small stew-pan.

With these Warlock was laden like a pack-horse, leaving room in the saddle for me. Bareshanks held my stirrup; I mounted, shook hands with him, not daring to attempt a word, and, with tears blinding me, turned my horse's head south on the Albany post-road.

Mr. Duncan, standing near the stables, gazed at me in astonishment.

"Ho!" he called out. "More wood-running, Mr. Cardigan? Faith, the scalp-trade must be paying in these humming days of peace!"

I tried to smile and gave him my hand.

"It's good-bye forever," I said, choking. "I cannot use the same roof that shelters my kinsman, Sir John Johnson."

He looked at me very gravely, asking me where I meant to go.

"To Boston," I replied. "I have affairs with one Thomas Foxcroft."

There was a silence, he still holding my hand as though to draw me back.

"Why to Boston?" he repeated, gently.

"To wed Miss Warren," I replied, looking him in the eyes.

He stared, then caught my hand in both of his.

"God bless her!" he said, again and again. "I give you joy, lad! She's the sweetest of them all in County Tryon!"

"And in all the world beside!" I muttered, huskily.

And so rode on.

CHAPTER XXI

My journey to Albany was slow, easy, and uneventful; I spared Warlock because of his added burdens, though he would gladly have galloped the entire distance, for the poor fellow was bitterly ashamed of playing pack-horse and evinced the greatest desire to finish and have done with it as soon as convenient.

His mortification was particularly to be noticed when he met other horses: he would turn his head away when he passed a pretty mare, he would hang his head when gay riders cantered past, and, when he met a peddler's horse, he actually shuddered.

But Warlock need not have taken it so to heart: he was the peer of any horse we met, which truly is no great recommendation, for the people of Albany do exhibit the most sorry horseflesh I have ever seen, and so Sir William had always said, laughing frequently at the patroons' nags until Sir Peter Warren wrote him to be careful else he might offend the entire town.

As for Albany itself I found it very large, though smaller than New York or Boston, they said, and I marvelled to see so many troops in various bright uniforms hitherto unfamiliar to me. The people themselves were somewhat stupid, being full o' Dutch blood and foodstuffs, and appeared somewhat mean in their dealings with strangers, though they call this penny-clipping thrift. Still, gentle blood never yet warmed at the prospect of under-feeding a stranger to save a shilling, and I found myself out of touch with those honest burghers of Albany who crowded the sleepy tap-room of the "Half-Moon Tavern" where I lodged.

I had no great difficulty in finding Peter Weaver, or in recommending myself to his good offices. He informed me that my uncle, Sir Terence Cardigan, was dying o' drink in Ireland, and wished me to go to him. I politely declined, and told him why. He was a pleasant, kindly, over-fed man, somewhat given to long and pointless discourse, yet a gentleman in bearing and a courteous friend. In his care I deposited my childish treasures for safe-keeping, taking with me only three extra articles, namely, my silver-gray clothes with underwear befitting, Sir William's leather book, and the knot of ribbon from Silver Heels's sleeve.

In Albany I bought a ring of plain gold to fit half-way on my little finger, judging Silver Heels's finger to be of that roundness. I also purchased a razor, though I had no present use for such an article. Still, I could not tell how soon my cheeks might require it, and it would not do to be caught unawares.

I stayed but one day in Albany, paying dearly for bait at the "Half-Moon Tavern," but my joy in my freedom and my happiness in expectancy left no room for rancour against these stolid, thrifty people who, after all, were but following the instincts of their breed.

Sir William was the most liberal man I had ever known, always cautious in condemnation, though he unknowingly did poor Cresap injustice; but I have often heard him say that to choose between the Dutch and the French for thrift and ferocity was totally beyond his power.

What I have seen of the Dutch or of those in whose veins runs Dutch blood confirms this. Since the Spaniards perpetrated their crimes in the New World, no people have ever been guilty of such shocking savagery towards the Indians as have the Dutch. Placid, honest in their own fashion, cleanly, sober, almost passionless, they yet have, deep within them, a ferocity and malignity scarcely conceivable—scarcely credible unless one has read that early history of their occupation here, of which little of the truth now remains on record.

The Albany people appear to have little sympathy to spare for unfortunate Boston. However, of that I cannot speak with authority, seeing that the whole town is soldier-ridden, and Tories everywhere holding forth in tap-room and marketplace. Besides, a company of Colonel John Butler's irregulars and a body of ne'er-do-well Onondagas were camped across the river, and their behaviour to the country people is drunken and scandalous.

Before I left Albany to set out on the Boston high-road, I visited Mr. Livingston's house, knowing that such a courtesy I owed for Sir William's sake, yet scarcely pleased at the prospect of again meeting Mrs. Hamilton. However, I had my journey for my pains, Mr. Livingston being lately deceased, and Mrs. Hamilton having left the day before to visit in Boston. Thus free of further obligation, Warlock and I took the Boston road at dawn; and how the dear fellow did gallop, though he carried but a buckskin dragoon without company or colours or commission to bear arms!

The first two days of my travel were almost without incident, lovely, calm October days through which sunlit clouds sailed out of the west, and the wild ducks drifted southward like floating banners in the sky.

In the yellow sunlight of the fields the quails were whistling, the heath-hens thundered through the copse, the crested partridge, with French ruff spread, stepped dainty as a game-cock through the briers, with his breathless menace: "Quhit! Quhit! Quhit!"

Once, riding on a treeless stretch of sandy road under the hot sun, a vast company of wild pigeons began to pass high overhead, thousands on thousands, thicker and ever thicker, till as far as the eye could reach from east to west they covered the sky in millions and millions, while the sun went out as in a thunder-cloud, and the air whistled and rang with their wings.

Their passage lasted some twenty minutes; a fine flight, truly, yet in Tryon County, near Fonda's Bush, Sir William and I had marked greater flights, lasting more than an hour.

This and Warlock's narrow escape from being bitten by one of those red snakes which pilot the rattlesnake and go blind in September were the only two noteworthy incidents of the first two days' journey on the Boston highway.

On the third day Warlock cast both hind shoes, and I was obliged to lead him very carefully, mile after mile, until, towards sundown, I entered a little village, where in a smithy a forge reddened the fading daylight.

The smith, a gruff man, gave me news of Boston, that the Port Bill was starving the poor and driving all decent people towards open rebellion. As for himself, he said that he meant to march at the first drum-beat and carry his hammer if firelocks were lacking.

He spoke sullenly and with a peculiar defiance, doubtless suspicious of me in spite of my buckskins. I told him that I knew little concerning the wrongs of Boston, but that if any man disturbed my native country, the insolence touched me as closely as though my own door-yard had been trampled. Whereat he laughed and gave me a brawny, blackened fist to shake. So I rode away in the dusk.

To make up for the delay in travelling afoot all day, I determined to keep on until midnight, Warlock being fit and ready without effort; so I munched a quarter of bread to stay my stomach and trotted on, pondering over the past, which already seemed years behind me.

The moon came up, but was soon frosted by silvery shoals of clouds. Then a great black bank pushed up from the west, covering moon and stars in sombre gloom, touched now and again by the dull flicker of lightning. The storm was far off, for I could hear no thunder, though the increasing stillness of the air warned me to seek the first shelter offered.

The district through which I was passing was well populated, and I expected every moment to see some light shining across the road from possibly hospitable windows. So I kept a keen outlook on every side, while the fields and woods through which I passed grew ominously silent, and that delicate perfume which arises from storm-threatened herbage filled my nostrils.

After a while, far away, the low muttering of thunder sounded, setting the air vibrating, and I cast Warlock free at a hand-gallop.

Imperceptibly the dark silence around turned into sound; a low, monotonous murmur filled my ears. It rained.

Careless of my rifle, having of course no need for it on such a populous highway, I let the priming take care of itself and urged Warlock forward towards two spots of light which might come from windows very far away, or from the lamps of a post-chaise near at hand.

Reining in, I was beginning to wonder which it might be, and had finally decided on the distant cottage, when my horse reared violently, almost falling on his back with me, and at the same moment I knew that somebody had seized his bridle.

"Stand and deliver!" came a calm voice from the darkness. I already had my rifle raised, but my thumb on the pan gave me warning that the priming was soaking wet.

"Dismount," came the voice, a trifle sharply.

I felt for the bridle, which had been jerked from my hands; it was gone. I gave one furious glance at the lights ahead, which I now saw came from a post-chaise standing in the road close by. Could I summon help from that? Or had the chaise also been stopped as I was now? Certainly I had run on a nest of highwaymen.

"How many have you?" I asked, choking with indignation. "I'll give three of you merry gentlemen a chance at me if you will allow me one dry priming!"

There was a dead silence. The unseen hand that held my horse's head fell away, and the animal snorted and tossed his mane. Again, not knowing what to expect, I cautiously felt around until I found the bridle, and noiselessly began to work it back over Warlock's head.

"Now for it!" I thought, gathering to launch the horse like a battering-ram into the unknown ahead.

But just as I drew my light hatchet from my belt and lifted the bridle, I almost dropped from the saddle to hear a meek and pleading voice I knew call me by name.

"Jack Mount!" I exclaimed, incredulous even yet.

"The same, Mr. Cardigan, out at heels and elbows, lad, and trimming the highway for a purse-proud Tory. Are you offended?"

"Offended!" I repeated, hysterically. "Oh no, of course not!" And I burst into a shout of uncontrollable laughter.

He did not join in. As for me, I lay on my horse's neck, weak from the reaction of my own laughter, utterly unable to find enough breath in my body to utter another sound.

"Oh, you can laugh," he said, in a hurt voice. "But I have accomplished a certain business yonder which has nigh frightened me to death—that's all."

"What business?" I asked, weakly.

"Oh, you may well ask. Hell's whippet! I lay here for the fat bailiff o' Grafton, who should travel to Hadley this night with Tory funds, and—I stopped a lady in that post-chaise yonder, and she's fainted at sight o' me. That's all."

"Fainted?" I repeated. "Where are her post-boys? Where's her footman? Where's her maid? Is she alone, Jack?"

"Ay," he responded, gloomily; "the men and the maid ran off. Trust those Dutch patrooners for that sort o' patroonery! If I'd only had Cade with me—"

"But—where's the Weasel?"

"I wish I knew," he said, earnestly. "He left me at Johnstown—went away—vanished like a hermit-bird. Oh, I am certainly an unhappy man and a bungling one at that. You can laugh if you like, but it's killing me. I wish you would come over to that cursed post-chaise and see what can be done for the lady. You know about ladies, don't you?"

"I don't know what to do when they faint," I replied.

"There's ways and ways," he responded. "Some say to shake them, but I can't bring myself to that; some say to pat their chins and say 'chuck-a-bunny!' but I have no skill for that either. Do you think—if we could get her out o' the chaise—and let her be rained on—"

"No, no," I said, controlling a violent desire to laugh. "I'll calm her, Jack. Perhaps she has recovered."

As we advanced through the rain in the dim radiance of the chaise-lamps, I looked curiously at Mount, and he up at me.

"Lord," he murmured, "how you have changed, lad!"

"You, too," I said, for he was haggard and dirty and truly enough in rags. No marvel that the lady had fainted at first sight o' him, let alone his pistol thrust through the chaise-window.

"Poor old Jack," I said, softened by his misery. "Why did you desert me after you had saved my life? I owe you so much that it were a charity to aid me discharge the debt—or as much of it as I may."

"Ho!" he muttered. "'Twas no debt, lad, and I'm but a pottle-pot after all. Now, by the ring-tailed coon o' Canada, I care not what befalls me, for Cade's gone—or dead—and I've the heart of a chipmunk left to face the devil."

"Soft," I whispered; "the lady's astir in her chaise. Wait you here, Jack! So!— I dismount. Touch not the horse; he bites at raggedness; he'll stand; so—o, Warlock. Wait, my beauty! So—o."

And I advanced to the chaise-window, cap in hand.

"Madam," I began, very gently, striving to make her out in the dim light of the chaise; "I perceive some accident has befallen your carriage. Pray, believe me at your disposal and humbly anxious to serve you, and if there be aught wherein I may—"

"Michael Cardigan!" came a startled voice, and I froze dumb in astonishment. For there, hood thrown back, and earnest, pale face swiftly leaning into the lamp-rays, I beheld Marie Hamilton.

We stared at each other for a moment, then her lovely face flushed and she thrust both hands towards me, laughing and crying at the same moment.

"Oh, the romance of life!" she cried. "I have had such a fright, my wits ache with the shock! A highwayman, Michael, *grand Dieu!*—here in the rain, pulling the horses up short, and it was, 'Ho! Stand and deliver!'—with pistol pushed in my face, and I to faint—pretence to gain a wink o' time to think—not frightened, but vexed and all on the qui vive to hide my jewels. Then comes the great booby, aghast to see me fainted, a-muttering excuse that he meant no harm, and I lying perdu, still as a mouse, for I had no mind to let him know I heard him. But under my lids I perceived him, a great, ragged, handsome rascal, badly scared, for I gathered from his stammering that he was waiting for another chaise bound for Hadley.

"*Vrai Dieu*, but I did frighten him well, and now he's gone, and I in a plight with my cowardly post-boys, maid, and footman fled, Lord knows whither!"

The amazing rapidity of her chatter confounded me, and she held my hands the while, and laughed and wept enough to turn her eyes to twin stars, all dewy in the lamp-shine.

"Dear friend," she sighed; "dear, dear friend, what happiness to feel I owe my life to you!"

"But you don't," I blurted out; "there never was any danger."

"Lord save the boy!" she murmured. "There is no spark o' romance in him!" And fell a-laughing in that faint, low mockery that I remembered on that fatal night at Johnson Hall.

"You are mistaken," I said, grimly. "Romance is the breath of my life, madam. And so I now plead freedom to present to your good graces my friend, Jack Mount, who lately stopped your coach upon the King's highway!"

And I caught the abashed giant by his ragged sleeve and dragged him to the chaise-window, where he plucked off his coon-skin cap and stared wildly at the astonished lady within.

But it was no easy matter to rout Marie Hamilton. True, she paled a little, and took one short breath, with her hand to her breast; then, like sunlight breaking, her bright eyes softened and that sweet, fresh mouth parted in a smile which spite of me set my own pulse a quickstep marching.

"I am not angry, sir," she said, mockingly. "All cats are gray at midnight, and one post-chaise resembles another, Captain Mount—for surely, by your exploits, you deserve at least that title."

Mount's fascinated eyes grew bigger. His consternation and the wild appeal in his eyes set me hard a-swallowing my laughter. As for Mrs. Hamilton, she smiled her sweet, malicious smile, and her melting eyes were soft with that false mercy which deludes apace and welcomes to destruction.

"Jack," said I, smothering my laughter, "do you get your legs astride the leader, there, and play at post-boy to the nearest inn. Zounds, man! Don't stand there hanging your jaw like a hard-run beagle! Up into the saddle with you! Gad, you've a ride before you with those Albany nags a-biting at your shins! Here, give me your rifle."

"And you, Michael," asked Mrs. Hamilton, "will you not share my carriage, for old time's sake?"

I told her I had my horse and would ride him at her chaise-wheels, and so left her, somewhat coolly, for I liked not that trailing tail to her invitation—"for old time's sake."

"What the foul fiend have I to do with 'old time's sake'?" I muttered, as I slung myself astride o' Warlock and motioned Jack Mount to move on through the finely falling rain. "'Old time's sake'! Faith, it once cost me the bitterest day of my life, and might cost me the love of the sweetest girl in earth or heaven! 'Old time's sake'! Truly, that is no tune to pipe for me; let others dance to it, not I."

As I rode forward beside her carriage-window, she looked up at me and made a little gesture of greeting. I bowed in my saddle, stiffly, for I was now loaded with Mount's rifle as well as my own.

What the deuce is there about Marie Hamilton that stirs the pulse of every man who sets eyes on her? Even I, loving Silver Heels with my whole heart and soul, find subtle danger in the eyes of Marie Hamilton, and shun her faint smile with the instant instinct of an anchorite.

Perhaps I was an anchorite, all ashamed, for I would not have it said of me, for vanity.

In a day when the morals of the world were rotten to the core, when vice was fashion, and fashion marked all England for her own, the overflow from those same British islands, flooding our land, stained most of those among us who could claim the right to quality.

I never had been lured by those grosser sins which circumstances offered—even in our house at Johnstown—and I would make no merit of my continence, God wot, seeing there was no temptation.

I had been reared among those whose friends and guests often went to bed too drunk to snuff their candles; cards and dice and high play were nothing strange to me, and, perhaps from their sheer familiarity, left me indifferent and without desire.

A titled drab I had never seen; the gentlemen whom I knew discussed their mistresses over nuts and wine, seeming to think no shame of one another for the foolishness they called their "fortune." Had it not been for Sir William's and Aunt Molly's teachings, I might have grown up to think that wives were wedded chiefly to oblige a friend. But Sir William and Aunt Molly taught me to abhor that universal vice long before I could comprehend it. I did not clearly comprehend it yet; but the thought of it was stale ashes in my mouth, so unattractive had I pictured what I needs must shun one day.

Riding there through the fine rain which I could scarcely feel on my skin, so delicate were the tiny specks of moisture, I thought much on the smallness of this our world, where a single hour on an unknown road had given me two companions whom I knew.

God grant the end of my journey would give me her for whose dear sake the journey had been made!

Thinking such thoughts, lost in a lover's reverie, I rode on, blind to all save the sweet ghosts I conjured in my brooding, and presently was roused to find the chaise turning into a tavern-yard, where all was black save for a lanthorn moving through the darkness.

Mount called; a yawning ostler came with a light, and at the same instant our host in shirt and apron toddled out to bid us welcome, a little, fat, toothless, chattering body, whose bald head soon was powdered with tiny, shining rain-drops.

Mrs. Hamilton gave me her hand to descend; she was as fresh and fragrant as a violet, and jumped to the ground on tiptoe with a quick flirt of her petticoat like the twitch of a robin his tail-feathers.

"Mad doings on the road, sir!" said our host, rubbing his little, fat hands. "Chaise and four stopped by the penny-stile two hours since, sir. Ay, you may smile, my lady, but the post-boys fought a dreadful battle with the highwaymen swarming in on every side. You laugh, sir? But I have these same post-boys here, and the footman, too, to prove it!"

"But, pray, where is the lady and her maid and the chaise and four?" asked Mrs. Hamilton, demurely.

"God knows," said the innkeeper, rolling his eyes. "The villains carried it off with the poor lady inside. Mad work, my lady! Mad work!"

"Maddening work," said I, wrathfully. "Jack, borrow a post-whip and warm the breeks of those same post-boys, will you? Lay it on thick, Jack; I'll take my turn in the morning!"

Mount went away towards the stable, and I quieted the astonished landlord and sent him to prepare supper, while a servant lighted Mrs. Hamilton to her chamber. Then I went out to see that Warlock was well fed and bedded fresh; and I did hear sundry howls from the villain post-boys in their quarters overhead, where Mount was nothing sparing of the leather.

Presently he came down the ladder, and laughed sheepishly when he saw me.

"They're well birched," he said. "It's God's mercy if they sit their saddles in the morning." Then he took my hands and held them so hard that I winced.

"Gad, I'm that content to see you, lad!" he repeated again and again.

"And I you, Jack," I said. "It is time, too, else you'd be in some worse mischief than this night's folly. But I'll take care of you now," I added, laughing. "Faith, it's turn and turn about, you know. Come to supper."

"I—I hate to face that lady," he muttered. "No, lad, I'll sup with my own marrow-bones for company."

"Nonsense!" I insisted, but could not budge him, and soon saw I had my labour for my pains.

"A mule for obstinacy—a very mule," I muttered.

"I own it; I'm an ass. But this ass knows enough to go to his proper stall," he said, with a miserable laugh that touched me.

"Have it as you wish, Jack," I said, gently; "but come into my chamber when you've supped. I'll be there. Lord, what millions of questions I have to ask!"

"To be sure, to be sure," he murmured, then walked away towards the kitchen, while I returned to the inn and cleansed me of the stains of travel.

We supped together, Mrs. Hamilton and I, and found the cheer most comforting, though there was no wine for her and she sipped, with me, the new brew of dark October ale.

A barley soup we had, then winter squash and a roast wild duck, with little quails all 'round, and a dish of pepper-cresses. Lord, how I did eat, being still gaunt from my long sickness! But she kept pace with me; a wholesome lass was she, and no frail beauty fed on syllabubs and suckets. Flesh and blood were her charms, a delicate ripeness, sweet as the cresses she crunched between her sparkling teeth. And ever I heard her little feet go tap, tap, tap, under the lamplit table.

I spoke respectfully of her losses; she dropped her eyes, accepting the condolence, pinching a cress to shreds the while.

She of course knew nothing of my journey to Pittsburg, nor of any events there which might have occurred after she had left, when her husband fell with many another stout frontiersman under Boone and Harrod.

I told her nothing, save that Felicity was in Boston and that I was journeying thither to see her.

"Is she not to wed the Earl of Dunmore?" asked Mrs. Hamilton.

"No," said I, quietly.

"La, the capricious beauty!" she murmured. "Sure, she has not thrown over Dunmore for that foolish dragoon, Kent Bevan?"

"I hope not," said I, maliciously.

"Who knows," she mused; "Mr. Bevan is to serve on Gage's staff this fall. It looks like a match to me."

"Is Mr. Bevan going to Boston?" I inquired.

"Yes. Are you jealous?" she replied, saucily.

I smiled and shook my head.

"But you once were in love with your cousin," she persisted. "*On aime sans raison, et sans raison l'on hait! Regardez-moi, monsieur.*"

"Your convent breeding in Saint-Sacrement lends to your tongue a liberty that English schools withhold," I said, reddening.

"Nay, now," she laughed, "do you remember how you played with me at that state dinner held in Johnson Hall? You rode me down rough-shod, Michael, and used me shamefully there, under the stairs."

"I'll do the like again if you provoke me," I said, but had not meant to say it either, being troubled by her eyes.

"The—the like—again? And what was that, pray?"

"You know," I said, sulkily.

"I think you—kissed me—"

"I think I did," said I; "and left you all in tears."

It was brutal, but I meant to make an end.

"Did you believe that those were real tears?" she asked, innocently.

"By Heaven, I know they were," said I, with satisfaction, "and small vengeance to repay the ill you did me, too."

"What ill?" she asked, opening her eyes in real surprise.

But I was silent and ashamed already. Truly, it had been no fault but my own that I had taken up the gage she flung at me that night so long ago.

"But I'll not take it up this time," thought I to myself, cracking filberts and looking at her askance across the table.

"I do not understand you, Michael," she said, with a faint smile, ending in a sigh.

"Nor I you, bonnie Marie Hamilton," said I. "Suppose we both cry quits?"

"Not yet," she said; "I have a little score with you, unsettled."

"What score?" I asked, smiling. "Cannot you appeal to the law to have it settled?"

"*La loi permet souvent ce que défend l'honneur,*" she said, with an innocent emphasis which left me sitting there, uncertain whether to laugh or blush. What the mischief did she mean, anyhow?

She picked up a filbert, tasted the kernel, dropped it, clasped her hands, elbows on the cloth, and gave me a malicious sidelong glance which still was full of that strange sweetness that ever set me on my guard, half angry, half bewitched.

"I wish you would let me alone!" I blurted out, like a country yokel at a quilting.

"I won't," she said.

"Remember what you suffered the first time!" I warned her.

"I do remember."

"Do you—do you dare risk that?" I stammered.

"*Et d'avantage—encore*," she murmured, setting her teeth on her plump white wrist and watching me uncertainly.

The game was running on too fast for me and my pulse was keeping pace.

"Safely they defy who challenge those in chains," I said, commanding my voice with an effort. "If that is your revenge, I cry you mercy; you have won."

After a long silence she raised her eyes, dancing with a mocking light in each starry pupil.

"I give you joy, Michael," she said, "if, as I take it, these same chains and fetters that you lately wear are riveted by Cupid."

But I answered nothing, attending her to the door, where she dropped me what I do believe was the slowest and lowest curtsey ever dropped by woman.

So I to my own chamber in no amiable frame of mind, and still tingling with the strange charm of my encounter. Head bent, hands clasped behind me, I walked the floor, striving to analyze this woman who had now twice crossed me on the trail of fate, this fair woman whose bright eyes were a menace and a challenge, and whose sweet, curved mouth was set there as eternal provocation to saint and sinner.

Thus for the first time in my life I had known what temptation might have been. Nay, I knew a little more than what it *might have* been, and, in the overwhelming flood of loyalty to Silver Heels, I cursed myself for a man without faith or shred of honour. For I was too unskilled in combats with the fair temptation to understand that it is no disgrace to falter, yet not fall.

There came a timid scratching at the door; I opened it and Mount sidled in, coy as a cat in a dairy with its chin still wet with cream. He regarded me doubtfully, but sat down when bidden and began to complain:

"Now, if you are minded to chide me for taking the road, I'm going out again. I can't bear any more, lad, that I can't!—what with Cade gone and me in rags, and stopping Councillor Bullock near Johnstown with pockets bare of aught but a cursed sixpence and that crooked as Lady Shelton's legs—and now I must needs fright a lady into a faint like a bad boy with a jack-o'-lanthorn—"

"What on earth is the matter with you?" I broke in, peevishly. "I'm not finding fault, Jack. If you mean to spend your life in endeavours to impoverish every Tory magistrate in America, it's your affair, and I can't help it, though you must know as well as I that there's a carpenter's tree and a rope at the end of your frolic."

"No, there isn't," he said, hastily. "I'm done with the highway save to pat it smooth with my feet. Lord, lad, it's not for the money, but for sport. And soon there'll be fighting enough to fill my stomach; mark me, the crocus that buds white this spring will wither red as blood ere its fouled petals fall!"

"War?" I asked, thrilling to hear him.

He rose and gazed at me most earnestly.

"Ay, surely, surely in the spring. Gad! Boston is that surfeited with redcoats now that when they cram down more next spring she can but throw them up to keep her health. Wait! Boston is sick in bone and body, but in the spring she takes her purge. Oh, I know," he cried, with a strange, prophetic stare in his eyes; "I have word from Shemuel. Now he's off to Boston with the news from Cresap. And I tell you, lad, that the first half-moon of April will start a devil loose in this broad land that state or clergy cannot exorcise!

"Not a devil," he corrected himself, slowly, "no, not a thing from hell, but that same swift angel sent to chasten worlds with fire. Dunmore will burn, and Butler. As for the rest, the honest, the rascals, the witless, the soulless, thieves, poltroons, usurers, and the vast army of well-meaning loyal fools, they will be cleared out o' this our world-wide temple whose roof is the sky and whose pillars are our high pines!—cleared out, scoured out, uprooted, driven forth like those same money-changers in the temple scourged by Christ,—and God is witness I, a sinner, mean no blasphemy, spite of all the sweating load o' guilt I bear."

"Where got you such phrases, Jack?" I asked. "It is not Jack Mount who speaks to me like a crazed preacher in the South who shouts the slaves around him to repent."

Mount looked at me; the dazed, fanatic light in his eyes faded slowly.

"I have a book here," he muttered, "a book I purchased in Johnstown of a man who sold many to patriots. Doubtless grief for Cade and my privations and my conning this same book while starving make me light-headed yet."

"What book is that?" I asked.

"*The Rights of Man.*"

"I, also, would be glad to read it."

"Read, lad. 'Tis fodder for King George's cattle—such as we. And the little calves our wenches cast, they, too, shall feed on it, though they cannot utter moo! for their own mothers' milk!"

"Jack, Jack," I cried, "you are strangely changed! I do not know you in this bitter mood, and your mouth full o' words that burn your silly lips. Wake to life, man! Gay! Gay! Jack! A pest on books and those who write 'em! I have ever despised your printed stuff, and damme if I'll sit and hear it through your lips!"

But it was like rousing a man from a sleeping-draught, for the book had so bewitched his senses in these long weeks he had wandered alone that I had all I could do to drag him out of his strange, dreamy enthusiasms, back into his old, guileless, sunny, open-hearted self. And I feel sure that I could not have succeeded at all had not the shock of his encounter with Mrs. Hamilton on the highway first scared him back to partial common-sense. Added to this my entreaties, and he became docile, and then, little by little, dropped his preacher's mad harangue to talk like a reasonable creature and wag his tongue unlarded with his garbled metaphors and his half-baked parables which no doubt no simple forest-runner could digest on the raw printed page. I pitied him sincerely. Truly, a little learning makes one wondrous kind.

I put the book in my shirt-front, meaning to be of those who ride and read, even as Jack was of those others who both read and run.

"Why did you desert me, Jack?" I asked, sitting chin on hand to watch him smoke the pipe which no kind fate had filled for him since he left Johnstown.

"Faith, I hung about with Cade, doing no harm, sitting in the sun to wait for news from you. Mr. Duncan, a kind officer, gave us news and made us welcome on the benches in front of the guard-house. And Mistress Warren would have us to eat with her—only I was ashamed. But Cade went and supped with her.

"Lad, Sir John Johnson is not a gentleman I should grow too fond of. His courtesy is a shallow spring, I'm thinking, dry at the first taste, and over-sour to suit my teeth."

"What did Sir John do?" I asked, growing red. "Surely he thanked you and Cade for saving his kinsman's life; surely he made you welcome at the Hall, Jack?"

"Surely, he did nothing of the kind," grunted Mount, puffing his pipe. "Sir John sent word to the guard that we had best find quarters in Johnstown taverns and not set the hounds barking in his kennels."

It was like a blow in the face to me. Jack saw it and laughed.

"It's not your fault," he said; "show me two eggs and I'll name two birds, but I won't swear they'll fight alike. If he's your kin, it's to be borne, lad, and that's all there is to it."

I set my teeth and swallowed my shame.

"So we went to Rideup's old camp," he continued; "a fair inn where a man may drink to whom he pleases and no questions asked nor any yokel to bawl 'God save the King!' or turn your ale sour with Tory whining. And there I lay and—tippled, lad. I'll not deny it, no! Like a fish in sweet water my gills did open and shut while the ale flowed into me, day and night perdu.

"Cade never drank. God! how that man changed—since he saw your sweet Mistress Warren there on the hillock at Roanoke Plain! Mad, lad, quite mad. But such a dear, good comrade—I—I can scarce speak o' him but I wink with tears."

The great fellow dug one fist into his eyes, and then the other, replacing his pipe in his mouth with an unmistakable snivel.

"Quite mad, Mr. Cardigan. He thought he saw his little daughter in Miss Warren, without offence to any one in all the world and least of all to you, and he waited all day to see her come out to the guard-house and give the news of your sick-bed to your Lieutenant Duncan. So one day, when you were surely out of danger and ready to fatten, comes Cade to the tavern and bids me good-bye, talking wildly of his lost daughter, and I, Heaven help me, lay abed with my head like a top all humming for the ale I'd had, and thinking nothing of what he said save that his madness grew apace.

"And that night he went away while I slept in my cups. When he came not I hunted the town for him as I had never hunted trail in all my life before. And I warrant you I left no stone unturned in that same town. I was half-crazy; I could not think he'd left me there of his own free will. Many a fight I had with the soldiers, many a bruise and broken head I left behind me ere I shook my moccasins free o' dust in Johnstown streets. They'll tell you, and that fat, purple-pitted councillor—Bullock, I mean—why, he would have me jailed for a matter of damaging his Tory constable. So I gave him a fright on the highway and left your Tryon County for a quieter one. That's all, lad."

What he had told me of Cade Renard troubled me. If Felicity had been strangely lost to her own family, and had been restored, doubtless she was now happy and full of wonder for the dear, amazing chance that had brought to her those honoured parents she had so long deemed to be with God. Yet she must be shy and over-sensitive also, having been brought up to believe she had no nearer kin than Sir Peter Warren. And now that he, after all, was no kin to her, nor she to us, if a mad forest-runner like Cade Renard should come to vex her with his luny fancies, it might hurt her or seem like reproach and mockery for her new parents.

"Do you think Cade followed Miss Warren to Boston?" I asked.

"My journey is to find that out," he said. "Ah, lad, a noble mind was wrecked in Renard's head. *I* know—others know nothing. What fate sent him like a wild thing to the forests, I only know, as you know, nothing but what he has told us both. If his madness has waxed so fiercely since he saw Miss Warren, it may be a sign that the end is near. I do not know. I miss him, and I must look for him while I can move these clumsy feet of mine."

My candle was burning very low now. Mount laid his pipe in the candle-pan, rose, shook himself, and said good-night.

"Good-night," I said, and sat down to light another candle. This done, I did undress me, and so would have been in bed had I not chanced to open the book he left me, thinking to glance it over and forget it.

But sunrise found me poring over its pages, while the candle, a pool o' wax, hardened in the candle-stick beside me.

CHAPTER XXII

By noon we were well on our way towards Boston, I riding beside Mrs. Hamilton's carriage wheels, Jack Mount perched up on the box, and very gay in a new suit of buckskins which he bought from a squaw in the village, the woman being an Oneida half-breed and a tailoress by trade.

So gorgeous was this newly tailored suit that, though my own buckskins were also new and deeply fringed on sleeve and leg, even to the quill and wampum embroidery on the thigh, I did cut but a dingy figure beside Jack Mount. His shoulders were triple-caped with red-fox fur edges; he wore a belted hunting-shirt, with scarlet thrums; breeches cut to show his long legs' contour to the clout, also gay with scarlet thrums; and Huron moccasins, baldric, holster, and sporran, all of mole-skin, painted and beaded with those mystic scenes of the False-Face's secret rites, common to the Six Nations and to other Northern and Western clans.

Proud as a painted game-cock with silver steels was Jack. Poor gossip, how different his condition now, with a rasher o' bacon and a cup of ale under his waist-band, a belt full of money outside of it, and his scarlet thrums blowing like ribbons in the wind! A new fox-skin cap, too, with the plumy white-tipped tail bobbing to his neck, added the finish to this forest dandy. Truly it did warm me to behold him ruffling it with the best o' them; and it was a wink and a kiss for the pretty maid in the pantry, and a pinch o' snuff with mine host, and "Your servant, ma'am," to Mrs. Hamilton, with cap sweeping the dust in a salute that a Virginian might envy and mark for imitation.

The post-boys slunk past him with rueful, sidelong glances; the footman gave him wide berth, obeying the order to mount with an alacrity designed to curry favour as soon as possible, and let the painful past go bury itself.

"You had best," muttered Mount, with pretence of a fierceness he loved to assume. "Gad! I'm minded to tan your buttocks to line my saddle—ho!—come back! I'm not going to do it, simpleton! I only said I was so minded. Into your saddles, in Heaven's name. Salute!—you mannerless scullions! Do you not see your mistress coming?"

I handed Mrs. Hamilton to her chaise, and stood in attendance while she tied on her velvet sun-mask, watching me steadily through the eye-holes the while, but not speaking. Yet ever on her lips hovered that smile I knew so well; and from her hair came that fresh scent which is of itself like the perfume of Indian swale-herb, and which powder and pomatum can neither add to nor dissimulate.

Over her gown of shimmering stuff, garlanded with lilac-tints, she wore a foot-mantle, for the road was muddy from the all-night rain, and this I disposed around her ankles when she had seated herself in the chaise, and wrapped her restless little feet in a thick, well-tanned pelt.

"*Merci*," she said, in a whisper, with her bright eyes sparkling under her velvet mask; and I closed the carriage and mounted Warlock nimbly, impatient to be gone.

"Michael," she said from the chaise window, nose in the air to watch me ride up.

"Madam," I replied, politely.

"Let Captain Mount ride your horse, and do you come into the carriage. I have so much to tell you—"

I made what excuse I could. She tossed her chin.

"I shall die of ennui," she said.

"Count the thraves in the stubble," said I, laughing.

"And talk to my five wits of the harvest? How amusing!" she retorted, indignantly.

"Repent the past, then," I suggested, smiling.

"Ay—but 'tis one blank expanse of white innocence, with never a stain to mark for repentance. My past is spotless, Michael—spotless—like a fox-pelt, all of a colour."

Now, though we call foxes red, their ear-tips are jet black and their brushes and bellies touched with white. But she was right; your spotless fox can have no dealings with a dappled fawn.

I signalled the footman and post-boys; the chaise creaked off down the road, and I dropped behind, turning a sober face to the rain-washed brightness of the world.

So we journeyed, coming into dry roads towards noon, where no rain had fallen. And already it seemed to me my nostrils savoured that faint raw perfume of the mounting sea, which only those who have lived their whole lives inland can wind at great distances. It is not a perfume either; it is a taste that steals into the mouth and tingles far back, above the tongue. And it is strange to say so, but those who never before have tasted the scent know it for what it is by instinct, and fall into a restless reverie, searching to think where they have savoured that same enchanted ocean breath before.

At Grafton we baited at the "Weather-cock Tavern"; then on along the Charles River, with the scent o' the distant sea in every breath we drew, through Dedham, past Needham, and north into a most lovely country of rolling golden stubble and orchards all red with apples, and bridges of stone, neatly fashioned to resist the freshets. Alas, that this fair province of Massachusetts Bay should lie a-gasping amid plenty, with the hand of Britain upon the country's thrapple to choke out the life God gave it.

On the straight, well-laid high-road we passed scores of farmers' wains, piled with corn and yellow pumpkins, cabbages, squashes, barrels of apples, sacks o' flour, and thraves, all bound for Boston, where the poor were starving and the rich went hungering because the King of England had been angered to hear men prate of human rights.

Since the 1st day of June the Boston Port Bill was in full effect, and the city was sealed to commerce. Not a keel had stirred the waters of the bay save when the great bulging war-ships shifted their moorings to swing their broadsides towards the town; not a sail was bent to the shore breeze in this harbour where a thousand vessels had cleared in a single year from its busy port.

So when the city felt the punishment heavy upon her, and the poor starved and the rich suffered, and the hot sun poured down on the empty rotting wharves, the farmers of Massachusetts Bay brought their harvests by land to the famine-stricken city, and sister colonies sent generously of their best with the watchword: "Stand fast, Boston! A King's anger is a little thing, but human rights shall not perish until we perish, every one!"

It was sunset as we turned into the Roxbury road, with the salt wind blowing the marsh-reeds and ruffling the shallow waters of the harbour to the north and east. It was ebb-tide; beyond the eastern bog, far out in the yellow shallows, the harbour channel ran in a darker streak, glittering under the red blaze of sunset.

Wet marshes spread away to the north; the wind was heavy with the salty stench of mud-flats uncovered at low-water, and all alive with sea-fowl hovering. Northeast the steeples of Boston rose, blood-red in the setting sun; distant windows flashed fire; weather-vanes turned to jets of flame.

The red glow enveloped the road over which we travelled, now in company with scores of other vehicles, all bound for Boston—coaches, flies, chaises, wagons, farm wains—all moving slowly as though the head of the column had been checked by something which we could not yet see.

I rode forward to where Jack Mount was sitting on the box of the chaise, and he motioned me to his side.

"We're close to Boston Neck," he said. "Tommy Gage has been making some forts ahead of us since I last smelled the mud-flats yonder."

I rode on slowly, passing along the stalled line of vehicles, until, just ahead, I caught a glimpse of an earthwork flying the British flag. The red banner stood straight out in the sea-wind, rippling, and snapping like a whip when the breeze freshened. Under it a sentry moved, bayonet glittering as he turned, paced on, turned again, only to retrace his endless path on the brown rampart of earth.

I shall never forget that first coming to Boston, and the first glimpse of the round city, set there in the sea with only a narrow thread of land to fasten it to the continent which had made the city's cause its own. Nor shall I forget my first sight of the city's landward gate, closed by British earthworks, patrolled by British bayonets, with the red standard flying in the setting sun.

The Providence coach was standing in the road to my left, the six horses stamping restlessly, the outside passengers shivering in the harbour wind, while the red-nosed coachman muttered and complained and craned his short bull-neck to see what was blocking the highway ahead.

"It's them darned cannon," he explained to everybody who cared to listen; "they're a-haulin' some more twenty-four pounders into the right bastion. Ding it! My horses are ketchin' cold an' bots an' ring-bone while we set here in a free land waitin' his Majesty's pleasure!"

"The cannon will come handy—some day," called out a passenger from the Philadelphia coach, stalled just behind.

"You'd better get your cannon out of the south battery before you lay plans to steal these!" retorted a soldier, derisively, making his way towards the city between the tangle of wheels and horses which almost choked the road.

"We'll get 'em yet, young red-belly!" shouted a fat farmer, cracking his whip for emphasis. His horses started, and he pulled them in, shouting: "Whoa, lass! Whoa, dandy! Don't shy at a redcoat; he can't harm ye!"

"Gad!" burst out an old gentleman on the Roxbury coach, "is this rebel impudence to be endured?"

A chorus of protestations broke from the tops of neighbouring coaches, but the sturdy old gentleman shook his cane, defying every Yankee within hearing, while the protests around grew to angry shouts and cries of: "Enough! Tar the Tory! Pitch the old fool into the mud!"

In the midst of the bawling and uproar the line of vehicles ahead suddenly started, and those behind moved on, rumbling over the planked road with creaking wheels and thunder of a hundred hoofs, drowning the voices of disputing Whig and Tory.

I looked up at the passengers as the huge mail-coaches with their four, six, or eight horses rumbled past. Many of the people glanced somewhat curiously down at me, smiling to see a forest-runner mounted on so fine a horse as Warlock. And I was proud to sit the saddle under their gaze, not minding the quips and jests directed at me from above; though, when once a mealy faced post-boy shouted at me, I fetched him a cuff on the ear which nigh unseated him, and drew a roar of laughter from the people near.

The Philadelphia coach with passengers from Maryland and Virginia came swaying up, horses dancing, guard standing by the boot, and sounding his long coaching-horn—a gallant equipage, with its blue gear and claret body showing through a skin of half-dry mud.

I glanced up at the outside travellers, thinking I might know some face among them, yet not expecting it. There were no familiar faces. I wheeled my horse to watch the coach go by, glancing idly at the window where a young girl leaned out, sucking a China orange. Our eyes met for a moment; the girl dropped the orange and stared at me; I also eyed her sharply, certain that I had seen her somewhere in the world before this. The coach passed. I sat on my horse, looking after it, cudgelling my wits to remember that red-cheeked, buxom lass, who seemed to know me, too.

Then, as our chaise rattled by, with the post-boys urging the horses, and Jack Mount on the box, it came to me in a flash that the girl was the thief-taker's daughter from Fort Pitt.

I rode up beside Mount and told him in a low voice that Billy Bishop's buxom lass was ahead of us in the Philadelphia coach, and that he had best keep his wits and eyes cleared for Billy Bishop himself.

He shrugged his shoulders, not answering, but I noticed he was alert enough now, unconsciously fingering his rifle, while his quick eyes roamed restlessly as the chaise passed in between the British earthworks on the Neck.

Truly this Captain-General Thomas Gage, whom the King of England loved so well, had cut Boston from the land as neatly as his royal master had cut it from the sea.

The Roxbury road ran through a narrow passage between two bastions of earth, surrounded with a heavy abatis and *trous de loup*. In the left bastion I could see magazines and guard-houses, and beyond it, near the shore, a small square redoubt, a block-house, and a battery of six cannon. In the right bastion there was a guard-house, and beyond that a block-house on the shore of the mud-flats, while farther out in the shallow water lay a floating battery.

Our chaise rolled in through the earthworks and down a causeway surrounded by water. This was Boston Neck, a strip of made land not wider than a high-road, and blocked at the northern extremity by a solid military work of stone and earth, bristling with cannon.

The gate guards eyed us sullenly as we drove into the city and up a long, dusty road called Orange Street. We continued to Newbury Street, to Marlborough Street, Mount directing us, thence through Cornhill to Queen Street, where we drew up at a very elegant mansion.

Dismounting, I took Mrs. Hamilton from the carriage, and she unmasked, for the fire was dying out in the western heavens.

"If," she began slowly, "I should bid you to supper at my house, would you hurt me with refusal, Michael?"

"Is this your house?" I asked, in surprise.

"Yes—my late husband's. Will you come?"

I explained that I cared not to leave Mount, and that also we must seek a tavern as soon as might be, for we had much business on the morrow which could not wait.

She listened, with a faintly mocking air, then thanked me for my escort, thanked Mount for his share in providing me as her escort by stopping her carriage, and finally curtseyed, saying in a low voice: "Your charming Miss Warren is doubtless impatient. Pray believe me that I wish you joy of your conquest."

I thought she meant it, and it touched me. But when I stepped to her door-yard to conduct her, she turned on me like a flash, and I saw her eyes all wet and brilliant, and her teeth crushing her under-lip.

"For a charming journey in my own company, I thank you," she said; "for your conceit and your insufferable airs, I will find a remedy—remember that! My humiliation under your own roof is not forgotten, Mr. Cardigan, and it shall not be forgotten until you pay me dearly!"

Astonished at her bitterness, I found not a word to answer. A man-servant in purple livery opened the door. Mrs. Hamilton turned to me with perfect composure, returning my bow with the smile of an angel, and tripped lightly into her house.

The post-chaise had driven off into the mews when I returned to the street, but Jack Mount was waiting for me, patting Warlock, whose beautiful head had swung around to watch for my coming.

"Well, Jack?" I asked, wearily.

"The 'Wild Goose Tavern' is ours," he said—"good cheer and company to match it."

I walked out into the paved street, leading Warlock. Mount swaggered along beside me, squaring his broad shoulders whenever we passed a soldier, and whistling lustily "Tryon County Men," till the stony streets rang with the melody.

We now crossed into Treamount Street, passed Valley Acre on our right into Sudbury Street, then northwest through Hilliers Lane, crossing Cambridge Street to Green Lane, and west again along Green Lane to the corner of Chambers Street, where it becomes Wiltshire Street and runs due north.

There was enough of daylight left for me to see that we were not in an aristocratic neighbourhood. Warehouses, ship-chandlers, rope-walks, and scrap-iron shops lined the streets, interspersed with vacant, barren plots of ground, rarely surrounded by wooden fences.

The warehouses and shops were closed and all the shutters and doors fast bolted. There was not a soul abroad in the streets, not a light to be seen save from one long, low building standing midway between Chambers and Wiltshire Streets—an ancient, discoloured, rambling structure, with a weather-vane atop, and a long, pillared porch in front, from which hung a bush of sea-weed, and a red sign-board depicting a creature which doubtless was intended for a wild goose.

"Lord, Jack!" I said, "Shemuel's 'Bear and Cubs' appeared preferable to your 'Wild Goose' yonder. I'm minded to seek other quarters."

"Never trust to the looks o' things," he laughed. "God made woodchucks to live on the ground, but they climb trees, too, sometimes. Do I think on the hog-pen when I eat a crisped rasher? Nenny, lad. Come on to the cleanest tap-room in Boston town and forget that the shutters yonder need new hinges!"

I led Warlock into the mews to a clean, well-aired stable, where an ostler bedded and groomed him, and shook out as pretty a handful of grain as I had seen since I left Johnson Hall.

Then Mount and I went into the tavern, where half a dozen sober citizens in string-wigs sat, silently smoking clay pipes with stems full three feet long.

"Good-evening, the company!" said Mount, pleasantly.

The men repeated his salutation, and looked at us sleepily over their pipes.

"God save our country, gentlemen," said Mount, standing still in the centre of the room.

"His mercy shall endure," replied a young man, quietly removing the pipe from between his teeth. "What of the Thirteen Sisters?"

"They sew that we may reap," said Mount, slowly, and sat down, motioning me to take a chair in the circle.

The men looked at us curiously, but in silence, although their sleepy, guarded air had disappeared.

After a moment Mount asked if there was anything new.

"Yes," replied the young man who had spoken before; "the Lawyers' and Merchants' Club met at Cooper's in Brattle Square last night to receive instructions from the Committee of Safety. I do not know what new measures have been taken, but whatever they may be we are assured that they will be accepted and imitated by every town in Massachusetts Bay."

"Who were present?" asked Mount, curiously.

"The full committee, Jim Bowdoin, Sam Adams, John Adams, John Hancock, Will Phelps, Doctor Warren, and Joseph Quincy. Paul Revere called a meeting at the "Green Dragon" the same night, and the Mechanics' Club sent invitations to the North End Caucus, the South End Caucus, and the Middle District, to consider the arrival of British transports from Quebec with the Tenth and Fifty-second regiments."

"What! more troops?" exclaimed Mount, in amazement.

"How long have you been absent from Boston?" asked the young man.

"Since April," replied Mount.

"Would you care to hear a few facts that have occurred since April, gentlemen?" asked the young man, courteously including me in his invitation. Mount called the tap-boy and commanded cakes and ale for the company, with a harmless swagger; and when the tankards were brought we all drank a silent but significant toast to the dark city outside our windows.

The young man who had acted as spokesman for his company now produced a small leather book, which he said was a diary. Pipes were filled, lips wet in the tankards once more, and then the young man, who said his name was Thomas Newell, opened his little note-book and read rapidly:

1774, May 18.—Man-o'-war *Lively* arrived with Gen. Gage. Town meeting called. *A.* sent Paul Revere to York and Philadelphia. *H.* very anxious.

May 17.—Gage supersedes Hutchinson as Governor. *S. A.* has no hopes.

June 1.—Three transports here with redcoats. *Thirteen Sisters* notified.

June 14.—The Fourth Regiment (King's Own) landed at the Long Wharf and marched to the Common. No riot.

June 15, A.M.—Stores on Long Wharf closed. Forty-third Regiment landed. We are already surrounded by a fleet and army, the harbour is shut, all navigation forbidden, not a sail to be seen except war-ships.

July 1.—Admiral Graves arrived with fleet from London, also transports with Fifth and Thirty-eighth Regiments.

July 2.—Artillery landed with eight brass cannon. Camped on Common. *S. A.* notified *Thirteen Sisters.*

July 4.—Thirty-eighth Regiment landed at Hancock's Wharf, with a company of artillery, great quantity of ordnance, stores, etc., three companies of the Royal Irish Regiment, called the Eighteenth Foot, and the whole of the Forty-seventh Regiment. Also bringing news that the Tenth and Fifty-second Regiments would arrive in a few days! *S. A.* sent riders to York and Philadelphia. Much hunger in town. Many young children dying.

Newell paused, glanced over the pages again, then shut the little book and placed it in his breast-pocket.

Mount sat grim and silent, twisting the scarlet thrums on his sleeves; the others, with painful, abstracted faces, stared at vacancy through the mounting smoke from their long clay pipes.

Presently the landlord came in, glanced silently around, saluted Mount with a quiet bow, paid his respects to me in a similar manner, and whispered that we might sup at our pleasure in the "Square Room" above.

So, with a salute to the company, we rose and left the tap-room to the silent smokers of the long pipes.

The so-called "Square Room" of the "Wild Goose Tavern" was a low, wainscoted chamber, set with small deep windows. It was an ancient room, built in the fashion of a hundred years ago, more heavily wrought than we build in these days; and although the floor-beams had settled in places, and the flooring sagged and rose in little hillocks, yet the place suggested great solidity and strength. Nor was it to be wondered at, for this portion of the tavern had at one time been a detached block-house pierced for musketry, and the long loopholes were still there above the wainscoting.

Spite of its age and fortified allure, the "Square Room" was cheerful under its candle-light and illuminated sconces. Rows of framed pictures hung along the walls, the subjects representing coaching scenes in England and also many beautiful scenes from the sporting life of country gentlemen.

Relics of the hunting field also adorned the walls, trophies of fox-masks, with brush and pads, groups of hunting-horns, whips, and spurs, with here and there an ancient matchlock set on the wall, flanked by duelling-pistols, powder-horns, and Scottish dirks.

The furniture was of light oak, yet very clumsy and old-fashioned, being worn shiny like polished Chinese carvings. Pipe-racks of oak were screwed into the wainscoting under long shelves, well stored with pewters, glass tankards, punch-bowls, and tobacco-jars.

There were a few small square tables scattered along the walls, but the centre of the room was taken up with a long table, some three dozen chairs placed, and as many covers spread for guests.

To this long, tenantless table our host conducted us, seating us with a silent civility most noteworthy, and in sharp contrast to the majority of landlords, who do sicken their guests with obsequious babble.

"Well, Clay," said Mount, hitching his heavy chair closer to the white cloth, "I left brother Jim in good spirits at Pitt."

The landlord bowed, and seemed gratified to hear it.

"You should know," said Mount, turning to me, "that our host is Barclay Rolfe, brother to Jim Rolfe, of the 'Virginia Arms' in Fort Pitt." And to the landlord he said, "Mr. Cardigan, late ward of Sir William Johnson, but one of us."

"I owe your brother much," said I, "more than a bill for a chaise and four. Possibly you have heard from him concerning that same chaise?"

"I have heard through Saul Shemuel," he said, gravely. "I guess my brother was tickled to death to help you out of that pickle, Mr. Cardigan."

"He shall not lose by it either," said I. "My solicitor, Peter Weaver, of Albany, has sent your brother full recompense for the carriage and animals."

The elder Rolfe thanked me very simply, then excused himself to go to the kitchen where our dinner should now be ready.

It was truly a noble dinner of samp soup, roast pork, beans, a boiled cod, most toothsome and sweetly salt, and a great wild goose, roasted brown, with onion and sage dressing, and an aroma which filled the room like heavenly incense.

With this we drank October ale, touching neither Madeira nor sherry, though both were recommended us; but I wished not to mix draughts to set that latent deviltry a-brewing in Jack Mount, so refused all save ale for himself and for me, though I allowed him a hot bowl with his hazel nuts.

We now withdrew to one of the small tables in a corner of the room, a servant bringing thither our nuts and hot bowls, and also some writing materials for me.

These I prepared to use at once, pushing the nut-shells clear, and seized the pen to cramp it in my fist and set to work, tongue-moistening my determined lips:

"October 28, 1774.

"Thos. Foxcroft, Esquire,
Solicitor, Queen Street,
Boston.

"My dear Sir,—At what hour this evening will it prove convenient for you to receive the undersigned upon affairs of the utmost urgency and grave moment concerning Miss Warren whose interests I believe you represent?

"The instant importance of the matter I trust may plead my excuse for this abrupt intrusion on your privacy.

"Pray consider me, Sir,
"Y^r most obliged and obedient Servt
"Michael Cardigan.

"At the Wild Goose
near Wiltshire and Chambers Streets."

Sealing the letter, I bade the servant take it and bring an answer if the gentleman was at home, but in any event to leave the letter.

Mount had taken a pipe from the stranger's rack, and now lighted it, peering out of the window, and puffing away in vast contentment.

Northward, across the water, the lights of Charlestown glimmered through a thin fog. Nearer, in mid-stream, rose the black hull of a British war-ship, battle-lanthorns set and lighted, stabbing the dark tide below with jagged shafts of yellow light, cut by little black waves which hastened seaward on the sombre ebbing tide.

As for Boston, or as much of it as we could see over the shadowy roofs and slanting house-tops, it was deathly dark and still. Fort Pitt, with its hundreds of people, which Boston could match with thousands, was far more stirring and alive than this dumb city of shadows, with never a stir in its empty streets, and never a light from a window-candle. Truly, we sat in a tomb—the sepulchre of all good men's hopes for justice from that distant England we had loved so well in kinder days.

Somewhere, deep in the dim city's heart, a fire was burning, and we could see its faint reflection on chimneys in the northwest.

"Doubtless some regimental fire on the Common," muttered Mount, "or a signal on Mount W—d—m, where the Light Horse camp. They talk to the war-ships and the castle from Beacon Hill, too. It may be that."

Musing there by the window, we scarcely noticed that, little by little, the room behind us was filling. Already at the long table a dozen guests were seated, some conversing, some playing absently with their glasses, some reading the newspapers through round horn-rimmed spectacles.

Many of them glanced sharply at us; some looked at Mount, smiled, and nudged others.

"Do you know any of these gentlemen, Jack?" I asked, in a low voice.

He swung around in his chair and surveyed the table.

"Ay, all o' them," he said, returning their amused salutations; "they all belong to the club that meets here."

"Club? What club?" I asked.

"The Minute Men's. I meant to tell you that you're a member."

"I a member?" I repeated, in astonishment.

"Surely, lad, else you never could ha' passed these stairs. I am a member; I bring you, and now you're a member. There's no oath to take in this club. It's only when you go higher into the secret councils like those o' the three caucuses, the Mechanics', and some others I shall not mention, by your leave."

Mount watched the effect of his words on me and grinned.

"You didn't know that I am one of the Minute Club's messengers? That's why I went to Pitt. Did you think I went there for my health? Nenny, lad. I had a message for Cresap as well as you, and I gave it, too."

He laughed, and moistened his lips at the hot bowl.

"Paul Revere, the goldsmith—he who made the print of the Boston Massacre—is another messenger, but not of the Minute Club. He is higher—goes breakneck to York for *S. A.*, you know."

"What is S. A.?" I broke in, petulantly. "You all talk of J. H. and S. A. and the Thirteen Sisters, and I don't understand."

"S. A. is Sam Adams," said Mount, surprised. "J. H. is John Hancock, a rich young man who is with us to the last gasp. The Thirteen Sisters mean the thirteen colonies. They're with us, too—at least we hope they are, though York is a hell for Tories, and Philadelphia's full o' broad-brims who may not fight."

"But what is this Minute Men's Club?" I asked, curiously.

"Headquarters for delegates from the Minute Men and all alarm companies in Massachusetts Bay. You know that every town, village, and hamlet in the province is organized, don't you? Well, besides the regular militia we have alarm companies, where half of the men are ready to march at a minute's notice. One officer from every company throughout the province is delegated to attend the Minute Club here, so that he can keep his company in touch with the march of events.

"Besides that, the club has a corps of runners, like me, to travel with orders when called on. I'm in for a rest now, unless something pressing occurs."

"And—what am I in this club?" I asked, smiling to see how well Jack Mount had kept his secrets since I first knew him.

"You? Oh, you are a recruit for Cresap's battalion," said Mount, much amused. "We recruit here, for certain companies."

"Is Cresap coming here?" I asked, eagerly.

"He marches in the spring with his Maryland and Pennsylvania Rangers—to pay his respects to Tommy Gage? Nenny! To help turn this pack o' bloody-backs out of Boston, lad, and that's the truth, which you should know."

I sat silent, pondering on the strange circumstances of these months which had brought me so swiftly, from my boyhood's isolation, into the thick of the tremendous struggle between King and colony, a struggle still bloodless, save for the so-called Boston Massacre of some years past.

That Mount had coolly recruited me without my knowledge or consent disturbed me not at all: first, because I should have offered my poor services anyway; second, because, had I been free to select, I should have chosen to serve with Cresap's men, knowing him, as I did, for a brave and honourable young man.

I told Jack as much, and his face brightened with pleasure. He insisted on presenting me to the company—which was now fast filling the room—as one of Cresap's Rangers; and he further did most foolishly praise me for my bearing in certain common dangers he and I had shared, which made me red and awkward and vexed with him for my embarrassment.

The gentlemen I met were all most kind and polite; some appeared to be gentlemen bred, others honest young men—over-silent and sober for their years, perhaps, but truly a sturdy, clean-limbed company, neatly but not fashionably attired, and the majority characterized by a certain lankness of body which tended to gauntness in a few.

All were officers of alarm companies belonging to the numerous towns of the province; all were simple in manner, courteous to each other, and thoughtful of strangers, inviting us to wine or punch, and taking no offence when I prudently refused, for my own sake as well as for Jack's.

Two soldiers of the Lexington militia entertained me most agreeably; they were Nathan Harrington and Robert Monroe, the latter an old soldier, having been standard-bearer for his regiment at Louisburg.

"For years," he observed, quietly, "the British have said that all Americans are cowards, and they have so dinned it into their own ears that they believe it. It is a strange thing for them to believe. Who was it stood fast before Duquesne when Braddock's British fled? Who took Louisburg? What men have fought for England on our frontiers from our grandfathers' times?"

"Ay," broke in Harrington, "they tell us that we are yokels without wit or knowledge to fire a musket. Yet, to-day, two-thirds of the men in our province of Massachusetts Bay have served as soldiers against the French or the savages."

"That we are under the King's displeasure," said Monroe, "I can well understand; but that he and his ministers and his soldiers should wish to deem us cowards—we who are English, too, as well as they—passes my understanding."

"Mayhap they will learn the truth ere winter," observed Harrington, grimly.

"If I or my friends be cowards, I do not know it," added Monroe, simply. "It is not well to boast, Nathan, for God alone knows what a man may do in battle; yet I myself have been in battle, and was afraid, too, but never ran. I carried England's flag once. It is not well that she foul her own nest."

"I have never smelled powder; have you, sir?" said Harrington, turning to me.

"Not to boast of," I replied.

"Mount says you conducted most gallantly under fire," said Monroe, smiling.

"No more gallantly than did all at Cresap's fort," said I, annoyed. "We were behind ramparts and dreaded nothing save an arrow or two."

"But you had some warm work with certain Tories, too," began Monroe—"one Walter Butler, I believe."

"How did you hear of that?" I asked, in astonishment.

"Benny Prince brought the news," he replied. "Where he heard it I do not know, but it is noised abroad that you laid no kind hands on Walter Butler and Lord Dunmore. Nay, sir, you should not be surprised. We have our agents everywhere, listening, watching, noting all facts and rumours for those whom I need not name. We know, for instance, that Walter Butler has travelled north in a litter. We know that Dunmore scarce dare show his head in Virginia for the shame you put upon him and the growing hatred of the people he governs. We know that Sir John Johnson is fortifying Johnson Hall and gathering hordes of savages and Tories in Tryon County. Ay, Mr. Cardigan, we know, too, that the son of your father will fight to the death for the cause which his honour demands that he embrace."

"My father died for his King," I said, slowly.

"And mine, too," said Monroe; "but were he not with God to-day, I know where he would be found."

Others began to join our group. Mount, who had been conversing with a handsome and very fashionably dressed young man, approached our table with his companion, and presented me to him.

I had, of course, heard more or less of John Hancock, but had pictured him as an elderly man, sober of costume and stern and gray. Therefore my first meeting with John Hancock was a disappointment. He was young, handsome, decidedly vain, though quite free from affectation of speech or gesture. He appeared to lack that gravity of deportment and deliberation which characterized the company around us; gestures and words were at times impetuous if not whimsical; he appeared not too free from an egotism which, I thought, tinged all he said, so that, somehow, his words lost a trifle of the weight they deserved to carry.

His style of dress was not to my taste, savouring of the French, I thought. He wore an apple-green coat, white silk stockings, very large silver buckles on his pumps, smallclothes of silver-net tied at the knees with pea-green ribbons, which fell to his ankles, and much expensive lace at his throat and cuffs.

His hair was frizzled and powdered, and worn in a French club with black ribbon, and the hair on his temples was loaded with pomatum and rolled twice.

He certainly was most civil to me, mentioning his pleasure that Captain Cardigan's son should embrace the patriots' cause, and inquiring most respectfully concerning the last moments of Sir William Johnson, a man, he said, for whom he had entertained the highest possible respect and admiration.

Our conversation was of short duration, Mr. Hancock being addressed and solicited by so many who had business with him in his capacity of delegate from the secret club at the "Green Dragon Tavern."

I learned from the hints dropped that Boston was literally crowded with clubs, some open, some secret, but all organized to discuss politics, and pledged to combat the acts of the British Parliament to the bitter end.

Many clubs were formed among the Boston mechanics, of which the Mechanics' Society or Club was the centre. The Boston mechanics, I learned, were the earliest and most constant supporters of the patriot cause. Neither threats, temptations, Tory arguments, nor loyalist bribes could shake their fidelity; and they were the people, too, who had most to lose when the city was closed to commerce. Starvation faced them; troops thickened in Boston; but the mechanics remained true. And although, when in dire need, to sustain their wives and little ones, they thoughtlessly started work on the new barracks, at a word of warning and explanation from the Committee of Safety, they left their work in a body, to the rage and chagrin of General Gage and every soldier and Tory in Boston.

I further learned that the patriots carried on their political action not only by clubs and through the newspapers, but also by public meetings in defiance of Governor Gage.

All men know that we Americans have inherited the right of public meeting. But when the "regulating act" came from England to prohibit that right, it missed fire, for though it did forbid such meeting unless authorized by Governor Gage, it did not provide for adjourning meetings already in progress. Therefore the assemblies in all the provincial towns had begun meetings in anticipation of the 1st of August, the date set for their prohibition, and the meetings were carried over that date, and kept alive day after day by not being officially declared adjourned.

It was useless for Gage to fume; he had no authority under the law to adjourn them.

In Boston the people flocked in crowds to Faneuil Hall and the Old South Church, where Samuel Adams, James Otis, and Josiah Quincy were the orators. And the government, in secret dread, watched the people thronging around these fiery orators, whose theme was liberty and equal rights for all.

The Committees of Donation and of Correspondence were most active. The former was organized to distribute relief to the poor in the stricken city; the latter was formed to keep all patriots in all of the thirteen colonies in touch with each other, and to observe the approach of the great current which was surely bearing war upon the waves that formed its crest.

This Committee of Correspondence was the great executive of our party. It watched unceasingly: it received information from all the societies, clubs, town assemblies, caucuses, and local committees. It distributed all information, all warnings, all rumours, not only from America, but also, through its agents, from abroad.

Many of its members were also members of the "Green Dragon." John Hancock was such a member, and therefore his presence here at the "Wild Goose" was perhaps significant.

That he was about to address the company was apparent, for everybody had now taken chairs and formed a semi-circle around Mr. Hancock, who stood leaning against the great centre-table, coolly taking snuff, and glancing over a written sheet of paper which he held in his left hand.

"It may be," he said, "a trifle premature to discuss here in open meeting those measures of resistance contemplated and now under discussion in the Committee of Correspondence, the Provincial Congress, and the Continental Congress.

"It is sufficient, therefore, for the moment, that you should know that Virginia and South Carolina are at last aroused to the necessity of taking thought for their local defences. I may also add that my Lord Dunmore's government increases in rigour and also in disfavour.

"The Committee of Correspondence has received word direct from Mr. Patrick Henry that he regards the cause of peace as already lost, and urges us to rely on Virginia, at least, for loyal support in whatever measures we may deem necessary to maintain our manhood in the face of all the world."

A murmur of applause swept like a whisper through the room, hushed immediately by cautious gestures and glances at the street outside, which might harbour a spy in its heavy gloom and impenetrable, brooding shadows.

"There is a certain document embodying a proposed declaration," continued Hancock, "which, although at present merely under discussion, I expect to see one day printed, completed, and framed, and hung in every home in these thirteen colonies. You may perhaps imagine what document I refer to, and doubtless many of you sitting here are not yet prepared for that supreme step forward in our manifest destiny. Neither, I may say, are many who have the framing of that declaration under discussion. Time alone will show that future of which I, for one, am so certain.

"I am not here to discuss with you the proposed declaration in question, which is not even yet existent save in the hearts of those who have dared to dream of it.

"I am here to submit to you a list of crimes against our colony of Massachusetts Bay, committed or contemplated by the King of England."

He unrolled his bit of paper, took a fresh pinch of scented snuff, and read, somewhat carelessly:

"The history of the present King of Great Britain:

"He refuses his assent to necessary laws for the public good.

"He forbids his Governors to pass laws of immediate importance, unless suspended in their operation till his assent be obtained; and when so suspended he has utterly neglected to attend to them.

"He has called together legislative bodies at places unusual with intent to fatigue, discourage, and annoy the members of such bodies.

"He has repeatedly dissolved representative houses for opposing his invasions of the people's rights.

"He obstructs the administration of justice.

"He makes judges dependent on his will alone for tenure of office and payment of salaries.

"He has created a multitude of new offices and sent hither swarms of officers to harass our people.

"He keeps among us, in times of peace, standing armies, without consent of our legislature.

"He renders his military independent of and superior to civil power.

"He protects these troops, by mock trials, from punishment for murders committed on the inhabitants of this province.

"He has cut off our trade with the whole world.

"He taxes us without our consent.

"He deprives us of the benefits of trial by jury.

"He transports us beyond the seas for trial for pretended offences.

"He takes away our charters, abolishes our laws, suspends our legislatures."

Hancock looked up, still holding the paper unrolled.

"Why," he said, lightly, "this is no King, but a Cæsar amid his prætorians! Faith, I have been reading some history of the tyrants—surely not the history of our beloved monarch, George the Third!"

There was a grim silence. Hancock's manner changed. He folded the paper, placed it in the bosom of his white waistcoat, and turned soberly to the rows of silent, seated men.

"Yesterday," he said, "a carpenter was arrested for stealing bread for his little children. May I request, gentlemen, that you send a delegate to the committee which will wait upon the Governor to-morrow to intercede for the starving man?"

Then, with a brief inclination, he turned and left the room ere anybody was aware of his purpose.

The effect of his unexpected appeal was as dramatic as his sudden exit. With one impulse the company rose, grave, pale, tight-lipped; little groups formed on the floor; few words passed; but Hancock had done his work, and every alarm company in Massachusetts would know, ere many hours, that they were to fight one day, not for their honour, but to prevent the King of England from driving them to dishonour, so that their children might not die of want before their eyes.

It was not an orator's effort that Hancock had accomplished; it was a mere statement of a truth, yet so skilfully timed and so dramatic in execution that it was worth months of oratory before the vast audiences of Faneuil Hall. For he had startled the representatives of hundreds of villages, and set them thinking on that which was closest to them—the danger to the welfare of their own households. Such danger makes panthers of men.

If Hancock was theatrical at moments, the end justified the means; if he was an egotist, he risked his wealth for principle; if he was a dandy, he had the bravery of the true dandy, which clothes all garments with a spotless, shining robe, and covers the face of vanity under a laurelled helmet.

It was late when the servant returned from Mr. Foxcroft, with a curt note from that gentleman, promising to receive me at one o'clock in the afternoon of the day following.

As I stood twisting the letter in my fingers, and staring out into the black city which perhaps sheltered the woman I loved somewhere amid its shadows, Jack Mount came up, peering through the window with restless eyes.

"Cade has never returned to this tavern," he said, gloomily. "No one here has either seen or heard of him since he and I left last April for Cresap's camp."

CHAPTER XXIII

Like a red lamp the sun swung above the smoky east, its round, inflamed lens peering through the smother beneath which Boston lay, blanketed by the thick vapours of the bay.

From my window I could distinguish the shadowy ship-yards close by. Northeast, across Green Lane, lay the Mill Pond, sheeted in mist, separated from the bay by an indented causeway.

On Corps Hill the paling signal-fires went out, one by one; a green light twinkled aloft in the dusky tangle of a war-ship's rigging; the smoky beacon in its iron basket flared, sank, glimmered, and went out.

Across the street, through the white mist lifting, spectral warehouses loomed, every shutter locked, iron gates dripping rust.

Jack Mount came in, and sat down on the edge of the bed with a silent nod of greeting, clasping his large hands between his knees.

"I have been thinking of that damned thief-taker," he said, yawning. "If he's tracked me from Pitt he's a good dog, and his wife should cast a prime dropper some day."

A servant brought us a bowl of stirabout and some rusks and salted codfish, and we breakfasted there in my chamber, scarcely speaking. Instead of exultation at my nearness to Silver Heels, a foreboding had weighed on me since first I unclosed my eyes. The depression deepened as I sat brooding by the window where the white sea-fog rolled against the sweating panes. Mount ate in silence; I could scarcely swallow any food. Presently I pushed away my plate, drew paper and ink before me, and fell to composing a letter. From the tap-room below a boy came to bring us our morning cups, and we washed the salty tang from our throats. Mount lighted his yard of clay and lay back, puffing smoke at the smeared window-panes. I wrote slowly, drinking at intervals.

The morning draught refreshed us; and when at length sunshine broke out over the bay, something of our dormant spirits stirred to greet it.

"How silent is the world outside," said I, listening to the sea-birds' mewing, and mending my quill with my hunting-knife.

"Misery breeds silence," he said.

"Are men starving here around us?" I asked, trying to realize what I had heard.

"Ay, and dying of it. The sun yonder no longer signals breakfast for Boston. Better finish your fish while you may."

He pulled slowly at his pipe. "If I am right," he drawled, "it would be close to mid-day now in England—the King's dinner-hour. His Majesty should be greasing his chin with hot goose-gravy."

His blue eyes began to shine; the long pipe-stem snapped short between forefinger and thumb; the smoking bowl dropped, and he set his moccasined heel upon it, grinding clay and fire into the stone floor. I watched him for a moment, and then resumed my writing.

"God save the King," he sneered, "and smear his maw thick with good fat meat! Let the rebel babes o' Boston die snivelling at their rebel mothers' dried-up breasts! It's a merry life, Cardigan. I dreamed last night a naked skeleton rode through Boston streets a-beating a jolly ringadoon on his bones:

"'Yankee doodle came to town

A-riding on a pony—'

But the pony was all bones, too, like the Pale Horse, and sat Death astride, beating ever the same mad march:

"'Yankee doodle—doodle—do!

Yankee doodle—dandy!'

'Twas the bay wind shaking the weather-vane—nothing more, lad. Come, shall we steer au large?"

"I must first send my letter," said I; and began to re-read it:

BOSTON, *October 29, 1774.*

"*To Mistress Felicity Warren*:

"DEAR, DEAR SILVER HEELS,—Being cured of my hurts and having done with Johnson Hall and my dishonourable kinsman, Sir John Johnson, Bart: I now take my pen in hand to acquaint you that I know all, how that through the mercy of Providence you have been reunited with your hon[rd] parents, long supposed to have been with God, their name and quality I know not nor doubt that it is most honourable. I did think to receive a letter from you ere I left the Hall, yet none came, so I insulted Sir John and took Warlock who is mine of a right and I am come to Boston to pay my respects to y[r] hon[rd] parents and to acquaint them that I mean to wed you as I love you my hon[rd] cozzen but feel no happiness in as much as a deathly fear hath possessed me for some hours that I am never again to see you, this same haunting dread that all may not be well with you does not subdue and chill those ardent sentiments which of a truth burn as hotly now as they burned that sweet noonday at Roanoke Plain.

"I further acquaint you that my solicitor, Mr. Peter Weaver of Albany, hath news that my uncle, Sir Terence Cardigan, Bart, is at a low ebb of life being close to his Maker through much wine and excesses, and hath sent for me, but I would not stir a peg till I have found you dear Silver Heels to ask you if you do still love that foolish lad who will soon be Sir Michael Cardigan to the world but ever the same Micky to you, though if war comes to us I doubt not that my title and estate will be confiscated in as much as I shall embrace the cause of the colonies and do what harm I may to the soldiers of our King.

"My sweet Silver Heels, this letter is to be delivered to y^r solicitor Mr. Thomas Foxcroft and by him instantly into your own hands, there being nothing in it not honourable and proper. I strive in vain to shake off the depression which so weighs down my heart that it is heavy with the dread that all may not be well with you, for I do distrust Sir John his word, and I do despise him heartily and deem it strange that he did conduct you to Boston under pretence of a business affair which he has since refused to discuss with me.

"Dear maid, if y^r honourable parents will permit, I shall this day venture to present myself and formally demand your hand in that sweet alliance which even death cannot end but must perforce render immortal for all time.

"Your faithful and obedient
servant and devoted lover
Michael Cardigan."

The writing of this letter comforted me. I directed it to "Miss Warren, in care of Mr. Thomas Foxcroft, to be delivered immediately," and summoning a servant, charged him to bear it instantly to Mr. Foxcroft.

"It is but a step to Queen Street," I said to the lank lad; "so if by chance the young lady herself be living there, you shall wait her pleasure and bring me my answer." And I gave him three bright shillings fresh struck from the mint that year.

"You will go with me, Jack?" I asked, as the messenger vanished.

Mount, sprawling by the window, turned his massive head towards me like a sombre-eyed mastiff.

"Daylight is no friend o' mine," he said, slowly. "In Boston here they peddle ballads about me and Cade; and some puling quill-mender has writ a book about me, the same bearing a gallows on the cover."

"Then you had best stay here," I said; "I can manage very well alone, Jack."

"Once," continued Mount, thoughtfully, polishing his hatchet on his buckskin breeches—"once I went strolling on the Neck, yonder, and no thought o' the highway either, when a large, fat man came a-waddling with two servants, and a pair o' saddle-bags as fat as the man, every bit."

He licked his lips and slowly turned his eyes away from mine.

"The moon was knee-high over the salt-grass," he continued; "the devil's in the moon when it's knee-high."

"So you robbed him," I added, disgusted. Mount glanced guiltily around the room—anywhere but at me.

"I only asked him what his saddle-bags might weigh," he muttered, "and the fat fool bawled, 'Thief! Help!' If he had not put it in my mind to scotch him!—but the great booby must out with his small-sword and call up his men. So, when he fell a-roaring that he was a King's magistrate—why—why, I rubbed a pistol under his nose. And would you believe it, lad, the next thing I knew, Cade and I could scarce walk for the weight o' the half-crowns in our breeches-pockets! It amazes me even yet—it does indeed!"

"You'd best look to your neck, then," I said, shortly. "Remember Bishop's buxom daughter on the Philadelphia coach last night. Where the kitten runs the catamount prowls."

"Oh, I'll take the air by night," observed Mount, with perfect good-humour. "The night air o' Boston is famous medicine for troubles like mine."

"You will do no more tricks on the highway?" I demanded, suspiciously.

He buried his nose in a pot of beer without replying. An hour passed in silence, save for the continual trotting to and fro of the boy from the tap-room, bearing deep, frothing tankards for Mount.

"Have a care," I said, at length; "if you drink like that you'll be out and abroad and into every foolish mischief, as you were in Pittsburg. Be a man, Jack!"

"I'm all salty inside like a split herring," he said, reaching for a fresh pewter, and blowing the foam till it scattered over the floor like flakes of snow.

Two hours had dragged on towards their finish, and already the clocks in the tavern were tolling the death of another hour, when my lank messenger came breathless to the door with a letter for me, and at the first glance I saw that the writing was the hand of Silver Heels herself.

Mount gaped at me, then one of his rare and delicate instincts moved him to withdraw. I heard him leave the room, but did not heed his going, for I was already deep in the pages of the letter:

"Dear Lad, my old Comrade,—Mr. Foxcroft did summon me to consider your letter of last evening, how it were best to inform you of what you should know.

"Now comes your letter of this morning by your messenger, and leaves me a-tremble to breathe its perfume of the love which I had, days since, resigned.

"For I did write you constantly to Johnstown in care of Sir John, and no answer came save one, from Sir John, saying you cared not to answer me my letters. This cruel insult from Sir John could not have been the truth in light of the letter now folded in my bosom, and softly rustling nestled against my breast.

"But it is plain to me, dear heart, that you as yet know nothing of what great change has come to me. And so, before I dare give you the answer which burns my mouth and thrills this poor body o' mine which aches for you, I must, for honour's sake, reveal to you what manner of maid you would now court, and into what desperate conditions I am come; not that I doubt you, Michael, dear soul of chivalry and tender truth!

"Know then, my friend, that I am hopelessly poor in this world's goods; know, too, that the new name I bear is a name marked for pity or contempt by those few who have not long since forgotten it. It is the death of my pride to say this. Yet I say it.

"My father is old and broken. His faculties have failed; he is like a child who forgets what his tongue utters, even while voicing his harmless desires. His property is gone; he does not know it. He sees around him the shadows of the past; he talks with the dead as though they sat at his elbow.

"His house is an empty shell; his lands have grown into thickets; his estate is lost to him through taxes long unpaid. Yet everywhere the phantoms of dead scenes surround him; ghosts walk with him through spectral domains, ride with him to hounds, carry his colours to victory on the race-course, sit with him at table, pour water for him which, in his wrapped eyes, bubbles like wine.

"Believe me, dear friend, it is pitiful and sad—sad past all I have ever known.

"For me, too, it is so strange, so hopeless, that, even after these long days, it is still an untrue dream from which I seem too weary and stunned to rouse and drive the gray vision from me.

"Long ago, in a distant year of sunlight, I remember a child called Silver Heels, whose mad desire for rank and power crammed her silly head, till, of a sweet May day, love came to her. Love drove her to folly; love reclaimed her; love lies still in her heart, watching for you with tireless eyes.

"Dear heart, would you take me? Even after all you now know? Do you want me, Michael?—me?—when all the world lies before you?

"I once most wickedly said that if I had been humbly born, I would not for my pride's sake wed with you. It is not true, Michael; I will wed with you. But, if after what you have learned, you care no longer to wed me, do not write me; do not come to give me reasons.

"Mr. Foxcroft attends me. We will await you at his house, at noon, and if you come—as, God help me I believe you will—then I shall teach you what a maid's love can mean. Oh, to have you again, as I held you those long days on the trail; but you were too near death to know it!—too close to death to hear all I promised you if only you would live!

"Felicity."

"Mount!" I cried, all of a-tremble, "I shall wed this noon! Get me a parson, man!" And I began tearing off my buckskins and flinging them right and left, shouting for Jack the while, and dressing in my finest linen and my silver-gray velvet.

Now choking with the tears that I could not crush back, now smiling at the sunlight which yellowed the white walls of my chamber, I shouted at intervals for Mount, until the tap-boy came to say that Mount had gone out. So I bade the tap-boy hasten forth and buy me a large nosegay with streamers, and fetch it to me instantly; and then returned to my toilet with a feverish haste that defeated its own purpose.

At last, however, I hung my sword, dusted the hair-powder from frill and ruffle, buckled shoon and knees, and shook out the long soft lace over my cuffs. Then I found the ring I had bought in Albany, and placed it in my silver-webbed waistcoat with its flowered flaps of orange silk.

The inn clocks chimed for ten as the lad brought me a huge nosegay all fluttering with white silken streamers.

"Where is my companion?" I asked, red as a poppy under his grins.

"Below, sir," replied the lad, hesitating.

"Drunk?" I demanded, angrily.

"Tolerable," said the lad.

With that I seized my nosegay, set my small French hat on my head, and went down the side stairway to the street.

Mount, swaggering on the tap-room porch, spied me and rubbed his startled eyes. But I seized him by the painted cape of his fox-trimmed hunting-shirt, and jerked him to and fro savagely.

"Idiot! Tippler! Pottle-pot!" I cried, in a rage. "I'm to be married—d'ye hear? Married! Married! Get me a parson! Take my nosegay! So! Now walk behind me as if you knew what decent folk are accustomed to do at a sudden wedding!"

"How can I get you a parson if I'm to march here behind you, bearing this nosegay?" he remonstrated, sidling away towards the tavern again.

"You stay where you are!" I said; then I called a servant and bade him find a parson to go instantly to the house of Thomas Foxcroft in Queen Street, and there await my coming.

Mount, almost sobered, through sheer astonishment, regarded me wildly.

"Jack, old friend," I said, in a burst of happiness, "I've found her, and she will be my wife by noon! Give me joy, Jack!—and mind that nosegay, idiot! Hold it aloft, else the streamers will trail in the dust! Now, then! Follow me! Gingerly, idiot, gingerly!"

And away I marched, scarce knowing what I did in my excitement, but turning now and again to see that Mount followed, bearing the nosegay with proper care.

"If you are to be wedded at noon," he said, timidly, as we were hurrying through Cambridge Street, "what are we going to do until then—walk the streets like this? Lord, what a fool I feel!"

I stopped short. It was quite true that I was not expected at Mr. Foxcroft's before noon, and it was now but ten o'clock or a little after.

"I can't sit still in that tavern," I said. "Let us walk, Jack. Two hours are quickly past. Come, step beside me—and mind those ribbons! Jack! I am mad with happiness!"

"Then let us drink to it," suggested Mount, but I jerked him to my side, and scarcely knowing what to do or where to go, started on, with the vague idea of circling the city in a triumphal march.

I shall never forget my first glimpse of the city by daylight: its brick houses streaked with sea-fog, its bare wooden wharves glimmering in the sunshine, as Mount and I passed through Lyna Street and out along the water by Lee's ship-yard and Waldo's Wharf.

Northward across the misty water the roofs and steeples of Charlestown reddened in the sun; to the west the cannon on Corps Hill glittered, pointing seaward over the Northwest Water Mill. From somewhere in the city came the beating of drums and the faint squealing of fifes; the lion banner of England flapped from Beacon Hill; white tents crowned the summit of Valley Acre; the ashes of the beacon smoked.

In the northwestern portion of the city the quiet of death reigned; there was not a sign of life in the streets; the wooden houses were closed and darkened; the ship-yards and wharves deserted; not a living soul was to be seen abroad. Mount's noiseless moccasined tread awoke no echoes, but my smart heels clattered as we turned southeast through squalid Hawkins Street, through Sudbury, Hanover, Wings Lane, Dock Square, by the Town Dock, and then south, past the Long Wharf and Battery Marsh, above which, on Fort Hill, another British flag rippled against the blue sky.

"The damned rag flies high to-day," muttered Mount.

"Are you not done with cursing it?" I said, impatiently. "This is no day for bitterness."

"It's a slave's flag," retorted Mount—"parry that!"

"It flew for centuries above free men; let that plead for it!" I answered.

There was an inn on Milk Street, near Bishop's Alley, and the first open house we had encountered. Mount, before I could prevent him, had nosed out the tap-room, and I followed perforce, although I knew well enough that it was an ill-advised proceeding, the place being full of British soldiery and Mount in a quarrelsome mood.

The soldiers eyed Mount and his nosegay askance, and Mount cocked his fox-skin cap and ruffled it offensively, outstaring the most insolent of them. But presently, to my relief, the soldiers left without accepting the opportunity for a quarrel, and Mount, somewhat dejected, refilled his glass and emptied it, with a disagreeable laugh. Then we went out by way of Winter Street to the Mall, Jack bearing my nosegay as though it had been a hostile ensign to flaunt before all England.

There seemed to be many people abroad on Common Street; the shops were open all along Treamount and King streets, and the Boston citizens went about their affairs as soberly and quietly as though the city were not choking to death with England's heavy fist at its throat.

As for the Boston people, they resembled our good townsmen of Tryon County somewhat, though their clothes were of a more elegant cut, and even the snuffiest of them wore lace and buckles. Their limbs and features, however, appeared long and thin, a characteristic I had already noticed in New England folk.

Through the double rows of trees I could see the tents of the marines pitched on the Mall, and beyond them a park of artillery and some low redoubts. Soldiers were passing everywhere: here a company marching to the drum across the Common, black gaiters twinkling; there a squadron of Light Horse, in blue and silver, riding, two abreast, to their barracks on George

Street. Anon comes a company of red-necked Highlanders, bagpipes squawling, and it made me think of Johnson Hall to see their bare shins passing, sporrans a-swing, and the crawling whine of their pipes in my ears.

I looked at my watch; it was eleven o'clock. Mount and I leaned back against the railing of the south burying-ground, watching the busy life of the camp on the Common. I had never before seen so many soldiers together, nor such a brilliant variety of uniforms. The towns-people, too, lingered to watch the soldiers, some sullenly, some indifferently, some in open enjoyment. These latter were doubtless Tories, for in their faces one could not mistake the expression of sneering triumph. Also many of them talked to the soldiers, which earned them unconcealed scowls from passing citizens.

"Well," said Mount, "have you seen enough of the lobster-backs? The sight of them," he continued, raising his voice, "sours my stomach, and I care not who knows it."

Several people near us looked at him.

"Keep quiet!" I said, sharply. "I have no desire to spend the day in the provost cell yonder. Can you not remember what this day means to me?"

Mount shrugged his broad shoulders, lighted his pipe, and sat down on the grass under a tall elm.

"Sit beside me, lad," he said, "and I'll tell you all about these gay birds, and how to know them by their plumage. Mark! Yonder comes an officer in black and scarlet, wearing a single gold epaulette and a gold gorget, with the royal arms in gold on his white baldric. That's the royal artillery, Mr. Cardigan. That gay old buck beside him is a colonel of foot. He's all scarlet trimmed up with yellow and white. Most of them wear white breeches and black gaiters. There! That fellow in blue and silver, with orange cuffs and top-boots, is a trooper of Light Horse. See the steel head-piece with its roll of bear-skin and the orange plume on the left side. Some of 'em wear red cuffs and plumes, but you can tell them by their laced blue vests and jack-boots, and the officers by white baldrics and two silver epaulettes."

"What is that fellow there with the bear-skin cap and white plume and tassels?" I asked, with a pretence of interest which in my anxiety and excitement I could not feel. The splendid uniform which I pointed out glittered in stripes of silver and pale blue embroidery over a scarlet coat.

"That lad is a drummer of the Grenadiers," said Mount. "The soldier beside him with the green facings and green-and-gold stock is one of the Twenty-fourth Foot—a sergeant by his baldric and cross-spear. Oh, they're gay and godless, as the Weasel would say—"

He paused and looked down. The slightest tremor twitched his underlip. I laid my hand lightly on his shoulder.

"Ay, ay," he said, "I'm lost without him—I don't know what to do—I don't know. I see him in my sleep; he comes in dreams o' the woods. I wake laughing at his dry jests, and find my face twisted wi' tears. There's never a leaf stirs on a bough but I listen for Cade's padded footfall behind me; there's never a free wind blows but I hark for his voice a-calling me back to the sweet green forest and the spice o' the birch camp-fire. Lad! lad! He's dead and buried these long weeks, and I am but a weird-hound on a spectre trail, dogging his wraith."

We sat there on the grass watching the marines drilling; the artillery trotted clanking past for exercise at the Fox Hill redoubt, and presently we heard the dull boom-booming of their cannon along the west shore of the bay.

"They even shoot at the rebel fishes," sneered Mount, raising his voice for the benefit of his neighbours.

I sprang to my feet impatiently, adjusted my sword, and dusted the skirts of my coat.

"It's not half-past eleven yet," observed Mount.

"I don't care," I muttered; "I shall go to Queen Street now. Come, Jack! I cannot endure this delay, I tell you."

He did not answer.

"Come, Jack," I repeated, turning around to summon him. "What are you staring at, man?"

As I spoke a roughly clad man pushed in between me and Mount, swinging a knobbed stick; another man followed, then another. Mount had leaped to his feet and backed up to my side.

"It's Billy Bishop's gang!" he said, thickly. "Leave me, lad, or they'll take us both!"

Before I could comprehend what was on foot, half a dozen men suddenly surrounded Mount, and silently began to close in on him.

"Go!" muttered Mount, fiercely, pushing me violently from him.

"No, you don't!" said a cool voice at my elbow; "we want the Weasel, too, for all his fine clothes!"

The next instant a man in a red neck-cloth had seized my hands in a grip of iron, and, ere I knew what had happened, he clapped the gyves on one of my wrists. With a cry of rage and amazement I tore at my manacled hand, and, partly helpless as I was, I sprang at the fellow. He struck me a fierce blow with his cudgel, and ran around the edge of the swaying knot of human figures which was slowly bearing Mount to the ground.

Then Mount rose, hurling the pack from him, and striking right and left with his huge arms. I saw the nosegay fly into a shower of blossoms, and the silken ribbons flutter down under the trampling feet.

For a moment I caught Mount's eye, as he stood like a deeply breathing bull at bay, then swinging the steel manacle which was locked on my right wrist, I beat my way to Mount's side, and faced the thief-taker and his bailiffs.

They rushed us against the fence of the burying-ground, bruising us with their heavy cudgels, and knocking the war-hatchet from Mount's fist. I had my sword out, but could not use it, the manacles on my wrist clogging the guard and confusing me. In the uproar around us I heard cries of: "Death to the highwaymen!" "Kill the rogues!" A vast crowd was surging up on all sides; soldiers drew their hangers and pushed their way to the side of the baffled bailiffs.

"Give up, Jack Mount!" cried the stout man with the red neck-cloth—"give up, in the King's name! It's all over with you now! I've run you from Johnstown on a broad trail, God wot! and I want your brush and pads, old fox!"

Mount displayed his broad knife coolly. The sunlight played over the blade of the murderous weapon; the crowd around us broke into a swelling roar.

Suddenly a soldier struck heavily at Mount with his hanger, but Mount sent the sword whirling with the broad, short blade in his hand.

"If you'll let this gentleman go, I'll give up," said Mount, sullenly. "Answer me, Billy Bishop!"

"Come, come," said Bishop, in a bantering voice, "we know all about this gentleman, Jack. Don't you worry; we'll take care he has a view of the Roxbury Cross-road as well as you!"

The taunt of the cross-roads gallows transformed Mount into a demon. He hurled his huge bulk at the solid mass of people; I followed, making what play I could with my small-sword, but in a moment I was down in the dust, blood pouring from my face, groping blindly for the enemies who were already clapping the irons on my other wrist.

Through the roar and tumult of frantic voices I was dragged into a stony street, crushed into the pit of a crowd, which hurried me on resistlessly. White, excited faces looked into mine; hundreds of clinched fists tossed above the dense masses on either side. Again and again I plunged at those who drove me, but they thrust me onward. Far ahead in the throng I saw the head and shoulders of Jack Mount overtopping them all.

The mob halted at a cross-street to allow a cavalcade of horsemen to pass. Above the heads of the people I could see the cavalry riding, sabres bared, the riders glancing curiously down at the rabble and its prisoners. A coach passed, escorted by dragoons; a gentleman looked out to seek the reason of the uproar. From his coach window his head leaned so close to me that I could have touched it. The gentleman was Walter Butler.

"A thief, sir," cried a bailiff; "taken by Bishop on the Mall. Would your lordship be pleased to see his comrade, the notorious Jack Mount?"

"Drive on," said Butler, impassively. Then the crowd began to hoot and jeer as the bailiffs pushed me forward once more through the dust of Cornhill up Queen Street.

And so, crushed by the awful disgrace which had fallen on me, writhing, resisting, dishevelled, I was forced into the Court-house on Queen Street, across the yard, and into the gates of the prison, which crashed behind me, drowning the roars of the people in my stunned ears.

CHAPTER XXIV

I was taken, in company with Jack Mount, on Monday morning, the 29th of October, 1774, without warrant or process, without a shadow of legal right, without the faintest justification or excuse, save that I had been seen conversing with Mount on the Mall, and had resisted the thief-taker Bishop and his filthy gang of bailiffs.

From the 29th of October until the 15th day of December, chained ankle to ankle, wrist to wrist, and wearing a steel collar from which chains hung and were riveted to the rings on my legs, I lay in that vile iron cage known as the "Pirates' Chapel," in company with Mount and eight sullen, cursing ruffians, taken in piracy off the Virginia capes by his Majesty's ship *Hebe*, consort of the frigate *Asia*.

During those six weeks not a moment passed in which I despaired, not an hour dragged out its chain of minutes but I believed it must be the hour for my delivery from this hideous injustice.

From the minute I had entered the "Chapel," the dull amazement which had fettered mind and body in a strange paralysis gave way to a deadly patience. My benumbed faculties grew clear; every sense became abnormally alert. Calmly I faced the terrible dilemma; I probed its consequences coolly; I understood that while Walter Butler held the Governor's ear, and while the Governor held the civil power at his own pleasure, and used it as whim or caprice moved him, I could neither hope for a hearing before a magistrate nor dare expect a trial by my countrymen. The soiled hand of England had polluted the ermine of the judges; the bayonets of England cleared the court-rooms; the mocking Governor brooded in Province House, watching the structure of civil rights crumble and collapse, while his judges, his sheriffs, his bailiffs, and his soldiers prowled through the débris of a structure which had been reared by my own people's martyrdom.

As for communication with the outside world, with friends, even with hostile relatives, or with the Governor himself, there was no possible chance. Our steel cage was set in the centre of a stone chamber, the barred windows of which opened on a bare stony parade, bounded on the east by Cornhill, on the west by Treamount Street, and on the south by School Street and the dead wall enclosing King's Chapel. There was not a soul to be seen in the prison or outside save the marine sentinels, the jailers, the warden of the prison, and the eight ruffians who were caged with us, among whom there was but a single Englishman.

Our cage was bedded with straw like a kennel; our food was brought us three times a day, in earthen bowls. A wooden spoon went with each bowl, otherwise the feed differed nothing from the feed of dogs.

Mount, in the beginning, had conducted like a madman, passing swiftly up and down his cage, pacing to and fro along the ranks of steel bars, blank fury glaring from his eyes, jaw hanging like the jowl of a committed panther.

All that first night he stalked the cage, brushing the bars with brow and thigh, and deep in his blue eyes there burned a terrible light, like the livid witch-fires which flare in haunted swamps.

At first the manacled ruffians who lay about us in the straw watched him doggedly, but as the night wore on and his pacing never ceased, they growled sullen protest. Then he slowly turned on them, baring his white teeth.

From that moment they gave him room and he ruled the cage as a silent, powerful beast rules, scarcely conscious of the cringing creatures who huddle around his legs, and whose presence cannot invade the solitude of his own fierce misery.

The light in the stone chamber was cool and gray—clear enough, yet never tinged with sunlight. Night brought thick, troubled shadows creeping around the single candle which dripped from an iron socket riveted to the wall. Then the shades of the jailers fell across the floor as the large lanthorn was set outside in the corridor, and all night long the shuffling tread of the sentry marked the dead march of time.

For three days, now, I had not touched the broth which was set on the straw beside me; I do not know that I should have made the effort to eat at all, except for an accident. It happened in this manner: one day, towards the middle of December, I had been lying on my belly, trying to think out something of that future which I had not yet despaired of. Musing there, nose buried in my arms, I lay almost on the verge of slumber, yet with one eye on the corridor beyond, when I saw distinctly a woman's face peer through the thick grating which separated the corridor from our stone chamber.

After a while the face disappeared; I lay still a moment, then touched Mount's arm.

He turned his haggard face to me.

"Bishop's daughter is in the corridor," I whispered.

"Where?" asked Mount, vacantly.

"Out there behind the grating. She may do something for—for you. If she should, I think we had better try to eat."

"Yes," he said, "we must eat." And he turned with a snarl on one of the caged wretches behind us who for days had been battening on the food that neither Jack nor I touched.

The man was in the act of dragging Mount's bowl and spoon towards his own nest in the straw, but he dropped the food and shrank back as Mount seized it with an oath.

I also secured my own bowl of bread and broth, and, together, we ate as animals eat, eying the others malevolently and askance.

That night Mount lay awake, watching the grating. At dawn I awoke to watch, and Mount rolled himself up into a ball of buckskin and slept the first peaceful sleep which had come to him since his taking.

The day passed in horrible monotony; our straw had become so foul that my head swam with the stench. But towards evening came a jailer and two soldiers, who raked the filthy straw from our cage, mopped the reeking floor, and when it had partly dried, shook us down a bedding of sweet rye-straw, into which we burrowed like dogs.

That night we heard the noise of hammers overhead, and at first terror seized on all in the cage, for we believed that workmen had come to build gibbets. In the morning, when our jailer arrived to fetch us water, I spoke to him, scarcely expecting a reply, for he had never before paid the faintest attention to questions from any of us.

I was surprised, therefore, when he hesitated, glanced up at me, and finally informed me that the hammering we heard was made by masons and carpenters who were reconstructing the upper tiers of the prison for the new warden and his family.

Presuming on his pleasant manner, I continued my questioning, but he soon silenced me with a shake of his head.

"I know nothing about your case," he said. "Matters move slowly here; the prison is crowded with rebels who have defied the Governor's edict against public assemblies. Their cases come before yours, young man."

"And the others here?" I asked.

He paid no attention to my question.

I asked for news of the outside world, but he would give me none.

Mount, whose morbid curiosity had been aroused by the sight of some workmen digging holes in the yard outside the prison, stood up to watch them. The other prisoners also huddled to the south side of the cage, their chains making a great clanking as they moved. At the moment when their backs were turned the jailer looked at them significantly, then at me, and, to my horror, passed his withered fingers over his corded throat.

I stared at him, fascinated, but he shrugged his stooping shoulders, shuffled off to the wicket, let himself out, and slammed the grating.

That night I sat close to Jack Mount, my hand on his broad shoulder, crushing back the lump in my throat. I believed he was to die soon; when, I did not know; but the grim gesture of the jailer had conveyed a hint that could not be mistaken.

At dawn I stood up to gaze fearfully out into the prison yard. Snow had fallen; workmen were digging at the holes with pick and crow.

When the jailer brought breakfast to us, he laid two bundles of sail-cloth on the floor under the windows beyond our cage. Later he returned and carefully nailed each strip of cloth over the windows, hiding our view of the prison yard.

Mount asked him why he did that; the other prisoners became restless and suspicious, calling out to the jailer in Spanish and Portuguese; even the Englishman broke his long silence with a sneering inquiry as to the reason of cutting off our view. The jailer continued his task without answering or even glancing at the imprisoned men, who now crowded against the bars, clamouring, gesticulating, and clanking their manacles. They were stunted, swarthy fellows, bull-necked, shaggy of hair and beard, clothed in filthy shreds of finery to which the straw stuck.

Some were frightfully scarred; some were still swathed in bandages, greasy with filth, tied over unhealed sores or wounds. One of them, who wore large gold hoops in his ears, had lost his right hand, but he beat against the steel bars with the mangled stump, and cried ever: "Listen, señor, you good fellow! Hé! Señor! I say, señor! They will to do me no harm, eh? I am innocent, what? And thus I say to your señor Governor; eh, you good fellow? What? It is the holy truth, by Jesu!"

The Englishman laughed scornfully: "They're planting trees in the yard outside. We'll all climb them soon, won't we, jailer?"

"By God," muttered Mount, "they are planting gallows!"

When he had shrouded the windows, the jailer scrambled briskly to the floor and hastened out through the wicket, unheeding the shouts and shrill cries of the ruffians, who had rushed to the other side of the cage. When the wicket slammed the panic ceased; a dead silence followed, then one of the Spaniards uttered a piercing scream and fell down into the straw, tearing and biting at his chains.

"Die like a man! Die like a man!" said the Englishman, contemptuously; but terror had seized another of the ruffians, and he began hobbling around the cage, shrieking out prayer on prayer.

Mount, pale and composed, lay at full length in our corner, watching the wicket, a straw between his white teeth. I sat beside him, my heart hammering under my torn shirt, resolutely crushing back the terror which was feeling my throat with icy fingers.

"Do you believe they are setting the gibbets?" I asked.

"Yes," he said.

After a moment he added: "Why did you not leave me, lad? This is foul company for a gentleman to die in."

Terror choked me. I sank face downward in the straw, blind with fright, and lay there shaking till the candle was lighted and the lanthorn in the corridor sent its yellow rays through the wicket.

Black, whirling thoughts swarmed through my brain; again and again I fought the battle for courage, only to lose it and again find myself faint with horror, tearing silently at my chains.

"Now that I know I am to die," said Mount, calmly, "I shall die easily enough. It was hope that hurt. I shall die easily."

"I shall die hard," I stammered; "no one will know it, but I shall die hard out there in the snow."

"I will stand next to you if I can," said Mount. "If you feel weak, reach out and touch me. I shall jest with the hangman. It is easy; you will see how easy it can be." I raised my head to look at him.

"You care nothing," I said, fiercely; "you will see Cade Renard, and you care nothing! But I am leaving *her*!"

"God will right all that," said Mount, gravely.

"As for death," I blurted out, pronouncing the word with an effort, "I can die as coolly as you. But—but a gentleman's son—on the gibbet—hanging in chains between thieves—the disgrace—"

Shame strangled the voice in my throat, my head reeled.

"Our Lord so died," said Mount, slowly.

I sat still as a stone. Mount gathered his knees in his hands and chewed his straw peacefully, blue eyes fixed on vacancy.

Presently I plucked his sleeve. "Yes, lad," he said, without turning.

"You are not afraid that I will not know how to meet—it?" I asked.

"No."

"I am—am not afraid," I whispered. "I mean to bear myself without fear. I shall speak to you when—we are ready. You shall see I am not afraid. Will they pray, Jack?"

"When? Now?"

"No, to-morrow."

"They will say a prayer on the gallows, lad."

"Will they take off our chains?"

"No."

"How—how long shall we hang?"

"A long time, lad."

"Could anybody know our features?"

"The weather will change them. Have you never seen a cross-roads gibbet?"

"No. Have you?"

"Yes, lad."

After a silence I said, "I hope no one will know me."

He did not reply; the candle-flame in the dripping socket swayed in icy draughts from the wicket; the Spaniards muttered and moaned and cried like sick children; the Englishman stood in silence, staring at the windows through which he could not see.

Presently he came over to our corner. We had never before spoken to him, nor he to us, but now Mount looked up with a ghost of a smile and nodded.

"It's all behind that window," said the Englishman, jerking his thumb over his shoulder; "we'll know all about it this time to-morrow. Is the young one with you afraid?"

"Not he," said Mount.

The Englishman sat down on his haunches.

"What do you suppose it is?" he asked.

"What? Death?"

"Ay."

"I don't know," said Mount.

"Nor I," said the Englishman, with an oath; "and," he added, "I have dealt it freely enough, too. Have you?"

"Yes," said Mount.

"And he?" glancing at me.

"Once," I replied, hoarsely.

"I've watched men die many times," continued the Englishman, rubbing his thumb reflectively over his irons, "and I'm not a whit the wiser. I've seen them hang, drown, burn, strangle—ay, seen them die o' fright, too. Puff! Out they go at last, and—leave me gaping at their shells. I've slid my hanger into men and the blood came, but I was none the wiser. What makes the dead look so small? Have you ever killed your enemy? Is there satisfaction in it? No, by God, for the second you stop his breath he's gone—escaped! And all you've got is a thing at your feet with clothes too large for it."

He looked at me and played with his wrist-chains. "You're six feet," he said, musingly; "you'll shrink to five foot six. They all do. I'll wager you are afraid, young man!"

"You lie!" I said.

"Spoken well!" he nodded. "You'll die smiling, yet. As for the Spaniards yonder, they'll sail off squalling. It's their nature; I know."

He rose and glanced curiously at Mount.

"You have not followed the sea?" he asked.

Mount shook his head absently.

"Highway?"

"At intervals."

"Well, do you know anything about this place called Death?" asked the Englishman, with a sneer.

"I expect to find a friend there," said Mount, looking up serenely.

At that moment a faint metallic sound broke on our ears. It seemed to come from the depths of the prison. We listened; the Spaniards also ceased their moaning and sat up, alert and quiet. The sound came again—silence—then the measured cadence of footfalls.

Mount had risen; I also stood up. The Spaniards burrowed into the straw, squealing like rats. Tramp, tramp, tramp, came the heavy footfalls along the corridor; the ruddy gleam of lanthorns played over the wicket.

"Halt! Ground arms!"

Lights blinded our dazzled eyes; bayonets glittered like slender flames.

An officer stepped to the lanthorn; a soldier raised it; then the officer unrolled a parchment and began to read very rapidly. I could not distinguish a word of it for the cries of the Spaniards, but I saw the jailer unlocking our cage, and presently two soldiers stepped in and drove out a Spaniard at the point of their bayonets.

Shrieking, sobbing, supplicating, the Spaniards were thrust out into the corridor; the Englishman went last, with a contemptuous nod at Mount and me, and a cool gesture to the soldiers to stand aside.

Mount followed; but, as he stepped from the cage, a soldier pushed him back, shaking his head.

"Not yet?" asked Mount, quietly.

"Not yet," said the soldier, locking the cage and flinging the iron key to the jailer.

Into the prison passed the tumult; the solid walls dulled it at last; then came the far echo of a gate closing, and all was silent.

I turned to the draped windows. Dawn whitened the sail-cloth that hung over them. A moment later I heard drums in the distance beating the "Rogues' March."

CHAPTER XXV

We were condemned to death without a hearing by a military court sitting at Fort Hill, before which we appeared in chains. The 19th of April was set for our execution; we were taken back to the south battery in a coach escorted by light horse, and from there conveyed through the falling snow to the brick prison on Queen Street.

This time, however, we were not led into the loathsome "Pirates' Chapel," but the jailers conducted us to the upper tier of the prison, recently finished, and from the barred windows of which we could look out into Long Acre and School Street across the eight gibbets to the King's Chapel. It appeared that England treated condemned highwaymen with more humanity than coast pirates, for our cells were clean and not very cold, and our food was partly butcher's meat. Besides this, they allowed us a gill of rum every three days, an ounce of tobacco once every twenty-four hours, and finally unlocked our irons, leaving us without manacles, in order that the sores on our necks, wrists, and legs might heal.

It was now the 1st of January, 1775. The New Year brought changes to the prison, but the most important change, for us, was the appointment of Billy Bishop as warden of our tier, to replace Samuel Craft, now promoted to chief warden in the military prison on Boston Neck.

The warden, his wife, and his children occupied the apartment at the west end of our corridor; and the day that Craft, the former warden, moved out, and the Bishop family moved in, I believed firmly that at last our fighting chance for life had come.

All day long I watched the famous thief-taker installing his family in their new dwelling-place; doubtless Mount also noted everything from his cell, but I could not communicate with him without raising my voice.

Mrs. Bishop, a blowsy slattern with a sickly, nursing child, sat on a bundle of feather bedding and directed her buxom daughter where to place the furniture. The wench had lost her bright colour, and something, too, in flesh. Her features had become thinner, clean-cut, almost fine, though her lips still curved in that sensual pout which so repels me in man or woman.

That she knew Mount was here under sentence of death was certain; I could see the sorrowful glances she stole at the grating of his cell as she passed it, her bare, round arms loaded with household utensils. And once her face burned vivid as she stole by, doubtless meeting Mount's eyes for the first time since he had bent in his saddle and kissed her in the dark mews behind the "Virginia Arms"—so long, so long ago!

All day the thief-taker's family were busied in their new quarters, and all day long the girl passed and repassed our cells, sometimes with a fearful side glance at the gratings, sometimes with bent head and lips compressed.

My heart began singing as I watched her. Surely, here was aid for us—for one of us at all events.

The early winter night fell, darkening our cells and the corridor outside; anon I heard Bishop bawling for candle and box, and I looked out of my grating into the darkening corridor, where the thief-taker was stumping along the entry bearing an empty candle-stick. Mrs. Bishop followed with the baby; she and her husband had fallen to disputing in strident tones, charging each other with the loss of the candles. As they passed my cell I moved back; then, as I heard their voices growing fainter and fainter down the corridor, I stepped swiftly forward and pressed my face to the grating. Dulcima Bishop stood within two feet of my cell.

"Will you speak to me?" I called, cautiously.

"La! Is it you, sir?" she stammered, all a-tremble.

"Yes; come quickly, child! There, stand with your back to my cell. Are you listening?"

"Yes, sir," she faltered.

"Do you still love Jack Mount?" I asked.

Her neck under her hair crimsoned.

"Will you help him?" I demanded, under my breath.

"Oh yes, yes," she whispered, turning swiftly towards my grating. "Tell me what to do, sir! I knew he was here; I saw him once in the 'Chapel,' but they boxed my ears for peeping—"

"Turn your back," I cut in; "don't look at my grating again. Now, listen! This is the 1st of January. We are to die at dawn on the 19th of April. Do you understand?"

"Yes, sir."

"You are to get us out, do you understand, child?"

"Yes—oh yes, yes! How, Mr. Cardigan? Tell me and I'll do it; truly, I will!"

"Then go to Jack's cell and let him talk to you. And have a care they do not catch you gossiping with prisoners!"

The girl glanced up and down the corridor; a deeper wave of red stained her face, but already I heard Mount calling her in a cautious voice, and she went, timidly, with lowered eyes.

I laid my ear to the grating and listened; they were whispering, and I could not hear what they said. Once an echoing step in the entry sent the girl flying across the corridor into her room, but it was only a night keeper on his rounds, and he went on quickly, tapping the lock of each cell as he passed. When the glimmer of his lanthorn died away in the farther passages, the girl flew back to Mount's grating. I listened and watched for a sign of Bishop and his wife.

"Jack," I called out in a low voice, "tell her to find Shemuel if she can."

"Quiet, lad," he answered; "I know what is to be done."

Before I could speak again, a distant sound warned the girl to her room once more; presently Bishop came stumping back, holding a lighted candle and still disputing with his slattern wife.

"You did! I tell you I seen you!" he grunted. "You left them candles in the wood-box."

"Well, why didn't you say so before you tore up all the parcels?" demanded his wife, shrilly.

"Oh, quit your nagging!" he snarled. "All the rogues in the prison will be laughing at you!"

"Let 'em laugh! Let 'em laugh!" she panted, waddling along furiously beside him; "I can't help it. I know I married a fool. Bishop, you're a fool, and you know it, and everybody knows it, so don't pick on me, for I won't have it!"

I saw the termagant as she passed my door, tagging after the thief-taker, who looked surly enough, but evidently was no match for the dirty shrew at his heels. How pitiful and petty their anger to a man in the shadow of death! But their wrangling voices were presently shut out as their door slammed. I waited a while, but heard nothing more, so took myself off to the corner, there to lie on my iron cot and try to think.

A young moon hung over King's Chapel, shedding a tremulous light on the snowy parade. Very dimly I could make out the tall shapes of eight gibbets, stark and black against the starry sky. There was no wind; the pendent bundles of bones and chains which hung from each gibbet did not sway as they had swayed that morning in a flurry of wind-driven snow, while the brazen drums of the marines played eight souls into hell eternal.

I watched the stars, peacefully, thinking of the stars that lighted our misty hills in Johnstown; I thought of Silver Heels and my love for her, and how, by this time, she must deem me the most dishonourable and craven among men. I thought of this calmly; long since I had weathered the storms of grief and rage impotent, which had torn me with their violence night after night as I lay in chains in the "Chapel."

No; all would yet be well; some day I should hold her in my arms. All would be well; some day I should hold the life of Walter Butler on my sword's point, and send his red soul howling! Yes, all would be well—

A ray of light fell on my face; I turned and sat up on the edge of my cot as the key in the cell door gritted.

Full under the flare of a lanthorn stood a man in a military uniform of scarlet and green. Behind him appeared Warden Bishop, holding the lanthorn.

"This is the Weasel, sir," he said, "at least he goes by that name, although the Weasel I have chased these ten years was a different cut of a rogue. But it's all one, captain; he was took with Jack Mount, and he'll dance a rope-jig the 19th of April next."

"Why not sooner?" asked the officer, gravely.

I started, quivering in every limb.

"Why not hang him sooner?" inquired Walter Butler, moving back a step into the corridor. He limped as he walked and leaned on a cane. My mark was still upon him.

"Well, sir," said Bishop, scratching his ears, "we hung eight coast-scrapers in November, and two sheep-thieves in December. We've got three pickpockets to swing this month, then Symonds, the wharf-robber, is to go in February. There's no room in March either, because the Santa Cruz gang goes up the 13th—seven o' them in chains—and the gallows yonder ain't dropped last year's fruit yet, and the people hereabouts complains o' the stench of a hot day and a south wind—"

"Can't he change places with some other rogue?" interrupted Butler, impatiently.

"Lord, no!" cried Bishop, horrified. "Leastways, not unless the court-martial directs it, sir. They don't do no such things in Boston, sir."

"They do in Tryon County," observed Butler, eying me coolly. Presently a ghastly smile stretched his pallid face, but his yellow eyes glared unchanging.

"Well, well," he said, "so you are to sail to glory at a rope's end, eh? You wouldn't burn, you know. But the flames will come later, I fancy. Eh, Mr.—er—Mr. Weasel?"

"Are your broken bones mended?" I asked, quietly.

"Quite mended, thank you."

"Because," I said, "you will need them some day—"

"I need them now," he said, cheerfully; "I am to wed a bride ere long. Give me joy, Weasel! I am to know the day this very night."

I could not utter a sound for the horror which froze my tongue. He saw it; fastened his eyes on my face, and watched me, silent as a snake with its fangs in its paralyzed prey.

"Would you care to see the famous Jack Mount, captain?" asked Bishop, swelling with pride. "I took him myself, sir. All the papers had it—I have the cuttings in my room; I can fetch them, sir—"

Butler did not appear to hear him.

"Yes," he continued, thoughtfully, "I ride this night to Lexington. She's a sweet little thing—a trifle skinny, perhaps. I think you have seen her—perhaps picked her pocket. When we are wed we shall come to Boston—on the 19th of April next."

I sprang at him; I had gone stone-blind with rage, and knew not what I did; the steel door crashed in my face; the locks rattled.

Outside the door I heard Butler's cool voice, continuing: "But if she pleases me not, to-night, I may change my mind and take her for my mistress—as Sir William took your aunt—as my friend General Gage has taken your old sweetheart, Mrs. Hamilton. One wench is like another in silken petticoats. Sleep soundly, Master Weasel. If I find her too thin for my taste I'll leave her for Dunmore."

All that night I lay on the stone floor of my cell, by turns inert, stupid, frantic.

When Bishop came to me in the morning he thought me ill and summoned the prison apothecary to cup me; but ere that individual appeared with his pills and leeches, I was quiet and self-possessed, ready to argue with the pill-roller and convince him I needed no nostrums. All that day I watched for Dulcima; twice I saw her go to Mount's cell, but could hear nothing of what they whispered.

Now as I was standing, looking out of the grating, I chanced to glance down, and saw that the apothecary had left his case of herbs and drugs on a bench which stood just outside my cell door.

Idly I read the labels on the bottles and boxes: "Senna, Jalap, Brimstone, Es. Cammomile, Saffron Pills, Tinc. Opium—"

Opium? An easy death.

I gazed at the dark flask, scarcely a foot below me, but as safe from me as though under lock and key. Presently I turned around; my cell contained a cot, an iron table, a bowl for washing, and a towel.

After a moment's thought I caught up the coarse towel, drew from it some threads, twisted them, tied on more threads, and then, greasing the cord with a bit of soap, made a running noose at the end.

There was nobody in the corridor. I heard voices in Bishop's room, whither the apothecary had gone to examine the baby at Mrs. Bishop's summons. Very carefully I let down my thread, fishing for the bottle's neck with my slip-noose; but the neck was so placed that I could not snare it, and I drew up another bottle instead, bearing the label: "*Ex. S. Nigrum.*"

What *Ex. S. Nigrum* might be I did not know, but hid the tiny flask under a loose fragment of stone in my flooring where a black beetle had his abode. Scooping out for it a little hole in the damp earth, I buried it, not harming my friend the beetle; then I returned to fish for my opium flask, but could not snare it. Finally I drew in my string just as the apothecary came out with Mrs. Bishop at his heels.

He stood a moment, talking, then picked up his cow-hide case, closed it, and took himself off.

That night, when the corridor was dusky and Bishop sprawled outside his door to smoke his evening pipe, I called to him and asked him for a jug of water. He fetched it and seemed disposed to linger and chat a bit, but I was uncommunicative, and presently he left me to my own devices, lighting the lanthorn in the corridor ere he retired to his room with his long pipe.

I now unearthed my flask containing the *Ex. S. Nigrum*, poured a single drop into my basin, filled it up with water, and then returned the flask to its hiding-place.

"We shall see," I muttered, "whether there be any virtue of poison in my *Nigrum*," and I caught the poor little black beetle who had come out to enjoy the lamplight.

Now as the drop of *Ex. S. Nigrum* had been diluted many hundreds of times by the water in my bowl, I argued that, if this solution dealt death to the beetle, a few drops, pure, would put Jack Mount and me beyond the hangman's hands.

Poor little beetle! how he struggled! I was loath to sacrifice him, but at last I dropped him into the bowl.

He did not swim; I watched him for a moment, and finally touched him. The little thing was stone dead.

That I had a terrible and swift poison in my possession I now believed; and my belief became certainty when the apothecary came next day in a panic, crying out to Bishop that he had lost a flask of nightshade syrup, and feared lest the infant might find it and swallow the poison.

I watched Bishop and his wife rummaging their rooms in a spasm of panic, and finally saw them go off with the puling pill-roller to report the loss to the head warden.

Later that day a turnkey searched my cell, but did not see the cracked corner of the stone slab, which I covered with one foot.

When all was quiet, I called to Dulcima and bade her tell Jack Mount that I had the poison and would use it on us both if we could not find other means to escape the gallows.

The poor child took the message, and presently returned, wiping her tears, to say that Jack had every hope of liberty; that I must not despair or take the life which no longer was at my own disposal, and that she, Dulcima, had already communicated with Shemuel.

She handed me a steel awl, telling me to pick at the mortar which held the stones on my window-ledge, and to fill these holes with water every night, so that the water might freeze and crack the stones around the base of the steel bars.

I had never thought of such a thing! I had often seen the work of frost on stones, but to take advantage of nature in this manner never occurred to me.

Eagerly and cautiously I set to work with my little steel pick, to drill what holes I might before Bishop came. But it was heart-breaking labour, and so slow that at the end of a week I had not loosened a single bar.

The next week the weather was bitterly cold. I had drilled some few holes around the base of an iron stanchion, and now I filled them with water and plugged them with a paste of earth from beneath my flooring, threads from my towel, and some soap.

At dawn I was at my window, and to my delight found the stone cracked; but the iron bar was as firm as ever, so I set to drilling my holes deeper.

At the end of that week Dulcima let me know that Jack had loosened one bar of his window, and could take it from its socket whenever I was ready. So I worked like a madman at my bar, and by night was ready to charge the holes with water.

It was now the middle of March; a month only remained to us in which to accomplish our liberty, if we were to escape at all.

That night I lay awake, rising constantly to examine my work, but to my despair the weather had slowly changed, and a warm thaw set in, with rain and the glimmer of distant lightning. In vain I worked at my bar; I could see the dark sky brighten with lightning; presently the low mutter of thunder followed. An hour later the rain fell hissing into the melting snow in the prison yard.

I sent word to Mount that I could not move my bar, but that he must not wait for me if he could escape from the window. He answered that he would not stir a peg unless I could; and the girl choked as she delivered the message, imploring me to hasten and loose the bar.

I could not do it; day after day I filled the cracks and holes, waiting for freezing weather. It rained, rained, rained.

Weeks before, Mount had sent the girl to seek out Mr. Foxcroft and tell him of my plight. I also had sent by her a note to Silver Heels.

The girl returned to report that Mr. Foxcroft had sailed for England early in November, and that nobody there had ever heard of a Miss Warren in Queen Street.

Then Butler's boast came to me, and I sent word to Shemuel, bidding him search the village of Lexington for Miss Warren. I had not yet heard from him.

Meanwhile Mount communicated, through Dulcima, with the Minute Men's Club, and already a delegation headed by Mr. Revere had waited on Governor Gage to demand my release on grounds of mistaken identity.

The Governor laughed at them, asserting that I was notorious; but as the days passed, so serious became the demands from Mr. Revere, Mr. Hancock, and Mr. Otis that the Governor sent Walter Butler to assure these gentlemen that he knew Mr. Cardigan well, and that the rogue in prison, who pretended to that name, was, in fact, a notorious felon named the Weasel, who had for years held the highway with the arch-rogue, Mount.

At this, Shemuel came forward to swear that Mr. Butler and I were deadly enemies and that Butler lied, but he was treated with scant ceremony, and barely escaped a ducking in the mill-pond by the soldiers.

Meanwhile Mr. Hancock had communicated with Sir John at Onondaga, and awaited a reply to his message, urging Sir John to come to Boston and identify me.

No reply ever came, nor did Sir John stir hand or foot in my behalf. Possibly he never received the message. I prefer to think so.

Matters were at this pass when I finally gave up all hope of loosening my window bars, and sent word to Jack Mount that he must use his sheets for a cord and let himself out that very night. But the frightened girl returned with an angry message of refusal from the chivalrous blockhead.

The next day it was too late; Bishop's suspicions somehow had been aroused, and it took him but a short time to discover the loosened bars in Jack Mount's cell.

How the brute did laugh when he came on the work accomplished. He searched Mount's cell, discovered the awl and a file, shouted with laughter, summoned masons to make repairs, and, still laughing, came to visit me.

I had not dared to leave my poison-flask in the hole under the stone. What to do with it I did not know; but, as I heard Bishop come chuckling towards my cell, I drove the glass stopper into the flask firmly as I could, then, wiping it, placed it in my mouth, together with the small gold ring I had bought in Albany, and which I had, so far, managed to conceal.

It was a desperate move; I undressed myself as he bade me, and sat on my bed, faint with suspense, while Bishop rummaged. He found the hole where I had hidden the flask. The awl lay there, and he pouched it with a chuckle.

When Bishop had gone, I drew the deadly little flask from my mouth, trembling, and chilled with sweat. Then I placed it again in its hiding-place, hid the ring in my shoe, and dressed slowly, brushing my shabby clothes, and returning the pockets and flaps which Bishop in his careful search had rifled. He did not search my cell again.

And now the days began to run very swiftly. On the 18th of April, towards five o'clock in the evening, a turnkey, passing my cell, told me that General Gage was in the prison with a party of ladies, and that he would doubtless visit my cell. He added, grimly, that the death-watch was to be set over us in an hour or two, and that, thereafter, I could expect no more visitors from outside until I held my public reception on the gallows.

Laughing heartily at his own wit, the turnkey passed on about his business, and I went to the grating to listen and look out into the twilight of the corridor.

Mrs. Bishop, whose sick baby was squalling, lighted the lanthorn above the door of her room, and retired, leaving me free to converse with Mount.

"Jack," I called, hoarsely, "the death-watch begins to-night."

"Pooh!" he answered, cheerfully. "Wait a bit; there's time to cheat a dozen gibbets 'twixt this and dawn."

"Yes," said I, bitterly, "we can cheat the hangman with what I have in this little flask."

"You must give it to the girl," he said. "She will flavour our last draught with it if worst comes to worst. She will be here in a moment."

At that instant I caught sight of Dulcima Bishop, her cloak all wet with rain, passing quickly along the corridor towards Mount's cell; and I called her and gave her my flask, glad to have it safe at least from the search which the death-watch was certain to make.

The poor child turned pale under the scarlet hood of her witch-cloak when I bade her promise to serve us with a kinder and more honourable death than the death planned for us on the morrow.

"I promise, sir," she said, faintly, raising her frightened white face, framed by the wet cloak and damp strands of hair. She added timidly: "I have a knife for—for Jack—and a file."

"It is too late for such things," I answered, quietly. "If it is certain that you cannot get the keys from your father, there is no hope for us."

Her face, which in the past month had become terribly pinched and thin, quivered; her hands tightened on the edge of the grating. "If—if I could get the keys—" she began.

"Unless you do so there is no hope, child."

There was a silence; then she cried, in a choking voice: "I can get them! Will that free Jack? I will get the keys; truly, I will! Oh, do you think he can go free if I open the cell?"

"He has a knife," I said, grimly; "I have my two hands. Open the cells and we will show you."

She covered her eyes with her hands. Jack called to her from his grating; she started violently, turned and went to him.

They stood whispering a long time together. I paced my cell, with brain a-whirl and hope battering at my heart for the admittance I craved to give. If she could only open that door!—that rusted, accursed mass of iron, the very sight of which was slowly crushing out the last spark of manhood in me!

"Are you listening?" whispered Dulcima at my grating again.

"Yes," I answered.

"Watch our door at seven to-night!" she said. "Be ready. I will open your door."

"I am ready," I answered.

At that moment the sound of voices filled the corridor; the girl fled to her room; a dozen turnkeys shuffled past, bowing and cringing, followed by Collins, the chief warden, an old man whom I had not before seen. Then came a gentleman dressed in a long dark cloak which hung from twin epaulettes, his scarlet and gold uniform gleaming below. Was that the Governor?

He passed my cell, halted, glanced around, then retraced his steps. After a moment I heard his voice distinctly at some distance down the corridor; he was saying:

"The highwaymen are here, Mrs. Hamilton—if—if you would care to see them."

I sat up in my cot, all a-tremble. Far down the corridor I heard a woman laughing. I knew that laugh.

"But," persisted the Governor, "you should really see the highwaymen, madam. Trust me, you never before beheld such a giant as this rogue, Jack Mount."

The voices seemed to be receding; I sprang to my grating; the Governor's bland voice still sounded at some distance down the passage; Mrs. Hamilton's saucy laughter rang faintly and more faintly.

Half a dozen keepers were lounging just outside of my cell. I summoned one of them sharply.

"Tell General Gage that Mrs. Hamilton knows me!" I said. "A guinea for you when she comes!"

The lout stared, grinned, and finally shambled away, pursued by the jeers of his comrades. Then they turned their wit against me, begging to know if I had not some message for my friends the Grand Turk and the Emperor of China.

I waited in an agony of suspense; after a long time I knew that the keeper had not delivered my message.

In the fierce returning flood of despair at the loss of this Heaven-sent chance for life, I called out for Bishop to come to me; I struck at the iron bars until my hands were bathed in blood.

At length Bishop arrived, in a rage, demanding to know if I had lost my senses to create such an uproar when his Excellency, Governor Gage, had come to inspect the prison.

In vain I insisted that he take my message; he laughed an ugly laugh and refused. Mrs. Bishop, whose infant was now very sick, came out, wrapped in her shawl, carrying the baby to the prison hospital for treatment, and a wrangle began between her and Bishop concerning supper.

My words were lost or ignored; Bishop demanded his supper at once, and his wife insisted that she must take the child to the hospital. The precious moments flew while they stood there under my grating, disputing and abusing each other, while the sick child wailed ceaselessly and dug its puny fingers into the sores on its head.

Presently a keeper passed, saying that the Governor wished to know what such indecent noise meant; and Bishop, red with rage, turned on his wife and cursed her ferociously until she retreated with the moaning child.

"Draw me a measure o' buttry ale; d'ye hear, ye slut?" he growled, following her. "If I'm to eat no supper till you get back, I'll want a bellyful o' malt to stay me!"

But Mrs. Bishop waddled on contemptuously, declaring she meant to go to the hospital, and that he could die o' thirst for aught she cared.

Dulcima, who stood in her doorway across the corridor, watched the scene stolidly. Bishop turned on her with an oath, and ordered her to draw his evening cup; she unhooked the tankard which hung under the lanthorn, hesitated, and looked straight at her father. He gave her a brutal shove, demanding to know why she dawdled while he thirsted, and the girl moved off sullenly, with flaming cheeks and eyes averted.

When she returned from the buttry I saw the warden take the frothing tankard, brush the foam away with his forefinger, and drain the measure to the dregs.

He handed the empty tankard to his daughter, smacking his lips with a wry face, and drawing the back of his hand across his chin. Then he became angry again.

"Ugh!" he muttered; "the ale's spoiled! What's in it, you baggage?" he demanded, suddenly swinging around on his daughter. "Draw me a cider cup to wash this cursed brew out o' me!"

There was a crash. The girl had dropped the tankard at her feet.

Quick as a flash Bishop raised his hand and dealt his daughter a blow on the neck that sent her to her knees.

"Break another pot and I'll break your head, you drab!" he roared. "Get up or I'll—"

He choked, gasped, lifted his shaking hand to his mouth, and wiped it.

"Curse that ale!" he stammered; "it's sickened me to the bones! What in God's name is in that brew?"

He turned and pushed open his door, lurching forward across the threshold with dragging feet. A moment later Dulcima passed my cell, her trembling hands over her eyes.

I went to my cot and lay down, face buried, teeth set in my lip. A numbness which at moments dulled the throbbing of my brain seemed to settle like chains on every limb.

Dully I waited for the strokes of the iron bell sounding the seventh hour; a lassitude crept over me—almost a stupor. It was not despair; I had long passed that; it was Hope, slowly dying within my body.

A few moments afterwards a strange movement inside my cell aroused me, and I opened my hot eyes.

In the dusk I saw the figure of a man seated beside my cot; peering closer, I perceived his eyes were fixed steadily on me. I sat up on my bed and asked him what he desired.

He did not answer. A ray of candle-light stealing through the barred window fell on the bright barrel of a pistol which lay across his knees.

"What do you wish?" I repeated, the truth dawning on me. "Can you not watch me from the corridor as well as in my cell?"

There was no reply.

Then at last I understood that this gray shape brooding there at my bedside was a guard of the death-watch, pledged never to leave me, never to take his eyes from me for an instant until the warden of the prison delivered me into the hands of the sheriff on the morrow for my execution.

Ding-dong! Ding-dong! The prison bell was at last striking the seventh hour. I lay still in my blanket, counting the strokes which rang out in thin, peevish monotony, like the cracked voice of a beldame repeating her petty woes.

At the last jangle, and while the corridor still hummed with the thin reverberations, I rose and began to pace my narrow cell, head bent on my breast, but keeping my eyes steadily on the grating.

The guard of the death-watch observed me sullenly. I drank from my pot of water, bathed my feverish face, and walked to the grating.

The lanthorn above Bishop's doorway burned brightly; the corridor was quiet. No sound came from Mount's cell. I could hear rain drumming on a roof somewhere, that was all.

Bishop was due at seven o'clock to inspect our bolts and bars; he had always arrived punctually. I watched his door. Presently it occurred to me that I had not seen Bishop since six o'clock when he had gone into his room, cursing the ale which his daughter had fetched him. This was unusual; he had never before failed to sit there on his threshold after supper, smoking his long clay pipe, and blinking contentedly at our steel bolts.

Minute after minute passed; behind me I heard my guard beating a slight tattoo with his heavy boots on the stones.

Suddenly, as I stood at my grating, I saw Dulcima Bishop step from the warden's door, close it behind her, and noiselessly lock it on the outside. The light of the lanthorn fell full on her face; it was ghastly. The girl stood a moment, swaying, one hand on the door; then she made a signal towards Mount's cell; and the next instant I saw Jack Mount bound noiselessly into the corridor. He caught sight of me, held up a reddened, dripping knife, pointed to my cell door, and displayed a key.

Instantly I turned around and sauntered away from the grating towards my tumbled bed. As I passed the death-watch, he rose and walked over to the outer window where my pot of water stood to cool.

Eying me cautiously he lifted the jug and drank, then set the pot back and silently resumed his seat, laying his pistol across his knees.

How was I to get at him? If Mount made the slightest noise in the corridor, the guard was certain to go to the grating.

Pretending to be occupied in smoothing out my tumbled bedding, I strove to move so that I might get partly behind him, but the fellow's suspicions seemed to be aroused, for he turned his head as I moved, and watched me steadily.

To spring on him meant to draw his fire, and a shot would be our undoing. But whatever I did must be done now; I understood that.

As I hesitated there, holding the blanket in my hands as though I meant to fling it on the bed again, the lamp in the corridor suddenly went out, plunging my cell in darkness.

The guard sprang to his feet; I fairly flung my body at him, landing on him in a single bound, and hurling him to the stone floor.

Instantly the light of the lanthorn flooded my cell again; I heard my iron door opening; I crouched in fury on the struggling man under me, whose head and arms I held crushed under the thick blanket. Then came a long, silent struggle, but at last I tore the heavy pistol from his clutch, beat him on the head with the steel butt of it until, through the blanket over his face, red, wet stains spread, and his straining chest and limbs relaxed.

Pistol in hand, I rose from the lifeless heap on the floor, and turned to find my cell door swinging wide, and Dulcima Bishop watching me, with dilated eyes.

"Is he dead?" she asked, and broke out in an odd laugh which stretched her lips tight over her teeth. "Best end him now if he still lives," she added, with a sob; "death is afoot this night, and I have done my part, God wot!"

I struck the man again—it sickened me to do it. He did not quiver.

She lifted the lanthorn from the floor and motioned me to follow. At the end of the corridor Mount stood, wiping his reeking knife on the soft soles of his moccasins.

"The trail's clear," he whispered, gayly; "now, lass, where is the scullions' stairway? Blow out that light, Cardigan! Quiet, now—quiet as a fox in the barn! Give me your hand, lass—and t'other to the lad."

The girl caught me by the arm and blew out the light, then she drew me into what seemed to be an impenetrable wall of darkness. Groping forward, I almost fell down a steep flight of stone steps which appeared to lead into the bowels of the earth. Down, down, then through a passage, Mount leading, the girl fairly dragging me off my feet in her excitement, and presently a wooden door creaked open, and a deluge of icy water dashed over me.

It was rain; I was standing outside the prison, ankle-deep in mud, the free wind blowing, the sleet driving full in my eyes.

"Oh, this is good, this is good!" muttered Mount, in ecstasy, spreading out his arms as though to take the world to his sick heart once more. "Smell the air, lad! Do you smell it? God! How sweet is this wind in my throat!"

The girl shivered; her damp, dishevelled hair blew in her face. She laid one shaking hand on Mount's wet sleeve, then the other, and bowed her head on them, sobbing convulsively.

Mount bent and kissed her.

"I swear I will use you kindly, child," he said, soberly. "Come, lass, gay! gay! What care we for a brace o' dead turnkeys? Lord, how the world will laugh at Billy Bishop when they hear I stole his girl, along with the prison keys! Laugh with me, lass! I mean honestly and kindly by you; I'm fit for a rope at the gibbet's top if I use you ill!"

"Would—would you truly wed me?" she stammered, raising her white face to his.

He swore roundly that he would wed her and end his days in serving her on his marrow-bones for gratitude.

And, as he made his vow, a startling change passed over her face; she laughed, turned her bright, feverish eyes on us with a reckless toss of her head, and drew the poison-flask from her bosom.

"You think," she said, "that we no longer need this little friend to sorrow? You are wrong!"

And, ere Mount or I could move, she raised the tiny flask betwixt forefinger and thumb, and dropped the dark scarlet contents between her teeth.

"I drink to your freedom, Jack," she said, blindly, reeling into Mount's arms. "Your—freedom—Jack," she gasped, smiling; "my father drank to it—in ale. He lies dead on the floor of it. All this—for—for your freedom, Jack!"

Mount was kneeling in the mud; she lay in his arms, the sleet pattering on her upturned face.

"For your freedom," she murmured, drowsily—"a maid must burn in hell for that. I burn, I burn! Oh, the fire in me, Jack!"

Her body writhed and twisted; her great bright eyes never left his. Presently she lay still. A moment later the prison bell broke out wildly through the storm, and a gunshot rang from the north guard-house.

We placed the dead child under a tree in the new grass, and covered her face with willow branches, all silky with the young buds of April. Then, bending almost double, we ran south along the prison wall, turning west as the wall turned, and presently came to the wooden fence of King's Chapel.

Mount gained the top of the fence from my shoulders, and drew me up. Then we dropped.

There were lights moving in Governor's Alley and the mews; through the sleet great snow-flakes whirled into the slush of the filthy street. The prison bell rang frantically behind us.

"It's the alarm, Jack!" I whispered.

He gave me a dull look, then shivered in his wet buckskins.

"She can't lie out there in the sleet," he muttered, blood-shot eyes roving restlessly in the darkness. "I am going back!"

"For God's sake, don't do that!" I begged; but he cursed me and brushed me aside.

Back over the wall he dropped. I started to follow, but he shoved me roughly and bade me mind my own concerns.

I leaned against the foot of the wall; the sleet pelted me; I bared my throat to it. After a while I heard Mount's labouring breath on the other side of the wall, and I climbed up to aid him.

He held the dead child in his arms; I took the body from him; he climbed over, and received it again, bearing it as though it were but a snow-flake's weight in his great arms.

"Go you and find a pick and spade in the mews, yonder," he said. There was a fixed stare in his eyes that alarmed me. "Damn you," he said, "it is the least we can do!"

"Jack," I said, "we cannot stay here to be taken again! You cannot bury her now; the ground is frosted; people will hear us!"

He glared at me, then swung his heavy head right and left. The next moment he started running through the storm, cradling the burden in his arms. I followed, not knowing what he meant to do.

At the King's Chapel gate he turned in along a dim gravel path, hedged with dripping box. Around us lay the headstones of the dead, with here and there a heavy tomb looming up in the storm around us.

For a moment he halted, peering about him. A square white sepulchre surmounted a mound on his right; he motioned me to hold the dead child and stepped forward, laying his hands on the slab. Then, with a heave of his powerful back, he lifted the huge stone, laying open the shadowy sepulchre below.

Again he took the dead in his arms, wiped the rain-drops from the face, laid the limp form in the sepulchre, and smoothed the clothing. Together we replaced the slab; it taxed all my strength to lift one end of it. The bell of the prison clanged frantically.

Mount stood back, breathing heavily, hands hanging. I waited in silence.

"What a little thing she was!" he muttered; "what a child—to—do—that! Do you think she will lie easy there?"

"Yes," I said.

At the sound of my voice Mount roused and turned sharply to me.

"The thief and the thief-taker's daughter!" he whispered, with a ghastly laugh. "They'll make a book of it—I warrant you!—and hawk it for a penny in Boston town!"

He touched the slab, all glistening with sleet, gripped the edge of the sepulchre, turned, and shook his fist at the prison. Then, quietly passing his arm through mine, he led the way out of the chapel yard, guiding me between the soaking hedges to the iron gate, and so out into the black alley.

Almost immediately a man shouted: "Stop thief! Turn out the guard!" and a soldier, in the shadow of the wall, fired at us.

Mount glared at him stupidly, hands dangling; the soldier ran up to him and presented his bayonet, calling on us to give up.

The sound of his voice appeared to rouse Mount to fury; he seized the musket, wrenched it from the soldier, and beat him into the mud. Then swinging the weapon by the barrel, he knocked down two bailiffs who were closing in on us, and started after another, with a yell of rage.

"Jack! Jack!" I cried. "Are you mad? Follow me; quick! We can't stay here, you great fool!"

He heard me, halted, hurled the musket after his flying foe, and broke out into a harsh laugh.

"Come on, lad," he said. "I did but mean to warm my blood and purge it of the prison rust. Truly I think we must make for the purlieus till they lose our trail!"

Through reeking lanes, foul alleys, and muddy mews where gaunt dogs battled over scraps with gaunter children, we ran, or lurked to listen, shunning the bleared lanthorn-light, shining through the storm.

At times the horror of that flight even now appalls me—that flight through the starving town o' Boston, where old women mouthed at us with their scurvy-cankered gums; where, slinking along dead walls, we stumbled over old men patiently picking with skinny fingers in the rotted herbage for roots to stay their starved stomachs' craving; where, in doorways, naked children, with bellies bloated by famine, stared at us out of hollow eyes.

The town appeared to be alive with British soldiery; mounted pickets roved through the streets; parties of officers passed continually; squad after squad of marines crossed our path, and at first we thought that all this show of troops was due to us and our escape, the hour being late for so many troops to be abroad.

"There's something else in the wind," muttered Mount, as we hid in Belcher's Lane to avoid a party of dragoons; "all this pother is never made on our account. There's deviltry a-brewing, lad. We had best start for the 'Wild Goose.'"

Through the mud of Cow Lane, Flounder Mews, and Battery Marsh we crept on, on, along back roads and shiny lanes, then, alarmed by a galloping dragoon, we threaded the marshy alleys to the north, from Hancock's Wharf clear around the peninsula to Back Street and Link Alley.

From thence through Hog Alley and Frog Lane south towards the Neck, only to be frightened north once more by the mad gallop of dragoons, and so to hide in Mackerel Lane.

And I am minded, as I recall that night's skulking flight, of a bandy little watchman who, at the mere sight of us, did drop his lanthorn and make off, bawling for aid, until Jack came up with him and fetched him a clip which knocked him and his noisy rattle into the mud of Mackerel Lane.

We fled as though all Boston ran snapping at our shin-bones, and at last we turned, unmolested, into Green Lane, and so came in sight of the "Wild Goose Tavern." Then, as we dropped into a breathless trot and began to plod across Chambers Street, a man, standing in the shadow of a tree, started forward as we came up.

Mount halted and drew his knife, snarling like a jaded wolf.

"Mount! Cardigan!" cried the man.

"Paul!" exclaimed Mount, eagerly.

The goldsmith wrung our hands with a grip of iron.

"It is the beginning of the end," he said. "The Grenadiers are to march. I've a horse on the Charlestown shore. Gage has closed the gates on the Neck."

"What do the Grenadiers want?" asked Mount, all on fire again, fagged and exhausted as he was.

"They want the cannon and stores at Concord," replied Revere, in a low, eager voice. "I'm waiting for Clay Rolfe. If the Grenadiers march by land, Rolfe hangs a lamp in the steeple of the Old North; if they take boats, he hangs two lamps. I guess they mean to cross the bay. The boats have been moored under the sterns of the war-ships for a week. I've a good horse across the water; I'll have the country-folk out by daylight if the troops stir an inch to-night. Wait; there's Rolfe now!"

A dark cloaked figure came swiftly out of the mews, swinging two unlighted lanthorns. It was Clay Rolfe, our landlord at the "Wild Goose," and he grasped our hands warmly, laughing in his excitement.

"Your boatman is ready under Hunt's Wharf, Paul," he said. "You had best row across the bay while the rain lasts. It will clear before midnight, and the *Somerset* is moored close to the *Lively* to-night."

"Yes," said Revere, "I've no mind to run the fleet yonder under a full moon." And he offered his hand to us, one after another, giving our hands a terrific squeeze.

"Don't forget, Rolfe," he said—"one if by land; two if by sea!"

Rolfe turned to us.

"Gage has officers watching every road outside of Boston; but Paul will teach them how fast news can travel." He glanced at the sky; rain fell heavily. "It won't last," he muttered; "there'll be a moon to-night; Paul, you had best row across now. The oars are muffled."

They saluted us and walked rapidly down Green Lane, wrapped to the eyes in their riding-cloaks.

"If Shemuel is at the 'Wild Goose,'" I said, "perhaps he has news for me."

We entered the inn and found it deserted by all save a servant, who recognized us and bade us welcome.

"The Grenadiers are out to-night, sir," he said to me. "All our company has gone to join the Alarm Men at Lexington and Concord. There is not a soul here, sir, except me."

"Where is Shemuel?" I asked.

"He is watching the Province House, sir; General Gage entertains to-night. It is all a ruse to quiet suspicion, sir. But we know what is on foot, Mr. Cardigan!"

Mount had dropped into a chair; the rain dripped from the red thrums of his buckskins; his fox-skin cap was soaked. There was blood on his hands; the servant brought a basin and towel.

"God knows what will happen at Concord," he said; "Mr. Hancock has gone there; Mr. Revere is to ride through Middlesex to raise the farmers. Have you seen the dragoons, sir? They do be riding and capering about town, stopping all mounted travellers. They stopped the Providence coach an hour since, and there was a fight with the towns-people in Beacon Street. The tents of the marines are down on the Mall; some say the storm tore them down."

So gossiping, the lad served us with bread, cheese, pickled beef, and a noggin of punch, and we listened, tearing at our food, and gulping it like famished beasts o' the woods.

He brought me my clothes of buckskin, and I tore my rotten prison rags from me—alas! the shreds of that same silver-velvet suit which I had put on six months since, to wed with Silver Heels.

We stripped to the buff; the lad soused us well with steaming water and again with water like ice.

Mount encased his huge frame in his spare buckskins. I once more dressed in my forest dress, refreshed and fortified by food and water which seemed truly to wash away the prison taint from our skins as the hot bowl of spirits washed the stale prison cheer from within.

The lad brought us our arms, and I could have shouted aloud my joy as I belted in my knife, hatchet, and bullet-pouch, and flung my rifle across my shoulder.

"Where is my horse?" I asked. "Have you looked to him, lad? By Heaven, if aught of mischance has come to him—"

"The great black horse Warlock, sir?" cried the lad. "He is stabled in the mews, sir. Mr. Rolfe has had him cared for like a baby; the head groom takes him out every day, Mr. Cardigan, and the horse is all satin and steel springs, sir."

"Where is he? Get a lanthorn," I said, huskily.

A moment later, in the mews, I heard a shrill whinny, and the tattoo of shod hoofs dancing.

"Warlock!" I cried.

The next instant my arms were around his neck.

CHAPTER XXVI

It was nearly ten o'clock; a freezing rain still swept the black Boston streets, with now and again a volley of hail, rattling on closed shutters and swinging shop-signs.

In the dark mews behind the "Wild Goose Tavern" had gathered a shadowy company of horsemen, unfortunate patriots who had not been quick enough to leave the city before the troops shut its landward gates.

Caught by the Governor's malignant move, separated from their companies of Minute Men, these half-score gentlemen had met at the "Wild Goose" to consult how best they might leave the city and join their comrades at Lexington and Concord.

Some were for riding to the Neck and making a dash across the causeway; some wanted boats, among the latter, Jack Mount, who naturally desired to rid the town of his person as speedily as might be.

"There's a hempen neck-cloth to fit my pipes in Queen Street," he said, plaintively, "and I desire it not, having no mind for flummery. Let us find a flat-boat, in God's name, and get us to Charlestown with our horses while the rain endures."

"Ay," replied an officer of Roxbury Minute Men, "but what if our horses neigh in mid-stream?"

"The *Somerset* ran out her deck-guns at sunset," added another. "What if she turned her swivel on us?"

"And how if they swept us off the causeway with a chain-shot?" asked Mount.

"What think you, Mr. Cardigan?" demanded an officer of Sudbury militia, leaning forward in his wet saddle to pat the dripping neck of his roan.

"I only know that I shall ride this night to Lexington," I said, impatiently, "and I am at your service, gentlemen, by land or sea. Pray you, decide quickly while the rain favours us."

"Is there a man among us dare demand a pass of the Governor?" asked the Sudbury officer, abruptly. "By Heaven, gentlemen, it is death by land or by sea if we make to force the lines this night!"

"And it is death to me if I stay here cackling," muttered Mount, as we caught the distant gallop of dragoons through stony Wiltshire Street.

We sat moodily in our saddles, huddled together in the darkness and rain, listening to the sound of the horses' feet on the pavement.

"I'd give a thousand guineas if I were on the Charlestown shore with Revere," muttered an officer.

"The Governor might sell you a pass for ten," observed another, sneeringly. "It will cost him a penny to keep his pretty bird o' paradise in plumes."

"If John Hancock were here he would get us a pass from Mrs. Hamilton," remarked the Sudbury officer.

There was a silence, then one or two men laughed.

"Is Mrs. Hamilton at Province House?" I asked, not understanding the careless handling of her name among these gentlemen.

Again came laughter.

"It is easy to see that you have been in prison," observed the Sudbury officer. "Mrs. Hamilton rules at Province House, and leads Tommy Gage by the nose—"

"By the *left hand*," interrupted another, maliciously.

"You mean that Mrs. Hamilton is—is—" I began.

"Town scandal," said the officer.

"It may be a lie," observed a young man mounted on a powerful gray.

"It is a lie," I said, with an ugly emphasis.

"Is that remark addressed to me, sir?" demanded the Sudbury officer, sharply.

"And to company, also," I replied.

"Gentlemen!" cried the Roxbury officer, "are we to have quarrels among us at such a time?"

"Certainly," said I, "if you or your company affront me. Tattle is dirty work for a gentleman's tongue, and the sooner that tongue is stopped with honest mud the better."

"I've called a gentleman out for less than that," said an old officer, dryly.

"I am at your service," I replied, disgusted.

"And I'm with you, lad," said Mount, walking up to my stirrup. "I have no stomach for those who wink at a woman's name."

"I also," said the young man on the gray, gravely.

A constrained silence followed, broken by the Sudbury officer.

"Hats off to the beautiful Mrs. Hamilton, gentlemen! Cardigan is right, by God! If we stand not for our women, who will?"

And he stretched out his hand in the rain. I took it; others offered me their hands.

"I ride to Province House," I said, briefly. "Jack, fetch a cloak to hide your buckskins and wait me here. Gentlemen, I wish you fortune in your journey."

As I rode out into Cambridge Street, thunder boomed in the east, and I saw the forked lightning racing through inky heavens, veining the storm with jewelled signs.

"God writes on heaven's wall!" I said, aloud.

A strange exultation stirred me; the dark world lay free and wide before me, and I would ride it, now, from end to end, till Silver Heels was mine and Butler's soul had dropped back into that pit from whence it had crawled to hide within his demon's body.

In Hillier's Lane I put Warlock to a gallop, but drew bridle in muddy Sudbury Street, where, from the darkness, a strident voice called on me to halt.

"Who comes there?" repeated the voice. I heard the trample of horsemen and the clink of sabres striking stirrups.

"Coureur-de-bois for Province House!" I answered, calmly. A chafing temper began to heat my blood; I gathered my bridle and dropped one hand on my hatchet.

"On whose affairs ride you?" demanded the spectral dragoon, laying his horse broadside across mine.

"On my own affairs!" I cried, angrily; "pull out there!—do you hear me, fellow?"

A lanthorn was lifted to my face.

"Let the forest wild-cat go," muttered an officer, riding back to the picket as I crowded my horse against the dragoon who had hailed me.

Without giving them a glance I pushed through the cluster of horsemen, and heard them cursing my insolence as I wheeled into School Street and cantered along Governor's Alley.

There were torches lighted in the mews; an hostler took Warlock; I swung out of the saddle and stepped back to a shelter from the storm.

Through the rain, up Marlborough Street, down School Street, and along Cornhill, drove the coaches and carriages of the Tory quality, all stopping at the brilliantly lighted mansion, where, as an hostler informed me, the

Governor was giving a play and a supper to the wealthy Tory families of Boston and to all the officers of the British regiments quartered in the city. I knew the latter statement was false.

I stood for a while in the rain among the throng of poor who had come to wait there, in patience, on the chance of a scrap from the servants' quarters after the servants had picked the bones their surfeited masters would scarcely deign to lick.

At first, as the coaches dashed up and the chairs jogged into the gateway, a few squalid watchers in the crowd fought to open the carriage-doors, hoping for a coin flung to them for their pains; but the sentinels soon put a finish to this, driving the ragged rabble savagely, with thrusts of their musket-butts, out into Marlborough Street. Under the gate-lanthorn's smeared reflections I saw the poor things huddled in a half-circle, pinched and chattering and white with hunger, soaked to the bone with the icy rain, yet lingering, God knows why, for a brief glimpse of My Lady in pink silk and powder, picking her way from her carriage across the puddles, while My Lord minced at her side and the footman ran behind to cover them both with a glistening umbrella.

The stony street echoed with the clatter of shod horses, the rattle of wheels, the shouts of footmen, and the bawling of chair-bearers.

Once, when the wind sharpened, shifted, and blew the slanting rain from the north, a warm odour of roasted butcher's meats came to us, and I could hear a hollow sound rising from the throng, which was like a groan.

In the Province House fiddlers were fiddling; it was chill enough in the street, but it was doubtless over-hot within, for servants came and threw open the windows and we could hear the fiddles plainly and the sweet confusion of voices and a young girl's laughter.

A hoarse cry broke out, wrung from the very vitals of the wretches around me.

"Silence!" shouted the officer of the gate-guard, striding out in his long rain-cloak and glaring about him, with tasselled stick upraised. The rain powdered his gilded French hat and laced vest, and he stepped back hastily under shelter.

There was perfect quiet for an instant, then a movement near me, a mutter, a quick surging of people, a cry: "Give room! Back there! Bear him up!"

A voice broke out, "He is starving; the smell o' meat sickens him!"

Two men staggered past, supporting a mere lad, whose deathly face hung on his rain-soaked cotton shirt.

"He has the spotted sickness!" muttered a chair-bearer near me; "it's death to take his breath! Let me pass!"

"The pest!" cried another, shrinking back, and stumbling away in a panic.

The officer watched the scene for a moment, then his heavy, inflamed face darkened.

"Back there! Be off, I say!" he bawled. "Ye stinking beggars, d'ye mean to poison us all with the pest? Turn out the gate-guard! Drive those filthy whelps up Cornhill!" he shouted to the corporal of the guard.

The soldiers came tumbling out of the gate-lodge, but before they could move on the throng another officer hurried up, and I heard him sharply recalling the soldiers and rebuking the officer who had given the order.

"No, no, that will not do," he said. "The town would flame if you drive the citizens from their own streets. Let them stand there. What harm are they doing?"

"The lout yonder fell down with the spotted pest," remonstrated the first officer. "Faugh! The rabble's rotten with scurvy or some filthy abomination—"

"They'll harm no one but themselves," replied the other in a sad voice, which sounded strangely familiar to me, so familiar that I involuntarily stepped out into the lighted space under the gate and peered at him through the rain, shielding my eyes with my hands.

The officer was Mr. Bevan.

Should I speak to him? Should I count on his friendship for me to get me an audience with the Governor? Here was a chance; he could vouch for me; so could Mrs. Hamilton.

As I hesitated somebody beside me clutched my elbow, and I swung around instantly, one hand on my hunting-knife.

The next moment Saul Shemuel almost rolled at my feet in an ecstasy of humble delight, sniffling, writhing, breathing hard, and clawing at my sleeve in his transports at sight of me.

I seized his arm, drew him along the wall, and into the dusky mews.

Impatient, yet touched, I suffered his mauling, demanding what news he might have, and he, beside himself with joy and excitement, could scarce find breath to pant out the news which concerned me. "I haf seen Foxcroft," he gasped. "Mr. Foxcroft he hass come to-day on dot *Pomona* frigate to Scarlet's Wharf, twelve weeks from Queenstown, sir. It wass printed in dot *Efening Gazette*, all apout Foxcroft how he iss come from Sir Peter Warren to make some troubles for Sir John Johnson mit dot money he took from Miss Warren, sir!"

"Foxcroft! Here?" I stammered.

"Yess, sir; I ran mit my legs to Queen Street, und I told him how you wass in dot prison come, und he run mit his legs to Province House, but too late, for we hear dot bell ring und dose guns shooting. Und I said, 'Gott of Isaac, I bet you Jack Mount he hass run avay!' Und Mr. Foxcroft he sees some dragoon soldiers come into Cornhill, calling out: 'Dose highwaymens is gone! Vatch 'em by dot Mall!' So Mr. Foxcroft he comes to Province House mit me, sir, und he iss gone in to make some troubles mit Governor Gage apout Sir John Johnson und dot money of Miss Warren! Ach, here iss Mr. Foxcroft, now, sir—"

I turned to confront a stout, florid gentleman, swathed in a riding-cloak, whose little, angry eyes snapped as he cried: "Governor Gage is a meddling ass! I care not who listens to me, and, I repeat, he is a meddlesome ass! Sir Peter Warren shall hear of this, damme! Am I a free agent, damme? I take it that I am a free agent, yet I may not leave this town to-night for lack of a pass. But I'll go! They shall not stop me! No, damme if they shall!"

The hostlers were all staring at him; I stepped towards him, eagerly, but the peppery and inflamed barrister waved me off.

"Damme, sir!" he bawled; "who the devil are you, sir? Take your hands from me, sir! I wish to go to my client in Lexington, and this Tory peacock will give me no pass! I will not suffer this outrage; I will appeal to—"

I gave him a jerk that shook the breath from his body, whispering in his ear: "Be silent, in Heaven's name, sir! I am Michael Cardigan!"

At first, in his passion, astonishment, and incredulity, he found no voice to answer me; but as Shemuel eagerly vouched for me, Mr. Foxcroft's fury and suspicion subsided.

"You? Cardigan?" he repeated. "Well, where the devil have you been, sir, and what the devil have you been about, sir? Eh? Answer me that, now!"

"I've been in prison, under sentence of death," I replied. "Where have *you* been, sir, to leave your client, Miss Warren, at the mercy of Walter Butler?"

At that he took fire, and, with trembling fist quivering towards heaven, he justified his absence in warm terms.

"I've been in England, sir, that's where I've been!" he cried. "I've been there to find out why your blackguard of a kinsman, Sir John Johnson, should rob my client of her property. And I've found out that your blackguard Sir John has not only robbed her of her means, but of the very name she has a right to! That's what I've done, sir. And if it does not please you, you may go to the devil!"

His impudence and oaths I scarcely noted, such a fierce happiness was surging through me to the very bones. I could have hugged the choleric barrister as he stood there, affronting me at every breath; I fairly beamed upon him when he bade me go to the devil, and, to his amazement, I seized his fat hands and thanked him so gratefully that the defiance died on his lips and he stared at me open-mouthed.

"My dear sir, my dear, dear friend," I cried, "I will get you your pass to clear the Neck to-night, and we will go together to find my cousin, Miss Warren. Wait me here, sir; I will leave Boston this night or my name is not Cardigan!"

Then bidding Shemuel keep an eye on Warlock, I hurried around to the gate-house, where the rabble still slunk, watching the lighted windows with famished eyes.

The clouds in mid-heaven had caked into snowy jets of fleece, and now the full moon of April flooded the soaked pavements with pools of silver.

The sentry halted me as I entered the court-yard, but when I asked for Mr. Bevan, he called to a comrade to take my message. The next moment Bevan stepped out into the moonlight.

"What is it, my man? Can I serve you?" he said, pleasantly, peering at me.

"Do you not know me, Mr. Bevan?" I asked.

"Cardigan!" he stammered, "is that you, Cardigan—"

He was close to me at a stride, both hands on my shoulders, his kindly, troubled eyes full of wonder and pity. Perhaps I appeared to him somewhat haggard and careworn, and then the rain had chilled and pinched me.

"I am not in want," I said, trying to smile.

"But—but why are you not among the guests at Province House?" he asked, quickly. "The son of Captain Cardigan needs no friend at court, I fancy."

He linked his gilded sleeve in my arm and drew me past the guard-house, and ere I could protest, I found myself inside the cloak-room among a company of old beaux and young fops, all in the hands of footmen and body-servants who were busily dusting the hair-powder from silken shoulders, smoothing out laces, hanging hats and cloaks to dry, and polishing sword-hilts for their languid, insolent-eyed masters.

"Can we not find a quiet corner hereabouts?" I asked. "I came to demand a pass for Lexington. Will you use your privilege with the Governor, Bevan?"

"A pass!" he exclaimed, stopping short in his tracks.

"To Lexington," I repeated.

"To-night?"

"Yes."

He raised his honest, perplexed eyes to me.

"I must have a pass; it concerns the welfare of Miss Warren," I began, then hesitated, remembering that I was also to take Jack Mount in my company, whose business in Lexington was very different from mine.

"Cardigan," he said, with troubled eyes on me, "I cannot lend myself to such a service, even for Miss Warren's sake, unless you first give me your word of honour that your journey concerns only Miss Warren's welfare."

My heart sank; I could not betray the comrade who counted on me. Jack Mount must get free o' Boston as well as I. But how could I lie to Bevan or requite his courtesy with treachery? Yet honour forbade me to leave Jack Mount, even for Silver Heels's sake.

"Pass or no pass, I go this night," I said, sullenly.

"Hush!" he said; "don't talk here."

He led me through the card-rooms, where a score of old bucks and purple-necked officers sat, all playing picquet in owlish silence, then through a partition, where a fountain sprayed beds of tall ferns, out into a lamp-illumined circular alcove, hung with China silks, and bowered deep in flowers and tiny, blossoming trees no higher than one's knee-buckle.

"The Chinese alcove," he observed. "Nobody will disturb us here, I fancy. You have heard of the Chinese alcove, Cardigan? There is the door to the famous golden gallery."

I glanced at the gilded door in the corner, half-hidden by Chinese drapery. I had heard that the Governor's sweetheart dwelt here.

Bevan reached up and pulled a velvet cord. Presently a servant brought us a silver bowl of steaming punch made with tea and fruit in the Regent's fashion.

"I drink no tea," I said, shortly.

"I suppose not," observed Bevan, laughing, and commanded the servant to fetch me a bowl without tea.

"Your courtesy to a rebel is extraordinary," I said, after an interval.

"Oh, I'm half rebel myself," he laughed. "I'd be in my shirt-sleeves out Middlesex way, drilling yokels—Minute Men, I believe—were it not that—that—oh, well, I'll wear the red jacket as long as I live and let the future weed out the goats from the sheep."

"It's different with you," I said. "You are English bred."

"Ay, and the red o' the uniform has dyed my flesh to the bone," he replied.

"You mean that you will fight—us?" I asked.

"Tooth and nail, my dear fellow," he said, gayly; "foot, horse, and dragoons! But what can I do to serve you—first?"

I tasted a glass of punch, then set it down impatiently. "I tell you I must ride to Lexington," I said, firmly, "and I mean to take friends if I choose—"

"Tell me no more, Cardigan," he broke in, "else I must refuse you what little service I may render. You know as well as I why the gates on the Neck are closed to-night. If you do not know, listen to me. The rebels have been storing war materials. Last October we gave their spokesmen full warning that we could no longer tolerate the collecting of arms and ammunition. We sent expeditions into the country to destroy what stores they had gathered."

He hesitated; a perplexed smile passed over his face. "You know perfectly well," he said, "that we have good reasons for closing the city gates to-night. I cannot give you a pass. Yet, for Miss Warren's sake"—he lifted his hat as he spoke—"I have done what I could in honour. Now I must leave you."

"What have you done?" I asked, angrily.

"I have conducted you to the Chinese alcove, my friend."

"The ante-chamber of the Governor's mistress," I retorted. "Am I to find my pass here among these flowers and blossoms?"

He looked down at the glasses on the table beside us, stirred the contents of his own, and nodded.

"What do you mean?" I demanded, hotly.

"I mean, Cardigan, that, except the Governor, there is only one person to-night in Boston who can secure you a pass for Lexington. If she chooses to do so, it is not my affair."

"If *who* chooses to do so?"

"She."

"Who?"

"Wait and—ask her," he said, gravely.

He was gone, wading waist-deep in flowers, ere I could compose my mind to think or protest, leaving me speechless; standing by the table.

A minute passed; through the thickets of sweet-smelling blossoms the candles flamed like those slender witch-lights that dance over nature's gardens, where bergamot and cardinal robe our dim woods in crimson glory under the October stars.

"What does he mean by leaving me here?" I muttered, pacing to and fro through the fragrant, flowering lane. Then, as I stood still, listening, far away I heard a glass door close with a crystalline clash; there came the rustle of brocade sweeping like a breeze along the passage; the door of the golden gallery swung outward; a figure all silk and lace stood poised on the step above me, screened to the knees behind the flowers.

"Where is the forest-runner who desires a pass to Lexington?" she began; then, perceiving my lank, dark form against the candle-light, she laughed a sweet, contented little laugh and bade me approach.

I saw that exquisite, indolent head bending towards me, the smiling eyes seeking my features, the jewels ablaze at her throat.

"Marie Hamilton!" I stammered.

All her neck and face flamed, then whitened to the hue of death as she stepped swiftly towards me, her brocade sweeping through the flowers with a sound like the wind tearing silken petals. Suddenly she stood still, clearing her startled eyes with one jewelled hand; her knees fell a-trembling; she swayed and caught at the stiff, golden curtains, half tearing them from the wall.

Into a carved chair, all glittering with dragon's wings, she fell, a crumpled heap of lace and jewels, and buried her face in her hands, pressing her fingers into the plump skin.

I watched her miserably; she twisted her white hands before her face; her quivering mouth, her delicate body bent and writhing, all these told me what no words could tell, and her agonized silence shouted her shame to the midnight skies of heaven.

In the hush that followed, the door of the golden gallery swung idly back and forth with a deadened, muffled beat like the noise of great wings flapping.

"Michael," she said, at last.

"Yes," I whispered, in hopeless grief.

Presently she sat up, wearily, one hand on her pale, smooth brow. I could not meet her eyes; I bent my head.

"Oh, God, what punishment is mine!" she sobbed.

She dropped her hands, clasped them, and looked wildly at me through her tears.

"If I am what I am, it was because I had lost you," she said. "I had eaten my heart out—you never came—I never thought you cared—I never thought you cared!" she wailed, twisting her interlocked fingers in helpless agony. "I had loved you so long; I tried to make you understand it, but you would not. I was mortally hurt—I said bitter things—but my heart was yours, Michael, yours for the asking, and so was I; you had only to take me; I would have gone with you from the first word you spoke to me in Johnson Hall—I would have followed you—from the first glance you gave me. Wrong? What is wrong? Love? It is *never* wrong! I would have died for a touch of your lips; I did almost die when you kissed me there, using me so shamelessly with your boyish cruelty! You went away in the night; I searched Johnstown, and I listened and questioned until I believed you had gone to Pittsburg. And I followed you, madly jealous of Felicity, crazed at the thought that she, too, was going to Pitt to be near you. But you were not at Fort Pitt; I waited, and I was calm because I believed that Felicity meant to wed with Dunmore. Then Harrod sent in his list of killed—my husband was among the dead. I went back to Albany. I meant to come to Boston to sell my house: I needed money. You found me there on the road that night; I could have died from happiness, but you would not understand me, Michael!" she ended, piteously.

I kept my eyes on the floor.

"And now, since you have been in Boston, all these long months," she cried, "I have not seen you; I could not find you, nor could I find anybody who had ever seen you. God knows I did not think to see you here since I, destitute, utterly desperate, caring nothing for life, took—this—shameful—step—"

She covered her hot face with her hands.

"Can you believe I love you still?" she sobbed.

I could endure no more; already I had stumbled through the flowery hedge towards the door, blindly forcing a path amid the blossoms which threw out a hundred tendrils to bar my way.

Once I looked back. She lay in the glittering chair, eyes following me. The next step, and a great bunch of roses blotted her face from my sight.

Through the card-room I hurried, aware of people around me, yet seeing nothing; down the stairway, jostled by people who were descending or mounting, and at last into the cloak-room and out through the court-yard, which was now bright with moonlight shining in the puddles of rain.

Shemuel came from the mews to meet me, leading Warlock. Mr. Foxcroft stalked behind him.

"Where is the pass?" he demanded. "Did you procure the pass, sir? What! Empty-handed! Now, by Heaven!" he cried, in a towering fury, "this Tory Governor presumes too far!"

"Be silent!" I said, sharply; "do you wish to have us all arrested? I shall go to Lexington to-night, I tell you, pass or no pass; and, before I go, you shall tell me where I may find Miss Warren."

"A mile out of Lexington on the Bedford Road," he replied. "How can you pass the Neck guard, without the Governor's leave, sir?"

"I will show you," said I, "if you choose to accompany me."

"You mean to ride for it?" he asked, excitedly.

I was silent.

"And risk a chain-shot from their twenty-four-pounders?" he persisted.

"Mr. Foxcroft," I said, "you may do as you please, but there is nothing under the moon, yonder, which can keep me from going to Lexington. Have you a horse stabled here? No? Can you hire one? Then hire him, in Heaven's name, and get into your saddle if you mean to go with me. Shemuel, find a good horse for Mr. Foxcroft, and another for Jack Mount. You must pay for them; I have no money. It is half-past ten o'clock; I will wait ten minutes."

Shemuel scurried back into the mews; Foxcroft followed, and in a moment his portly figure was lost to sight in the dusky alley.

I looked up at the lighted windows of Province House, wondering how on earth I was to go to Lexington. Music was sounding from the ballroom; I looked out across the dark city; the moon hung over the bay; the rigging of a war-ship rose black against the silvery disk. Instinctively I turned my eyes towards the steeple of the Old North Meeting-House. The steeple was dark; the troops had not yet started.

Musing there in the moonlight, hands clasped on the pommel of my saddle, the dull thunder of hoofs from the stable aroused me, and presently Mr. Foxcroft came clattering out of the mews, followed by Shemuel, also mounted, a grotesque lump of a shape, crouched on the saddle, his flat, three-cornered hat crammed over his great ears, his nose buried in his neck-cloth. He led a third horse behind him.

"Now, sir," panted Foxcroft, "I am prepared to ride to the devil with you and put this Tory Governor's nose out o' joint!"

"Do you also ride with us, Shemuel?" I asked.

He replied faintly in the affirmative. The little creature was frightened. His devotion touched me very deeply.

Walking our horses along Common Street, we were almost immediately accosted by dragoons, who, on learning that our destination was the "Wild Goose Tavern," cursed us roundly, promising to clean out that nest of rebels at no distant date. Their officer also began to harangue us, but I pushed my horse past him and cantered on into the Mall and out through Green Lane, wheeling into the alley behind the "Wild Goose."

Of the half-score gentlemen whom I had left there, sitting their rain-drenched horses, none remained. However, Mount was in the tavern, and he came at my whistle, explaining that the balance of the company had chosen to risk crossing the bay under the guns of the *Somerset*, rather than attempt to force the Neck.

"God go with them!" said I; "here's Shemuel with a horse for you. We'll ride to the shore and see what can be done."

Mount, who had been busily embracing Shemuel, gave the little Jew a mighty slap of affection, vaulted into his saddle, passed my rifle to me, and fell back beside the peddler, while Mr. Foxcroft and I rode through the Mall once more, down towards the shore, where, in the darkness, faint flashes through the trees came and went as the waves of the bay caught the moonlight.

"Is it too far to swim?" I asked Mr. Foxcroft.

"Too far," he replied, with a shiver. "All is marsh beyond; the mud would smother us ere we landed. That shoal yonder is dry at low-water."

"Mr. Foxcroft," said I, "we must swim for it somewhere. Could we not make the Charles River at a pinch?"

"No, nor Stony Brook," he said. "A good swimmer might circle the floating battery and make his way outside the Neck, but he could not last, Mr. Cardigan."

We had been slowly approaching the shore while we spoke. For some time I had fancied I heard sounds in the darkness like the stirring and movement of a body of men assembling. At first I fancied the swelling murmur of the tide deceived me, yet at moments it seemed as though I could distinguish a trampling sound which could not have been the beat of the ocean's steady squadrons on the beach.

Then, as we came out through the fringe of trees from which the land fell away to the water's edge, a stirring sight lay spread before us: below, in the dazzling moonlight, the shore swarmed with soldiers, teamsters, and boatmen, moving hither and thither along the water's edge. Companies of grenadiers were marching towards the wooden wharf at the end of Hollis Street; companies of light infantry and marines were embarking in the boats which lay rocking along the shore; horses snorted, gathered in groups, while boatmen poled flat-boats towards a cove from which already a scow, freighted with horses, was being pushed out into the bay.

Although there was no talking, save the half-whispered commands of the officers, the movement of so many boats, the tread of a thousand men, the stamping and noises of horses, all swelled into a heavy, ceaseless sound, which mingled with and intensified the murmur of the mounting tide, stirred to its flood by the silver magic of the rising moon.

Hundreds of soldiers had already embarked; we could distinguish the dark line of their boats, all strung out as though fastened together, stem and stern, rising and falling on the glittering surface of the bay, ever lengthening, as new boats, loaded deep with soldiers, put out to fall into line and sail bobbing away into the darkness, only to reappear again under the flood of moonlight.

"Suppose," whispered Mount, "we lead our horses aboard that scow yonder!"

In another moment, scarcely aware of what I was actually about, I had dismounted, and was leading Warlock straight down to the shore towards a cove, where half a dozen boatmen were standing in a scow, resting on their long sea-poles.

"If they ask questions, knock them into the water!" said Mount, calmly.

He repeated the instructions to Foxcroft and Shemuel as we filed along the dim shore past a throng of boatmen, grooms, officers' servants, and teamsters, and made straight towards the scow that lay a few yards off shore in the little, shadowy cove.

It was a desperate attempt; had I given myself one minute's reflection, I should rather have risked a dash across the Neck and a chain-shot on the causeway. Yet its very audacity was in our favour; the boatmen, when they saw us leading our horses down to their cove, hastily lowered a plank bridge from their heavy scow, and Mount coolly waded out into the water, guiding his horse aboard as calmly as though it were his own stable, and these Tory boatmen his paid grooms.

I followed with Warlock, who snorted and pawed when the salt water rose to his fetlocks, but he danced up the plank incline and entered the boat without coaxing. Shemuel's horse, a sleek, weasel-bellied animal, with a wicked eye and a bunch o' hackle for a tail, swung round in the water, slinging the little Jew on his face in the mud, and then, with a vicious squeal, flung up his heels and cantered off, scattering a company of marines drawn up a hundred yards down the shore.

Draggled and dripping, Shemuel, standing knee-deep in salt water, watched the flight of his horse, but I bade him come aboard at once, and he did so, casting sidelong glances at the boatmen, who regarded him with astonishment.

Mr. Foxcroft, meanwhile, had dragged his horse aboard, and Mount ordered the boatmen to push off at once.

As the men took up their heavy sea-poles, I heard them whispering to each other that Mount and I must be scouts sent ahead to spy for the soldiers, and I caught them eying our buckskins curiously as they lay on their poles, pushing out towards the broad belt of moonlight which glistened beyond.

The wind whipped our cheeks as we swung clear of the land; the boatmen presently took to their oars, which I noticed were muffled midway between blade and handle. The row-locks, also, had been padded with bunches of wheat-straw and rags.

Now that we were safely afloat, misgivings seized me. I had never before been on salt water; the black waves which came slapping on our craft disturbed me; the shadowy hulk of the war-ship which lay athwart our course loomed up like doom, seeming to watch us with its wicked little green and red eyes, marking us for destruction.

The wind freshened furiously in my face; the waves came rolling in out of the darkness, rap! rap! slap! rap! crushing into stinging gusts of spray, soaking us to the skin.

Far to our left the line of boats floated, undulating across the bay; the beacon in Boston flared out red as we rounded Fox Hill; the light on Mount Wh-d-m twinkled.

Presently Mount touched my arm and pointed. High up in the dark haze above the city two bright lights hung. So we knew that Rolfe was watching from the belfry of the Old North Meeting-House, and that Paul had read the twin lamps' message and was now galloping west through the Middlesex farms.

Shemuel, shivering in his wet and muddy garments, crept up beside me to ask where we were to be landed.

I did not know, nor dared I ask, fearing to awake suspicion. Besides, we were close under the sprit of a tall, black frigate, so close that I could see the candles flaring in the battle lanthorns and the dead bay-weeds hanging from the chains, and I could even read her name, the *Falcon*.

Then, suddenly, out of the shadow under the black frigate's hulk, a cockle-shell came dancing towards us, with an officer in the stern, who played his lanthorn on us and waved his arm.

"Move into line with the ship's boats!" he called out, with many a strange sea-oath; and our brawny oarsmen pulled northeast once more towards the long line of boats which now stretched almost across the bay.

"You land at Phipps's Farm, sir?" inquired a sweating boatman of Mount.

"Phipps's Farm!" broke in Mr. Foxcroft. "It's in the marshes o' Lechemere! I'm damned if I'll be landed at Phipps's!"

"Isn't that where the troops land, sir?" asked the boatman, resting his oar.

Mount shook his head mysteriously.

"We are on special service, lads," he said. "Ask no questions, but put us ashore at Willis Creek, and tell the colonel to give you a guinea apiece for me."

At this impudent remark the boatmen began to row with renewed vigour; the salt spray drove aboard in showers, the wind roared in our ears, the horses huddled together.

Once more we swung across the line of boats; in the craft just ahead of us I could see the marines sitting with their muskets on their knees, right hands covering the flints and pans.

As the distance slowly increased between us and the troop-boats, I began to breathe more freely. Mount stood by his horse, coolly chewing a straw from the wadded oar-locks, his fox-skin cap pushed back on his head, the fluffy tail blowing wildly in the wind.

Slowly the dark shore took shape before us; already I could smell the land smell, and hear the wind among the reeds.

Oh, the happiness to be free from that prison city, lying there in the gloom across the water!—the joy to tread free ground once more, to scent free winds, to move unrestrained across the world again!

Mount, too, was sniffing restlessly at the marsh, wreathed in sea-mist; I fancied his eyes glowed in the moonlight like the eyes of a waiting hound.

Something touched my hand; Shemuel came cowering to my side.

"Courage," I whispered.

"I haf done all I could," he said, in a shaking voice.

"I know that, lad," I muttered.

His wet fingers sought mine.

"I shall nefer be safe no more," he whispered.

"What do you mean?" I asked.

"I don't know. I shall nefer set foot on shore no more. I don't live long now, Mr. Cardigan."

He was trembling from head to foot as I laid my hand on his shoulder.

The boatmen had dropped their oars and taken to their poles once more; the tall reeds rustled as our scow drove its square nose into the shallows and grounded with a grating jar. Startled curlews, round about us, uttered their querulous cries.

"There's a road swings northwest through the marshes," said Mount, wading out into the water and leading his horse up through the rushes. "Follow me, lad. I should know this country from Cobble Hill to Canada."

Foxcroft had mounted; Jack climbed stiffly into his saddle; I threw Warlock around in the reeds, prepared to set foot to stirrup, when Shemuel seized my arm convulsively. A patrol of British light horse, riding in single file, came picking their way down the shore in the moonlight.

Mount and Foxcroft saw them and drew bridles; I slung my legs across Warlock, just as they hailed us.

"Get up behind! Quick!" I whispered to Shemuel, watching the horsemen riding towards Mount, who was ahead of Foxcroft.

Shemuel's strength appeared to have left his limbs; he struggled to mount behind me; Warlock, alarmed at his contortions, began to dance restlessly.

Impatient, I stooped to grasp Shemuel, and I already had him by the collar when an exclamation and a sudden trampling of horses made me turn my head just in time to see a British officer seize Jack Mount and attempt to drag him from his saddle.

Before I could straighten up, the cavalry were upon us; I saw Foxcroft snap his pistol, wheel, and gallop into the reeds; I saw Jack Mount fling the officer off and fetch him a cracking blow with the barrel of his rifle. Two men rode at me; I raised my rifle with one hand, calling to Shemuel to mount behind me, but the frightened peddler squirmed out of my clutch and rushed off headlong into the marsh.

A horseman followed him, cursing; the other trooper, mired in the rushes, struggled to get at me.

I swung my rifle to my cheek; it flashed in the pan; the brute set his horse at a gallop, and, leaning forward, deliberately shot at the unarmed peddler. Shemuel dodged, ran a few yards, doubled on the horseman, and came rushing back towards Mount. He gained a little hillock of rising ground; he could have escaped into the fringing willows, but, to my horror, he turned and waved his arms to me, shouting:

"Ride! Ride! Mr. Cardigan! For Miss Warren's sake, ride, sir!"

"Touch that man and I'll brain you!" I roared at the horseman who had now drawn his sabre.

Again I tried to shoot the trooper, but the flint sparks died out in the damp pan. With a groan I rode after him, calling out to Shemuel to seek cover in the brush, but he only ran about on his hillock, dodging the infuriated trooper, and calling frantically to me that I must save myself for Miss Warren's sake.

Then, while my horse was floundering in the marsh, slowly drawing his mired limbs to firm ground, I saw Shemuel dart towards me with a shriek, and, ere I could reach him, I saw the trooper bend down from his saddle and slash the poor, frightened creature's head with one terrible blow of his heavy sabre.

Down into the mud plunged Shemuel; the trooper's horse trampled and passed over his body, then swung in a rushing circle and bore down on me, just as the other rider came splashing at me from the right.

My rifle a third time flashed in the pan; the priming had been wet with spray. I struck Warlock on the flanks, whirled him head on against Shemuel's murderer, and, whipping out my war-hatchet, aimed a furious blow at the fellow's head. The keen hatchet blade sank into the trooper's shoulder; he tumbled out of his stirrups and landed heavily among the cat-tails.

Instantly I checked Warlock, poised myself in my stirrups, and launched the hatchet straight at the other horseman, striking him full in the chest, but whether with blade-edge, handle, or flat, I know not, for, as his horse swerved wide, passing me at a tearing gallop, Mount and Foxcroft flew past, calling out that Shemuel was dead and that I must follow them for my life.

Up the shore we crashed through the rushes, driving straight out into the marsh, our horses floundering, and the light horsemen firing their pistols at us from the firmer ground above.

A ball grazed Warlock; his neck was wet with blood.

"They'll murder us all here!" cried Foxcroft; "charge them, in God's name!"

Mount heard him and bore to the left; I followed; knee to knee we lifted our crazed horses out of the marsh and hurled them into the little patrol of light horse, bursting upon them ere they could wheel to meet us.

In the moonlight their sabres flashed before our eyes, but no lunging point found its billet of flesh, though their blades rang out on our rifle-barrels; then we were on them, among them, plunging through them, and pounding away northward over a hard gravel road.

They discharged their pistols at us; a few of them followed us, but all pursuit ceased below Prospect Hill; we galloped, unmolested, into the old Charlestown and West Cambridge Road, and flew onward through the night.

In lonely stretches of road, which ran rivers of moonlight, I could see Mount riding, head on his breast, square jaw set, and I knew he was brooding on Shemuel's dismal end.

The swift murder of the little peddler shocked me terribly; Shemuel's strange premonition of his own approaching death fairly made me shiver in my stirrups as I rode. Like a doomed man the Jew had gone to his end, with what courage God had lent him. He had been a friend to me. For all his squalid weakness of limb, his natural fear of pain, his physical cowardice, he had not swerved from the service of his country, nor had he faltered or betrayed the confidence of men whose peril imperilled himself. Nothing save his fidelity to us had forced him to leave the city with us; nothing save the innate love of liberty in his grotesque and dirty body had lured this errant child of Israel to risk his life in bearing messages for those who watched the weighted hours creep on towards that bloody dawn already gathering under the edges of the sleeping world.

Now, as we rode, from behind us the sound of bells came quavering across dim meadows; out of the blue night bells answered; we heard the reports of guns, the distant clamour of a horn blowing persistently from some hidden hamlet.

"The alarm!" panted Foxcroft, at my elbow, as we pounded on. "Hurrah! Hurrah! The country lives!"

"Jack!" I called, through the rushing wind, "the whole land is awaking behind us! Do you hear? Our country lives!"

"And England dies!" cried Mount, passionately. With both hands uplifted, and bridle flung across his horse's neck, he galloped in the lead. On his huge horse, towering up in the saddle, he swept on through the night, a gigantic incarnation of our people militant, a colossal shape embodying all that we had striven for and suffered for from the hour when the first pioneer died at the stake.

On he swept astride his rushing horse, the fox-tail on his cap streaming, the thrums on his sleeves blowing like ripe grain; and ever he tossed his arms towards the sky and shook his glittering rifle above his head, till the moonshine played on it like lightning.

"Ring! Ring out your bells!" we shouted, as we tore through a sleeping village; and behind us we could see candle-light break out from the dark houses, and, ere the volleying echoes of our horses' hoofs struck the last spark from the village streets, the meeting-house bell began swinging, warning the distant farms that the splendid hour had come.

And now, unexpectedly, we encountered a check in our course. Full in the yellow moonlight, on a little hill over which our road lay, we caught sight of a body of horsemen drawn up, and we knew, by the moon shining on their gorgets, that we had before us a company of dragoons with their officers.

At a word from Jack I dismounted and pulled the rails from the road fence on our right. Through the aperture we filed, out into a field of young winter wheat well sprouted, and then west, as quietly as we might, with watchful eyes on the dragoons.

But the British horsemen had also turned, and were now trotting along parallel to our course, which manœuvre drove us off eastward again across the meadows, deep starred with dandelions. For us to alarm Lexington was now impossible. We could already see the liberty-pole on the hill and make out where the village lay, by a gilt weather-vane shining in the moonlight above the trees. But there were no lights to be seen in Lexington, and we dared not ride through the dark town, not knowing but that it might be swarming with dragoons.

Still, if it were impossible for us to alarm Lexington, we could ride on across the fields and gain the Bedford Road.

Mr. Foxcroft undertook to pilot us. As I rode by his side I could scarce believe that, yonder, close at hand in the darkness, Silver Heels slept, nor doubted that I was near. My heart began a-drumming.

"You are sure she is there?" I asked, plucking Foxcroft's sleeve.

"Unless Captain Butler has prevailed," he said, grimly.

I choked and trembled in my saddle.

"Do you—do you believe she would listen to him?" I muttered.

"Do you?" he asked, turning on me.

We forced our horses through a belt of tasselled willows fringing a little thread of a meadow stream. The dew showered our faces like a flurry of rain. My cheeks were burning.

"How far is it? Are we near her house?" I asked again and again. I strove to realize that I was nearing Silver Heels; I could not, nor was I able to understand that I should ever again see her.

In moments of my imprisonment I had believed devoutly that I should live to see her; yet since my deliverance from that cage of stones I had not dared assure myself that I should find her; I had not given myself time to think of the chances that might favour me or of the possibilities of failure. Dormant among my bitter memories lay that vile threat of Walter Butler; I dared not stir it up to examine it; I let it lie quiet, afraid to rouse it. By what hellish art could he, my mortal enemy, inspire aught but hatred in the woman who had loved me and who must have known how I had suffered at his hands?

Yet, if he had not lied to me, she had at least given him an audience. But his boast that she had consented to fix a day to wed with him I believed not, deeming it but a foolish attempt at cruelty on a man who, truly enough, at that time, seemed doomed to die upon the gibbet behind Queen Street court-house.

We now came to a stony pasture in which cattle lay, turning their heavy heads in the dim light to watch us. I dismounted to let down the bars. In vain I looked for a house; there were no lights to be seen.

Foxcroft moved slowly; I nearly rode him down in my rising anxiety, now almost beyond control.

At length, however, he discovered a narrow, overgrown lane, lined with hazel, and we turned into it, single file, leading our horses. The lane conducted us to an orchard, all silvery in the moonbeams, and now, through the long rows of trees, I saw the moon shining on the portico of a white mansion.

"Is that the house?" I whispered.

Foxcroft nodded.

We led our horses through a weedy garden up to the pillared portico. Even in the moonlight I could see the neglect and decay that lay over house and grounds. In the pale light clusters of yellow jonquils peeped from the tangle about the doorsteps; an owl left a hemlock tree with a whistle of broad wings and wheeled upward, squealing fiercely.

And now, as I leaped to the porch, I became aware of a light in the house. It streamed from a chink in the wooden shutters which were closed over the window to the right of the door.

Foxcroft saw it; so did Mount; we tied our hard-blown horses to the fluted wooden pillars, and, stepping to the door, rapped heavily.

The hard beating of my heart echoed the rapping; intense silence followed.

After a long time, pattering, uncertain steps sounded inside the hallway; a light, dim at first, grew brighter above the fanlight over the door.

The door opened to its full width; the candle flared in the draught of night wind, smoked, flickered, then burned steadily. A little, old man stood in the hallway; his huge shadow wavered beside him on the wall.

It was the Weasel!

The cuffs of his coat, guiltless of lace, were too large for his shrunken arms; his faded flowered waistcoat hung on his thin body like a sack; yet his hair was curled and powdered over his sunken forehead. On his colourless, wasted face a senile smile flickered; he laid his withered hand on his breast and bowed to us, advancing to the threshold.

With a gesture he welcomed us; he did not speak, but stood there smiling his aged smile, expectant, silent, the pattern of threadbare courtesy, the living spectre of hospitality.

"Cade!" whispered Mount, with ashy lips; "Cade, old friend! How came you here?"

The Weasel's meaningless eyes turned on Mount; there was no light of recognition in them.

"You are welcome, sir," said Renard, in the ghost of his old voice. "I pray you enter, gentlemen; we keep open house, ah yes!—an old custom in our family, gentlemen—you are welcome to Cambridge Hall, believe me, most welcome."

The thin, garrulous chatter awoke petulant echoes through the silent hall; he raised his childish voice and called out the names of servants, long dead. The hollow house replied in echoes; the candle-flame burned steadily.

"My servants are doubtless in their hall," he said, without embarrassment; "that the office of hospitality devolves on me I must count most fortunate. Pray, gentlemen, follow. The grooms will take your horses to the stables."

Leading us into a room, where were a few chairs set close to a small, shabby card-table, he begged us to be seated with a kindly smile, then seated himself, and fell a-babbling of ancient days, and of people long since in their graves, of his kennels and stables, of the days when the world was younger, and hearts simpler, and true men loved their King.

Nor could we check him, for he would smile and talk of the fleet in the downs, and the fête to be given in Boston town when Sir Peter Warren and his old sea-dogs landed to dine at Province House. And all the while Jack Mount sat staring with tear-smeared eyes, and lips a-quiver, and great fists clasped convulsively; and Foxcroft leaned, elbow on knee, keen eyes watching the little madman who sat serenely babbling of a household and a wife and a life that existed only in his stricken brain.

His wines he brought us in cracked glasses—clear water from a spring that was older than human woe, but, like his hospitality, unfailing.

At intervals he spoke to empty space, as though servants waited at his back; and it was the "Blue Room" for Mr. Foxcroft, and the "South Chamber" for "you, sir, Captain Mount, I believe, of his Majesty's Grenadiers?" Oh, it was heart-breaking to see the agony in Mount's eyes and the ghastly by-play of the little, withered man, the light of whose mind had gone out, leaving a stricken body to be directed by the spirit of a child.

Never shall I forget that candle-lit scene as I saw it: Mount, dumb with grief, sitting there in his buckskins, rifle on knee and fox-skin cap twisted in his great brown hands; Foxcroft, his black smalls splashed with clay, his heavy, red face set in careworn lines; and the little, shabby Weasel, in his mended finery, shrunken fingers interlocked on his knee, smiling vacantly at us over a cracked glass of spring-water, and dispensing hospitality with a mild benevolence which was truly ghastly in its unconscious irony.

"What in God's name is he doing here?" I whispered to Foxcroft.

"Quiet," motioned Foxcroft, turning his head to listen. I, too, had caught the sound of a light footfall on the stair. Instinctively we all rose; the Weasel, muttering and smiling, ambled to the dark entry.

Then, out of the wavering shadows, into the candle-light, stepped a young girl, whose clear hazel eyes met ours with perfect composure. Her face was deadly white; her fingers rested in the Weasel's withered palm; she saluted us with a slow, deep reverence, then raised her steady eyes to mine.

"Silver Heels! Silver Heels!" I whispered.

Her eyes closed for a moment and she quivered from head to foot.

"My daughter, gentlemen," said the Weasel, tenderly; bending, he touched her fingers with his shrivelled lips, smiling to himself.

Her gray eyes never left mine; I stepped forward; she gave a little gasp as I took her hand.

"Who is this young man?" said the Weasel, mildly. "He is not Captain Butler, dear—or my memory fails—ay," he babbled on, "it fails me strangely now, and I had best sit quiet while younger heads think for me. Yet, this young man is not Captain Butler, dear?"

"No, father."

In the silence I heard my heart beat heavily. A minute passed; the Weasel peered at me with his dim eyes and clasped his daughter's hand closely.

"Silver Heels! Silver Heels!" I cried, with a sob.

"Do you want me—now?" she whispered.

I caught her fiercely in my arms; she hung to me with closed eyes and every limb a-tremble.

And, as I stood there, with my arms around her, and her face against mine, far away I heard the measured gallop of a horse on the highway, nearer, nearer, turning now close outside the house, and now thundering up to the porch.

Instantly Jack Mount glided from the room; Foxcroft, listening, silently drew his pistol; I reached out for my rifle which leaned against the chair, and, striking the butt heavily against the floor, glanced at the pan. The rifle had primed itself.

Then I turned smiling to Silver Heels.

"Do you know who is coming?" I asked.

"Yes."

I stepped to the centre of the room; the door opened gently; a motionless shape stood there in the moonlight, the shape of my enemy, Walter Butler.

CHAPTER XXVII

He hesitated, poised on the threshold, his yellow eyes contracting, dazzled by the candle; then, like lightning, his sword glittered in his hand, but Mount, behind him, tore the limber blade from his grip and flung it ringing at my feet. Now, weaponless and alone, Butler stood confronting us, his blank eyes travelling from one to another, his thin lips twitching in an ever-deepening sneer. Nor did the sneer leave his face when Mount slammed and locked the door behind him, and unsheathed his broad hunting-knife.

"Something is dreadfully wrong, gentlemen," quavered poor Cade Renard; "this is Captain Butler, my daughter's affianced. I pray you follow no ancient quarrel under my roof, gentlemen. I cannot suffer this affront—I cannot permit this difference between gentlemen in my daughter's presence—"

Mount quietly drew the little man aside to the door and led him out, saying tenderly: "All is well, old friend; you have forgotten much in these long days. You will remember soon. Go, dream in the moonlight, Cade. She was ever a friend to us, the moon."

Suddenly Butler turned on Silver Heels, his darkening face distorted.

"You have played the game well!" he whispered, between his teeth.

"What game?" I asked, with deadly calmness. "Pray say what you have to say at once, Mr. Butler."

Again his evil gaze shifted from face to face; there was no mercy in the eyes that met his; his visage grew loose and pallid.

"That she-devil swore to wed me!" he broke out, hoarsely, pointing a shaking finger full at Silver Heels. "She—swore it!" His voice sank to a hiss.

"To save my father from a highwayman's death!" said Silver Heels, deathly white.

She turned to me, quivering. "Michael, I am a thief's daughter. This is what I am come to!—to buy my father's life with my own body—and fling my soul at that man's feet! *Now will you wed me?*"

A cold fury blinded me so I could scarcely see him. I cocked my rifle and drew my hand across my eyes to clear them.

"This is not your quarrel!" he said, desperately; "this woman is the daughter of Cade Renard, a notorious highwayman known as the Weasel! I doubt that Sir Michael Cardigan—for your uncle is dead, whether you know it or not!—would care to claim kinship in this house!"

He turned like a snake and measured Mount from head to foot.

"Give me my sword!" he said, harshly, "and I will answer for myself against this other thief!" His glaring eyes fell on Foxcroft.

"What the devil are you doing here?" he snarled. "Are you knave or fool, that you stand there listening to this threat on my life? You know that this woman is Renard's child! You have Sir John's papers to prove it! Are you not his attorney, man? Then tell these gentlemen that I speak the truth, and that I will meet them both, singly, and carve it on their bodies lest they forget it!"

"It is too late," I said; "a gentleman's sword can never again be soiled by those hands."

"Ay!" cried Foxcroft, suddenly, "it is too late! You say I have papers to prove the truth? I have; and you shall hear the truth, you cursed scoundrel!"

"She is the Weasel's child!" cried Butler, hoarsely.

"If she were the child of Tom o' Bedlam, she is still betrothed to me! God knows," I said, "whether you be human or demon, and so perhaps you may not burn in hell, but I shall send you thither, with God's help!"

And I laid my hand on his arm, and asked him if he was minded to die quietly in the garden; while Mount, knife at his throat, pushed him towards the door.

"Do you mean it?" he burst out, shuddering. "Am I not to have a chance for life? This is murder, Mr. Cardigan!"

"So dealt you by me at the Cayuga stake," I said.

"Yet—it is murder you do. If my hands are not clean, would you foul your own?"

"So dealt you by me in Queen Street prison," I said, slowly.

"Yet, nevertheless, it is murder. And you know it. This is no court of law, to sit in judgment. Are the Cardigans the public hangmen?"

"Give him his sword!" I cried, passionately. "I cannot breathe while he draws breath! Give him his sword, or I will slay him with naked hands!"

"No!" roared Foxcroft, hurling me back.

Butler scowled at the lawyer; Foxcroft scowled at him, and placed his heavy shoe on the fallen sword. Then he suddenly stooped, seized the gilded hilt, and snapped the blade in two, casting the fragments from him in contempt.

"The sword of a scoundrel," he said; "the sword of a petty malefactor—a pitiful forger—"

"Liar!" shrieked Butler, springing at him. Mount flung the maddened man into a chair, where he lay, white and panting, staring at Foxcroft, who now stood by the table, coolly examining a packet of documents.

"It is all here," he said—"the story of two cheap dabblers in petty crime—Sir John Johnson and Mr. Walter Butler—how they did conspire to steal from Miss Warren her wealth, her fair fame, and the very name God gave her. A shameful story, gentlemen, but true on the word of an honourable man."

"Lies!" muttered Butler, between ashen lips. His cheeks became loose and horrible; his lips shrivelled up above his teeth. Foxcroft turned to me, purple with passion.

"Sir William Johnson, your honourable kinsman, left Miss Warren property in his will. Sir John found, in the same box which held the will, a packet of documents and letters addressed to Sir William, apparently proving that Miss Warren was the child of a certain lady who had left her husband to follow the fortunes of Captain Warren—her child by her own husband, Cade Renard, a gentleman of Cambridge."

"The Weasel!" burst out Jack Mount.

"But she is not, sir!" cried Foxcroft, turning on Mount. "She is Captain Warren's own child; I journeyed to England and proved it; I have papers here in my pocket to prove it!" he said, slapping the flaps of his brass-buttoned coat. "It was a lie from beginning to end; the letters supposed to have been written to Sir William by Sir Peter Warren were forged; the documents supposed to have been unearthed from the flooring in the captain's cabin of his Majesty's ship *Leda* were forged. I can prove it! I can prove that Walter Butler was the forger! I can prove that Sir John Johnson knew it! And to that end Sir John and Captain Butler conspired to make her believe herself to be the child of a half-crazed forest-runner who had been besetting Sir John with his mad importunities, calling himself Cade Renard, and vowing that Miss Warren was his own child!"

He glared at Butler; the wretched man's lips moved to form the word, "Lies!" but no sound came. Then Foxcroft turned to me.

"In my presence these three men broke the news to her; they hoodwinked me, too. By God, sir, I had never suspected villany had not that contemptible fool, Sir John, attempted to bribe silence, should anything ever occur to cast doubt on the relationship betwixt this fellow Renard and Miss Warren!"

The lawyer paused, grinding his teeth in rage.

"I accepted the bribe! I did, gentlemen! I did it to quiet suspicion. Sir John believes me to be his creature. But I set out to follow the matter to the bitter end, and I have done it! It's a falsehood from A to Zed! I shall have the pleasure of flinging Sir John's bribe into his face!"

He laid his hand on my arm, speaking very gently and gravely.

"Mr. Cardigan, Miss Warren is the truest, bravest, sweetest woman I have ever known. She received the news of her dreadful position as a gallant soldier receives the fire of the enemy. When it was made hopelessly clear to her that this lunatic Renard was her father, and that she was not a Warren, not an heiress, that she must now give up all thought of the family on which she had so long imposed—and give up all pretensions to *you*, sir—she acquiesced with a dignity that might have become a princess of the blood, sir! No whining there, Mr. Cardigan! Not a whimper, sir; not a reproach, not a tear. Her first thought was of pity for her father—this little, withered lunatic, who sat there devouring her with his eyes of a sick hound. She went to him before us all; she took his hand—his hard, little claw—and kissed it. By God, gentlemen, blood tells!"

After a long silence I repeated, "Blood tells."

Mount, head in his hands, was weeping.

"Then came Butler, the forger," said Foxcroft, pointing at him. "And when he found that, after all, Miss Warren honoured herself too highly to seek a rehabilitation through his name, he came here and threatened this poor old man's life—threatened to denounce him as a thief, and have him hung at a cross-roads, unless she gave herself to him! Then—then she consented."

Butler was sitting forward in his chair, his bloodless face supported between his slim fingers, his eyes on vacancy. He did not seem to hear the words that branded him; he did not appear to see us as we drew closer around him.

"In the orchard," muttered Mount; "we can hang him with his own bridle."

We paused for an instant, gazing silently at the doomed man. Then Mount touched him on the shoulder.

At the voiceless summons he looked up at us as though stunned.

"You must hang," said Mount, gravely.

"Not that! No!" I stammered; "I can't do it! Give him a sword—give him something to fight with! Jack—I can't do it. I am not made that way!"

There was a touch on my arm; Silver Heels stood beside me.

"Let them deal with him," she murmured, "you cannot fight with him; there is no honour in him."

"No!—no honour in him!" I repeated.

He had risen, and now stood, staring vacantly at me.

"Damnation!" cried Mount, "are you going to let him loose on the world again?"

"I cannot slay him," I said.

"But a rope can!" said Mount.

"Do you then draw it," I replied, "and never rail more at the hangman!"

After a moment I unlocked and opened the door. As in a trance, Butler passed out into the moonlight; Mount stole close behind him, and I saw his broad knife glimmer as he followed.

"Let him go," I said, wearily. "I choke with all this foul intrigue. Is there no work to do, Jack, save the sheriff's? Faugh! Let him go!"

Butler slowly set foot to stirrup; Mount snatched the pistol from the saddle-holster with a savage sneer.

"No, no," he said. "Trust a scoundrel if you will, lad, but draw his fangs first. Oh, Lord above!—but I hate to let him go! Shall I? I'll give him a hundred yards before I fire! And I'll not aim at that! Shall I?"

If Butler heard him he made no sign. He turned in his saddle and looked at Silver Heels.

Should I let him loose on the world once more? God knows I am no prophet, nor pretend to see behind the veil; yet, as I stood there, looking on Walter Butler, I thought the haze that the moon spun in the garden grew red like that fearsome light which tinges the smoke of burning houses, and I remembered that dream I had of him, so long ago, when I saw him in the forest, with blood on him, and fresh scalps at his belt—and the scalps were not of the red men.

Should I, who had him in my power, and could now forever render the demon in him powerless—should I let him go free into the world, or send him forever to the dreadful abode of lost souls?

War was at hand. War would come at dawn when the Grenadiers marched into Concord town. To slay him, then, would be no murder. But now?

Mount, watching me steadily, raised his rifle.

"No," I said.

What was I to do? There was no prison to hale him to; the jails o' Boston lodged no Tories. Justice? There was no justice save that mockery at Province House. Law? Gage was the law—Gage, the friend of this man. What was I to do? Once again Mount raised his rifle.

"No," I said.

So passed Walter Butler from among us, riding slowly out into the shadowy world, under the calm moon. God witness that I conducted as my honour urged, not as my hot blood desired—and He shall deal with me one day, face to face, that I let loose this man on the world, yet did not dream of the hell he should make of Tryon County ere his red soul was fled again to the hell that hatched it!

So rode forth mine enemy, Walter Butler, invulnerable for me in his armour of dishonour, unpunished for the woe that he had wrought, unmarked by justice which the dawn had not yet roused from her long sleep in chains.

Again Mount raised his rifle.

"No," I said.

A little breeze began stirring in the moonlit orchard; our horses tossed their heads and stamped; then silence fell.

After a long while the voice of Mount recalled me to myself; he had drawn poor Renard to a seat on the rotting steps of the porch.

"Now do you know me, Cade?" asked Mount, again and again.

The Weasel folded his withered hands in his lap and looked up, solemnly.

"Cade? Cade, old friend?" persisted Mount, piteously, drawing his great arm about the Weasel's stooping shoulders.

The Weasel's solemn eyes met his in silence.

Mount forced a cheerful laugh that rang false in the darkness.

"What! Forget the highway, Cade? The King's highway, old friend? The moon at the cross-roads? Eh? You remember? Say you remember, Cade."

The blank eyes of the Weasel were fixed on Mount.

"The forest? Eh, Cade? Ho!—lad! The rank smell o' the moss, and the stench of rotting logs? The quiet in the woods, the hermit-bird piping in the pines? Say you remember, old friend!" he begged; "tell me you remember! Ho! lad, have you forgot the tune the war-arrow sings?"

And he made a long-drawn, whispering whimper with his lips.

In pantomime he crouched and pointed; the Weasel's mild eyes turned.

"The Iroquois!" whispered Mount, anxiously. "They wear O-Kwen-cha!—red paint! Hark to the war-drums! Do you not hear them chanting:

"Ha-wa-sa-say!

Ha-wa-sa-say!"

The Weasel's eyes grew troubled; he looked up at Mount trustfully, like a child who refuses to be frightened.

"I hear Che-ten-ha, the mouse; he gnaws, gnaws, gnaws."

"No, it is the Iroquois!" urged Mount. "You have fought them, Cade; you remember? Say that you remember!"

"I—I have fought the Iroquois," repeated the Weasel, passing his hand over his brow; "but it was years ago—years ago—too long ago to remember—"

"No, no!" cried Mount, "it was but yesterday, old friend—yesterday! And who went with you on the burnt trail, Cade? Who went with you by night and by day, by starlight and by sun, eating when you ate, starving when you starved, drinking deep when you drank, thirsting when you thirsted? It was I, Cade!" cried Mount, eagerly; "I!"

"It was Tah-hoon-to-whe, the night-hawk," murmured the little man.

"It was I, Jack Mount!" repeated the forest-runner, in a loud voice. "Hark! The Iroquois drums! The game's afoot, Cade! Rouse up, old friend! The trail is free!"

But the Weasel only stared at him with his solemn, aged eyes, and clasped his trembling hands in his lap.

Mount stood still for a long while. Slowly his eager head sank, his arms fell, hopelessly. Then, with a gulping sob, he sank down beside his ancient comrade, and hid his head in his huge hands.

The Weasel looked at him with sorrowful eyes; then rose, and came slowly towards Silver Heels.

"They say you are not my daughter," he said, taking Silver Heels's hands from mine. "They tell me I have forgotten many things—that you are not my little girl. But—we know better, my child."

He bent and kissed her hands. His hair was white as frost.

"We know better, child," he murmured. "You shall tell me all they say—for I cannot understand—and we will smile to remember it all, in the long summer evenings—will we not, my child?"

"Yes," said Silver Heels, faintly.

"There is much, sir, that I forget in these days," he said, turning gravely towards me—"much that I cannot recall. Age comes to us all with God's mercy, sir. Pray you forgive if I lack in aught of courtesy to my guests. There are many people who stay with us—and I cannot remember all names of new and welcome guests—believe me, most welcome. I think your name is Captain Butler?"

"Sir Michael Cardigan," whispered Silver Heels.

"And welcome, always welcome to us here in Cambridge Hall," murmured the old man, staring vacantly about him.

Foxcroft, who had gone to the shabby barn, came back and whispered that there were no horses there, and no vehicle of any description; that we had best make ready for a journey to Albany immediately, and abandon the house and its scant furnishings to the mercy of chance.

I left it to him and to Jack Mount to persuade poor Renard that a journey was necessary that very night; and to them also I left the care of providing for us as best they might, saying that I had no money until I could reach Albany, and that my horse Warlock was to carry Miss Warren.

When Mount had drawn poor Cade away, and when Foxcroft began rummaging the great house for what necessaries and provisions it might contain, Silver Heels took me by the hand and led me up the creaking old stairs and across the gallery to her own chamber. The moonlight flooded the room as we entered, making its every corner sparkle.

Save for the great four-posted bed with its heavy canopy, there was in the room nothing but a pine table and a jug and basin.

"So poor am I," she whispered, close beside my face.

"Is this all?" I asked.

"All save the clothes on my body, Michael."

"Silver Heels! Silver Heels!" I said, sorrowfully, holding her by the hands and never moving my eyes from her tender eyes. And we looked and looked, nor gazed our fill, and the light of her sweet presence was like moonlight which swam in the silvery room, bathing me to the soul of me with deep content.

"All these piteous days!" she said, slowly.

"Ay—all of them! And each hour a year, and each nightfall a closing century. Silver Heels! Silver Heels! You are unchanged, dear heart!"

"Thin to my bones, and very, very old—like you, Michael."

"We have young souls."

"Yes, Michael. We are young in all save sorrow."

"And you are so tall, Silver Heels—"

"Span my waist!"

"My hand would span it. Ah! Your head comes not above my chin for all your willow growth!"

"Your hands are rough, Sir Michael."

"Your hands are satin, sweet."

"Yet I wash my kerchief and my shifts in suds."

How the moon glowed and glowed on her.

"You grow in beauty, Silver Heels," I said.

"When you are with me I do truly feel beauty growing in me, Michael."

We sat down together on the great bed's edge, her face against mine, and looked out at the faint stars which the glory of the moon had not yet drowned in light.

Far in the night a cock crowed in the false dawn.

"You have suffered, sweet?" I whispered.

"Ay. And you?"

"Much," I replied.

After a long while she spoke.

"You have never wavered—not once—not for one moment?"

"Once."

In a faint whisper, "When?"

"On the road from Albany, dear heart."

"You rode in company?"

"Not of my choice."

"Who?"

"Do not ask."

"Who?"

"I cannot tell—"

"Who?"

"In honour."

"You wavered?"

"There was no danger when I thought of you."

She raised her face; her mouth touched mine, then clung to it, and I breathed the sweetest breath a maid e'er drew, and all my soul grew dim and warm and faint, with her arms now around my neck, now clinging to my shoulders, and her face like a blossom crushed to mine.

Trembling in limb and body she stood up, brushing her gray eyes awake with slender fingers.

"Ah, what happiness, what happiness!" she whispered. "I am all a-quiver, and I burn to the soul of me. What strange, sweet mischief is there in your lips, Michael? Nay—do not touch me—dear, dear lad; not now—not yet."

She leaned from the open casement; in the intense stillness a voice broke out from below:

"Ready, Cardigan! The horses wait at the barn!"

As she had no cloak I wrapped her in mine, and, passing my arm around her, led her down to the porch and out across the orchard to the barn where Renard sat, mounted on his old comrade's horse.

Warlock came to my call; he nosed the little hand that Silver Heels held out, and laid his head close to hers.

"Bear her safely, Warlock!" I muttered, huskily, and lifted her to the saddle, bidding Foxcroft mount his own horse, as I would walk beside Miss Warren.

So we started, Foxcroft in the van, then the Weasel, with Mount afoot, leading the horse, then Silver Heels in her saddle, with one hand on my shoulder as I walked at her side, rifle trailed.

"There is a road which swings north," said Foxcroft. "We must circle Lexington."

"There is a road yonder," called out Mount.

Foxcroft hesitated.

"I think it leads to Roxbury," he said; "I cannot tell if it be the road."

"Is it the Roxbury Road, Cade?" asked Mount, cheerfully.

"Doubtless, doubtless," replied the Weasel, vacantly, staring at Silver Heels.

"He does not remember," whispered Silver Heels.

"Try it," said Mount; "I doubt not but that it swings far north o' Lexington. If this were the forest 'twixt Saint Sacrement and Pitt I'd vouch for us all, but the smell o' the town has dulled and blunted my nose, and I see no longer like a tabby in a dark pantry."

He moved into the road, following Foxcroft, and leading the horse on which Cade Renard was mounted. I came last with Silver Heels.

The moon was well on her journey towards the dark world's edge ere we came to a cross-roads; but the four finger-posts were missing, and we found ourselves no wiser than before. Foxcroft voiced his misgivings that we were on the Lexington Road after all, and not on the road to Roxbury, as we should surely have crossed the Concord Road ere this.

And he was right, for in a few moments we came in full view of the Lexington Meeting-house, with the Concord Road running into our road on the left and "Buckman's Tavern" on the right, all ablaze with candles set in every window, and a great stable lanthorn shining in the centre of the road.

"It is past three in the morning," said Foxcroft, looking at his watch. "The British should have been here ere this if they were coming at all."

Mount threw his rifle into the hollow of his left arm, and, tossing his horse's bridle to Foxcroft, walked towards "Buckman's Tavern" where, in the lanthorn light, a throng of men were standing.

I heard him greet them with a hearty "God save our country"; then he disappeared in the crowd.

The night had turned chilly; I buttoned my riding-coat across Silver Heels's throat and covered her head with the cape, tying it under her chin like a hood.

Presently Mount came striding back, rifle on shoulder, followed by an hostler with a stable light.

"The militia have been yonder under arms since midnight," he said. "A messenger rode in ten minutes since with news that the road was clear and no British coming. We can get a post-chaise here"—he nodded towards the hostler who stood swinging his lamp in one hand and his firelock in t'other.

"I guess the redcoats ain't a-coming, gentlemen," said the hostler, with a grin.

"Then we had best bait at the tavern," said Foxcroft, quickly; and he led the way, riding beside the Weasel, who seemed utterly indifferent to his surroundings.

As we threaded our path through the crowd of men and boys I noticed that all were armed with rifles or old-time firelocks, and some even with ancient blunderbusses and bell-muzzled matchlocks. They appeared to be a respectable company, mostly honest yokels from the village, clad in plain homespun. A few wore the militia uniform; one or two officers were dressed in the full uniform of the Third Suffolk Regiment. They eyed us curiously as we passed through their straggling ranks; one called out: "The forest-runners are with us! Hurrah!" But, for the most part, they regarded us quietly, readily making way for me as I came up, leading Warlock with Silver Heels in the saddle, cloaked to the eyes.

A servant, wearing a pistol in his belt, brought us bread and hot stirabout in a great blue bowl. This dry fare we washed with ale, Silver Heels tasting a glass of Madeira to warm her chilled body.

It was a silent, thoughtful repast. Mount, sitting close beside the Weasel, urged the old man to eat, and he did, mechanically, with dazed eyes fixed on space.

One thing I began to notice: he no longer watched Silver Heels with that humble, devoted, hungering mien of a guardian hound; he scarcely appeared to be aware of her presence at all. Once only he spoke, asking what had become of his rifle; and Mount, eager and hopeful, brought his own rifle to the stricken man. But the Weasel had already forgotten what he had asked for, and he glanced at the weapon listlessly, his hands folded before him on the cloth.

Though her life had nigh been wrecked forever by this poor madman, Silver Heels, sitting at his elbow, watched over him with a serious tenderness and pity, doing for him those little offices which do become the children of the aged and infirm, and which, God grant, our children shall fulfil towards us. And so I saw her with the salt-box, savouring his stirabout so that it should be seasoned to his liking, and, with the cone of sugar, chip such morsels with her knife as he might mumble when he chose.

Presently Foxcroft went to the stables to see that our post-chaise was well provisioned for the journey, and Mount led Renard away to watch the feed-bags filled for our horses' provender.

Silver Heels, still wrapped in my riding-cloak, laid her slim hand on my arm, and we walked together to the tavern porch.

The road from Boston divides in front of the Meeting-house, forming two sides of a grassy triangle, on the base of which stands the Meeting-house, facing down the Boston Road. Near this village green a few armed men still lingered in the faint light of dawn, conversing in low voices, and glancing often down the deserted Boston Road.

A score of men sat around us on the damp tavern steps, listlessly balancing their rifles between their knees, some smoking wooden pipes, some dozing, some drinking early milk from a bucket brought by a small, freckled lad who wore neither hat nor shoes.

"Do you desire some fresh milk, lady?" he asked, gazing solemnly up at Silver Heels.

She smiled faintly, took the proffered dipper, and drank a little.

"No pay, lady," he said, as I drew out some coins which Foxcroft had loaned me; "the redcoats are comin', and we need to for-ti-fy the in-ner man—and the in-ner lady," he added, politely.

A soldier looked up and laughed.

"That's what the little rascal heard Captain Parker say," he drawled, much amused, while the barefoot Ganymede withdrew, blushing and embarrassed, to act as cup-bearer to others who had beckoned him.

"We've got a hundred an' thirty militia here already," volunteered a drummer-boy who lolled on the porch, fondling his wet drum; "but Captain Parker, he let 'em go into the houses around the green because he guesses the redcoats ain't a-comin', but I'm to stay here an' drum like the devil if the redcoats come."

"An' I'm to fife if they come!" added another boy, stoutly.

I glanced down at the big, painted drum, all beaded with dew, and I read "Louisburg" written in white letters on the hoops.

"We have some old Louisburg soldiers here," said the urchin, proudly. "The redcoats say that we be all cowards, but I guess we have fit battles for 'em long enough."

"You are over-young to fight in war," said Silver Heels, gently.

"No, ma'am, we ain't!" they retorted, in a breath. "We'll give 'em 'Yankee Doodle' this time, my lady!"

"'Yankee Doodle,'" repeated Silver Heels, mystified.

"A foolish song the British play in Boston to plague us," I explained.

Presently Silver Heels touched my arm. "See yonder—look at that man, down there in the road! See him running now, Michael!"

I turned and looked down the Boston Road; the little barelegged drummer stood up.

Faintly came the far cry through the misty chill: "The British are coming! The British are coming!"

The next instant the wet, stringy drum banged and buzzed on the tavern porch, drowning all other sounds in our ears; a score of men stumbled to their feet, rifles in hand; the little fifer blew a whistling call, then ran out into the road.

At that same moment our post-chaise lumbered around the corner of the tavern yard and drew up before us, Mount acting as post-boy, and Foxcroft and the Weasel riding together in the rear.

Mount apprehended the situation at a glance; he motioned me to place Silver Heels in the chaise, which I did, with my eyes still fixed on the foggy Boston Road.

"Is it a false alarm?" inquired Foxcroft, anxiously, as a few of the militia came running past our chaise. "Ho! Harrington! Hey! Bob Monroe! Is it true they are coming, lads?"

Harrington and Monroe, whom I had met in Boston at the "Wild Goose," waved their arms to us, and called out that it was doubtless true.

"Which way?" cried Foxcroft, standing up in his stirrups.

But the militia and Minute Men ran out without answering, and joined the line which was slowly forming on the green, while the old Louisburg drum rolled, vibrating sonorously, and the fife's shrill treble pierced the air.

There was a uniformed officer in front of the ragged line, shouting orders, gesticulating, pushing men into place; some sidled nearer to their comrades as though for shelter, many craned their necks like alarmed turkeys, a few huddled into groups, charging and priming their pieces—some threescore yokels in all, though others were running from the houses and joining the single rank, adding to the disorder and confusion. And all the while the old Louisburg drum thundered the assembly.

"Cardigan, which way are they coming?" cried Foxcroft, still standing up in his stirrups. "They say there are redcoats behind us and more in front of us!"

"Do those ragged rascals mean to face a British army?" exclaimed Mount, reining in his horse, which had begun to rear at the noise of the drum.

"Turn your horses, Jack!" I said, holding Warlock by the head; "turn back towards Concord!"

"There's redcoats on the Concord Road!" cried a woman, running out of a house close by. I saw her hurry across to the village green, carrying a sack of home-moulded bullets.

Jonathan Harrington caught her arm, took the bullet-pouch, kissed her; then she hastened back to the little house and stood at the window, peering out with white face pressed to the dark glass.

I flung myself astride Warlock, wheeled the restless horse, and ranged up alongside Mount.

"Can we not take the Bedford Road?" I asked, anxiously.

"They say the British are betwixt us and the west," replied Mount. His eyes had begun to burn with a steady, fierce light; he sat astride the off horse, cocking and uncocking his rifle.

"Then we should make for the Boston Road!" I said, impatiently; "we can't stay here—"

"Look yonder!" broke in Foxcroft, excitedly.

Out into the Boston Road, in the gray haze of dawn, trotted a British officer, superbly mounted. The pale light glimmered on his silver gorget; the gold on his sleeves and hat sparkled.

Straight on his heels marched the British infantry, moving walls of scarlet topped with shining steel, rank after rank, in magnificent alignment, pouring steadily into the square, with never a drum-beat to time the perfect precision of their black-gaitered legs.

"Halt!" cried a far voice; the red ranks stood as one man. An officer galloped alongside of the motionless lines, and, leaning forward in his saddle, shouted to the disordered group of farmers, "Stop that drum!"

"Fall in! Fall in!" roared the captain of the militia; the old Louisburg drum thundered louder yet.

"Prime! Load!" cried the British officers, and the steady call was repeated from company to company, and yet to companies unseen, far down the Boston Road.

Twoscore of spectators had now so hemmed in our post-chaise that we could not move without crushing them, yet I struggled ceaselessly to back the vehicle into the stable-yard, and Foxcroft begged the crowd to move and let the chaise pass.

We had scarcely succeeded in reaching the corner of the yard, and the body of the chaise was now safe from bullets, when a British major galloped into the green, motioning violently to the militia with his drawn sword.

"Disperse! Disperse!" he called out, angrily.

"Stand your ground!" roared the militia captain. "Don't fire unless fired upon! But if they mean to have a war, let it begin here!"

"Disperse!" shouted the British major. "Lay down your arms! Why don't you lay down your arms and disperse—"

A shot cut him short; his horse gave a great bound, backed, lashed out with both hind feet, then reared in agony.

"My God! they've shot his horse!" cried Foxcroft.

"'Tis his own men, then," broke in Mount; "I marked the smoke."

"Disperse!" bellowed the maddened officer, dragging his horse to a standstill—"disperse, ye rebels!"

Behind a stone wall a farmer rose and presented his firelock, but the piece flashed in the pan. A shot rang out, but I could not see who fired.

Far down the Boston Road the solid front of a second British column appeared.

Already some of the Minute Men were quitting the single, disordered rank on the green which still wavered, facing the regulars; but their captain continued in front of his men, and the drummer still drummed his hoarse challenge.

Then a British officer fired his pistol from the saddle, and, before any one could move or lift a finger, a bright sheet of flame girdled the British front, and the deafening roar of musketry shook the earth.

Through the low rushing billows of smoke that gushed out over the ground like foam, I saw the British major rise in his stirrups, and, reversing his sword, drive it downward as signal to cease firing. Other officers rode up through the smoke, shouting orders which were lost in the dropping shots from the militia, now retreating on a run past us up the Bedford Road.

"Look at Harrington," cried Mount; "he's down under that smoke!"

But Harrington rose, and reeled away towards his own house. I saw his wife at the door; the wounded man also saw her, and feebly stretched out his hands as though calling for aid, then he pitched forward on his face and lay still, one hand clutching his own door-step.

"Halt!" shouted the British major, plunging about on his wounded horse through the smoke. "Stop that firing! D'ye hear what I say? Stop it! Stop it!" And again and again he reversed his sword in frantic signals which no one heeded.

An officer cantered up, calling out: "Major Pitcairn! Major Pitcairn! Are you hit, sir?"

A volley from the British Tenth Foot drowned his voice, and the red-coated soldiers came bursting through the smoke on a double-quick, shouting and hoisting their mitre-caps on the points of their bayonets. Behind them the grenadiers rushed forward, cheering.

A soldier of the light infantry in front of the Meeting-house flung up his musket and fired at an old man who was hobbling across the street; shots came quicker and quicker; I saw my acquaintance, Monroe, attempt to traverse the road towards the tavern; he was rolling in the mud ere he had taken two steps. A grenadier ran after a lank farmer and caught him by the collar; the farmer tripped up the redcoat and started to run, but they brought him to his knees in the road, and then shot him to death under their very feet.

I galloped to the chaise and jerked the horses back, then wheeled them westward towards Bedford, where the remnants of the militia were sullenly falling back, firing across at the British, now marching on past the Meeting-house up the Concord Road.

"No! No!" cried Foxcroft, "we cannot risk it! Stay where you are!"

"We cannot risk being butchered here!" I replied. Silver Heels was standing straight up in the chaise, one hand holding to the leather curtain. Her face had grown very white.

"They've killed a poor young man behind that barn!" she whispered, as I leaned from my saddle and motioned her to crouch low. "They shot him twice, and struck him with their muskets!"

I glanced hastily towards the barn and saw a dark heap lying in the grass behind it. Three red-coated soldiers stood near, loading their muskets and laughing.

"Look at the Weasel!" muttered Mount, jerking my arm as my horse ranged up beside his.

The Weasel was hastily climbing out of his saddle, rifle in hand. His face, which a few moments before had been haggard and vacant, had grown flushed and eager, his eyes snapped with intelligence, his head was erect, and his movements quick as a forest-cat's.

"Cade!" quavered Mount. "Cade, old friend, what are you doing?"

"Come!" cried the Weasel, briskly; "can't you see the redskins?"

"Redcoats! Redcoats!" cried Mount, anxiously. "Where are you going, Cade? Come back! Come back! They can't hit us here! Redcoats, Cade, not redskins!"

"They be all one to me!" replied the Weasel, briskly, scuttling away to cover under a tuft of hazel.

"Don't shoot, Cade!" bawled Mount. "Wait till we can gather our people! Wait! Hell and damnation! don't fire!"

"Bang!" went the Weasel's long brown rifle; a red-coated soldier on the Concord Road dropped.

"He's done it! God help us!" groaned Foxcroft.

"Hold those horses!" said Mount, desperately. I seized the leaders, Mount slipped from his saddle to the ground, and ran out to the long, dead grass behind the Meeting-house. I could see him catch the Weasel by the arm and attempt to drag him back by force, but the mad little creature clung obstinately to his patch of hazel.

"He won't come!" shouted Mount, turning towards me.

As he turned, I saw the entire British column marching swiftly up the Concord Road, a small flanking party thrown out on the right. The Weasel also saw the troops and made haste to level his rifle again, but Mount fell upon him and dragged him down into the marsh-grass.

From the Bedford Road our militia fired slowly across at the fast vanishing troops on the Concord Road; the British flanking party returned the fire, but the main column paid no heed to the shots, and pressed on in silence, without music, without banners, without a drum-tap to mark their rapid march. No British soldiers came our way; they appeared to disdain the groups of militia retreating along the Bedford Road; their rear-guard fired a few scattering shots into "Buckman's Tavern" at long range, then ran on to keep in touch with the main body.

Both the Weasel and Mount were now deliberately firing at the British flanking party, which had halted on a bit of ploughed ground, and seemed to be undecided whether to continue their march or return and punish the two foolhardy riflemen whose bullets had already knocked one big soldier flat on his back across the fresh furrows.

All at once six red-coated soldiers started running towards Jack Mount and the Weasel. I shouted to warn the infatuated men. Silver Heels caught my arm.

"I cannot leave them there!" I stammered; "I must go to them!"

"Foxcroft will guard me!" she murmured. "Go to them, dearest!"

"Foxcroft! Hold these horses!" I cried, flinging Warlock's bridle to him, and slipping out of my saddle.

Rifle a-trail, I ran across the road, leaped the fence, and plunged into the low bushes. Jack Mount turned a cool, amused eye on me as I came up.

"The Weasel is right," he said, triumphantly; "we'll catch a half-dozen red-birds now. Be ready when I draw their fire, lad; then drop and run forward through the swamp! You know how the Senecas fight. We'll catch them alive!"

Over the tops of the low bushes I could see the soldiers coming towards us, muskets half raised, scanning the cover for the game they meant to bag, thrusting their bayonets into bushes, beating the long grass with their gunstocks to flush the skulking quarry for a snap-shot.

Without warning, Mount rose, then sank to the ground as a volley rattled out; and instantly we three ran forward, bent double. In a moment more I sprang up from the swamp-grass beside a soldier and knocked him flat with a blow from my rifle-stock. Mount shot at another and missed him, but the fellow promptly threw down his musket, yelling lustily for quarter.

The four remaining soldiers attempted to load, but the Weasel tripped up one, with a cartridge half bitten in his mouth, and the other three were chased and caught by some Acton militia, who came leaping across the swampy covert from the Bedford Road.

When the Acton men returned with their prisoners, the soldier whom I had struck was sitting up in the swamp-grass, rubbing his powdered head and staring wildly at his sweating and anxious comrades.

"That's the fellow who murdered Harrington!" said one of the militia, and drew up his rifle with a jerk.

"Use these prisoners well, or I'll knock your head off!" roared Mount, striking up the rifle.

An officer of Minute Men came up; his eyes were red as though he had been weeping.

"They butchered his brother behind the red barn yonder," whispered a lean yokel beside me. "He'll hang 'em, that's what he'll do."

"That's it! Hang 'em!" bawled out a red-headed lout, flourishing a pitchfork. "Hang the damn—!"

"Put that fool under arrest," said the officer, sharply. Some Acton Minute Men seized the lout and hustled him off; others formed a guard and conducted the big, perspiring, red-coated soldiers towards "Buckman's Tavern."

"You will treat them humanely?" I asked, as the officer passed me.

He gave me a blank glance; the tears again had filled his eyes.

"Certainly," he said, shortly; "I am not a butcher."

I gave him the officer's salute; he returned it absently, and walked on, with drawn sword and head sunk on his tarnished brass gorget.

A restless, silent crowd had gathered at "Buckman's Tavern," where two dead Minute Men lay on the porch, stiffening in their blood.

The sun had not yet risen, but all the east was turning yellow; great clouds of red-winged blackbirds rose and settled in the swampy meadows, and filled the air with their dry chirking; robins sang ecstatically.

Back along the muddy Bedford Road trudged the remnants of the scattered Lexington company of militia; the little barelegged drummer posted himself in front of the Meeting-house once more, and drummed the assembly. Men seemed to spring from the soil; every bramble-patch was swarming now; they came hurrying across the distant fields singly, in twos and threes, in scores.

Far away in the vague dawn bells rang out in distant villages, and I heard the faint sound of guns and the throbbing of drums. I passed the Lexington company re-forming on the trodden village green. Their captain, Parker, called out to me: "Forest-runner! We need your rifle! Will you fight with us?"

"I cannot," I said, and ran towards the post-chaise, rifle on shoulder.

The women and children of Lexington were gathered around it. I saw at a glance that Silver Heels had given her seat to a frightened old woman, and that other women were thrusting their children into the vehicle, imploring Mount and Foxcroft to save them from the British.

"Michael," said Silver Heels, looking up with cool gray eyes, "the British are firing at women in the farm-houses on the Concord Road above here. We must get the children away."

"And you?" I asked, sharply. She lifted a barefooted urchin into the chaise without answering.

A yoke of dusty, anxious oxen, drawing a hay-cart, came clattering up, the poor beasts running heavily, while their driver followed on a trot beside them, using his cruel goad without mercy.

"Haw! Haw! Gee! Gee! Haw!" he bellowed, guiding his bumping wagon into the Bedford Road.

"The children here!" called out Silver Heels, in her clear voice, and caught up another wailing infant, to soothe it and lift it into the broad ox-wagon.

In a moment the wagon was full of old women and frantic children; a young girl, carrying a baby, ran alongside, begging piteously for a place, but already other vehicles were rattling up behind gaunt, rusty horses, and places were found for the frightened little ones in the confusion.

Some boys drove a flock of sheep into the Bedford Road; a herd of young cattle broke and ran, scattering the sheep. Mount and I sprang in front of

Silver Heels, driving the cattle aside with clubbed rifles. Then there came a heavy pounding of horses' hoofs in the mud, a rush, a cry, and a hatless, coatless rider drew up in a cloud of scattering gravel.

"More troops coming from Boston!" he shouted in his saddle. "Lord Percy is at Roxbury with three regiments, marines, and cannon! Paul Revere was taken at one o'clock this morning!" And away he galloped, head bent low, reeking spurs clinging to his horse's gaunt flanks.

Silver Heels, standing beside me in the hanging morning mist, laid her hand on my arm.

"If the British are at Roxbury," she said, "we are quite cut off, are we not?"

I did not answer. Mount turned a grave, intelligent eye on me; Foxcroft came up, wiping the mud and sweat from his eyes.

At that moment the drum and fife sounded from the green; the Lexington company, arms trailing, came marching into the Bedford Road, Indian file, Captain Parker leading.

Beside him, joyous, alert, transfigured, trotted the Weasel. "We've got them now!" he called out to Mount. "We'll catch the redskins with our hands at Charlestown Neck!"

The little barelegged drummer nodded seriously; the old Louisburg drum rumbled out the route-march.

Into "Buckman's Tavern" filed the Lexington men and fell to slamming and bolting the wooden shutters, piercing the doors and walls for rifle-fire, piling tables and chairs and bedding along the veranda for a rough breastwork.

"You must come with the convoy," I said, taking Silver Heels by the hand.

Her grave, gray eyes met mine in perfect composure.

"We must stay," she said.

"They are bringing cannon—can you not understand?" I repeated, harshly.

"I will not go," she said. "Every rifle is required here. I cannot take you from these men in their dire need. Dear heart, can you not understand me?"

"Am I to sacrifice you?" I asked, angrily. "No!" I cried. "We have suffered enough—"

Tears sprang to her eyes; she laid her hand on my rifle.

"Other women have sent their dearest ones. Am I less brave than that woman whose husband died yonder on his own door-sill? Am I a useless, passionless clod, that my blood stirs at naught but pleasure? Look at those dead men on the tavern steps! Look at our people's blood on the grass yonder! Would you wed with a pink-and-white thing whose veins run water? I saw them kill that poor boy behind his own barn!—these redcoat ruffians who come across an ocean to slay us in our own land. Do you forget I am a soldier's child?"

A loud voice bellowing from the tavern: "Women here for the bullet-moulds! Get your women to the tavern!"

She caught my hand. "You see a maid may not stand idle in Lexington!" she said, with a breathless smile.

CHAPTER XXVIII

Silver Heels stood in the tap-room of "Buckman's Tavern" casting bullets; the barefoot drummer watched the white-hot crucible and baled out the glittering molten metal or fed it with lumps of lead stripped from the gate-post of Hooper's house in Danvers.

Near the window sat some Woburn Minute Men, cross-legged on the worn floor, rolling cartridges. From time to time the parson of Woburn, who had come to pray and shoot, took away the pile of empty powder-horns and brought back others to be emptied.

The tavern was dim and damp; through freshly bored loopholes in the shutters sunlight fell, illuminating the dark interior.

In their shirts, barearmed and bare of throat to the breast-bone, a score of Lexington Minute Men stood along the line of loopholes, their long rifles thrust out. They had no bayonets, but each man had driven his hunting-knife into the wall beside him.

Jack Mount and the Weasel lay, curled up like giant cats, at the door, blinking peacefully out through the cracks into the early sunshine. I could hear their low-voiced conversation from where I stood at my post, close to Silver Heels:

"Redcoats, Cade, not redskins," corrected Mount. "British lobster-backs—eh, Cade? You remember how we drubbed them there in Pittsburg, belt and buckle and ramrod—eh, Cade?"

"That was long ago, friend."

"Call me Jack! Why don't you call me Jack any more?" urged Mount. "You know me now, don't you, Cade?"

"Ay, but I forget much. Do you know how I came here?"

"From Johnstown, Cade—from Johnstown, lad!"

"I cannot remember Johnstown."

Presently the Weasel peered around at Silver Heels.

"Who is that young lady?" he asked, mildly.

Silver Heels heard and smiled at the old man. The faintest quiver curved her mouth; there was a shadow of pain in her eyes.

The fire from the crucible tinted her cheeks; she raised both bared arms to push back her clustering hair. Hazel gray, her brave eyes met mine across the witch-vapour curling from the melting-pot.

"Do you recall how the ferret, Vix, did bite Peter's tight breeches, Michael?"

"Ay," said I, striving to smile.

"And—and the jack-knife made by Barlow?"

"Ay."

She flushed to the temples and looked at my left hand. The scar was there. I raised my hand and kissed the blessed mark.

"Dear, dear Michael," she whispered, "truly you were ever the dearest and noblest and best of all!"

"Unfit to kiss thy shoon's latchet, sweet—"

"Yet hast untied the latchets of my heart."

A stillness fell on the old tavern; the Minute Men stood silently at the loopholes, the barefoot drummer sat on his drum, hands folded, watching with solemn, childish eyes the nuggets of lead sink, bubble, and melt.

A militiaman came down-stairs for a bag of bullets.

"They be piping hot yet," said the drummer-boy, "and not close pared."

But the soldier carelessly gathered heaping handfuls in his calloused palms, and went up the bare, creaking stairs again to his post among the pigeons.

The heat of the brazier had started the perspiration on Silver Heels's face and neck; tiny drops glistened like fresh dew on a blossom. She stood, dreamily brushing with the back of her hand the soft hair from her brow. Her dark-fringed eyes on me; under her loosened kerchief I saw the calm breathing stir her neck and bosom gently as a white flower stirs at a breath of June.

"The scent of the sweet-fern," she murmured; "do you savour it from the pastures?"

I looked at her in pity.

"Ay, dear heart," she whispered, with a sad little smile, "I am homesick to the bones of me, sick for the blue hills o' Tryon and the whistling martin-birds, sick for the scented brake and the smell of sweet water babbling, sick for your arm around me, and your man's strength to crush me to you and take the kiss my very soul does ache to give."

A voice broke in from the pigeon-loft above, "Is there a woman below to sew bandages?"

"Truly there is, sir," called back Silver Heels.

"I'll take the mould," said the small drummer, "but you are to come when the fight begins, for I mean to do a deal o' drumming!"

She started towards the stairway, then turned to look at me.

"My post is wherever you are," I said, stepping to her side.

I took her little hand, all warm and moist from the bullet-moulding, and I kissed the palm and the delicate, rounded wrist.

"There is a long war before us ere we find a home," I said.

"I know," she said, faintly.

"A long, long war; separation, sadness. Will you wed me before I go to join with Cresap's men?"

"Ay," she said.

"There is a parson below, Silver Heels."

Her face went scarlet.

"Let it be now," I whispered, with my arm around her.

She looked up into my eyes. I leaned over the landing-rail and called out, "Send a man for the parson of Woburn!"

An Acton man stepped out on the tavern porch and shouted for the parson. Presently the good man came, in rusty black, shouldering a fowling-piece, his pockets bulging with a Bible and Book of Common Prayer, his wig all caked and wet from a tour through the dewy willows behind the inn.

"Is there sickness here—or wounds?" he asked, anxiously. Then he saw me above and came wheezing up the stairs.

"Heart-sickness, sir," I said; "we be dying, both of us, for the heart's ease you may bring us through your holy office."

At length he understood—Silver Heels striving to keep her sweet eyes lifted when he spoke to her, and I quiet and determined, asking that he lose no time, for no man knew how long we few here in the tavern had to live. In the same breath I summoned a soldier from the south loophole in the garret, and asked him to witness for me; and he took off his hat and stood sheepishly twirling it, rifle in hand.

And so we were wedded, there in the ancient garret, the pigeons coo-cooing overhead, the blue wasps buzzing up and down the window-glass, and our hands joined before the aged parson of Woburn town. I had the plain gold ring which I had bought in Albany for this purpose, nor dreamed to wed my sweetheart with it thus!—and O the sweetness in her lips and eyes when I drew it from the cord around my neck and placed it on her smooth finger at the word!

Little else I remember, save that the old parson kissed her, and the soldier kissed her outstretched hand, and let his gun fall for bashful fright. Nor that we were truly wedded did I understand, even when the parson of Woburn went away down the creaking stairs with his fowling-piece over his shoulder, leaving us standing mute together under the canopy of swinging herbs. We still held hands, standing quiet, in a vague expectation of some mystery yet to come. Children that we were!—the mystery of mysteries had been wrought, never to be undone till time should end.

A pigeon flew, whimpering, to the beam above us, then strutted and bowed and coo-cooed to its startled, sleek, white sweetheart; a wind blew through the rafters, stirring the dry bunches of catnip, mint, and thyme, till they swung above, scented censers all, exhaling incense.

There was a pile of cotton cloth on the floor; Silver Heels sank down beside it and began to tear it into strips for sewing bandages.

I looked from the window, seeing nothing.

Presently the Minute Man at the south loop spoke:

"A man riding this way—there!—on the Concord Road!"

Silver Heels on the floor worked steadily, ripping the snowy cotton.

"There is smoke yonder on the Concord Road," said the Minute Man.

"AND SO WE WERE WEDDED"

I roused and rubbed my eyes.

"Do you hear firing," he asked, "far away in the west?"

"Yes."

"Concord lies northwest."

Silver Heels, absorbed in her task, hummed a little tune under her breath.

"The smoke follows the road," said the Minute Man.

The firing became audible in the room. Silver Heels raised her head with a grave glance at me. I went and knelt beside her.

"It is coming at last, little sweetheart," I said. "Will you go, now? Foxcroft will take you across the fields to some safe farm."

"You know Sir William would not have endured to see me leave at such a time," she said.

"Yes, dear heart, but you cannot carry a rifle."

"But I can make bullets and bandages."

"The British fire at women; you must go!" I said, aloud.

"I will not go."

"I command."

"No." She bent her fair, childish head and the tears fell on the cloth in her lap.

"Look! Look at the redcoats!" called out the Minute Man at the attic window.

As I rose I heard plainly the long, resounding crash of musket firing, and the rattle of rifles followed like a hundred echoes.

"Look yonder!" he cried.

Suddenly the Concord Road was choked with scarlet-clad soldiers. Mapped out below us the country stretched, and over it, like a blood-red monster worm, wound the British column—nay, like to a dragon it came on, with flanking lines thrust out east and west for its thin red wings, and head and tail wreathed with smoke.

And now we could see feathery puffs of smoke from the road-side bushes, from distant hills, from thickets, from ploughed fields, from the long, undulating stone walls which crossed the plain. Faster and faster came the musket volleys, but faster yet rang out the shots from our yeomanry, gathering thicker and thicker along the British route, swarming in from distant towns and hamlets and lonely farms.

The old tavern was ringing with voices now—commands of officers, calls from those who were posted above, clattering steps on the porch as the Acton men ran out to their posts behind the tufted willows in the swamp.

He who had been placed in charge at the tavern, a young officer of the Woburn Alarm Men, shouted for silence and attention, and ordered us not to fire unless fired upon, as our position would be hopeless if cannon were brought against us. Then he commanded all women to leave the tavern and seek shelter at Slocum's farm across the meadows.

"No, no!" murmured Silver Heels, obstinately, as I took her hand and started for the stairs, "I will not go,—I cannot—I cannot! Let me stay, Michael; for God's sake, let me stay!" And she fell on her knees and caught at my hands.

"To your posts!" roared the Woburn officer, drawing his sword and coming up the stairs two at a jump. He stopped short when he saw Silver Heels, and glanced blankly at me; but there was no time now for flight, for, as he stepped to the window beside me, pell-mell into the village green rushed the British light infantry, dusty, exhausted, enraged. In brutal disorder they surged on, here a squad huddled together, there a company, bullied, threatened, and harangued by its officers with pistols and drawn swords; now a group staggering past, bearing dead or wounded comrades, now a heavy cart loaded with knapsacks and muskets, driven by hatless soldiers.

Close on their heels tramped the grenadiers. Soldier after soldier staggered and fell from the ranks, utterly exhausted, unable to rise from the grass.

The lull in the firing was broken by a loud discharge of musketry from Fiske's Hill, and presently more redcoats came rushing into the village, while at their very heels the Bedford Alarm Men shot at them, and chased them. Everywhere our militia came swarming—from Sudbury, Westford, Lincoln, Acton; Minute Men from Medford, from Stowe, from Beverly, and from Lynn—and their ancient firelocks blazed from every stone wall, and their long rifles banged from the distant ridges.

Below me in the street I saw the British officers striving desperately to reform their men, kicking the exhausted creatures to their feet again, striking laggards, shoving the bewildered and tired grenadiers into line, while thicker and thicker pelted the bullets from the Minute Men and militia.

They were brave men, these British officers; I saw a young ensign of the Tenth Foot fall with a ball through his stomach, yet rise and face the storm until shot to death by a dozen Alarm Men on the Bedford Road.

It was dreadful; it was doubly dreadful when a company of grenadiers suddenly faced about and poured a volley into our tavern, for, ere the crashing and splintered wood had ceased, the tavern fairly vomited flame into the square, and the British went down in heaps. Through the smoke I saw an officer struggling to disengage himself from his fallen and dying horse; I saw the massed infantry reel off through the village, firing frenziedly right and left, pouring volleys into farm-houses, where women ran screaming out into the barns, and frantic watch-dogs barked, tugging at their chains.

It was not a retreat, not a flight; it was a riot, a horrible saturnalia of smoke and fire and awful sound. As a maddened panther, wounded, rushes forth to deal death right and left, even tearing its own flesh with tooth and claw, the British column burst south across the land, crazed with wounds, famished, athirst, blood-mad, dealing death and ruin to all that lay before it.

Terrible was the vengeance that followed it, hovered on its gasping flanks, scourged its dwindling ranks, which withered under the searching fire from every tuft of bushes, every rock, every tree-trunk.

Already the ghastly pageant had rushed past us, leaving a crimson trail in its wake; already the old tavern door was flung wide, and our Minute Men were running down the Boston Road and along the ridges on either side, firing as they came on.

I, with Mount and the Weasel, hung to their left flank till two o'clock, when, about half a mile from Lexington Meeting-house, we heard cannon, and understood that the relief troops from Boston had come up.

Then, knowing that there were guns enough and to spare without ours, we shouldered our hot rifles and trudged back to "Buckman's Tavern," through the dust, behind a straw-covered wain which was driving slowly under the heat of an almost vertical sun.

Mount, parched with thirst, hailed the driver of the wain, asking him if he carried cider.

"Only a wounded man," he said, "most dead o' the red dragoons."

I stepped to the slowly moving wagon and looked over the tail-board down into the straw.

"Shemuel!" I cried.

"Shemuel!" roared Mount.

The little Jew opened his sick eyes under his bandage. The Weasel climbed nimbly over the tail-board and settled down beside the wounded man, taking his blood-smeared hand.

"Shemuel! Shemuel! We saw them split your head!" stammered Mount, in his astonishment and joy.

"Under my hat I did haff a capful of shillings," replied Shemuel, weakly; "I— I go back—two days' time to find me my money by dot Lechemere swamp— eh, Jack?"

"God bless you, old nosey!" cried Mount; "we'll get your money, lad! Won't we, Cardigan?"

The little Jew turned his heavy eyes on me.

"You haff found Miss Warren?" he gasped. "Ach, so iss all well. I go back— two days' time—find me my money." He smiled and closed his eyes.

So we re-entered Lexington, Jack Mount, the Weasel, Saul Shemuel, and I; and on the tavern steps Silver Heels stood, her tired, colourless face lighted up, her outstretched hands falling on my shoulders; and I to take her in my arms, for she had fallen a-weeping. Above us the splendid blue of the sky spread its eternal tent, our only shelter, our only home on the long trail through the world; our lamp was the sun, our fireplace a continent, and the four winds our walls, and our estates were bounded by two oceans, washing the shores of a land where the free, at last, might dwell.

In the south the thunder of the British cannon muttered, distant and more distant; the storm had passed.

Had the storm passed? The smoke hung in the north where Concord town was burning, yet around us birds sang.

And now came Jack Mount, riding postilion on the horses which drew the post-chaise; behind him trotted the Weasel, leading out Warlock. Silver Heels saw them and stood up, smiling through her tears.

"Truly, we stayed and did our duty, did we not, dear heart?"

"With your help, sweet."

"And deserted not our own!"

"Yours the praise, dear soul."

"And did face our enemies like true people all; is it not so, Michael?"

"It is so."

"Then let us go, my husband. I am sick for my own land, and for the happiness to come."

"Northward we journey, little sweetheart."

"To the blue hills and the sweet-fern?"

"Ay, home."

And so we started for the north, out of the bloody village where our liberty was born at the first rifle-shot, out of the sound of the British cannon, out of the land of the salt sea, back to the inland winds and the incense of our own dear forests, and the music of sweet waters tumbling where the white pines sing eternally.

I rode Warlock beside the chaise; Shemuel lay within; Silver Heels sat beside the poor, hurt creature, easing his fevered head; but her eyes ever returned to me, and the colour came and went in her face as our eyes spoke in silence.

"Good-bye," said Foxcroft, huskily.

Mount squared himself in his saddle; the Weasel, rifle on thigh, set his horse's head north.

Slowly the cavalcade moved on; the robins sang on every tree; far to the southward the thunder of the British cannon rolled and re-echoed along the purple hills; and over all God's golden light was falling on life, and love, and death.

CHAPTER XXIX

We entered Albany on the 22d of April; the town had heard the news from Lexington ere we sighted the Albany hills, the express having passed us as we crossed the New York line, tearing along the river-bank at a breakneck gallop.

So, when we rode into Albany, the stolid, pippin-cheeked Dutchmen had later news than had we, and I learned then, for the first time, how my Lord Percy's troops had been hurled headlong through Cambridge Farms into Charlestown, where they lay like panting, slavering, senseless beasts under the cannon of the *Somerset* and *Asia*. And all Massachusetts sat watching them, gun in hand.

We lay at the house of Peter Weaver, my lawyer, Silver Heels and I; Jack Mount and Cade Renard lay at the "Half Moon," where poor Shemuel could procure medicine and such medical attendance as he so sorely stood in need of.

With Peter Weaver I prepared to arrange my affairs as best I might, it being impossible for me to undertake a voyage to Ireland at this time, though my succession to the title and estates of my late uncle, Sir Terence, made it most necessary.

For the first time in my life I now became passably acquainted with my own affairs, though when we came to figure in pounds, shillings, and pence, I yawned, yet made pretence of a wisdom in mathematics which, God knows, is not in me.

Silver Heels, her round chin on my shoulder, listened attentively, and asked some questions which caused the ponderous lawyer to address himself to her rather than to me, seeing clearly that either I cared nothing for my own affairs or else was stupid past all belief.

Sir William's legacies to me and to Silver Heels were discussed most seriously; and Mr. Weaver would have it that the law should deal with my miserable kinsman, Sir John, for the fraud he had wrought. Yet, it was exactly *that*; and, because he *was* my kinsman, I could not drag him out to cringe for his infamy before the rabble.

The land and the money left to us by Sir William we would now, doubtless, receive, but it was only because Sir William had desired it that we at length made up our minds to accept it at all.

This I made plain to Mr. Weaver, then relapsed into a dull inspection of his horn spectacles as he discoursed of mortgages and bonds and interests and liens with stupefying monotony.

"It is like the school-room, Micky," murmured Silver Heels, close to my ear, and composed her countenance to listen to a fluent peroration on percentage and investments in terms which were to me as vain as tinkling cymbals.

"Then I am wealthy?" I interposed, again and again, yet could draw from that fat badger, Weaver, neither a "yes" nor "no," nor any plain speech fit for a gentleman's comprehension.

So when at length we quitted Mr. Weaver a sullen mood possessed me and I felt at bay with all the learned people in the world, as I had often felt, penned in the school-room.

"Am I?" I asked Silver Heels.

"What?"

"Rich or poor? Tell me in one word, dear heart, for whether or not I possess a brass farthing in the world, I do not know, upon my honour!"

"Poor innocent," she laughed; "poor unlearned and harassed boy! Know, then, that you have means to purchase porridge and a butcher's roast for Christmas."

"I be serious," said I, anxiously, "and I would know if I have means to support a large family—"

"Hush!" said Silver Heels. What I could see of her face,—one small ear,—was glowing in rich colour.

"Because—" I ventured. But she plucked at my arm with lowered eyes, nor would hear me to explain that I, newly wedded, viewed the future with a hopeful gravity that befitted.

"As for a house," said I, "there is a pleasant place of springs called Saratoga, dearly loved by Sir William."

"I know," said she, quickly; "it comes from 'asserat,' sparkling waters."

"It comes from 'Soragh,' which means salt, and 'Oga,' a place—"

"It does *not*, Micky!"

"It does!"

"No!"

"It does!"

"Oc-qui-o-nis! He is a bear!" said Silver Heels, to herself.

We stopped in the hallway, facing each other. Something in her flushed, defiant face, her bright eyes, the poise of her youthful body, brought back with a rush that day, a year ago, when I, sneaking out of the house to avoid the school-room, met her in the hallway, and was balked and flouted and thrust back to the thraldom of the school. Here was the same tormentor—the same child with her gray eyes full of pretty malice, the same beauty of brow and mouth and hair was here, and something added—a maid's delicate mockery which veiled the tenderness of womanhood; a sweetheart and a wedded wife.

"I am thinking of a morning very, very long ago," I said, slowly.

"I, too," said Silver Heels.

"Almost a year ago," I said.

"A year ago," said Silver Heels.

"You little wild-cat thing!" I whispered, tenderly, and took her by the waist so that her face lay upturned on my shoulder.

"Stupid," she said, "I loved you that very day."

"What day?"

"The day we both are thinking on: when you met me in the hall with your fish-rod like a guilty dunce—"

"You wore a skirt o' buckskin and tiny moccasins and stockings with scarlet thrums; and you were a-nibbling a cone of maple-sugar," said I.

"And you strove to trip me up!"

"And you pushed me!"

"And you thrust Vix at me!"

"And you kicked my legs and ran up-stairs like a wild-cat thing."

There was a silence; she looked up into my face from my shoulder.

"This, for a belt of peace betwixt those two children who live in memory," said I, and kissed her.

"Oonah! All is lost," she said; "he does with me as he will!" and she rendered me my kiss, saying, "Bearer of belts, thy peace-belt is returned."

So was perfect peace established, not only for the shadowy children of that unforgotten past, but for us, and for all time betwixt us; and our belts were offered and returned, and the sign was the touching of her lips and mine.

For Shemuel's sake, and because we would not desert him, we continued in Albany until near the end of April.

Taking counsel together, we had determined to build a mansion, when the times permitted, midway on the road 'twixt Johnstown and Fonda's Bush, our lands joining at that place. But I feared much that the war which now flamed through Massachusetts Bay might soon creep northward into our forest fastness and set the border ablaze from the Ohio to Saint Sacrement. Much, too, I feared that the men of the woods whose skin was red would league with the men whose coats were red. All his later days Sir William had striven to avert this awful pact; Dunmore played against him, Butler betrayed him, Cresap was tricked, and Sir William lost. Now, into his high place sneaked a pygmy, slow, uncertain, sullen, treacherous—his own son, who would undo the last knot which bound the Indians to a fair neutrality. Perhaps he himself would even lead them on to the dreadful devastation all men dreaded; and, if he, men must also count on the Butlers, father and son, to carry terror through our forests and hunt to death without mercy all who stood for freedom and the rights of man.

One of these I had held in my hand and released. Yet still that old certainty haunted me, the belief that one day I was to meet and kill him, not in honourable encounter, now, for he had lost the right to ask such a death from me; but in the dark forest, somewhere among the corridors of silent pines, I would slay him as sachems slay ferocious beasts that track men through ghost-trails down to hell.

Then should we be free at last of this fierce, misshapen soul, we People of the Morning, Tierhansaga, and the shrinking forest should straighten, and Oya should be Oyabanh, and the red witch-flower should wither to a stalk, to a seed, and sprout a fair white blossom for all time, Ahwehhah.

That night, as I stood on the steps of Peter Weaver's red brick house, turning to look once more into the coals of the setting sun ere I entered the door, a hand twitched at my coat-skirt, and, looking down, I saw below me on the pavement an Indian dressed in the buckskins of a forest-runner.

"Peter!" I cried, for it was he, my dusky kinsman on the left hand; then my eyes fell on his companion, a short, squat savage, clad in red, and painted hideous with strange signs I could not read.

"Red Jacket," said Peter, calmly.

I looked hard at Peter; he had grown big and swart and fat like a bear-cub in November; Red Jacket raised his sullen eyes, then dropped them.

Suddenly, as I stood there, at a loss what next to say, came a heavy man, richly clothed, flabby face bent on the ground. Nor would he have discovered me, so immersed in brooding reverie was he, had not Peter touched his elbow.

A bright flush stained his face; he looked up at me where I stood. Then I descended the steps, shoving Peter from between us, and Sir John Johnson, for it was he, moved back a pace and laid his heavy hand on his sword-belt as I came close to him, looking into his cold eyes.

"Liar!" I said; "liar! liar!" And that was all, for he gave ground, and his hand fell limply from his dishonoured hilt.

So I left him, there in the darkening street, the Indians watching him with steady, kindling eyes.

We started next day at dawn, Silver Heels riding Warlock in her new kirtle and little French three-cornered hat with its gilt fringe, to which she had a right, as she was now My Lady Cardigan, if she chose.

I rode a bay mare, bought in Albany, yet a beauty, and doubtless the only decent horseflesh in all that town of rusty rackers and patroons' sorry hacks. Mount and the Weasel, leather-clad, and gay with quilled moccasins and brilliant thrums, journeyed afoot, on either side o' Shemuel, who bestrode a little docile ass.

His noddle, neatly mended and still bound up, he had surmounted with a Quaker hat so large that it rested on his large flaring ears; peddlers' panniers swung on either flank, crammed deep with gewgaws; he let his bridle fall on the patient ass's neck, and, thumbs in his armpits, joined lustily the chorus raised by Mount and Renard:

"Come, all ye Tryon County men,

And never be dismayed;

But trust in the Lord,

And He will be your aid!"

Roaring the rude chorus, Jack Mount marched in the lead, his swinging strides measured to our horses' steady pacing; beside him trotted the little Weasel, his hand holding tightly to the giant's arm; and sometimes he took three steps to Mount's one, and sometimes he toddled, his little, leather-bound legs twinkling like spokes in a wheel, but ever he chanted manfully as he marched:

"O trust in the Lord,

And He will be your aid!"

And Shemuel's fervent whine from his lowly saddle rounded out the old route-song.

An hour later I summoned Jack Mount, and he fell back to my stirrups, resting his huge hand on my saddle as he walked beside me.

"Jack," I said, "is poor Cade cured o' fancy and his mad imaginings?"

"Ay, lad, for the time."

"For the time?"

"A year, two years, three, perhaps. This is not the first mad flight o' fancy Cade has taken on his aged wings."

"You never told me that," I said, sharply.

"No, lad."

"Why not?"

"Do you spread abroad the sorry secrets of your kin, Mr. Cardigan?"

"He is not your kin!"

"He is more," said Mount, simply.

After a silence I asked him on what previous occasion the little Weasel had gone moon-mad.

"On many—every third or fourth year since I first knew him," said Mount, soberly. "But never before did he leave me to follow his poor mad phantoms—always the phantom of his wife, lad, in divers guises. He saw her in a silvery bush o' moonlight nights, and talked with her till my goose-flesh rose and crawled on me; he saw her mirrored in cold, deep pools at dawn, looking up at him from the golden-ribbed sands, and I have laid in the canoe to watch the trouts' quick shadows moving on the bottom, and he a-talking sweet to his dear wife as though she hid under the lily-pads like a blossom."

He glanced up at me pitifully as he walked beside my stirrup; I laid my hand on his leather-tufted shoulder.

"Sir, it is sad," he muttered; "a fair mind nobly wrecked. But grief cannot deform the soul, Mr. Cardigan."

"He knows you now?"

"Ay, and knows that he has dwelt for months in madness."

"Does he know that it was me he loved so deeply in his madness?" asked Silver Heels, gently.

"I think he does," whispered Mount.

Silver Heels turned her sorrowful eyes on poor Cade Renard.

Riding that afternoon near sunset, at the False Faces' Carrying-Place upon the Mohawk, we spoke of Johnson Hall and the old life, sadly, for never again could we hope to enter its beloved portals.

Naught that belonged to us remained in the Hall, save only the memories none might rob us of.

"If only I might have Betty," said Silver Heels, wistfully.

"Betty? Did she not attend you to Boston with Sir John?" I asked.

"Yes, but she was slave to Sir John. I could not buy her; you know how poor I awoke to find myself in Boston town."

"Would not that brute allow you Betty?" I asked, angrily.

"No; I think he feared her. Poor, blubbering Betty, how she wept and roared her grief when Sir John bade her pack up, and called her 'hussy.'"

That night we lay at Schenectady, where also was camped a body of Sir William's Mohawks, a sullen, watchful band, daubed in hunting-paint, yet their quivers hung heavy with triple-feathered war-arrows, and their knives and hatchets and their rifles were over-bright and clean to please me.

Some of them knew me, and came to talk with me over a birch-fire. I gave them tobacco, and we tarried by the birch-fire till the stars waned in the sky and the dawn-stillness fell on land and river; but from them I could learn nothing, save that Sir John and Colonel Guy had vowed to scalp their own neighbours should they as much as cry, "God save our country!" Evil news, truly, yet only set me firmer in my design to battle till the end for the freedom that God had given and kings would take away.

Silver Heels, quitting the inn with Mount, came to warn me that I must sleep if we set out at sunrise. Graciously she greeted the Mohawks who had risen to withdraw; they all knew her, and watched her like tame panthers with red coals in their eyes.

"But they are panthers yet; forget it not," muttered Jack Mount.

At sunrise we rode out into the blue hills. Homeless, yet nearing home at last, my heart lifted like a singing bird. Dew on the sweet-fern exhaling, dew on the ghost-flower, dew on the scented brake!—and the whistle of feathered wings, and the endless ringing chorus of the birds of Tryon! Hills of pure sapphire, streams of gems, limpid necklaces festooned to drip diamonds from crags into some frothing pool! Pendent pearls on vines starred white with bloom; a dun deer at gaze, knee-deep in feathering willow-grass; a hermit-bird his morning hymn, cloistered in the vaulted monastery where the great organ stirs among the pines!

Hills! Hills of Tryon, unploughed, unharrowed, save by the galloping deer; hills, sweet islands in the dark pine ocean, over whose waste the wild hawk's mewing answers the cry of its high-wheeling mate; hills of the morning, aromatic with spiced fern, and perfumed of the gum of spruce and balsam; hills of Tryon; my hills! my hills!

"The spring is with us," said Jack Mount, stooping to pluck a frail flower.

"Ka-nah-wah-hawks, the cowslip!" murmured Silver Heels.

"Savour the wind; what is it?" I asked, sniffing.

"O-neh-tah, the pine!" she cried.

"O-ne-tah, the spruce!" I corrected.

"The pine, silly!"

"The spruce!"

"No, no, the pine!"

"So be it, sweet."

"No, I am wrong!"

And we laughed, and she stretched out her slender hand to me from her saddle.

Then we galloped forward together, calling out greeting to our old friends as we passed; and thus we saluted Jis-kah-kah, the robin, and Kivi-yeh, the little owl, and we whistled at Koo-koo-e, the quail, and mocked at old Kah-kah, the watchful crow.

Han-nah-wen, the butterfly, came flitting along the roadside, ragged with his long winter's sleep.

"He should not have slept in his velvet robe for a night-shift," said Silver Heels; "he is a summer spendthrift, and Nah-wan-hon-tah, the speckled trout, lies watching him under the water."

Which set me thinking of my feather-flies; and then the dear old river flashed in sight.

"I see—I see—there, very far away on that hill—" whispered Silver Heels.

"I see," I muttered, choking.

Presently the sunlight glimmered on a window of the distant Hall.

"We are on our own land now, dear heart," I said, choking back the sob in my throat.

I called out to Jack Mount and unslung my woodaxe. He drew his hatchet, and together we cut down a fair young maple, trimmed it, and drove a heavy post into the soil.

"Here we will build one day," said I to Silver Heels. She smiled faintly, but her eyes were fixed on the distant Hall.

I had leased, from my lawyer, Peter Weaver, a large stone mansion in Johnstown, which stood next to the church where Sir William lay; this until such time as I might return from the war and find leisure to build on my own land the house which Silver Heels and I had planned to stand on a hill, in full view of the river and of the old Hall where our childhood had been passed.

It was night when we rode into Johnstown. I could discover no changes in the darkness, save that a few new signs swung before lighted shops, and every fifth house hung out a lanthorn and a whole candle-light.

Our stone house was vast, damp, and scantily furnished, but Jack Mount lighted a fire in the hallway, and Silver Heels went about with a song on her lips, and Cade Renard sent servants from the nearest inn with cloth and tableware, and meats smoking hot, not forgetting a great bowl of punch and a cask of ale, which the scullions rolled into the great hall and hoisted on the skids.

So we were merry, and silent, too, at moments, when our eyes met in faint smiles or wistful sympathy.

Shemuel, with his peddling panniers, had strangely disappeared, nor could we find him high or low when Mount and Cade had set their own table by the fire and the room smelled sweet with steaming toddy.

"Thrift! Thrift!" muttered Mount, rattling his toddy-stick impatiently; "now who could have thought that little Jew would have cut away to make up time in trade this night!"

But Shemuel had traded in another manner, for, ere Mount had set his strong, white teeth in the breast-bone of a roasted fowl, I heard Silver Heels cry out: "Betty! Betty! Oh dear, dear Betty!" And the blubbering black woman came rolling in, scarlet turban erect, ear-rings jingling.

"Mah li'l dove! Mah li'l pigeon-dove! Oh Gord, mah li'l Miss Honey-bee!"

"You must keep her, lad," muttered Mount.

"I think Sir John will sell," I said, grimly.

And so he did, or would have, had not his new wife, poor Lady Johnson, whom I had never seen, writing from the Hall, begged me to accept Betty as a gift from her. And I, having no quarrel with the unhappy lady, accepted Betty as a gift, permitting Lady Johnson to secure from the incident what comfort she might.

All through the sweet May-tide, Jack Mount and Cade Renard sunned themselves under the trees in our garden, or sprawled on the warm porch like great, amiable wolf-hounds, dozing and dreaming of mighty deeds.

Ale they had for the drawing, yet abused it not, respecting the hospitality of the house and its young mistress, and none could point the shameful finger at either to cry: "Fie! Pottle-pot! Malt-worm! Painted-nose! Go swim!" At times, sitting together on the grass, cheek by jowl, I heard them singing hymns; at times strolling through the moon-drenched garden paths they lifted up their souls in song:

"The hunter has taken the trail to the East;

The little deer run! The little deer run!

Fear not, little deer, for he hunts the Red Beast;

Ye are not for his gun! Ye are not for his gun!

"The hunter lies cold on the trail to the East;

His bosom is rent! His bosom is rent!

He died for his country, to slay the Red Beast;

To Heaven he went! To Heaven he went!"

In the moonlight the doleful chant droned on, night after night, under the dewy lilacs; and the great horned-owl answered, hooting from the pines; and Silver Heels and I listened from the porch, hand clasping hand in fearsome content. For out in the dark world God was busy shaping the destiny of a people; even the black forest knew it, and thrilled like a vast harp at the touch of the free winds' fingers—unseen fingers, delicate, tentative, groping for the key to a chord of splendid majesty. And when at last the chord should be found and struck, resounding to the deep world's rock foundation, a free people's voices should repeat, singing forever and for all time throughout the earth:

"Amen!"

Meanwhile, stillness, moonlight, and a "*Miserere*" from the lips of two strange forest-runner folk, free-born and ready when the Lord of all led forth His prophet to command.

On that night I heard a man in the street repeat a name, Washington. And all that night I thought of it, and said it, under my breath. But what it might portend I knew not then.

May ended, smothered in flowers; and with the thickening leaves of June came to us there in the North rumours of the times which were to try men's souls. And again I heard, somewhere in the darkness of the village streets, the name I heard before; and that night, too, I lay awake, forming the word with silent lips, close to my young wife's breast.

The full, yellow moon of June creamed all our garden now; Mount and Renard sat a-squat upon the grass, chin on fist, to muse and muse and wait— for what? The King of England did not know; but all the world was waiting, too.

Then, one dim morning, while yet the primrose light tinted the far hills, I awoke to see Silver Heels in her white night-robe, leaning from the casement, calling out to me in a strange, frightened voice: "Michael! Michael! They are coming over the hills—over the hills, dear heart, to take you with them!"

At the window, sniffing the fresh dawn, I listened.

"Footfalls in the hills!" she said, trembling. "Out of the morning men are coming! God make me brave! God make me brave!"

For a long time we stood silent; the village slept below us; the stillness of the dawn remained unbroken, save by a golden-robin's note, fluting from a spectral elm.

"It is not yet time," I said: "let us sleep on, dear heart."

But she would not, and I was fain to dress me in my leather, lest the summons coming swift might find me all unready at the call.

Then she roused Betty and the maid and servants, bidding them call up Mount and Renard, for the hour was close upon us all.

"Dear love," I said, "this is a strange fear that takes you from your pillows there, at dawn."

"Strange things befall a blindly loving heart," she said; "I heard them in my dreams, and knew them, all marching with their yellow moccasins and raccoon-caps and green thrums blowing in the wind."

"Riflemen?"

"Ay, dear love."

"Foolish prophetess!"

"Too wise! Too wise!" she whispered, wearily, nestling within my arms, a second only, then:

"Sir Michael!" roared Mount below my window; "Cresap is on the hills with five hundred men of Maryland!"

Stunned, I stared at Silver Heels; her face was marble, glorified.

As the sun rose I left her, and, scarce knowing what I did, threw my long rifle on my shoulder and ran out swiftly through the garden.

Suddenly, as though by magic summoned, the whole street was filled with riflemen, marching silently and swiftly, with moccasined feet, their raccoon caps pushed back, the green thrums tossing on sleeve and thigh. On they came, rank on rank, like brown deer herding through a rock run; and, on the hunting-shirts, lettered in white across each breast, I read:

LIBERTY OR DEATH.

Mount and the Weasel came up, rifles shouldered, coon-skin caps swinging in their hands. Mount shyly touched the hand that Silver Heels held out; Cade Renard took the fingers, and, bending above them with a flicker of his aged gallantry, pressed them with his shrivelled lips.

"We will watch over your husband, my lady," he said, raising his dim eyes to hers.

"Ay, we will bring him back, Lady Cardigan," muttered Jack Mount, twisting his cap in his huge paws.

Silver Heels, holding them each by the hand, strove to speak, but the voice in her white throat froze, and she only looked silently from them to me with pitiful gray eyes.

"To kill the Red Beast," muttered Mount; "it is quickly done, Lady Cardigan. Then your husband will return."

"To kill the Beast," repeated Renard; "the Red Beast with twin heads. Ay, it can be done, my lady. Then he will return."

"I swear it!" cried Mount, flinging up his great arm. "He will return."

"To doubt it is to doubt God's grace, child. He will return," said Cade Renard.

She looked at me, at Mount, at the Weasel, then at the torrent of dusty riflemen steadily passing without a break.

"If he—he must go—" she began. Her voice failed; she caught my hands and kissed them.

"For our honour—go!" she gasped. "Michael! Michael! Come back to me—"

"Truly, dear heart—truly! truly!"

"Ho! Cardigan!" rang out a voice like a pistol-shot from the passing ranks.

Through my tear-dimmed eyes I saw Cresap, sword shining in his hand.

"We come," cried Mount, shaking his rifle towards the rising sun; "death to the Red Beast!"

"Death to the Beast!" shouted Cresap, shaking his shining sword.

Half a thousand heavy rifles shook high; half a thousand deep voices roared thunderously through the stony street:

"Liberty! Liberty or Death!"

THE END

And now that of a truth the Red Beast is slain, as all men know, follow these mellow years through which our children move, watching the world like a great witch-flower unfold. Content, I sit with her I love, at dusk, tying my soft feather-flies just as I tied them for Sir William in the golden time. The trout have nothing changed, nor I, though kings already live as legends.

Bitter-sweet on porch and paling, woodbine and white-starred clematis, and the deep hum of bees; and in the sunlit garden poppies, red as the blood of martyrs. Then moonlight and my dear wife at the door.

Betty, she hath cradled our tot, Felicity, to croon some soft charm of Southern sorcery, whereby sleep settles like gray dusk-moths on tired lids.

But for the boy, William, it serves not, and he defies us with his wooden gun, declaiming that a man whose grandsire died with Wolfe will not be taken off to bed at such an hour. And so my sweetheart cradles him, unheeding my stern hint of rods a-pickle for the wilful; and, in the moonlight, joining my fish-rod, I hear her from the nursery, singing the song of blessed days departed, yet with each dawn renewed:

"For courts are full of flattery,

As hath too oft been tried;

The city full of wantonness,

And both be full of Pride:

Then care away,

And wend along with me!"

"I know a trout," quoth Jack Mount, taking his cob-pipe from his teeth, "a monstrous huge one, lad, hard by the thunder-stricken hemlock where the Kennyetto turns upon itself. Shemuel did mark the fish, sleeping at noon three days since."

"Bring Cade along," said I, opening the garden gate, and gathering my rod and line lest the fly-hook catch in the rosebush; "and fetch the gaff, Jack, when you return."

But when he came again into the moonlit garden he came alone, swinging the bright steel gaff.

"Cade sleeps by the fire in the great hall," he said. "Truly, lad, we age apace, and the sly beast, Death, follows us, sniffing, as we go. Lord! Lord! How old we grow—how old, how old! All of us, save Lady Cardigan and you! Years freshen her."

"The years are kind," I said.

So we descended through the dusk to the sweet water flowing under the clustered stars.

www.ingramcontent.com/pod-product-compliance
Ingram Content Group UK Ltd.
Pitfield, Milton Keynes, MK11 3LW, UK
UKHW032028070225
454812UK00005B/432